Driving Germany

Studies in German History
General Editor:
Christof Mauch, *Director of the German Historical Institute, Washington, DC and Professor of Modern History, University of Cologne*

Volume 1
Nature in German History
Christof Mauch

Volume 2
Coping with the Nazi Past
Edited by Alan E. Steinweis and Philipp Gassert

Volume 3
Adolf Cluss, Architect: From Germany to America
Edited by Alan Lessof and Christof Mauch

Volume 4
Two Lives in Uncertain Times: Facing the Challenges of the Twentieth Century as Scholars and Citizens
Wilma and Georg Iggers

Volume 5
Driving Germany: The Landscape of the German Autobahn, 1930-1970
Thomas Zeller

DRIVING GERMANY

THE LANDSCAPE OF THE GERMAN AUTOBAHN, 1930–1970

Thomas Zeller

Translated by Thomas Dunlap

First published in 2006 by

Berghahn Books

©2006, 2010 Thomas Zeller
First paperback edition published in 2010

All rights reserved. Except for the quotation of short passages
for the purposes of criticism and review, no part of this book
may be reproduced in any form or by any means, electronic or
mechanical, including photocopying, recording, or any information
storage and retrieval system now known or to be invented,
without written permission of the publisher.

Library of Congress Cataloging-in-Publication Data

Zeller, Thomas, 1966–.
  Driving Germany: the landscape of the German autobahn, 1930–1970 / Thomas Zeller.
  p. cm.—(Berghahn monographs Studies in German History; v. 5)
  Includes bibliographical references and index.
  ISBN 978-1-84545-309-3 (hbk: alk. paper) ISBN 978-1-84545-271-1 (pbk: alk. paper)
  1. Landscape protection—Germany—History—20th century. 2. Express highways—Germany—History—20th century. 3. Roadside improvement—Germany—History—20th century. 4. National socialism and architecture. 5. Landscape architecture—Environmental aspects—Germany—History—20th century.

QH77.G3 Z45 2006
333.720943/0904 22   2006023468

British Library Cataloguing in Publication Data

A catalogue record for this book is available
from the British Library.

Printed in the United States on acid-free paper.

ISBN 978-1-84545-309-1 hardback
ISBN 978-1-84545-271-1 paperback

Contents

Illustrations		vii
Acknowledgments		viii
1.	Introduction: Germany and its Autobahn	1
	A growing overlap: history of technology and environmental history	6
	Transportation history: the system of mobility	8
2.	Landscape: the Dual Construction	13
	Physically altered landscapes	14
	Culturally altered landscapes	15
3.	The Historical Habitat of Landscape-Friendly Roads	21
	The autobahnen in environmental history	22
	Building technological landscapes on the Rhine and Neckar	24
	Reconciling nature and technology in the interwar period	26
	Alwin Seifert and Fritz Todt: a biographic constellation	31
4.	Planning the Autobahn before and after 1933	47
	The failed autobahn project of the interwar period	47
	Building the Nazi autobahn	51
	The place of the autobahn in the Nazi dictatorship	55
	Propagandizing the Reichsautobahn	62
	German Technology (Deutsche Technik) and the Reichsautobahn	66
5.	Conflicts over the Harmonious Road	79
	Finding a niche for landscape architects	85
	Searching for a job description	98
	Pitting landscape architects against civil engineers	102
	Marginalizing conservation and spatial planning on the autobahn	109
	Legalizing the exclusion of conservation	115

6. The Myth of the Green Autobahn — 127
   Road alignment as a subject of controversy — 127
   "One drives faster than I can write": visual consumption on the Reichsautobahnen — 138
   The flora of the Nazi autobahn: contesting native plants — 142
   An ideology disintegrates: technology in the crisis of 1937 — 156
   The value and cost of landscaping — 162
   The landscape advocates seek power beyond the autobahn — 164

7. Reinterpretations: the West German Autobahn, 1949 to 1970 — 181
   Autobahnen and the politics of the Bonn Republic — 182
   Building a federal highway system — 185
   The postwar trust in numbers — 192
   "An autobahn is not a hiking path": roadside plantings as safety devices — 207
   Roadside greenery as a bone of public contention — 218

8. Conclusion — 235

Bibliography and Sources — 249

Index — 281

Illustrations

Map 4.1.   58
Diagram of the German autobahn system in 1948

Figure 4.2.   65
Fritz Bayerlein: autobahn painting from the 1930s, portraying the road in the 1970s

Figure 6.1.   130
Aerial view of a straight stretch of the Nazi autobahn (Frankfurt/Main to Darmstadt)

Figure 6.2.   138
View of the *Reichsautobahn* and Alpine scenery near Irschenberg, Bavaria

Figure 6.3.   158
The Nazi autobahn in the forest

Figure 7.1.   197
Guardrails on the postwar autobahn, 1971

Figure 7.2.   202
Transition curve (cover of a postwar civil engineering textbook, 1971)

Figure 8.1.   238
"No landscape is too good for the Führer's autobahn!" Poster, 1970s

Acknowledgments

The present book is a revised and translated version of my *Straße, Bahn, Panorama. Verkehrswege und Landschaftsveränderung in Deutschland 1930 bis 1990* (Frankfurt am Main/New York: Campus, 2002). To provide more context for an English-speaking audience, I have added chapter 3. A chapter on high-speed railways from the original version has been excised. I have added occasional references to new scholarly works that have come to my attention since the original publication date, but I have been unable to be comprehensive in this regard.

The translation owes its existence to the generous support of the German Historical Institute in Washington, D.C., for which I am most grateful. In particular, I am indebted to the Institute's director, Christof Mauch, who has been steadfast in championing environmental history. An anonymous reviewer suggested useful revisions, which have strengthened the manuscript. I was fortunate to work with Thomas Dunlap, a master in the art of translating, and I thank him for his creativity and diligence. At Berghahn Books, Michael Dempsey, Melissa Spinelli, Vivian Berghahn and Marion Berghahn guided me through the publication process.

The basis for the German version of this book was my dissertation thesis submitted to the Ludwig-Maximilians-University in Munich. During the dissertation stage, I benefited from a fellowship granted by the Alfried Krupp von Bohlen und Halbach-Foundation. My intellectual and physical home during the research and writing phase was the Research Institute for the History of Technology and Science at the Deutsches Museum in Munich. Helmuth Trischler, its director and my doctoral advisor, has been a steady source of advice and support. Ulrich Wengenroth agreed to serve as dissertation reader. Barbara Schmucki, with whom I shared an office during the Munich years, had to endure my feeble attempts at humor and still read parts of the original manuscript. I am thankful to her and to Martina Blum, Michael Dorrmann, Alex Gall, Luitgard Marschall, and Thomas Wieland for suggestions. In the United States, many colleagues offered insights and useful criticism, especially Tom Lekan. My fellow historians of technology at the University of Maryland, Robert Friedel and David Sicilia, have welcomed me to College Park. For help with the images, I thank Catherine Hays and Claire Kunkel.

This work would not have been possible without the hospitality and practical help of family and friends. My siblings Stephan Zeller, Rose Zeller-Hofer, and Martin Zeller, their families, and my father, Rupert Zeller, have aided me when I was on the road. Both when we were on the move and at home, Karen Oslund's love and support have been crucial.

Chapter 1

INTRODUCTION: GERMANY AND ITS AUTOBAHN

A German thinks of planting trees whenever he hears the word *Kultur*.[1]

– Eugen Rosenstock-Huessy (1938)

Together with *Kindergarten, Blitzkrieg,* and *Angst,* autobahn (pl. autobahnen) is one of a handful of German words that have migrated into the English language. Driving along one of these multilane, limited-access highways arouses in many foreign visitors feelings that vacillate between awed amazement at this efficient transportation machine and anxiety over the absence of speed limits. A few car dealerships in the United States, from Boston to the San Francisco Bay Area, even call their establishments "Autobahn USA" or "Autobahn Motors," in the hope, evidently, of generating higher sales by invoking the German road network. Recently, one American author even called for an "American autobahn" with no speed limit.[2] The electronic pop music band Kraftwerk made a major contribution to the ambivalent assessment of this technological artifact stretching over thousands of kilometers with its 1974 song "Autobahn": by using the most modern musical techniques to portray a fast-paced road trip, it surrounded the autobahnen with the aura of a modern sheen and cool technoromanticism.

Observers versed in history, however, tend to see in the German autobahnen and their external effects a thicket of motivations, myths, and interpretations. The spectrum ranges from false Internet rumors about the supposed military reasons behind the roadways (the aftereffects of Nazi propaganda legends), to personal driving experiences and even academic controversies. Many of the popular myths have been debunked by scholarship: the autobahnen did not serve primarily military purposes, nor did they solve the problem of unemployment to the degree the Nazis claimed. Yet the context of their creation left a lasting imprint. Like few other European technologies, these roadways have a

---

Notes for this section begin on page 9.

prominence that has a special link to Europe's turbulent history in the twentieth century in general, and to Germany in particular. Indeed, the specific shape they took is inconceivable without this context. Drawing on models from Italy and the United States, Hitler's Nationalist Socialist dictatorship assigned high priority to the long-dormant autobahn project during the first years of the regime. The autobahnen were elevated into a central icon of the Nazi State and its dictator as "Reichsautobahnen" and "Adolf Hitler's Roadways"; a massive propaganda campaign on many levels, from cigarette cards to art exhibitions, implanted the roadways and their cultural significance into the memory of several generations. After the Second World War and Germany's liberation, the autobahnen lay upon the German landscape like a hollow relic of past megalomania, until they were reinterpreted—in a more subtle but no less effective process—into central corridors of the economic reconstruction of a Western democracy.

Such efforts at interpretation and reinterpretation are the topic of the present book. It does not claim to be a comprehensive cultural or technological history of the autobahnen. Instead, using a central aspect of these roadways, it analyzes their changing social and professional meaning between 1930 and 1970 in two political systems, the Nazi dictatorship and the Federal Republic of Germany: at the center of the analysis is the relationship of the autobahnen to the landscape surrounding them and shaped by them. Especially under the Nazis, autobahn planners proclaimed that they were successfully reconciling nature and technology in the form of the roadways and were creating a model for a nature-friendly technology. Looking back today, it seems peculiar that roads were praised, beginning in the 1930s, as paths (literally) to open up nature. Yet that was precisely the claim advanced by the planners. By examining these claims, their cultural and political content, and the various strategies—successful or not—to implement these proposed designs, I seek in the present study to make a contribution chiefly to the history of technology and the environment, but also to German history in general. It is also my hope to raise the awareness of historians that landscapes—both their idea and reality—are phenomena subject to historical change.

Though historians of Germany have much to learn from paying attention to the autobahn as the largest peacetime infrastructure project of the National Socialists and its changing role in postwar Germany, little research on it has been published, at least in English. It is not only historians of technology who will find roads, like other infrastructure technologies, a highly rewarding field of research for investigating the relationship between technology and society. As the material realization of societal ideas, goals, and norms, they reflect their roots and the conflicts over their creation: they are thus 'socially constructed technology,' a phrase that many historians of technology have been using for nearly two decades.[3] At the same time, and no less importantly, such technologies reverberate back upon the societies in which they are embedded, whether through utilization, interpretation, or mythologization. Environmental historians also can benefit from such studies. As we shall see, the roadways in question represented, in the intention of the planners and for many users and interpreters, a window upon nature, and in the process they created landscapes. Nature, however, is not simply one of the most dazzling concepts of the Western imagination, but also a social fact that is constantly renegotiated.

A study of roads offers environmental historians a chance to explore, in all its complexity and subtlety, an important facet of the closely interconnected relationship of technology and nature. Especially in the United States, the notion of "wilderness"—historically inaccurate but culturally potent—has caused roads to be seen as intruders into untouched nature. Reality, whether in America or Europe, is more complicated and therefore more rewarding of study. Roads imparted to cultural landscapes shaped by people, forces, and institutions another layer of human activity; these alterations of the cultural landscape triggered vigorous debates and various design proposals. Examining such plans and structures is therefore an important topic for environmental history. The concept of cultural landscapes will be examined more deeply in the next chapter.

The present book also seeks to help overcome the previous thematic narrowing of some parts of environmental history to nature-protection movements. Especially in Germany, social actors such as landscape architects, with their own professional and aesthetic ideas and increasing state support, were often more important in carrying out their agendas than were environmentalists organized into relatively small groups and peripheral state bureaucracies. However, historians have paid much more attention to the latter than the former.

It is my hope, furthermore, that this book will address important aspects of the history of Germany in the twentieth century. Alongside the already-mentioned symbolic function of the roadways for the National Socialist dictatorship, the social history of the planners and of their clashing conceptions for the autobahnen is well worth a closer look. The discussion over the relative modernity of National Socialism, a debate that was prominent in the 1990s and keeps flaring up, offered a starting point for this study, as did the examination of the question regarding continuities and discontinuities of professional elites between Nazi Germany and the Federal Republic; I chose the period from 1930 to 1970 to answer that question. With different goals and political systems, both the Nazi dictatorship and the postwar republic used the autobahn to advance their particular versions of modernity.

Finally, the book seeks to contribute to the current discussion about the "green Nazis," that is, the question of whether, and if so to what degree, the Nazi regime was open to ideas today regarded as environmentally friendly, and they implemented corresponding policies.[4] Because the builders of the autobahnen claimed to have found an environmentally compatible technology, they have become prime exemplars in this debate. Michael Prinz and Rainer Zitelmann use the roadway's supposed closeness to nature as an example in their politically dubious attempt to claim National Socialism for modernity. But even authors who have other political or scholarly motivations have maintained to this day that the landscape history of the autobahnen is a success story. For Anna Bramwell and Jost Hermand, the roadways and the constellations of personnel to which they gave rise are evidence of a "green wing" in the NSDAP. William Rollins speaks in this context of a remarkable ecological sensibility. For Simon Schama, as well, it is a fact, however "painful to acknowledge," that National Socialism was "environmentally conscientious."[5] As the present study will show, such conclusions are premature, at best.

Even Gert Gröning and Joachim Wolschke-Bulmahn, landscape architects who, in numerous publications, uncovered their discipline's connections to National Socialism, which had been suppressed as late as the 1980s, saw the involvement of landscape architects in the construction of the autobahnen primarily as evidence for the closeness and ideological convergence between landscape architecture and National Socialism. This iconoclastic and personalizing approach serves a professional discipline's need for self-reassurance. While these references to landscape planning and nature protection before 1945 were certainly a benefit to historical scholarship, they illustrate the limitations of an approach that is engaged primarily in unmasking prominent figures in the field at the expense of contextualization.[6] These studies also fail to examine to what extent the ideas of landscape architects were realized, and whether the claimed closeness between landscape architecture and National Socialism was in fact as constant and consistent as contemporary pronouncements suggest. This weakness affects also the otherwise useful media history of the National Socialist autobahn by Erhard Schütz and Eckhardt Gruber, and the anthology edited by Rainer Stommer.[7]

These authors relied for the most part on the printed sources of the regime in studying the landscape of the autobahnen as a successful project, ignoring along the way the tension-filled history of their planning and construction. Archival sources allow us to paint a more precise and revealing picture of these roadways, thus offering a more nuanced account of their importance to the ideology of National Socialism and the reality of its regime. First approaches in this direction came from the classic work by Karl-Heinz Ludwig and the study by Annette Nietfeld, though both were limited to primary sources available in West German archives. The bulk of governmental sources on the building of the autobahn, however, remained in East Germany after 1945; an analysis of autobahn construction published in that country in 1975 took little interest in the landscape aspects of the roadways.[8] The present study drew not only on the now freely accessible files of the Reich government, but for the first time also on the extensive and informative papers of the Nazi autobahn's chief landscape architect, Alwin Seifert, and what I found there often contradicted Seifert's boastful and self-serving autobiography. The examination of these sources and the use of the landscape concept allowed for a more complex analysis. To put it in greatly oversimplified terms, I have found for the National Socialist autobahnen a declining importance of nature protection and a contradictory amalgam of technocratic planning and attempted landscape management, very much in contrast to authors like Rollins, for whom the autobahn, especially, is evidence of the regime's pro-environment attitude. An analysis that is based on the sources not only reveals the contradictions between intention and actual construction; even on the level of intentions, the simple clarity of propaganda conceals a clash of concepts, ideas, and goals. These conflicts carried over into the planning and building of the roadways and were not resolved by 1945.

During the first two decades of the Federal Republic, the autobahnen were reinterpreted from "Adolf Hitler's Roads" into a modern transportation infrastructure. Civil engineers were able to create professional continuity through methodological discontinuity, and to do so they engaged in their own kind of politics about the past. In the federal administrative system of the Federal Republic, and in the face of the trend to put construction methods on an increasingly scientific footing, the role of landscape architects was severely curtailed.[9]

*

An important goal of this book is to encourage historians to engage themselves more intensively with landscapes. The concept of "landscape" is back in fashion. Since the 1990s, scholars in the humanities and social sciences in Germany have devoted themselves more fully than before to the unwieldy construct of landscape, a spatial, cultural, natural, and also human phenomenon. This upswing is generating reissues of classic prewar works, stimulating new studies on the literary history of landscape, and leading this field of research out of its German defensiveness.[10] Compared to Great Britain and the United States, where "landscape studies" appear more frequently on the academic stage, though not in a leading role, the extent of the interest in landscape in Germany is still modest. It is sufficiently large, however, to address a central aspect of landscape: the technical formation and appropriation of landscape. Without being able to lay out this complex in all its breadth, the present book examines the relationship between landscape and technology by looking at a single example in the realm of transportation.

Let me make the axiomatic statement that transportation and landscape shape each other. The transportation infrastructures of the modern era discovered, partially defined, and always changed the landscapes they transected. Landscapes through which traffic moved were thus turned into landscapes of transportation. Transportation is far more than the economic and material mechanism by which persons and goods move about; rather, for passengers, airplane travelers, and motorists, it includes an experience of landscapes of various kinds. The historical changes in this process are what the present study examines.

In my approach, such landscapes of transportation are understood equally as technological and social constructions. This means, first of all, that these landscapes were by no means the inevitable result of an inherent logic. On the contrary: social groups with identifiable ideologies and interests determined the shape and cultural perception of landscapes. In other words, it is not possible to separate the production of knowledge about transportation and landscape as well as the planning and construction of roads from the level of their cultural meaning. As I will argue, the culturally charged phenomenon of landscape is especially well-suited to examining this interconnection of technology and culture. I will not attempt to probe into the essence of landscape and its specifically German manifestation (if such a thing exists), nor do I seek to analyze *the* experience of landscape in transportation. By the same token, I have not endeavored to write a complete history of the politics and construction of the projects that are mentioned. Rather, this is an attempt to render landscape manageable as a topic of study in the historical sciences, and to test this approach on one example.

The inherently banal statement that most experiences of landscape in the twentieth century were mediated technologically is one of the starting points for the present work. Whether through the train window, motorcycle goggles, or the windshield: in a motorized land like Germany, the ideas and experiences of nature are largely shaped by driving, traveling, and commuting. These everyday landscapes are no less memorable than tourist destinations. To put it more pointedly: what is of interest here is less the gaze from the top of the Alps, but rather the historically evolved, mobile gaze at the peaks of the Alps, at suburbs and noise barriers. In that respect the attention will rest on the everyday landscapes that are involuntary components of travel for passengers and drivers. Yet these landscapes are not accidental creations (let alone technically determined); instead, they are the result of historical decision-making processes based on an ideologically motivated assignment of values and on social conflicts. As we shall see, landscape was always contested and overlaid with various normative signs, and in that respect it was the opposite of a realm free of civilization that Romanticism had made of it. In this study, landscape functions as the stage and rhetorical resource for the clashes between various social groups such as motorists, civil engineers, conservationists, and landscape architects. These social groups competed for prestige, influence, and the power to define and shape the criteria of landscape; in the case of engineers and landscape architects, there was also a quarrel over where to draw the boundaries of institutions and their own disciplines. Who decided whose conception of landscape and transportation would be articulated, heard, and implemented? This question is one point of departure for this study. For the purpose of this book, landscape is therefore not a fixed entity with roots outside society, but a cultural product that must be continually redefined.

A growing overlap: history of technology and environmental history

Over the past few years, the two subdisciplines of history of technology and environmental history have drawn increasingly close, especially in the United States. That was not always so: the most recent détente was preceded by attempts to draw lines of epistemological and institutional separation. While the history of technology began to establish itself at American universities beginning in the 1950s, environmental history has institutionalized itself only during the last twenty-five years. The fact that both areas of research have a substantial overlap in methodology has been a topic of considerable discussion for only a very short time. According to a summary, elements common to both fields are city and environment, industry and natural resources, as well as the use of energy, water, and land.¹¹ In Germany, by contrast, the history of technology had been established as a discipline for decades when (West German) historians of the field published the first articles on the "historical study of the environment" in the early 1980s. This suggests that German historians of technology saw environmental history as a positive challenge in their own field of research, while in the United States there was a tendency toward institutional boundary-drawing and mutual disinterest, which were overcome only in the 1990s.¹² Bridges were built especially by those representatives of the two fields who drew inspiration from the methods of historical geography or who studied cultural representations of nature and technology.¹³

One obstacle along the way was the apparent epistemological clash between technology and environment. At first glance, these two realms are categorically distinct, the one representing that which is made by human hand (technology), the other that which lies outside of humanity (nature). However, this simplistic polarity is not very useful for historical studies that examine human action and perception in nature. Rather, it would seem that humans, technology, and nature are best studied as elements of a continuum. Relevant to environmental history are encounters and exchanges between what appear to be clearly and categorically separate groups. Most interesting in this regard seem to be the overlap and gray zones between nature and technology, where sharp demarcations lose their effectiveness and historical complexity is preferable to binary simplifications.¹⁴

There is also the added fact that it seems epistemologically highly problematic to use nature as a yardstick for evaluating human action.¹⁵ The concept of a wilderness devoid of humans is clearly just as unsuitable for studying the natural environment. More sustainable, for example, is the definition introduced by Joachim Radkau: environmental historians study how humans influence their conditions of life and reproduction and respond to changes. In the process, environmental history pays special attention to the unintended long-term consequences of human action.¹⁶

It should be briefly noted that the German methodological debate about what nature is and how one can grasp it as an environmental historian has a history of its own. Environmental history as practiced in Germany has never lacked such methodological differentiations until now. To put it somewhat pointedly, one might even say that a period of delayed self-reflectiveness on the part of German environmental history is only now coming to an end. In view of the difficulty of defining "environment or nature," one practicing environmental historian has warned of a "loss of the subject."¹⁷ Although nature seems to resist definition, this diversity of perspectives is by no means damaging: "It seems pointless to search for a specific definition; 'nature' clearly signals multifarious and complex experiences. The term 'nature' embodies history, and its substance is perhaps best explained in stories. Those stories would presumably revolve around the connection between the human way of life and the environment."¹⁸

One of the stories is the redefinition and shaping of landscapes for transportation. On the one hand, transportation routes have been dominated, ever since the Enlightenment, by the "ideology of circulation," which transcends space and whose goal is the exchange of persons, goods, and ideas. On the other hand, this circulation simultaneously levels local peculiarities and older cultural landscapes. By embracing this field of tension, the methodological convergence of technology history and environmental history is best suited to approaching the phenomenon of transportation landscapes.[19]

Transportation history: the system of mobility

At the same time, this study aims to make a contribution to the modern history of transportation. Unlike the study of individual carriers, this history seeks to look at transportation as a social, economic, cultural, and technological system, thus trying to integrate itself into the general discipline of history.[20] In the process, transportation history has given rise to various research areas, some of which are represented in this study. As one example, I will mention transportation policy as the focal point where decisions are made about the allocation of financial resources and about investment policies, but also as the regulatory force in the transportation sector. A number of studies on this theme exist. Furthermore, cities have attracted attention as the historical locus where transportation and traffic are concentrated.[21]

Overarching, comparative research approaches that transcend disciplinary boundaries are strongly represented in this subfield of the historical sciences. And the connection to current transportation and traffic planning is something that the discipline of history can at least point to. Because of the potential of existing transportation systems to shape society, and because of the long duration of transportation investments once they have been made, history is present in what happens every day in the realm of transportation and traffic. Behaviors, economic structures, spatial relationships, and cultural practices are all products of and preconditions for the emergence of a specific transportation system. Such historically mediated connecting effects are especially apparent when the discussion in contemporary transportation planning touches on the relationship between traffic and the environment. It would make no sense to deny the role of automobile traffic in today's environmental problems. Millions of dead and injured, millions of tons of pollutants, the effects of urban sprawl cemented in place by the automobile and its infrastructures, with consequences that extend all the way to the health care system—these are the only too-visible downsides of the automobilization of many societies, especially in the second half of the twentieth century.[22]

These observations are not intended as normative guidelines for the present study, however; against this background it is all the more remarkable that wide segments of the public shared the view that roads during the interwar period were able to help improve nature. Here we are not dealing merely with an irony of history, where the unintended side effects trumped the original intentions. Rather, this hoped-for reconciliation of landscape and technology through a certain kind of road construction is, in and of itself, a historical product whose context has far too long remained unclear within historical scholarship. In attempting such a contextualization on various levels, I hope to impart a new twist to Rosenstock-Huessey's caustic remark about the Germans and their trees by looking at the trees along the side of the road.

Notes

1. Eugen Rosenstock-Huessy, *Out of Revolution. Autobiography of Western Man* (Providence, RI/Oxford, UK, 1993 [orig.1938]), 423.
2. Mark Rask, *American Autobahn: The Road to an Interstate Freeway with no Speed Limit* (Minneapolis, 1999).
3. The locus classicus for the social positioning of technology is Wiebe E. Bijker, Thomas Parke Hughes, and T.J. Pinch, eds., *The Social Construction of Technological Systems: New Directions in the Sociology and History of Technology* (Cambridge, Mass, 1987). However, this volume shows little interest in the environmental aspects of technological change.
4. Franz-Josef Brüggemeier, Mark Cioc, and Thomas Zeller, eds., *How Green Were the Nazis? Nature, Environment, and Nation in the Third Reich* (Athens, Ohio, 2005); Joachim Radkau and Frank Uekötter, eds., *Naturschutz und Nationalsozialismus* (Frankfurt/Main and New York, 2003). On the more general debate see Riccardo Bavaj, *Die Ambivalenz der Moderne im Nationalsozialismus. Eine Bilanz der Forschung* (Munich, 2003).
5. Rainer Zitelmann and Michael Prinz, eds., *Nationalsozialismus und Modernisierung* (Darmstadt, 1991); Anna Bramwell, *Ecology in the 20th Century: a History* (New Haven, 1989); Jost Hermand, *Grüne Utopien in Deutschland. Zur Geschichte des ökologischen Bewußtseins* (Frankfurt/Main, 1991); William Rollins, *A Greener Vision of Home: Cultural Politics and Environmental Reform in the German Heimatschutz Movement, 1904–1918* (Ann Arbor, 1997); idem, "Whose Landscape? Technology, Fascism, and Environmentalism on the National Socialist Autobahn," *Annals of the Association of American Geographers* 85 (1995): 494–520. With a similar tendency: Dietmar Klenke: "Autobahnbau und Naturschutz in Deutschland. Eine Liaison von Nationalpolitik, Landschaftspflege und Motorisierungsvision bis zur ökologischen Wende der siebziger Jahre," in *Politische Zäsuren und gesellschaftlicher Wandel im 20. Jahrhundert. Regionale und vergleichende Perspektiven*, ed. Matthias Frese and Michael Prinz (Paderborn, 1996), 465–498. Simon Schama, *Landscape and Memory* (New York, 1995), 119–120.
6. Gert Gröning and Joachim Wolschke-Bulmahn: *Die Liebe zur Landschaft. Teil I: Natur in Bewegung. Zur Bedeutung natur- und freiraumorientierter Bewegungen der ersten Hälfte des 20. Jahrhunderts für die Entwicklung der Freiraumplanung* (Munich, 1986); *Die Liebe zur Landschaft. Teil III: Der Drang nach Osten. Zur Entwicklung der Landespflege im Nationalsozialismus und während des Zweiten Weltkrieges in den "eingegliederten Ostgebieten"* (Munich, 1987); *Grüne Biographien. Biographisches Handbuch zur Landschaftsarchitektur des 20. Jahrhunderts in Deutschland* (Berlin, 1997).
7. Erhard Schütz and Eckhard Gruber, *Mythos Reichsautobahn. Bau und Inszenierung der "Straßen des Führers" 1933–1941* (Berlin, 1996). Rainer Stommer, ed.,*Reichsautobahn. Pyramiden des Dritten Reiches. Analysen zur Ästhetik eines unbewältigten Mythos* (Marburg, 1982).
8. Karl-Heinz Ludwig, *Technik und Ingenieure im Dritten Reich* (Düsseldorf, 1979); idem, "Politische Lösungen für technische Innovationen 1933–1945. Eine antitechnische Mobilisierung,

Ausformung und Instrumentalisierung der Technik," *Technikgeschichte* 62 (1995): 333–344, 336; Annette Nietfeld, "Reichsautobahn und Landschaftspflege: Landschaftspflege im Nationalsozialismus am Beispiel der Autobahnen," Diploma thesis, Technische Universität Berlin, 1985. Karl Lärmer, *Autobahnbau in Deutschland* (Berlin: Akademie, 1975). Judging from the sources I have examined in the present study, the biography by Seidler depicts Todt in too positive a light: Franz W. Seidler, *Fritz Todt. Baumeister des Dritten Reiches* (Berlin, 1986). Important from an economic perspective are Hansjoachim Henning, "Kraftfahrzeugindustrie und Autobahnbau in der Wirtschaftspolitik des Nationalsozialismus 1933–1936," *Vierteljahrschrift für Sozial- und Wirtschaftsgeschichte* 65 (1978): 217–242; Richard J. Overy, "Cars, Roads, and Economic Recovery in Germany, 1932–1938," in his *War and Economy in the Third Reich* (Oxford, 1994),68–89.

9 By setting 1970 as the terminus of the present study, I was able to use the files of the Federal Transportation Ministry in the Bundesarchiv in Koblenz up to that year; because of the restrictive period that applies in Germany, the files from the years after that were not available to me.

10 Rudolf Borchardt, *Der Deutsche in der Landschaft* (Frankfurt, 1989 [orig. 1925]); Friedmar Apel, *Deutscher Geist und deutsche Landschaft. Eine Topographie* (Munich, 1998); Richard Muir, *Approaches to Landscape* (Lanham, Md., 1999) (on the weak foothold of "landscape studies" see xiii–xiv). For an examination from the perspective of cultural studies see Stefan Kaufmann, ed., *Ordnungen der Landschaft. Natur und Raum technisch und symbolisch entwerfen* (Würzburg, 2002).

11 Jeffrey K. Stine and Joel A. Tarr, "Technology and the Environment: The Historian's Challenge," *Environmental History Review* 18 (1994): 1–7; eidem, "At the Intersection of Histories. Technology and the Environment," *Technology and Culture* 39 (1998): 601–640. Additional titles in the Internet version of this article: http://www2.h-net.msu.edu/environ/historiography/ustechnology.htm, accessed 15 January 2005.

12 This view is supported by the fact that the (German-speaking) Society for the History of Technology (*Gesellschaft für Technikgeschichte*) chose "Nature and Technology" as the theme for its first conference in 1992. On the historiography see Norman Fuchsloch, "Einführung in 'Methodenfragen der Umweltgeschichte,'" in *Umweltgeschichte-Methoden, Themen, Potentiale*, ed. Günter Bayerl, Norman Fuchsloch, and Torsten Meyer (Münster, 1996), 1–12. Outside the purview of the present study is the question of why environmental history in Germany—in contrast with the United States—less often crosses the threshold of institutionalization in professorships within history departments.

13 William Cronon, *Nature's Metropolis. Chicago and the Great West* (New York and London, 1991); David E. Nye, *American Technological Sublime* (Cambridge, Mass., 1994); William Irwin, *The New Niagara. Tourism, Technology, and the Landscape of Niagara Falls, 1776–1917* (University Park, PA, 1996); Mark Fiege, *Irrigated Eden. The Making of an Agricultural Landscape in the American West* (Seattle and London, 1999). The classic work is by Leo Marx, *The Machine in the Garden. Technology and the Pastoral Ideal in America* (London, Oxford, and New York, 1964).

14 Rolf-Peter Sieferle, "Einleitung: Naturerfahrung und Naturkonstruktion," in *Natur-Bilder. Wahrnehmungen von Natur und Umwelt in der Geschichte*, ed. Rolf-Peter Sieferle and Helga Breuninger (Frankfurt and New York, 1999), 9–18; Richard White, *The Organic Machine* (New York, 1995), ix–xi; idem, "'Are You an Environmentalist or Do You Work for a Living?': Work and Nature," in *Uncommon Ground: Rethinking the Human Place in Nature*, ed. William Cronon (New York, 1996), 171–185.

15 The philosophical position which says that an epistemic anthropocentrism is unavoidable seems plausible: Ruth and Dieter Groh, "Natur als Maßstab-eine Kopfgeburt," in *Zum Naturbegriff der Gegenwart*, publ. by Landeshauptstadt Stuttgart, Kulturamt (Stuttgart-Bad Canstatt, 1994), vol. 2, 15–37; eidem, *Weltbild und Naturaneignung. Zur Kulturgeschichte der Natur* (Frankfurt/Main, 1991); Hans Lenk, "Der Macher der Natur? Über operativistische Fehldeutungen von Naturbegriffen der Neuzeit," in *Natur als Gegenwelt. Beiträge zur Kulturgeschichte der Natur*, ed. Götz Großklaus and Ernst Oldemeyer (Karlsruhe, 1983), 59–86.

16 William Cronon, "The Trouble with Wilderness; or, Getting Back to the Wrong Nature," in Cronon, *Uncommon Ground*, 69–90; Joachim Radkau, "Was ist Umweltgeschichte?," in *Umweltgeschichte. Umweltverträgliches Wirtschaften in historischer Perspektive*, ed. Werner Abelshauser (Göttingen, 1994), 11–28, 20–21. Review of the literature: Joachim Radkau, "Technik- und Umweltgeschichte," *Geschichte in Wissenschaft und Unterricht* 48 (1997): 479–497, 50 (1999): 250–258, 356–384; Arne Andersen, "Umweltgeschichte. Forschungsstand und Perspektiven," *Archiv für Sozialgeschichte* 33 (1993): 672–701; Verena Winiwarter, *Was ist Umweltgeschichte?* (Vienna, 1998); Joachim Radkau, *Nature and Power: A Global History of the Environment*, trans. Thomas Dunlap (Cambridge, forthcoming).

17 Franz-Josef Brüggemeier, *Das unendliche Meer der Lüfte. Luftverschmutzung, Industrialisierung und Risikodebatten im 19. Jahrhundert* (Essen, 1996), 10.

18 Radkau, "Was ist Umweltgeschichte?," 14. See also the by-now-classic statement of Raymond Williams: "The idea of nature contains, though often unnoticed, an extraordinary amount of human history"; quoted in William Cronon, "Introduction: In Search of Nature," in Cronon, *Uncommon Ground*, 23–56, 25.

19 Rosalind Williams, "Nature Out of Control: Cultural Origins and Environmental Implications of Large Technical Systems," in *Cultures of Control*, ed. Miriam R. Levin (Amsterdam, 2000), 41–68.

20 Barbara Schmucki, "Automobilisierung. Neuere Forschungen zur Motorisierung," *Archiv für Sozialgeschichte* 35 (1995): 582–597; Thomas Kühne, "Massenmotorisierung und Verkehrspolitik im 20. Jahrhundert: Technikgeschichte als politische Sozial- und Kulturgeschichte," *Neue Politische Literatur* 41 (1996): 196–229; Hans-Jürgen Teuteberg,"Entwicklung, Methoden und Aufgaben der Verkehrsgeschichte," *Jahrbuch für Wirtschaftsgeschichte* (1994): 173–194; Helmuth Trischler and Hans-Liudger Dienel,"Geschichte der Zukunft des Verkehrs. Eine Einführung," in *Geschichte der Zukunft des Verkehrs. Verkehrskonzepte von der Frühen Neuzeit bis zum 21. Jahrhundert*, ed. eidem (Frankfurt and New York, 1997), 11–39, 14–15; Wilfried Reininghaus, "Verkehr und Region," in *Verkehr und Region im 19. und 20. Jahrhundert. Westfälische Beispiele*, ed. Wilfried Reininghaus and Karl Teppe (Paderborn, 1999), 1–43; Christoph Maria Merki, "Die verschlungenen Wege der modernen Verkehrsgeschichte," *Schweizerische Zeitschrift für Geschichte* 45 (1995): 444–457; idem, "Unterwegs in unwegsamem Gelände. Historische Straßenverkehrsforschung in der Schweiz," *Traverse* 6, No. 2, (1999): 37–54; Michael Hascher and Stefan Zeilinger, "Verkehrsgeschichte Deutschlands im 19. und 20. Jahrhundert. Verkehr auf Straßen, Schienen und Binnenwasserstraßen. Ein Literaturüberblick über die jüngsten Forschungen," *Jahrbuch für Wirtschaftsgeschichte* (2001): 165–183; Christopher Kopper, *Handel und Verkehr im 20. Jahrhundert* (Munich, 2002).

21 Dietmar Klenke, *Bundesdeutsche Verkehrspolitik und Motorisierung. Konfliktträchtige Weichenstellungen in den Jahren des Wiederaufstiegs* (Stuttgart, 1993); idem, *"Freier Stau für freie Bürger." Die Geschichte der bundesdeutschen Verkehrspolitik* (Darmstadt, 1995); Thomas Südbeck, *Motorisierung, Verkehrsentwicklung und Verkehrspolitik in der Bundesrepublik Deutschland der 1950er Jahre. Umrisse der allgemeinen Entwicklung und zwei Beispiele: Hamburg und das Emsland* (Stuttgart, 1994); Hans-Liudger Dienel and Barbara Schmucki, eds., *Mobilität für alle. Geschichte des öffentlichen Personennahverkehrs in der Stadt zwischen technischem Fortschritt und sozialer Pflicht. Beiträge der Tagung "Öffentlicher Nahverkehr" in München, Dezember 1994* (Stuttgart 1997); Clay McShane, *Down the Asphalt Path. The Automobile and the American City* (New York, 1994); Barbara Schmucki, *Der Traum vom Verkehrsfluß. Städtische Verkehrsplanung seit 1945 im deutsch-deutschen Vergleich* (Frankfurt and New York, 2001).

22 John McNeill has subsumed the environmental impact of the automobile system under the heading "motown cluster" : J.R. McNeill, *Something New Under the Sun. An Environmental History of the Twentieth-Century World* (New York/London, 2000), 297–311.

Chapter 2

LANDSCAPE: THE DUAL CONSTRUCTION

More than 150 years ago, the conservative cultural theorist and folklorist Wilhelm Heinrich Riehl asserted that every age had its specific "eye for landscape." What seemed ugly to one century was beautiful to another. During the "pig-tail period" (the 1770s and 1780s), the Black Forest had been seen as barren and unpleasant, but in Riehl's day it was discovered as a picturesque landscape.[1] If this observation is true, Clio is beginning to develop a keener eye for landscape in our time. The changing landscape and the changing gaze at the landscape have been topics of historical study for some years now.

A study of the landscape of the autobahn requires that one address, at least conceptually, what is meant by landscape. For it was landscape, not environment or nature, that was the goal and effect—or at least the contested entity—for the roadway planning under examination here. All participating social groups—from landscape architects and roadway engineers to journalists, landscape painters, novelists, and the users of the autobahn—mostly had landscape in mind when they spoke or wrote about the spatial consequences of the roads. Consciously or not, they were tapping into one of the most complex discourses of modernity. A quick glance at the geographic, art-historical, philosophical, and historical literature about the concept of "landscape" already reveals that we are dealing with an ambiguous and multivalent term that resists a convenient definition. The landscape ecologist Ludwig Trepl has emphasized that landscape is at the heart of the most diverse discourses.[2] Since the contemporary landscape concept represents the confluence of various traditions, identifying an unbroken and coherent landscape concept would amount to an analytically useless narrowing.

The easiest approach for historians is to refer to landscape as a political entity. As early as the Frankish kingdom of the Middle Ages, landscape names acquired importance as jurisdictional, administrative, fiscal, or seigneurial elements for organizing space. In the estate-based structure of the territorial state, *Landschaft*

Notes for this section begin on page 17.

was seen as the totality of the estates vis-à-vis the prince. As late as 1953, administrative units of provincial self-administration in North Rhine-Westphalia were set up, following the Prussian model, as *Landschaftsverbände*. All these administrative and political conceptions of landscape will be intentionally ignored here, since this level of the landscape concept is of little help to an analysis of technological landscapes.[3]

Instead, it is useful, in the aftermath of the misleading dichotomy between technology and nature mentioned above, to posit landscape and technology not as a pair of opposites, but as a complementary continuum in which humans and nature have made a place for themselves. As David Nye has said: "Technology is not alien to nature, but integral to it." Landscapes, in other words, are not static places, but "changing sites where new meanings are constantly emerging."[4] It is therefore important to see landscapes as construed both physically and socially at the same time: they are not only imagined as pictures in the mind, but are simultaneously constructed with shovels, backhoes, tar, and concrete.

Physically altered landscapes

On the one hand, natural spaces, especially in densely settled Central Europe, have been used, altered, and shaped by humans for millennia.[5] Hardly a blade of grass grows without human influence or use. Historians would do well to neither celebrate nor lament this circumstance, but simply to note and examine it in all its complexity. Riehl coined the phrase "cultural landscape" (*Kulturlandschaft*) for such areas, and it is relevant for geography and landscape studies. Transportation routes such as railroads and roadways are prominent elements of these cultural landscapes.[6] Railroad embankments and autobahn tunnels profoundly alter the topography. Such infrastructures are superimposed upon other types of uses, such as agriculture, forestry, and commerce outside of urban agglomerations, and evolved cityscapes within cities. It would be false, however, to think of the growth of traffic corridors as the transformation of formerly static landscapes. Rather, changes to the landscape, though varying in intensity, have always been a consequence and companion of human history.[7] The notion that preindustrial landscapes are necessarily intact and harmonious, and that landscapes in the industrial age are always destructive, is therefore not tenable and a topic for scholarship rather than a heuristic device. Furthermore, Hansjörg Küster has shown that the dynamic of the human impact on landscape is added to the natural dynamic of landscape transformation. Already before the Neolithic revolution, and thus before the massive impact of humans on the landscape in Central Europe, landscape was in a fundamental process of change. As a result, the static idea of nature protection, the preservation of traditional landscape types, could thus have very ironic consequences—not only that protected landscapes are the product of human activity (as, for example, the Lüneburg Heath, one of Germany's oldest nature parks), but that constant interventions are necessary to preserve the appearance of the ensemble and retard the natural dynamic. The notion of a static landscape was given up in the biological sciences only in the second half of the twentieth century.[8]

Culturally altered landscapes

On the other hand, landscapes are socially constructed, since they privilege a particular "way of seeing," as the cultural geographer Denis Cosgrove put it. The contemplation of a landscape, whether from a moving car or a lookout tower, is a cultural practice that builds on other cultural practices. In art history, landscape was, from the late Middle Ages, a technical term for a painting depicting a slice of nature. Both the term and the genre emerged over five hundred years ago and dominated landscape painting into the twentieth century.[9] In the fifteenth century, landscape emancipated itself into an autonomous subject, turning from an illustrative background for narrative stories from nonreligious literature and the Bible into a theme in its own right. The formerly abstract landscape became recognizable and quotidian.[10] In the last years of the sixteenth century, *Landschaft* traveled from southwest German attestations via the Netherlands to England, where, as landscape, it became a genre term and loanword in the English language.[11] Since the Romantic period, in particular, certain types of landscapes were invested with national attributes as a way of simultaneously creating and illustrating the link between nature and nation.[12] The most prominent German example is the Romantic mystification and quasireligiosity in some of the paintings by Caspar David Friedrich, whom contemporary critics already accused of "pathological emotion."[13] This kind of criticism did not detract from the tremendous public reception of these works. In fact, Friedrich's readily accessible and understandable symbolism allowed his elevation of nature into the realm of the metaphysical to become one of the best-known facts of German landscape painting.

Informative and revealing from the perspective of the history of the environment and of technology are the depictions of railroad journeys in the nineteenth century in the paintings of Adolph von Menzel and Joseph Mallord William Turner. In the face of the alleged destruction of space through transportation that was noted by contemporaries, these painters, like Claude Monet, sought to pictorialize a temporal perspective. In twentieth-century Modernism, landscape became, if not entirely obsolete, certainly increasingly uncommon. In 1925, Ferdinand Léger formulated the apodictic statement that landscape no longer existed.[14]

The art historian Martin Warnke has looked at "political landscape," a topic that is close to my own theme. He tries to examine visual depictions for their political and social changes. Warnke is intent on showing that an eye for and perception of the landscape need not suffer from political conditions, but can in fact be sharpened by them. In the fine arts we can find various interpretative claims made on landscape, beginning with political order, which correlates with the order of the landscape. Monuments, boundary stones, and roads convey meanings and, as Warnke puts it, "demand certain statements from the landscape." In spite of the overloading of nature in landscape painting, he has argued, the former held its own as "nature *qua* nature." This link of politics and landscape, which points to the political function of landscape and the landscape function of politics, will have a prominent place in the subsequent analysis.[15]

Equally useful in this context are the impulses from cultural geography—especially the work of Cosgrove—for an understanding of landscape as scenery. In the 1990s, the subjective experiential quality of landscape, its interpretative openness, made it more attractive to broad segments of cultural studies. More recently, cultural geography has also begun to see landscape as more than a dialogue and to study also its physical qualities.[16]

In the meantime, history rediscovered landscape as a field of research in the last ten years. The motivations behind this have been varied, ranging from the rediscovery of the region as a historical entity, to Schama's broadly conceived, though not always reliable, general history of the myth of landscape.[17] Most stimulating for the present study were those works that relate the examination of conceptions of landscape to concrete changes in the landscape. Large-scale technological projects of the nineteenth and twentieth centuries have attracted numerous historical analyses. One of the first studies that examined landscape as an experience and its technological change was Wolfgang Schivelbusch's classic work on the railway journey in the nineteenth century, published nearly thirty years ago. Schivelbusch noted that the railroad created "panoramic travel," where the travelers, because of the increased speed, could no longer perceive the foreground of landscape and therefore concentrated on the background or new kinds of travel reading.[18] It was only in the 1990s, and especially in the Alpine countries of Switzerland and Austria, that landscape changes through transportation routes became again a topic of research. All these studies are based on the assumption that the perception of landscape is both technologically constructed and charged with various cultural values. It was precisely during a journey—whether by car or train—that landscape pictures were created that were interpreted as specifically Austrian or specifically Swiss. Wolfgang König has also pointed out that different technological alternatives for the construction of such transportation arteries existed and that their planning was the topic of controversies.[19] Separate landscape histories dealt with the surveying of landscape as a social practice, the reshaping of the Rhine, the landscape history of an industrial region, and landscape changes through oil drilling.[20]

Building on these examples from historical scholarship, the present study is interested in the dual—physical and discursive—construction of landscape in the planning and construction of the autobahnen. The methodological approach by way of both environmental history and the history of technology is intended to do justice to the interweaving of landscape and technology. That is why this study will focus on the treatment of landscape and on the technological means for changing it that were chosen and those that were not. Technology and nature were constructed both topographically and in the imagination of their creators and consumers. At the same time, I have sought to shed light on those conceptions of landscape that were created or obstructed by these changes or static efforts. These conceptions can be found in the utterances of the actors; in part they become visible only after the conclusion of a construction project as unintended consequences. The multifaceted history of the term "landscape" that I have sketched here provides some sense of the various ideological and social claims that were brought to bear on landscape. Conflict, not consensus, was the hallmark of landscape design.

Yet attention will be given not only to the production side of landscape. Traffic routes were used by motorists who—similar to other processes of consumption—appropriated the groomed landscape, invested it with meaning, and in the process changed it.[21] The effect of landscape in the form of an individual driving experience will also be examined; in this way, landscape will be made usable for environmental history as a term that contemporaries defined in individually different ways.

Notes

1. Wilhelm Heinrich Riehl, "Das landschaftliche Auge," in his *Culturstudien aus drei Jahrhunderten*, 2nd ed. (Stuttgart, 1859), 57–79.
2. Trepl, Ludwig: "Was ist Landschaft?," *Der Bürger im Staat* 44 (1994): 2–6, 6; Werner Flach, "Landschaft. Die Fundamente der Landschaftsvorstellung," in *Landschaft*, ed. Manfred Smuda (Frankfurt/Main, 1986), 11–28; Gerhard Hard, *Die "Landschaft" der Sprache und die "Landschaft" der Geographen. Semantische und forschungslogische Studien zu einigen zentralen Denkfiguren in der deutschen geographischen Literatur* (Bonn, 1970).
3. Gunter Müller, "Zur Geschichte des Wortes Landschaft," in *"Landschaft" als interdisziplinäres Forschungsproblem. Vorträge und Diskussionen des Kolloquiums am 7./8. November 1975 in Münster*, ed. Alfred Hartlieb von Wallthor and Heinz Quirin (Münster, 1977), 4–12; Rainer Piepmeier, "Landschaft," in *Historisches Wörterbuch der Philosophie*, ed. Joachim Ritter and Karlfried Gründer (Basel and Stuttgart, 1980), vol. 5: cols. 11–28, 12. See also the reference to the interweaving of aesthetic and legal definitions of landscape in Kenneth Olwig, *Landscape, Nature, and the Body Politic: From Britain's Renaissance to America's New World* (Madison, 2002).
4. David E. Nye, "Technologies of Landscape," in Nye, *Technologies*, 3–17, 10, 16.
5. Werner Konold, ed., *Naturlandschaft-Kulturlandschaft. Die Veränderung der Landschaften nach der Nutzbarmachung durch den Menschen* (Landsberg, 1996).
6. Ulrich Troitzsch, "Die technikgeschichtliche Entwicklung der Verkehrsmittel und ihr Einfluß auf die Gestaltung der Kulturlandschaft," *Siedlungsforschung. Archäologie-Geschichte-Geographie* 4 (1986): 127–143; Thomas Lekan and Thomas Zeller, "Introduction: The Landscape of German Environmental History," in *Germany's Nature: Cultural Landscapes and Environmental History*, ed. eidem (New Brunswick, 2005), 1–14; Denis E. Cosgrove, "Landscape and *Landschaft*," *Bulletin of the German Historical Institute Washington D.C.*, No. 35 (Fall 2004): 57–71.

7. Andreas Dix, "Vorindustrielle Kulturlandschaften. Leitlinien ihrer historischen Entwicklung," in *Die Veränderung der Kulturlandschaft. Nutzungen-Sichtweisen-Planungen*, ed. Günter Bayerl and Torsten Meyer (Münster and New York, 2003), 11–31.
8. For an example of this natural dynamic see Hansjörg Küster, *Geschichte der Landschaft in Mitteleuropa. Von der Eiszeit bis zur Gegenwart* (Munich, 1995), 10, 69–70. Küster evidently regards the concept of landscape as so unproblematic that he does not define it in any detail. On the methodological change in ecology see Michael G. Barbour, "Ecological Fragmentation in the Fifties," in Cronon, *Uncommon Ground*, 233–255.
9. Müller, "Zur Geschichte," 9.
10. Erich Steingräber, *Zweitausend Jahre europäische Landschaftsmalerei* (Munich, 1985), 73, has identified the painting "St. Peter's Miraculous Fish Catch" (1444) by the Rottweil painter Konrad Wirtz as an intermediate step and the "first reliably identifiable 'landscape portrait' in European painting." The painting is shown in Steingräber, plate 34. The Danish art historian Wamberg, by contrast, dates the transition to the 1420s: Jacob Wamberg, "Abandoning Paradise. The Western Pictorial Paradigm Shift around 1420," in Nye, *Technologies*, 69–86, here 71.
11. Erich Steingräber, "Zur Einführung. Über Natur, Landschaft und Landschaftsmalerei," in Steingräber, *Zweitausend Jahre europäische Landschaftsmalerei*, 9–17, 9.
12. Barbara Novak, *Nature and Culture. American Landscape and Painting 1825–1875*, (New York and Oxford, 1995); W.J.T. Mitchell, *Landscape and Power* (Chicago, 1994): landscape as the "dreamwork of imperialism" (p. 19); Peter Howard, "Painter's Preferred Places," *Journal of Historical Geography* 11 (1985): 138–154. See the attempt to look at landscape paintings from the perspective of art history and environmental history in Bernhard Buderath and Henry Makowski, *Die Natur dem Menschen untertan. Ökologie im Spiegel der Landschaftsmalerei* (Munich, 1986). On Friedrich ibid., 120–130, 171–175; Gottfried Boehm, "Das neue Bild der Natur. Nach dem Ende der Landschaftsmalerei," in Smuda, *Landschaft*, 87–110.
13. Oskar Bätschmann, *Entfernung der Natur. Landschaftsmalerei 1750–1920* (Cologne, 1989), 297. On Friedrich see Simon Schama, *Landscape and Memory* (New York, 1995), 106.
14. Schama, *Landscape and Memory*, 102. On travel by train see the following discussion of Schivelbusch. Fernand Léger, "Sehr aktuell sein" (1925), quoted in Bätschmann, *Entfernung der Natur*, 210.
15. Martin Warnke, *Political Landscape: The Art History of Nature*, trans. David McLintock (Cambridge, Mass, 1995), 145–146. The author erroneously attributes military intentions to the German autobahnen (13). See Chapter 4.
16. Denis E. Cosgrove, *Social Formation and Symbolic Landscape* (Totowa, NJ, 1985), 1. See the preface to the new edition of the book and the literature cited there: *Social Formation and Symbolic Landscape*, 2nd ed. (Madison, Wisc., 1997), xi–xxxv. Also, see Don Mitchell, *Cultural Geography. A Critical Introduction* (Oxford, 2000); Muir, *Approaches*; Cosgrove, "Landscape and *Landschaft*"; George F. Thompson, ed., *Landscape in America* (Austin/Tex., 1995); George Henderson, "'Landscape is Dead, Long Live Landscape': A Handbook for Sceptics," *Journal of Historical Geography* 24 (1998): 94–100; Alexander Wilson, *The Culture of Nature. North American Landscape from Disney to Exxon Valdez* (Cambridge and Oxford, 1992); Anne Whiston Spirn, "Constructing Nature: The Legacy of Frederick Law Olmsted," in Cronon, *Uncommon Ground*, 91–113. For a further discussion on German-language geography see Thomas Zeller, *Straße, Bahn, Panorama. Verkehrswege und Landschaftsveränderung in Deutschland 1930 bis 1990* (Frankfurt/New York, 2002), 28–35.
17. Norbert Fischer, "Der neue Blick auf die Landschaft," *Archiv für Sozialgeschichte* 36 (1996): 434–442; Sabine Doering-Manteuffel, *Die Eifel: Geschichte einer Landschaft* (Frankfurt and New York, 1995); Schama, *Landscape*. On Schama's problematic characterization of landscape practices under National Socialism, see the following chapter.

18. Wolfgang Schivelbusch, *Geschichte der Eisenbahnreise* (Munich, 1977); English translation *The Railway Journey. The Industrialization of Time and Space in the 19th Century* (Berkeley, 1986); John R. Stilgoe, *Metropolitan Corridor. Railroads and the American Scene* (New Haven and London, 1983).
19. Georg Rigele, *Die Wiener Höhenstraße. Autos, Landschaft und Politik in den dreißiger Jahren* (Vienna, 1993); idem, *Die Großglockner-Hochalpenstraße: Zur Geschichte eines österreichischen Monuments* (Vienna, 1998); Wolfgang Kos, ed., *Die Eroberung der Landschaft: Semmering, Rax, Schneeberg. Katalog zur Niederösterreichischen Landesausstellung Schloss Gloggnitz 1992* (Vienna, 1992); idem, *Über den Semmering. Kulturgeschichte einer künstlichen Landschaft* (Vienna, 1984); Walter Zschokke, *Die Straße in der vergessenen Landschaft: Der Sustenpass* (Zurich, 1997); Wolfgang König, *Bahnen und Berge. Verkehrstechnik, Tourismus und Naturschutz in den Schweizer Alpen 1870–1939* (Frankfurt and New York, 2000).
20. David Gugerli, ed., *Vermessene Landschaften. Kulturgeschichte und technische Praxis im 19. und 20. Jahrhundert* (Zurich, 1999); Traude Löbert, *Die Oberrheinkorrektion in Baden. Zur Umweltgeschichte des 19. Jahrhunderts* (Karlsruhe, 1997); Mark Cioc, *The Rhine: An Eco-Biography* (Seattle and London, 2002); Gerhard Lenz, *Verlusterfahrung Landschaft. Über die Herstellung von Raum und Umwelt im mitteldeutschen Industriegebiet seit der Mitte des neunzehnten Jahrhunderts* (Frankfurt and New York, 1999); Brian Black, *Petrolia: The Landscape of America's First Oil Boom* (Baltimore and London, 2000).
21. John Urry, *Consuming Places* (London and New York, 1995), 187–210; Scott Lash and John Urry, *Economies of Signs and Space* (London, Thousand Oaks, and Delhi, 1994), 252–278.

Chapter 3

THE HISTORICAL HABITAT OF LANDSCAPE-FRIENDLY ROADS

One of the most important attributes that the National Socialist regime bestowed on the autobahn of the 1930s was its novelty. The purpose, design, and scale of the roads were thoroughly new—at least that is how the accompanying propaganda presented it. While the constructed autobahn network was indeed more extensive than all other comparable road systems, it certainly did not grow out of the German soil overnight and without deeper roots. Moreover, the novelty that the Nazis claimed for their most prominent technological project was part of the intended mythologizing. It was only through constant emphasis on the unprecedented that the modernity of the roads and thus of the regime could be established. From the historian's perspective, however, it is important to place the origin, design, and goal of the autobahn into larger contexts. Although the attempt to completely untangle the web of project and myth would be futile, it is imperative for a deeper study to identify and examine related ideas, discourses, and projects.

The landscape history of the autobahnen is largely embedded within two frameworks of research. For one, this study builds on the reassessment that began in the 1990s of the nature conservation and *Heimatschutz* (homeland protection) movements in Germany in the twentieth century; for another, the political history of the roads itself offers a historiographic context. To make it easier to shed light on the significance of the autobahn's landscape for German history as well as the history of technology and the environment, the discussion that follows will lay out these two backgrounds. Also needed are brief biographical references to Alwin Seifert, the chief landscape architect of the Nazi autobahn, in whose work these two currents flowed together and the conflicts over the design of the roads became visible.

Notes for this section begin on page 41.

The autobahnen in environmental history

Examining the relationship between landscape and technology by using the German autobahnen as an example allows one to draw deeper inferences about the history and significance of historical currents in Germany that were focused on the environment. A reassessment of the nature conservation and *Heimatschutz* movements is beginning to emerge today within the historical sciences. As in similar movements in other European countries, mostly educated middle-class urbanites formed local, regional, and finally national alliances to protect their *Heimat* from what they saw as the encroachments of modernity. *Heimat* encompassed not only regionally distinct landscapes, but also regional dialects, cuisine, and dress and signified a deep emotional attachment to place.

While these movements were simply dismissed as reactionary and hostile to progress a generation ago, they are now increasingly seen as more complex social developments. A more differentiated analysis of their ideology and impact points to tensions between various currents within the organizations, to their beginning scientization and their changing political importance. Alongside the generally accepted, almost trivial, love of *Heimat* and the urge to protect nature, these organizations provided a platform for such contrary currents as the international nature park movement and an increasingly insular racism after the end of the First World War. Added to this is the fact that the *Heimatschutz* movement both acted as a conduit and prepared the way for the penetration of conceptions of landscape protection into the road-building plans of the Nazis. As I will show, many of the landscape architects involved in the construction of the autobahnen were members of the *Heimatschutz* movement or were at least grounded in its tradition. In fact, contact between the Nazi state and the group in question occurred via the *Heimatschutz*.

Further, ideas that had already been discussed within the *Heimatschutz* movement exerted an influence on the design of the freeways. However, I want to avoid seeing the *Heimatschutz* movement as a mere precursor to the ideas and policies of conservation within National Socialism, or, conversely, to examine the conceptions of this time as late projections of *Heimatschutz*. Instead, road planners were interested in replacing the "old" conservation and *Heimatschutz* movements with a professional elite of ideologically motivated designers. This has been overlooked by previous scholarly literature, which saw in the autobahnen merely the continuation of a *Heimatschutz* tradition and did not shed enough light on the emerging split between landscape architects and conservationists.

At the beginning of the *Heimatschutz* movement there stood, without a doubt, the conservationist idea of nature. The belief in progress and sense of optimism in Germany's comparatively late process of industrialization went hand in hand in the late nineteenth century with complaints that some members of the educated bourgeoisie voiced about this surging economic growth. They identified the landscape as the victim of the economic upswing. In an 1880 essay entitled "On the Relationship of Modern Life to Nature," the Dresden music professor

Ernst Rudorff noted accusingly that industrialization was destroying the "picturesque and poetic" in the landscape.[1] Rudorff's critique blended the yearning for unspoiled nature with an invocation of the "Germanic essence"; the nation was the motivation behind the protection of nature. It was not the destruction of landscape as such that was felt as a loss, but the disappearance of the German landscape.

By invoking mythical and fairy-tale figures, poets, and music, Rudorff elevated nature to the rank of a phenomenon that stood behind and above everything, whose final depths could apparently be plumbed only by artistic souls. This landscape was removed from and opposed to human activities, older than the latter and obeying inherent laws. Thomas Nipperdey discerns two countervailing and mutually complementary trends in the late nineteenth and early twentieth centuries: on the one hand there was the scientification and mathematization of the understanding of nature, which made the approach to nature increasingly difficult for the layperson.[2] This scientizing development led, on the other hand, to a further privatization of the experience of nature by the individual; at least the bourgeois understanding of nature was, as the example of Rudorff's pronouncements shows, aesthetic and sentimental.

Rudorff's contemplation of nature articulated dichotomies that provided many points for the agenda of subsequent discussions. *Heimatschützer* countered a modernity that was felt to be discomforting with their critique of civilization: feeling and emotion were pitted against rational and economic thinking; German spirit was pitted against productivity gains and individual profit. Rural boundedness was the antithesis to the urban lack of culture as expressed in the workers who acted en masse. Behind this was the deep-seated conflict between culture and civilization. Rudorff evidently went further in his critique than the first chairman of the *Bund Heimatschutz*, Paul Schultze-Naumburg, an artist, architect, and writer.[3] Rudorff turned a blind eye to the developments of modernity in his own peculiar way. Although he joined many of his contemporaries in placing his hopes in the emerging electricity, which enhanced aesthetic qualities by separating the dirty site where it was generated from the clean place where it was consumed, Rudorff believed that a dam or other such installation "can never be seen as a beautification of nature; it is and remains under any circumstance the relinquishing of an ideal possession." He was equally categorical in his rejection of the use of the steam-operated threshing machine in agriculture: the peasants would merely use the free time gained through the machine for outings to urban entertainments; it would be far better if they kept the energy of their muscles fresh.[4] This paternalism of the urban educated bourgeoisie, with its deep-seated distrust of mass culture, remained a fundamental constant of the *Heimatschutz* movement well into the twentieth century, especially with respect to mass tourism.

With Rudorff as the driving force, a founding meeting in Dresden in March of 1904 established the *Bund Heimatschutz*.[5] While the original agenda ranged from the preservation of ancient monuments, to landscape protection, all the way to traditional costumes, practical work was dominated by activities involving architecture and the building trade.⁶ The *Heimatschützer* achieved partial victories with their demands for the establishment of nature preserves.⁷ In March of 1898, the parliamentary representative Wilhelm Wetekamp, a senior teacher (*Oberlehrer*) from Breslau, demanded in the Prussian House of Representatives protected areas modeled after Yellowstone National Park, which had been created in the United States in 1872. The *Heimatschützer*, to put it in pointed terms, were out to save landscapes they deemed valuable from the reach of an industrialization they perceived as threatening. This thinking in terms of refuges blended elements of a protective understanding of nature with ideas about a primal landscape under threat at a time of massive social, economic, and cultural upheaval.

The botanist and director of the West Prussian Provincial Museum in Danzig, Hugo Conwetz, following a proposal in that direction, was asked by the Prussian Ministry of Culture to produce a memorandum on the protection of natural monuments; it was published in 1904. In October 1906, the Prussian minister of religious, educational, and medical affairs asked Conwentz to establish and head a "State Office for the Protection of Natural Monuments in Prussia." The office, initially administered as a secondary activity, became an official agency in Berlin in 1911.⁸ Advisory committees were set up in Bavaria in 1906 and in Württemberg in 1908 as state-commissioned expert panels with a consultative function.⁹

In addition to state recognition, the organized *Heimatschutz*, a numerically small movement carried chiefly by the educated bourgeoisie and architects, sought changes to the built environment early on. When it came to practical work, the organization, which thought of itself as a *Heimat* lobby, did not adopt Rudorff's posture of withdrawal but an open engagement with modernity, especially in the shape of modern technology. I will examine the goals and breadth of *Heimatschutz* activities by looking at two examples: the hydroelectric power plant in Laufenburg and the barrages in the Neckar River.

Building technological landscapes on the Rhine and Neckar

The best-known example of early *Heimatschutz* activism is the debate between 1904 and 1908 over a hydroelectric power plant on the Rhine at Laufenburg in Baden—the acid test, as it were, of the newly organized *Heimatschutz*. A consortium of private companies and large banks, including the Berlin electric company AEG (Allgemeine Elektrizitäts-Gesellschaft or General Electric Company) and the Dresdner Bank, was planning a power plant whose original output of fifty-thousand horsepower was more than twice the size of comparable European projects at the time. Speaking for the *Heimatschutz*, Carl Johannes Fuchs, professor of National Economy at the University of Tübingen, argued that economic and aesthetic interests could be reconciled. The public campaign was aimed not at the hydroelectric power plants as such, but against its location: the chosen site threatened to destroy the Laufenburg rapids, which still existed despite the massive upgrading of the Rhine in the nineteenth century.¹⁰

On the other side stood the interests of the electrical industry, for whom the power plant promised to become an important part of the grid. In the battle against the electrical industry—in an interesting twist, AEG's Berlin headquarters was headed by Walter Rathenau, who was an intermittent critic of civilization—the organized *Heimatschutz* supporters eventually lost, even though they began a Germany-wide campaign to collect signatures and received the support from prominent intellectuals like Friedrich Naumann, Max Weber, and Werner Sombart. The *Heimatschutz* presented an alternative project that had been drawn up by an engineer. It envisaged redirecting the water of the Rhine into a side canal to produce electricity, thus saving the rapids. The government of Baden, however, gave the nod to the already planned, large-scale project, and construction began in 1908. Still, the defeat, as the supporters of the *Heimatschutz* saw it, was not total: at the expense of the electrical companies, the Interior Ministry of Baden commissioned a landscape painter to capture the rapids before their destruction. The painting was handed over to the state gallery in Karlsruhe, where it serves as a public testimony to the now vanished rapids.[11] What Warnke has called the compensatory function of landscape painting could not be any more striking than in this case, where the aesthetic losses were to be, if not compensated, at least preserved for posterity by the commissioned work of art.

Although the Laufenburg campaign meant that the first organized action on the part of the *Heimatschutz* against a large-scale technological project failed, the German-wide attention it attracted, the broad support it received from the educated bourgeoisie, and its use of publicity-effective forms of protest such as petitions, letters to the editor, and the collecting of signatures pointed the way to other forms of activism by the *Heimatschutz*. It was also clear that the aesthetic argument of the *Heimatschutz* supporters called at least for a response, and not just inside the circles of the educated bourgeoisie. These responses were a painting in the case of the Laufenburg rapids and a construction method cushioned by *Heimatschutz* concerns in the case of the Neckar.

The Neckar is a river in southwestern Germany that flows through Stuttgart on its way to the Rhine; it was made navigable for coal barges between the wars. Like other southern German states, Württemberg and Baden were looking to develop the river as a way of advancing local industrialization in spite of their geographic distance from the mining and steel industries in the Ruhr region. Coal itself was to reach the Southwest more quickly, and hydropower was to supply energy. *Heimatschutz* interests and local opposition delayed the project during the 1920s, with both sides engaging in a war of experts. As part of the compromise solution that was eventually worked out, the architect Paul Bonatz designed some of the barrages and weirs for the Neckar.

Bonatz had made a name for himself with the central train station in Stuttgart (completed in 1922), whose design sought to combine technical utility and regional architecture. In the case of the barrages for the Neckar, located directly beneath the well-known castle ruins at Heidelberg, Bonatz was eager to avoid "brutalizing the landscape," while emphasizing at the same time that the function of the weir had to be clearly evident to every observer. Local protest by those seeking to protect historical monuments and by university professors had been an attempt to prevent the development of the Neckar. A lobby of American alumni of Heidelberg University, who were now professors at Stanford University, spoke out, as "commissioned guardians of intellectual property," against the planned "despoliation" of the Neckar Valley.

Bonatz's aesthetic claimed to be functional and at the same time sought to accommodate regional concerns. It was intended not only to help mollify the opponents, but also to make the Neckar into the field of experimentation for architectural modernity. For that reason, Bonatz rejected romantic architectural citations such as gabled towers on the power plant, which would have created an obvious link to Heidelberg Castle, located above the Neckar. The architect's goal was accommodation to the landscape through appropriate designs and not through ornamentation. Bonatz craftily extracted the agreement to have the power plant initially built according to his ideas, with the option of adding neo-romantic towers after its completion. Once the barrages were finished, public opinion then swung in favor of the undecorated building and Bonatz won. The architect went on to design other barrages for the Neckar, realizing in them his vision of a modernity cushioned by landscape, a vision that adopted the primacy of function from the Bauhaus modernity, while emphasizing, however, that a building should fit into its landscape through simple, accommodated forms.[12] It comes as no surprise, therefore, that Bonatz was one of the chief architects of the autobahn bridges.

From the perspective of the *Heimatschützer* and of regionalist architecture, the controversies over the Laufenburg hydroelectric power plant and the Neckar barrages were clear signals that technological artifacts within the built environment were architecturally malleable. The *Heimatschützer* had made the architectural style of large infrastructure projects a subject of negotiation in the public sphere. In that respect, the vanished rapids of Laufenburg and the built barrages on the Neckar below the Heidelberg Castle reappeared again and again in various debates and proposed solutions concerning the shape of Germany's technologized cultural landscape in the twentieth century.

Reconciling nature and technology in the interwar period

The Laufenburg power plant and the Neckar barrages were not unique cases, but signs of a general vocabulary of compatibility between modern function and region-conscious design that was theoretically and practically articulated in the first quarter of the twentieth century. The publication most influential in the diffusion of this architectural language was Paul Schultze-Naumburg's "Cultural Works (*Kulturarbeiten*)," which appeared between 1901 and 1917 and was reprinted several times. Schultze-Naumburg presented house types, factories, developed rivers, and gardens. What became famous was the method of visually contrasting "good" and "bad" examples, which Schultze-Naumburg, as his own photographer, used for the first time in Germany and perfected. These informative, lavishly designed, and appealingly written books were widely read far beyond the *Heimatschutz* movement; with only the slightest exaggeration, the art critic Julius Posener, who had been trained in very different schools of thought, said that one could find the *Kulturarbeiten* in every bourgeois household "that wants to be seen as cultivated."[13]

Architectural historians have rightly noted that the *Heimatschutz* style was different from Bauhaus modernity. That became especially obvious in the debate over flat versus pitched roofs, which contemporary observers interpreted as a fight over an international or a national building style. Although this discussion was important to the self-conception of both sides, it alone is not representative. Schultze-Naumburg's publications were also received within the Bauhaus camp; the location of buildings within the landscape was also to the Dessau Bauhaus an important criterion for the success of its architecture. Schultze-Naumburg's goal was not the restoration of an untouched nature. Although "untouched" nature was inherently beautiful, this did not imply the reverse, namely that "reshaped" nature was inherently ugly. On the contrary: as long as natural and human forces worked together in the right way, touched nature was also beautiful, Schultze-Naumburg argued, in a clear allusion to the discourse about cultural landscapes within geography.[14]

Relevant for my purposes is that three of the nine volumes of *Kulturarbeiten* looked at the "shaping of landscape by man." Schultze-Naumburg presented a systematic and vivid array of factories, canals, power poles, and roads. When it came to the latter, Schultze-Naumburg praised sinuous lines as a way of doing justice to the contours of the topography. For him, dead straight road segments were appropriate only on plains and when they led, in the form of an avenue, to a visible goal like a castle. In hilly terrain, however, long, straight roads were an anathema to Schultze-Naumburg, since they ignored the rhythm of the landscape and impressed on it too much the stamp of technology. This preference for the curvy line was nothing new: already in the aesthetic discussion of the eighteenth century, William Hogarth had recommended sinus-shaped "lines of beauty," which were eagerly implemented in garden and park architecture. For Johann Wolfgang von Goethe in 1825, the design of parks necessarily involved "crooked paths"; so many private gardens with meandering paths were laid out in the nineteenth century that contemporary critics spoke derisively of "pretzel paths."[15] Schultze-Naumburg, however, placed the curvaceous line of the road in the context of a massive industrialization, whose infrastructure promised to reach into the last corner of Germany. In this context, sinuous lines in uneven terrain were for him an aesthetically appropriate response to the massive changes of the landscape; the circulation of individuals and machines was to be guided onto aesthetically acceptable paths.[16]

Given the wide circulation of the *Kulturarbeiten*, one may speculate that the designers of the autobahnen were familiar with these publications. Alwin Seifert, the most articulate among the landscape architects, was quite obviously trained on the work of Schultze-Naumburg and counted him among his most trusted correspondents. As we shall see, however, when it came to the autobahnen, the explanatory contexts for sinuous roads and other design features changed.

Schultze-Naumburg's widely read and influential writings were not the only indication that the organized *Heimatschutz* was increasingly accepting and paying attention to industrial architecture and infrastructure during the interwar period. There was a whole genre of publications that the designers of the autobahnen could fall back on for their arguments and plans. Previous scholarship on the landscape of the autobahnen has not paid sufficient attention to the existence and extent of this literature. That has contributed to the inaccurate assessment that the choice of design elements and their justificatory contexts were seen as genuinely National Socialist (that view, incidentally, was in agreement with the claims of the Nazi regime itself). In fact, the design efforts for the roads under the aegis of the Nazis represent the contradictory, mixed application of already existing stylistic elements and discussions.

One important publication in this regard was *Die Ingenieurbauten in ihrer guten Gestaltung* (Well-designed Civil Engineering Works, 1923). The associations of the *Heimatschutz*, the design alliance *Deutscher Werkbund*, and architects published this collection of what they regarded as 250 successful works of civil engineering, from the Tower of Babel to cement factories, electricity masts, and road bridges. Other examples included churches and salt works, single factory buildings, and massive dams. Because the Association of German Engineers (Verein Deutscher Ingenieure or VDI) joined this effort, the volume received the seal of approval, as it were, of the most important associations of architects, engineers, and *Heimatschutz* organizations. While it was remarkable that architects and engineers set aside for this occasion the institutional split that had occurred between them in the nineteenth century, it was more relevant still that the VDI supported this endeavor at all. In the interwar years, engineers were able to join forces with their erstwhile critics of the *Heimatschutz*.[17]

In contrast to Schultze-Naumburg's publications, only positive examples were shown in this volume. The brief accompanying text by Werner Lindner, managing director of the *Bund Heimatschutz*, highlighted the priority given to the building's function. Lindner listed three principles of good civil engineering works: a construction program that articulated the spatial needs and economic requirements; actual construction reflecting good craftsmanship; and a good design for both individual construction elements and the project as a whole. The book was blunt in its criticism of mere ornamentation and decoration such as "transformer stations that look like gingerbread houses." The important thing, rather, was to create "simple, factual (*sachlich*) beauty." The book was nothing less than an affirmation of the landscape-transforming power of technology, provided it was shaped by culturally adept experts: "Landscape has been altered by humans since time immemorial. And that is how it shall continue. For the respect for the irreplaceable treasures of nature and culture will always show us the right paths."[18]

Against Rudorff's fundamental opposition, this architectural primer held up an architectural modernity with a creative underpinning, a modernity that subordinated itself to architectural traditions and cultural landscapes. This justifying rhetoric and these design characteristics became enormously important to the autobahnen. There is good reason to assume that nearly all the landscape architects involved in the building of the autobahnen and many engineers were at least familiar with this literature, even if they may not always have agreed with it.

On the whole, the interwar years saw a growing interest in landscape-bound construction, and—in general—in a genealogy of technological infrastructures in their relationship to the environment. For the *Bund Heimatschutz* and the VDI, Lindner published in 1927 a volume exclusively on factory installations, with line drawings and photographs. Within the heated architectural quarrels in Germany in the 1920s about "The New Objectivity" (*Die Neue Sachlichkeit*) and Bauhaus modernity, Lindner clearly supported an integration into the "*Heimatbild*" (the look of the homeland), but at the same time he emphasized the "strongly counterbalancing tone of the international." As before, his strongest warning was directed against false sentimentality, and the strongest demand was for "adepts," that is, architecturally trained experts.[19] This was also the context for a collaboration between the VDI, the *Heimatschutz*, and the Deutsches Museum in Munich, the national museum of science and technology. In a volume published in 1932, the three institutions presented "technological cultural monuments" as equal to other cultural monuments. On display here was not only the aspiration of the organized engineers to overcome their cultural defensiveness and to capitalize on the concept of 'monument,' but also the affirmation of the historical landscaping of infrastructures such as bridges, which by their age, so it was argued, had virtually fused with the environment.[20]

A representative collection of texts on German *Heimatschutz*, published three years before the Nazis came to power, also proclaimed this organic language of forms to reconcile technology and nature as the quasi-official guideline of the *Heimatschutz*. One essay on "*Heimatschutz* and technology" explicitly distanced contemporary *Heimatschutz* from the founding years that had been marked by a hostility to technology, and it recommended that lovers of the *Heimat* and engineers engage in mutually respectful collaboration. An essay on transportation issues focused above all on water management and electricity transmission lines, surmising that highways could be most easily integrated into the terrain. (Although this was generally true in comparison to railroads, the disagreements about the autobahnen under the Nazi regime and in the Federal Republic show how controversial their design actually was.)[21]

In that volume, and this provides revealing insight into the history of the *Heimatschutz*, we find at the same time a growing frustration on the part of the *Heimatschützer*, who, in spite of their collaboration with other organizations, were not receiving the social recognition they believed they deserved. In Schultze-Naumburg's writings, and especially in his essay for the 1930 anthology, this frustration led to a growing rhetoric of gloom and doom. Differently from what he had still done in the *Kulturarbeiten*, Schultze-Naumburg now attributed the imperfections and ugliness in the landscape to the racial composition of German society, concretely, to the "increasing number of inferior people." In so doing, he provided an echo of contemporary "racial hygiene," which asserted a hierarchy of races and the growth of supposedly inferior elements of society. By the early 1930s, Schultze-Naumburg's thinking had become thoroughly racialized. Although this did not contradict his earlier publications, it did place them into a new explanatory context: instead of bad taste, it was now racially based bad taste that was producing so much ugliness in the landscape and therefore making the work of the *Heimatschutz* all the more urgent.[22] The rhetorical transition to National Socialism, whose ideology—all the syncretism notwithstanding—contained racial thinking as its central category, was therefore not particularly difficult for this current of the *Heimatschutz* movement. And so when Lindner, in a 1934 booklet, described the *Heimatschutz* as "not hostile to progress" and noted its "recognition of modern progress," this was not an empty gesture of deference to the new regime and its urge toward spatial expansion, but the continuation of what was by then an established architectural genre, which Lindner briskly praised as a "building mentality" (*Baugesinnung*). It comes as no surprise that one chapter in Lindner's booklet carries the title "The beauty of civil engineering."[23] Lindner was hoping that the autobahnen announced by the regime would not sacrifice treasures of landscape or urban architecture and would be planted with hedges and native trees.

*

There are two reasons why the context of the *Heimatschutz* movement and its development to 1933 is important for an understanding of the design of the autobahnen. First, the transition away from an antagonistic to a—at least theoretically—conciliatory relationship with technology and engineers created an architectural language, in both publications (as in Schultze-Naumburg) and in the landscape (as in Bonatz), that Nazi managers of technology could tap into. To put it concisely: the idea that the autobahnen should be "integrated into the landscape" was not a National Socialist invention, but the continuation of an established architectural discourse, even if—as we shall see—some of the basic elements of that discourse changed after 1933. The *Heimatschutz* movement, and especially the architects who belonged to it, saw in the embrace of technology a way of garnering the social recognition (and commissions) that would have been denied them had they struck a purely rejectionist stance. They shared this desire for social valorization with the engineers, who were still seeking to demonstrate their relevance by embracing the notion of technology as "cultural work" and a creative endeavor. This overlap of ideology and the quest for status was already considerable before 1933.[24]

Equally noticeable was the increasingly racial underpinning of the demands for a technology that was closely connected to the landscape. This was the second important tie-in with the collective ideology of the National Socialists. In this regard, the advocates of a technology that was cushioned by *Heimatschutz* considerations did not have far to go to find common ground with the new regime. At the same time, it is important to emphasize that the racist rationale behind this architectural style was not inevitable; it seems to have grown stronger under specific political conditions, like the increasing frustration with the Weimar Republic in general and with the advancing industrialization that was antithetical to *Heimat*, in particular. This contradictory amalgam becomes clearer still if one looks at the most important landscape architect of the Nazi autobahn, Alwin Seifert. He combined in a single person some of the developmental characteristics I have mentioned and the volatile history of conservation, landscape architecture, and *Heimatschutz*. Since he was one of the crucial actors in the construction of the roadways, it is worth taking a look at his biography, especially since it is now possible to shed a more revealing light on it with the help of previously unused sources. Through his role in the National Socialist autobahn project, he attained a position of remarkable influence in the Nazi regime. It is not the intent of the present study to provide a biographic account of Seifert. Still, before looking at the landscape advocates as a group, it is worthwhile to weigh the human factor of the professional collaboration between Seifert (1890–1972) and Fritz Todt (1891–1942), the engineer in charge of the Reich autobahnen.

Alwin Seifert and Fritz Todt: a biographic constellation

Alwin Seifert made his own contribution to the myths that emerged around the Nazi autobahn through his autobiography, first published in 1962. There, he presented his own role as central for the roadway's integration into the landscape and recounted this effort in general as a success.[25] An examination based on primary sources can qualify both claims. Born in 1890 into a middle-class family in Munich, Seifert had been personally shaped during the first three decades of his life by the *Wandervogel* (literally "hiking bird") movement with its specific nature experiences, and professionally by his training as an architect in the conservative academic climate of his hometown. His father owned a construction business. Beginning in the 1920s, Seifert was part of a small group of self-taught garden and landscape architects, though without playing a leading role in it.

His personal development was also shaped—as was that of his later mentor Todt (who was only a year younger)—by the fact that he grew up a Protestant in predominantly Catholic regions of southern Germany.[26] More important than the religious affiliation, however, was the deeply felt experience of nature in the Youth Movement, for which Seifert, as a member of the urban bourgeoisie, was predestined.[27] This movement, which took the children of the well-off middle class from the cities into the countryside, encouraged him to carefully study landscapes, especially those of the Isar River in Munich all the way to its source in the Alps, and of the mountains surrounding it. In and with the *Wandervogel* movement, Germany's most important youth hiking group, Seifert and his comrades had an opportunity to "become deeply immersed" in the landscape.[28] The experiences as *Wandervögel* shaped this generation and its understanding of nature, even though they did not predetermine a particular political orientation in adulthood—former *Wandervögel* could become Communists as well as National Socialists. Some of the erstwhile hiking buddies reunited after 1934 during the construction of the autobahn. One study has identified twenty professional representatives from the fields of landscape cultivation (*Landespflege*) and landscape planning (*Landesplanung*) who had been members of the bourgeois youth movement. Six of them worked as advisors to the Regional Planning Offices (*Oberste Bauleitung*) of the autobahn.[29] At least one-third of the "landscape advocates" had thus crisscrossed the land as *Wandervögel*. While it is problematic to reduce youthful hiking and later professional work to mere continuities, it is worthwhile to take a look at the ideas of nature within the Youth Movement.[30]

To begin with, the *Wandervogel*, as an opportunity for diversion outside of the home with one's peers, was attractive to many youngsters simply because it allowed them to escape domestic restrictions. The group experience was described as intoxicating, the kind of experience that only young people are able to have. The *Wandervögel* shared an enjoyment of nature with the excursion tourists from the city they so deeply scorned—though their enjoyment was on a very different level, as they would have insisted. In that sense the movement was also a form of protest against the institutions of what was perceived as a philistine and outmoded adult world. Against this background, the experience of unknown nature provided emotional access to one's own self, self-discovery, and a way of dealing with entry into adulthood. In the experience of nature, as a somewhat more general thesis puts it, "one's own otherness is sought, the path into the inner self is taken, to what is far-away inside, the inner unknown, which is supposed to reveal itself in and through nature."[31] For a person in such an elevated and solemn mood, the actual landscape that one passes through becomes, in the end, irrelevant.[32] The Sunday outing thus turned into an inner rebellion—the writer Kurt Tucholsky later coined the derisive term "*Innenrummel*" (internal carnival).[33]

The actual encounter with nature, as one scholar has noted, was not exactly respectful, as the boys and young men evidently had to be warned not to yell in the forest, tear off branches, or leave trash behind. Moreover, open nature served merely as a backdrop and a stage for group singing and dancing.[34] As for the published notions of landscape, the hikers clearly took their cues from the model of preindustrial landscapes with what was regarded as a harmonious alternation of field, forest, meadow, water, and rural architecture.[35] In this literature, nature was normatively charged and described as grand and sublime. Part of this was the—in the final analysis—metaphysical dimension of the experience of nature. According to George Mosse, those members of the Youth Movement who fought in the First World War experienced nature as a world that was the opposite of the reality of death. Nature was able to overarch victory or defeat.[36]

Historians agree that the notion of the *Wandervogel* movement as a mere escape from the large city into nature and away from civilization into naturalness is a cliché.[37] The arguments of the early *Heimatschutz* movement that were critical of civilization and, as a whole, harsh in tone hardly appeared in the publications of the *Wandervogel* even after the founding of the *Bund Heimatschutz* in 1904. They are found only later and then in a more subtle form. This is clearly evident in the polarity of city and countryside. The large city was not condemned in the Youth Movement—to the extent that one can make this kind of generalization based on its publications; on the contrary, it was "discovered as a *Heimat* to be discovered and shaped."[38] One element that played an important role in this qualified affirmation of the present was the understanding of technology, which was increasingly seen not as the destroyer of old values, but as a creative tool. At the first *Freideutscher Jugendtag* (Free German Youth Day) on the Hoher Meißner mountain near Kassel in October of 1913, the speaker, Gottfried Traub, noted that the Panama Canal had been completed that same day; for him, this sign of a "strong technological will" was a call to people "full of a free will," not a call for hostility to technology.[39] Traub, visibly impressed by this large-scale technological project, wanted to place technology into the hands of powerful, creative men who gave primacy to the will. This kind of declaration at a prominent event distinguished the nature image in the *Wandervogel* movement from the predominantly preservationist notions in the early *Heimatschutz*. The *Wandervögel* sought to give nature its due without completely condemning industrialization. The guiding images from the Youth Movement were aimed above all on an aesthetically mediated conception of nature, though this did not exclude its ecological-classificatory study. A quasi-touristic enjoyment of landscape within a group and a botanic understanding of nature went hand in hand, accompanied by the knowledge of technological infrastructures which—like the railroad—often made the trip into nature close to the city possible in the first place. This particular conception of technology and nature also shaped Alwin Seifert and many of his later colleagues in landscape architecture.

Seifert attended a humanistic *Gymnasium* from 1900 to 1903; acquired his *Abitur* (*Gymnasium* diploma) in 1909 at the Royal Theresengymnasium, a so-called *Realgymnasium* geared toward the sciences, "with an A in all subjects"; and subsequently began an apprenticeship as a bricklayer. After that he studied architecture at the Technical University in Munich, where he was a student of Theodor Fischer, one of the proponents of regionalist architecture. In the spring of 1912, Seifert completed his examination as a journeyman bricklayer, and in the summer of 1913 he passed his diploma examination as an architect "with the highest grade of A."[40]

Following a stint in a construction business, Seifert became an army railroad engineer in World War I; in his Bavarian Reserve Construction Company, he acquired a "great appreciation for truly skillful civil engineering construction." In his memoirs, Seifert combined his memory of battles and regions with thoughts of flowers and shrubs. As a second lieutenant, Seifert built bridges and railroads in Serbia, Poland, and France. South of Metz, he had a light railroad meander its way up a mountain through oak forests, calling it "a true work of art." This conformity to the landscape had a military rationale: a poorly camouflaged railroad would have been an easy target for the enemy.[41]

After the war, Seifert took over his father's construction business, which went bankrupt during the period of hyperinflation. From 1920 to 1923 he had a position as an assistant at the Technical University.[42] Beginning in 1923 he worked as a freelance architect, designing chiefly agricultural buildings and houses in the countryside, and trained himself to be a landscape architect. It was in this capacity that he began to publish essays in professional journals beginning in 1927.

Within landscape architecture, a fundamental transition had occurred since 1900 away from the landscape garden and toward an architecturally designed garden. Analogous to architecture, Paul Schultze-Naumburg rediscovered old, simple, and usable peasant gardens and made them into models. In his own writings, Seifert emphasized "nativeness" (*Bodenständigkeit*), that is, a close rootedness in the landscape and at the same time the unity of house and garden. The notion of "nativeness," chiefly because of its use within National Socialism (which I will examine later), has been reduced to plants that were regarded as native in botany. Within garden architecture, however, the word had already been used since the turn of the century with various meanings. Seifert's notion of "soil-rooted (*bodenständig*) garden art," which he articulated in a fundamental article in 1929, was strongly shaped by economic arguments, not by the exclusive use of certain groups of plants. Seifert's goal was to plan house and garden as a unified entity, in the process creating an organism whose maintenance was economically efficient. The call for nativeness included the choice of local construction materials such as wood, brick, or natural stones, and plants. A garden architect should be able to determine the plant community that was unique to each garden site, though at the same time he had the artistic freedom to design harmonious ensembles of autochthonous botany and non-native but well-suited plants. Revealing about Seifert's understanding of art and nature is also that in his view, every artistic task had only one correct solution. Intuition was the path to this solution, which the garden architect, thanks to his expertise, would be able to articulate and defend as the *non plus ultra*. While such a strategy was still relatively easy to implement when designing house gardens for individual clients, when it came to the construction of the autobahn it became increasingly part of more complicated negotiations.[43]

Let us return to the interwar period: other currents in garden architecture at the time underlined above all the functionality of the garden, going so far as to demand the utilization of every scrap of land during times of economic crisis.[44] This was not a fundamental contradiction, however: for Seifert, the use of native plants was usually more economically efficient than the cultivation of exotic ones. The rhetorical differences between the various garden styles are indications of attempts to carve out one's place within the group of garden architects rather than of radically different notions of design. However, this observation is true only for the period before 1933. After Seifert's rise within the ranks of the National Socialist dictatorship, the meaning of nativeness also changed, as we shall see.[45]

In 1932, Seifert assumed a lectureship at the Technical University for "Garden Architecture and Cemetery Design," previously held by the prolific Munich municipal architect Hans Grässel. The renaming of the seminar to "Practical Garden Design" went hand in hand with a substantive change in course. In his inaugural lecture, the freshly minted lecturer offered a cursory overview of the history of garden art and ended with an "outlook on great, imminent transformations," by which he meant a turning away from the large city, the spread of vegetarianism, and the growing importance of house gardens in the Great Depression. Seifert pointed to the great ethical values connected with gardening, and to the "immersion into the beauty and regularity of nature in the interest of the inner renewal of our people." He presented his academic program as something new, and embedded it within the vocabulary of the life-reform movement. However, what seems characteristic for the context of the early 1930s is the moderate economization of this critique; green politics was seen in connection with the Great Depression as a contribution to the food supply. This nexus of economic efficiency and aesthetics formed the basis of views that were limited to garden design. It was only when these were expanded to landscape design under National Socialism that the *völkisch* roots of such demands were strengthened in the rhetoric of justification.[46]

Beginning in 1930, Seifert became a proponent of biodynamic agriculture without the use of artificial fertilizers and insecticides, which the Austrian occultist and social reformer Rudolf Steiner (1861–1925) had introduced to his anthroposophical movement six years earlier. Anthroposophy was both a spiritual movement and concerned with issues such as education, alternative medicine, and agriculture. Although he did not adopt the anthroposophical worldview entirely, Seifert certainly felt inspired by it and turned his garden in the Munich suburb of Laim into a great biodynamic model garden, which some Nazi grandees visited later on.[47]

Through his aesthetic predilections and his professional activities, Seifert soon came into contact with the organized *Heimatschutz* movement and became a member. On his first larger commission, the building of a farmhouse near Weilheim in Upper Bavaria, he sought to combine the demands of a "highly modern enterprise" with the means of nativist (*bodenständig*) forms. In 1926, he was appointed to a building committee of the Bavarian *Heimatschutz* association. Seifert became active on the national level two years later, when he participated, as a Bavarian delegate, in talks between the German *Heimatschutz* Association (*Deutscher Bund Heimatschutz*) and the Association of Steel Works on the question about the use of steel sheets as a roofing material. Werner Lindner and Paul Schultze-Naumburg became acquaintances of Seifert's.[48]

Although some of Seifert's views changed over the years and some contradictions multiplied and shifted, a few basic constants can be identified. They include a general rejection of rationalistic thinking, and conversely a belief in forces that could not be ascertained by science; linked to this was an awareness of living in an age of upheaval. Through his early penchant for mathematics, chemistry, and technology, he became acquainted with the "mechanistic world view" according to Charles Darwin and Ernst Haeckel. Seifert later wrote that at the age of thirty, that is, in 1920, he severed all inner connections to this "prosaic and thoroughly a-musical world" and henceforth devoted himself to intuition. This sharply articulated dichotomy of emotion and reason, art and science, expression and calculation also shaped his understanding of landscape and technology.[49]

Seifert's critique of civilization, influenced by the *Wandervogel* and *Heimatschutz* movements, made what was measurable and countable, the pervasion of the world with reason and numbers, alongside free-market thinking and racial influences, the basic evils and the reasons behind the progressive destruction of nature. He rejected this kind of "mechanistic" thinking also because it reflected only part of the whole—a common figure of thought in the rhetoric of holism in ecology at the time. Seifert the landscape architect believed that an "age of the living" was beginning with the rule of National Socialism, an age that would overcome the polarities and lead to the ascendancy of feeling guided by intuition:

> In its most profound meaning, this radical change is nothing other than the beginning of a final conflict between, on the one hand, Western and bolshevist materialism, which is limited to a veneration of what is measurable and countable, and, on the other, a world view whose foundation includes the very simple truths of soul, faith, awe, *Heimat*, and nature. The very survival of the German people and thus of Aryan humanity as such depends on the spiritual rebuilding taking hold of all spheres of life and leading them away from the mechanistic worldview of yesterday ... A revaluation of all values is at hand. The countable and the measurable, which was yesterday still the absolute, the unalterable, has today become very relative; now only the unprovable is absolute, imperative.[50]

This anti-Enlightenment, antiscientific resentment was for Seifert one of the main reasons why he devoted himself to shaping the landscape, which escaped mathematical analysis and offered him a tailor-made point of contact with the ideology of National Socialism. Seifert borrowed the language of authenticity and stark dichotomies from the sloganeers of the conservative and *völkisch* movements of the interwar period. It is deeply ironic that these ideas prompted Seifert to participate in the most modern and extensive peacetime infrastructure project of the National Socialists. What is more, his goal was to make the holistic, "spiritual rebuilding" manifest in the form of concrete and hedges, that is, in the shape of a road, which could not have been built in its desired form without "mechanistic" planning. As so many other statements by Seifert, this one, too, involved a good deal of hyperbole. As an architect, Seifert's academic degree was in engineering, which meant that he had an understanding and mastery of the language and methodology of civil engineers. Moreover, it is no doubt safe to assume that the military light railways he built in the First World War, whether or not they were works of art, were subject to conventional technical design specifications. As we shall see, Seifert and the other landscape architects had an adequate knowledge of botany and made unhesitating use of the insights of phytosociology, which employed scientific methods and arguments. As practical gardeners they were quite familiar with classificatory ecology; indeed, the distinction between "alien" and "native" (*bodenständig*) plants presupposed knowledge of the botanical debates at the time. All of these contradictions were, consequently, too great for Seifert to resolve.

For Seifert's self-image, however, the all-embracing claim of his antirationalistic conceptualization was more than merely a rhetorical gesture. He asserted that he was able to produce valid artistic designs for technical problems—such as the routing of roads—in a purely intuitive manner. Since intuitive knowledge was tied to individuals, this raised the importance of personality, which manifested itself in an arrogant expert status. Seifert claimed that he had successfully learned how to grasp things intuitively. Two eccentricities highlight this tendency. He possessed, in his own words, a "calcium aura": his body sensed chalky soil and reacted to it with rheumatic pain. Even in a moving train he could tell whether the wagon was passing over new red sandstone or shell limestone.[51] His house in Munich was located on the Munich *Schotterebene* (gravel plain), and the resultant chronic lack of sleep had constantly spurred him to work. And for Seifert, one of the bones of contention still fought over today between rationalists and believers in intuition had a clear answer: there was no doubt that subterranean veins of water influenced the well-being of humans. Later, if there was a rash of accidents at a particular site following construction of a stretch of the autobahn, a dowser was allowed to probe the "pyramids of the Third Reich" for potential danger spots.[52] It would appear that Alwin Seifert and Fritz Todt shared this belief.

In his memoirs, the erstwhile Reich Landscape Advocate (*Reichslandschaftsanwalt*) left no doubt that strength of will and tenacity formed the foundations of his personality. His sense of humor, he wrote, had been grim, at best; he lacked charm or congeniality. Indeed, for the technicians with whom he had worked on the building of the autobahnen, he had at times "been a truly insufferable person." With his high opinion of himself, Seifert always preferred a robust quarrel to a vague exchange of opinions. One historian described him as "arrogant, brusque of manner, pragmatic and eccentric."[53] Even the obituary at the Technical University Munich in 1972 spoke of "never flagging courage and an unnerving persistence, the secret of his success." In other words: Seifert was a pushy and boastful individual, self-confident to the point of arrogance.[54]

When Seifert detected in himself traits such as determination and tenacity, he attributed them, remarkably enough, to the quality of his inherited tendencies. Evidently, he had learned early on in his life to think in such categories. It was not without some pride that he admitted, in 1938, when such a revelation could only be helpful, that he had been a member in a *völkisch* secret society in

Munich before the First World War. To Ilse Heß, wife of Hitler's deputy and with her husband a client who commissioned a house garden, Seifert wrote that since 1911 he had been educated by the authors of the NSDAP's racial program "to an overappreciation of the Nordic race."[55] At that time, he was certified to be more than 80 percent of Nordic race, and a corresponding "racial arrogance" had been the inevitable result. For this, he had "paid a substantial price" in more than one area, but after that he had straightened himself out again, apparently an allusion to the personal crisis of 1920. He attributed his successes within National Socialism to the "dogged tenacity of the Huguenot part of my blood" from his mother's side.[56] While Seifert continued to believe in 1938—as he no doubt had since the break with the Nordic racial theory at the beginning of the 1920s—that racial factors formed personality, he now also regarded races that were not strictly "Nordic," like the "Alpine" ones, as racial equals.[57] Seifert also mentioned having been a member of a "Widar Circle," a "small *völkisch* club," in which he allegedly met Rudolf Heß in 1919.[58] To be sure, the scholarly literature on the numerous *völkisch* organizations in Munich knows of no organization with such a name,[59] but it does suggest that the Widar Circle could have been one of the lodgelike circles around the Thule Society in Munich, the extreme right-wing secret society that was one of the precursors of the Nazi party. With elaborate rites of initiation and strict hierarchies, their goal was to counter the presumed circles of the Jewish world conspiracy.[60]

We are left with two things: first, there is the name of the group, whose roots in Nordic mythology point to the "high-Nordic men and women."[61] In Nordic mythology, Widar (also Vidar or Vidarr) is a son of Odin, who at the time of Ragnarök (what the composer Richard Wagner calls the Twilight of the Gods) avenges his father's death by tearing apart the jaws of the Fenrir wolf and plunging his sword into its body.[62] Second, Seifert retained a strident anti-Semitism from his days in the Widar Circle. He boasted in a letter to the Berlin landscape architect and competitor Heinrich Wiepking-Jürgensmann: "What you write about Jewish clients fortunately does not apply to me. Since I already joined a very anti-Semitic, *völkisch* secret society in 1911, I avoided Jews whenever possible. And the only one for whom I was willing to design a garden during the worst times, you took from me."[63]

Before 1933, Seifert was not present on the public political stage. During the Nazi dictatorship, he claimed that he had been a member of the antirepublican, reactionary German National People's Party (*Deutschnationale Volkspartei*) from at least 1919 to 1921.[64] The world economic crisis resulted for Seifert, as it did for others in the self-employed professions, in a dearth of commissions. He and his wife Maria, the sister of the composer Carl Orff, were deeply in debt.[65]

In sum, one can say that Seifert's ideological and professional inclinations predestined him for far-reaching coalitions of ideology and interest in the Third Reich. His personality—antirational, drawn to artistic ideals, and hardly ever plagued by self-doubts—prepared him ideologically for the National Socialist discourse on technology, and personally for the pronounced power struggles of the Third Reich. To this was added an assertive personality. One can surmise that while he probably did not yearn for the dictatorship, he also did not regret the end of the Weimar Republic. Yet his basic attitude—protective of his *Heimat*, elevating rootedness in the soil to a leitmotif, anti-Semitic, and *völkisch*—made him recognize that the new Reich offered a chance to realize his ideas about the shaping of landscape. Trained on the work of Schultze-Naumburg and Lindner, Seifert combined the ideas about nature and technology from the *Heimatschutz* of the 1920s with the creative will of the architect. He was much less interested in the mere protection of nature and the establishment of preserves than in the shaping of new landscapes. That landscapes changed and that the pace of these changes since industrialization was rapid was so obvious to Seifert that it hardly needed to be stated. In spite, and precisely because, of his bond to landscapes, he approved of the massive transformation of nature by the infrastructure projects of National Socialism, as long as they were guided by experts like himself who were motivated by *Heimatschutz* concerns. As a public project that was extensive and appeared in the guise of modernization, the building of the Reich autobahnen was a welcome opportunity for the freelance architect to improve his material circumstances and to alter the built landscape beyond the borders of his native Bavaria. To that extent, Seifert was an almost ideal embodiment of the attitude of the *Heimatschutz*, with its modernity-affirming architecture and emerging racism.

With the patronage of Rudolf Heß and Todt, Seifert quickly attained an informal position of some influence within the National Socialist power structure. He became an important contact person for the Anthroposophical movement. At the same time, the regime's confused administrative structures provided a platform for Seifert's skill at getting his way and for his rhetorical talents. The dictatorship rewarded him with honorary titles: in 1938, he was awarded the title of "Professor" on the occasion of Hitler's birthday. On Seifert's fiftieth birthday, Todt appointed him "Reich Landscape Advocate." Although this was neither a position nor an honorary office, and it didn't come with any defined powers, the Byzantine-sounding honorific title flattered its bearer's need to feel self-important. Seifert's influence waned after Heß's flight to England and Todt's death in a plane crash. For a while, he was under surveillance by the Reich Main Security Office (*Reichssicherheitshauptamt*). Personal constellations were more important to his position than institutionalized influence.[66] Hermann Giesler, one of Hitler's architects, rightly attests that Seifert had a penchant to "vivere pericolosamente."[67]

Seifert's ideas and his career under National Socialism were also connected with the rise of landscape architecture in Germany to the status of a formal profession. Since the rise of the bourgeoisie, a few designers had created gardens that they designed, depending on the prevailing taste and their own professional background, as landscape gardens, that is, imitations of forms regarded as natural; or as architectural gardens, that is, forms conceived deliberately in formal opposition to nature. Beginning around 1900, the architectural garden became the predominant choice for house gardens also in Germany. Seifert followed that trend, and he preferred to design his gardens in conjunction with the house.

In the twentieth century, garden architects like Seifert began to form associations. The precursor to the present *Bund Deutscher Landschafts-Architekten* (Association of German Landscape Architects) was founded in 1913. Designers took a growing interest not only in gardens or urban parks, but also in public landscapes and the landscaping that accompanied infrastructure projects.

Landscape architecture became institutionalized within academia only in 1929, when the first chair for garden art was established at the Agricultural University (Landwirtschaftliche Hochschule) in Berlin.[68] It would appear that the participation of landscape architects in the *Reichsautobahnen* played an important part in their professionalization process. Without anticipating the results of the present study, I will call attention to an internal, methodological tension within the field, one that is evidently latent to this day and reappears time and again—the dual function of landscape architecture as ecological expertise and as creative aesthetic. As late as the 1990s, landscape planning was in danger of foundering against the postulate of landscape as a unity of nature and aesthetic aspects, a danger that was reflected on the level of training in splits within university departments. On the one hand, ecosystems were studied for their complex structure of effects and interactions; on the other hand, the result of landscape planning was supposed to meet aesthetic demands. These two demands were not mutually exclusive, but neither were they contingent upon each other.[69] This inherent tension also marked landscape architecture under National Socialism and the landscape of the *Reichsautobahnen*. The tendency to prefer one side or the other served to legitimate positions in conflicts over policy within and outside the field. For example, in 1940, Wiepking-Jürgensmann, the holder of the above-mentioned chair in Berlin, wrote apodictically and not without inner contradictions:

> Aesthetic considerations play no role in modern landscape policy. We want a landscape that is sensible, used, and secured for all times. The more sensible it is, the more beautiful it will be. For the person of sound sensibility, aesthetics is not a question, but simply something self-evident; it is the visible expression of the harmony of things, including that of opposites. An unharmonious landscape is the visible expression of its faulty management.[70]

Although aesthetic is here seen merely as the product of "right" use, at the same time it was of such importance that it provided the endpoint for thinking about the relationship of cause and effect. The criterion of "right" or "false" use opened up a normative breach through which the social ascription of value could enter. It was no coincidence that the holder of a chair in a marginal field spoke of "landscape politics" when he offered a historical derivation of his research program. The discipline offered its services to the Nazi regime by way of the "health" label, which prior to 1945 was applied to humans and after that to landscape itself and provided a criterion for its evaluation. "Healthy landscape" thus became a normative goal.[71]

As a result, landscape was for landscape architects the constitutive substance of their field, one that was both self-evident as the core of their work and contested as to the claims that were advanced about it. The circumstance that offered Seifert and other landscape architects the possibility to expand their livelihood was the Nazi regime's pronounced receptiveness to infrastructure projects: in its first years, the regime pushed massive plans to transform the German landscape in favor of transportation, industry, and agriculture. In the case of the autobahnen, the Nazi regime's building activity was, propaganda proclamations notwithstanding, by no means radically new. Rather, what culminated in the frenzied construction activity after 1933 were many years of unsuccessful lobbying in the interwar period. These autobahn ideas will be examined in the following chapter.

Notes

1. Reprint of Ernst Rudorff's essay "Über das Verhältniß [sic] des modernen Lebens zur Natur," *Natur und Landschaft* 65 (1990): 119–125. For a now outdated interpretation see Arne Andersen, "Heimatschutz: Die bürgerliche Naturschutzbewegung," in *Besiegte Natur. Geschichte der Umwelt im 19. und 20. Jahrhundert*, ed. Franz-Josef Brüggemeier and Thomas Rommelspacher, 2nd ed. (Munich, 1989), 143–157. For differing accounts, see Edeltraud Klueting, ed., *Antimodernismus und Reform. Zur Geschichte der deutschen Heimatbewegung* (Darmstadt, 1991); Rolf-Peter Sieferle, "Heimatschutz und das Ende der romantischen Utopie," *Arch+* 81 (1985): 38–42; John Alexander Williams, "'The Chords of the German Soul are Tuned to Nature': The Movement to Preserve the Natural *Heimat* from the Kaiserreich to the Third Reich," *Central European History* 29 (1996), 339–384. The extensive literature on *Heimat* cannot be cited here in its entirety.
2. See the chapter "Natur" in Thomas Nipperdey, *Deutsche Geschichte 1866–1918. Erster Band: Arbeitswelt und Bürgergeist* (Munich, 1990), 182–186, quotes 182 und 183.
3. See Norbert Borrmann, *Paul Schultze-Naumburg 1869–1949. Maler-Publizist-Architekt* (Essen, 1989).
4. Andreas Knaut, "Ernst Rudorff und die Anfänge der deutschen Heimatbewegung," in Klueting, *Antimodernismus und Reform*, 20–49, quote 29.
5. The preparations had taken about two years, and the goal was to form, not an umbrella organization for the regionally already existing and very self-confident *Heimatwesen* clubs, but a true association. However, this attempt ended in 1908 with a reorganization, from which the regional *Heimat* clubs emerged even stronger: Knaut, "Ernst Rudorff," 41 and 43.
6. Knaut, "Ernst Rudorff," 42, 48. Winfried Speitkamp, "Denkmalpflege und Heimatschutz in Deutschland zwischen Kulturkritik und Nationalsozialismus," *Archiv für Kulturgeschichte* 70 (1988): 149–193; Christian F. Otto, "Modern Environment and Historical Continuity: The Heimatschutz Discourse in Germany," *Art Journal* 43 (1983): 148–157.
7. Michael Wettengel, "Staat und Naturschutz 1906–1945. Zur Geschichte der Staatlichen Stelle für Naturdenkmalpflege in Preußen und der Reichsstelle für Naturschutz," *Historische Zeitschrift* 257 (1993): 355–399, here 361–365.
8. Ibid., 365–366.

9. Ibid., 366–367. On the *Landesausschuß für Naturpflege* in Bavaria see Arne Andersen and Reinhard Falter, "'Lebensreform' und 'Heimatschutz,'" in *München—Musenstadt mit Hinterhöfen. Die Prinzregentenzeit 1886–1912*, ed. Friedrich Prinz and Marita Kraus (Munich, 1988), 295–300.
10. Mark Cioc, *The Rhine: An Eco-Biography* (Seattle/London, 2002).
11. Ulrich Linse, "'Der Raub des Rheingoldes': Das Wasserkraftwerk Laufenburg," in: Ulrich Linse et al., *Von der Bittschrift zur Platzbesetzung. Konflikte um technische Großprojekte. Laufen, Walchensee, Wyhl, Wackersdorf* (Berlin/Bonn, 1988), 11–62, here 33–34; idem, "Die Vernichtung der Laufenburger Stromschnellen. Ein 'klassischer' historischer Konflikt zwischen 'Volkswirtschaft' und 'Heimatschutz,'" *Geschichte in Wissenschaft und Unterricht* 48 (1997): 399–412; Rollins, *A Greener Vision of Home*, 141–143; Franz-Josef Brüggemeier, *Tschernobyl, 26. April 1986. Die ökologische Herausforderung* (Munich, 1998), 112–114. On Rathenau see Hans Wilderotter, ed., *Walter Rathenau, 1867–1922: Die Extreme berühren sich* (Berlin, 1994).
12. Bernhard Stier, "Auf der Wasserstraße in die Moderne. Der Bau des Neckarkanals im Spannungsfeld von Technik, Ästhetik und Politik 1920–1935," *Zeitschrift für Geschichte des Oberrheins* 143 (1995): 287–351, quote 307; Michael Hascher and Janine Maegraith, "Changing Face and Meaning of Rivers in Germany: Neckar, Moselle and Altmühl in the 20th Century," unpublished manuscript, 2003.
13. Borrmann, *Schultze-Naumburg*, 7 and 26.
14. Paul Schultze-Naumburg, *Kulturarbeiten*, vol. 7: *Die Gestaltung der Landschaft durch den Menschen*, Part I (Munich, 1915), 15; Borrmann, *Schultze-Naumburg*. On the roof debate, see Barbara Miller Lane, *Architecture and Politics in Germany, 1918–1945* (Cambridge, Mass., 1985).
15. On Hogarth's "Analysis of Beauty" (published in 1753), see Tom Turner, *Garden History. Philosophy and Design 2000BC-2000AD* (London and New York, 2005), 197–198. Goethe quote: Marie Luise Gothein, *Geschichte der Gartenkunst. Zweiter Band: Von der Renaissance in Frankreich bis zur Gegenwart* (Jena, 1914), 415. In 1889, the journalist Ferdinand Avenarius, founder of the journal *Kunstwart* of the Dürerbund, criticized sinuous "pretzel paths" as the design characteristic of the English landscape garden and of its imitators on the continent: Gothein, *Geschichte*, 454. Paul Schultze-Naumburg, *Die Gestaltung der Landschaft durch den Menschen*, 3rd ed. (Munich, 1928), 26.
16. One example for a long straightaway with a goal is the former "Olympia road," today a four-lane arterial road out of Munich toward Garmisch, which was built for the Winter Olympics in 1936 and is today part of the autobahn network as the A95. For many kilometers, drivers heading toward Munich on a perfectly level road see the towers of the Frauenkirche in the center of the city, their view framed by rows of trees on both sides.
17. Werner Lindner, *Die Ingenieurbauten in ihrer guten Gestaltung* (Berlin, 1923).
18. Ibid., 9, 11, 21.
19. Werner Lindner, *Bauten der Technik. Ihre Form und Wirkung. Werkanlagen* (Berlin, 1927), VIII.
20. Conrad Matschoss and Werner Lindner, eds., *Technische Kulturdenkmale* (Munich, 1932). See Uwe Beckmann, "Technische Kulturdenkmale als Objekte technischer Kultur bei deutschen Ingenieuren und Heimatschützern," *Technische Intelligenz und "Kulturfaktor Technik": Kulturvorstellungen von Technikern und Ingenieuren zwischen Kaiserreich und früher Bundesrepublik Deutschland*, ed. Burkhard Dietz, Michael Fessner, and Helmut Maier (Münster, 1996), 177–188. On monuments, see Rudy Koshar, *Germany's Transient Paths. Preservation and National Memory in the Twentieth Century* (Chapel Hill/London, 1998).
21. Gesellschaft der Freunde des deutschen Heimatschutzes, ed., *Der deutsche Heimatschutz. Ein Rückblick und Ausblick* (Munich, 1930). Friedrich Haßler, "Heimatschutz und Technik," ibid., 182–187; Franz Grüger, "Heimatschutz und die Probleme der modernen Kraft- und Verkehrswirtschaft," ibid., 174–182.
22. Paul Schultze-Naumburg, *Die Gestaltung der Landschaft*, 11–17. On the frustration of the *Heimatschützer* and the *Naturschützer* in the Weimar Republic see Dominick, *Environmental Movement*, 81–85; Lekan, *Imagining the Nation*, Chapter 4.

23. Werner Lindner, *Der Heimatschutz im neuen Reich* (Leipzig, 1934), 42–43, 63–65.
24. On the social status of engineers and their aspirations see Ludwig, *Technik und Ingenieure*; Kees Gispen, *New Profession, Old Order: Engineers and German Society, 1815–1914* (Cambridge and New York, 1989); Dietz, Fessner, and Maier, *Technische Intelligenz*.
25. Seifert, *Leben*. What Joachim Radkau has referred to as the "duo Todt-Seifert" seems to have been, rather, a quarrelsome couple with an unequal distribution of power: Joachim Radkau, *Natur und Macht: Eine Weltgeschichte der Umwelt*, 2nd ed. (Munich, 2002), 298.
26. Meetings between Todt and Seifert often took place in Munich, where both men lived. At the beginning of their collaboration, the engineer and the architect went on a mountain excursion together with their wives. Seifert to Todt, 23 August 1934, Bundesarchiv Potsdam [henceforth BAP] 46.01/1487.
27. Seifert, *Leben für die Landschaft*, 6–10; Alwin Seifert, in *Garten und Landschaft* 82 (1972): 340–344 (biography written by Seifert himself); Gertrud Schiegerl and Armin Stiegler, "Die Gärten Alwin Seiferts," diploma thesis at the Lehrstuhl für Landschaftsarchitektur und Entwerfen, Technische Universität München-Weihenstephan, 1985, 10–12; "Lebenslauf Alwin Seifert," 16 July 1942, Historisches Archiv der Technischen Universität München (HAU-TUM), personnel file Alwin Seifert, fol. 25–26; "Lebenslauf," 24 April 1920, Bayerisches Hauptstaatsarchiv Munich [hereafter BayHStA], MK 58957. For a somewhat more positive assessment see Reinhard Falter, "Widerstandskämpfer oder Nutznießer? Der 'Reichslandschaftsanwalt' Alwin Seifert als Beispiel für ein ambivalentes Verhältnis zum Nationalsozialismus." *Die Drei* 67, no. 11 (1997): 1074–1082.
28. Seifert, *Leben*, 20.
29. They were Josef Breloer, Hermann Göritz, Wilhelm Hübotter, Hermann Mattern, Max Müller, Alwin Seifert. Joachim Wolschke-Bulmahn, *Auf der Suche nach Arkadien. Zu Landschaftsidealen und Formen der Naturaneignung in der Jugendwebewegung und ihrer Bedeutung für die Landespflege* (Munich, 1990), 259–260.
30. Wolschke-Bulmahn (ibid.) also denies that membership in the Youth Movement had a generally shaping influence.
31. Walter Sauer, "Der Mythos des Naturerlebnisses in der Jugendbewegung," in *Typisch deutsch: die Jugendbewegung. Beiträge zu einer Phänomengeschichte*, ed. Joachim H. Knoll and Julius H. Schoeps (Opladen, 1988), 55–70, quote 65.
32. Ibid., 64.
33. Quoted by Jürgen Reulecke, "Wo liegt Falado? Überlegungen zum Verhältnis von Jugendbewegung und Heimatbewegung vor dem Ersten Weltkrieg," in Klueting, *Antimodernismus und Reform*, 17.
34. Sauer, "Mythos," 62.
35. Wolschke-Bulmahn, *Auf der Suche*, 66–72.
36. George L. Mosse, "War and the Appropriation of Nature," in *Germany in the Age of Total War. Essays in Honour of Francis Carsten*, ed. Volker Berghahn and Martin Kitchen (London and Towota, NJ, 1981), 102–122. See Gudrun Fiedler, *Jugend im Krieg. Bürgerliche Jugendbewegung, Erster Weltkrieg und sozialer Wandel 1914–1923* (Cologne, 1989).
37. Thus both Sauer, "Mythos des Naturerlebnisses," 59, and Reulecke, "Wo liegt Falado?," 13.
38. Reulecke, "Wo liegt Falado?," 15.
39. Quoted in Sauer, "Mythos des Naturerlebnisses," 60. According to George L. Mosse, Traub was a "leader of the *völkisch* movement" and later, as a member of the DNVP, he sharply rejected Hitler's politics: *The Crisis of German Ideology* (London, 1964), 245–247.
40. Seifert, *Leben*, 15, 20, 23. Alwin Seifert, in *Garten und Landschaft* 82 (1972): 340.
41. Seifert, *Leben*, 25, 27–28. With this project he had unknowingly "anticipated the basic laws of an autobahn that was perfect in terms of technology, artistry, and landscape": ibid., 27.
42. Winfried Nerdinger, ed., *Architekturschule München 1868–1993. 125 Jahre TU München* (Munich, 1993), 101–102.
43. Schiegerl and Stiegler, "Die Gärten Alwin Seiferts," 31–41.

44. Schiegerl and Stiegler, "Die Gärten Alwin Seiferts," 25–36, 123–129. In the 1920s, the Westphalian *Heimatschutz* movement emphasized the ideas formulated by the garden architect Leberecht Migge about the economic design of the garden in the sense of an internal colonization in the spirit of Frederick the Great: Birgitta Ringbeck, "Architektur und Städtebau unter dem Einfluß der Heimatschutzbewegung," in Klueting, *Antimodernismus*, 216–287, here 281–82. See Günther Uhlig, "Siedlungskonzepte Migges und ihre reformpolitische Bedeutung," in *Leberecht Migge 1881–1935. Gartenkultur des 20. Jahrhunderts*, publ. by the Fachbereich Stadt- und Landschaftsplanung der Gesamthochschule Kassel (Kassel, 1981).
45. See Chapter 6, section *The flora of the Nazi autobahn: contesting native plants.*
46. In a letter to a colleague, Seifert noted "an unexpectedly strong interest" on the part of the students in his lectures. Seifert to Hübotter, 31 August 1932, Alwin Seifert Papers at the Chair for Landscape Architecture and Design, Technical University of Munich-Weihenstephan (hereafter ASP) ASP15; Seifert to Hübotter, 14 May 1933, ibid.; "Praktische Gartenkunst an der Technischen Hochschule München," clipping from *Münchner Neueste Nachrichten*, 12 May 1932, HAUTUM, personnel file Alwin Seifert, fol. 10; Nerdinger, *Architekturschule München*, 101–102; Edelgard Voglmaier, *Hans Grässel: Architekt und städtischer Baubeamter in München 1860–1939* (Munich, 1994), 250.
47. The occasion was the lecture by the later autobahn landscape advocate Max K. Schwarz (Worpswede) about the biodynamic method, which he delivered in June of 1930 at the meeting of the Association of German Garden Architects in Heidelberg. At that same conference, Seifert spoke about soil-rooted gardening. It was his second lecture ever. *Verband Deutscher Gartenarchitekten* to its members, 14 April 1930, ASP 215; Seifert to Hirsch, 15 April 1930, ibid.; Seifert to Hirsch, 2 May 1930; Seifert to Hirsch, 7 July 1930, ibid. See Seifert, *Leben*, 34–35. Seifert attended Schwarz's courses in Worpswede near Bremen. For the connection between Steiner and organic agriculture, see Philip Conford, *The Origins of the Organic Movement* (Edinburgh, 2001), 65–80. On organic agriculture under National Socialism see Gesine Gerhard, "Breeding Pigs and People for the Third Reich: Richard Walther Darré's Agrarian Ideology," in Franz-Josef Brüggemeier, Mark Cioc, and Thomas Zeller, eds., *How Green Were the Nazis? Nature, Environment, and Nation in the Third Reich* (Athens, Ohio, 2005), 129–146.
48. Seifert to the Bavarian State Association for *Heimatschutz*, 11 June 1925, ASP 5; Bavarian State Association for *Heimatschutz* and the Association for Folk Art and *Volkstum* to Architect BDA Albin (sic) Seifert, 24 June 1926, ibid.; Seifert to the Bavarian State Association for *Heimatschutz*, 25 June 1926, ibid.; Lindner, "Eilige Rundmitteilung an die Heimatschutzvertreter gelegentlich der Leipziger Zusammenkunft am 6.6.28," 7 June 1928, ibid.; Seifert to the Bavarian State Association for *Heimatschutz*, 5 July 1928, ibid. A friendship seems to have developed with Lindner and his family. Eva-Marie Lindner greeted him in 1939 as "Dear uncle Seifert!" Arbeitsgemeinschaft Heimat und Haus, Eva-Marie Lindner, to Seifert, 3 March 1939, ibid.
49. Schiegerl and Stiegler, "Gärten Alwin Seiferts," 25–36 and 123–129; Seifert, *Leben*, 23. There is also an account of the "misfortune" into which the application of these purely scientific criteria had driven him. Seifert was evidently alluding to the fact that his first marriage, concluded in November of 1914, remained childless, "which is why it was divorced in 1920. My first wife died in July 1920." In 1924, Seifert married Maria Orff, "this marriage, too, remained childless." "Lebenslauf Seifert," 16 July 1942, HAUTUM, fol. 25–26.
50. Alwin Seifert, "Natur und Technik im deutschen Straßenbau," in Alwin Seifert, *Im Zeitalter des Lebendigen. Natur-Heimat-Technik*, 2nd ed. (Planegg near Munich, 1942), 9–23, 10.
51. Ibid., 23, 50–52.
52. After the surface of the autobahn near Münchberg had been struck by lightning, Todt asked the dowser Professor Wimmer from Munich-Pasing "to look at the site when you get a chance and to tell me about it in greater detail." Todt to Directorate *Reichsautobahn*, 6 July 1936, BAK NS 26/1188. After the outbreak of the war, Seifert pointed out to Todt that a dowser could sense mines only when they were directly below them: "At that point it is, needless to say, too late." Seifert to Todt, 13 November 1939, BAK NS 26/1188.

53. Seifert, *Leben*, 49–50, quote 50. John Charles Guse, "The Spirit of the Plassenburg," PhD Dissertation, University of Nebraska at Lincoln, 1981, 154.
54. Obituary, Technical University Munich, March 1972, HAUTUM, personnel file Seifert, fol. 322.
55. Seifert to Heß, 7 November 1938, Institut für Zeitgeschichte, Munich, Archive [henceforth IfZ] ED 32, fol. 48–49. See Seifert, *Leben*, 23–24: "One of the pioneers of racial hygiene was my spiritual guide for a long time, one of the most prominent representatives of the doctrine of human inheritance was a friend."
56. The Dauphiné in southeastern France, from where his mother's ancestors came, was a "core area of the Alpine race": Seifert to Heß, IfZ Archiv ED 32, fol. 49.
57. In the letter to Ilse Heß, he expressed his delight over an advertising poster for the Nazi female youth organization Bund Deutscher Mädel (BDM) in Austria, which showed a brown-haired, dark-eyed girl: "With the annexation of Austria, a more positive valuation of the Alpine races has taken on crucial *völkisch* significance": Seifert to Heß, fol. 49.
58. Seifert to Hauptdienstleiter Saur, Reichsministerium Speer, 21 September 1943, 4, Amtsgericht Munich, Denazification Files Alwin Seifert [hereafter AGM], Akte Amt für Technik. Gröning and Wolschke-Bulmahn, on the other hand, claimed in several articles, without any evidence, that Seifert had probably been a member of the Thule Society, in which Rudolf Heß and Fritz Todt were also supposedly active: Joachim Wolschke-Bulmahn and Gert Gröning, "The ideology of the nature garden. Nationalistic trends in garden design in Germany during the early twentieth century," *Journal of Garden History* 12 (1992): 73–80, on Seifert 80, note 17. There is nothing in the scholarly literature about Todt's membership in the Thule Society.
59. Nicholas Goodrick-Clarke, *The Occult Roots of Nazism. The Ariosophists of Austria and Germany 1890–1935* (Wellingborough, 1985); Hermann Wilhelm, *Dichter, Denker, Fememörder. Rechtsradikalismus und Antisemitismus in München von der Jahrhundertwende bis 1921* (Berlin, 1991); Jeffrey A. Goldstein, "On Racism and Anti-Semitism in Occultism and Nazism," *Yad Vashem Studies* XII (1979): 53–72; Dusty Sklar, *Gods and Beasts. The Nazis and the Occult* (New York, 1977).
60. Goodrick-Clark, *Occult Roots*, 126–27. One such circle existed in Magdeburg under the name Wotan Lodge.
61. Seifert to I. Heß, IfZ Archive ED 32, fol. 48.
62. *Der Große Brockhaus*, 15th ed., vol. 19 (Leipzig, 1934), 576.
63. Seifert to Wiepking-Jürgensman, 31 October 1939, 2, AGM, Akte Wiepking. For a more detailed examination see Thomas Zeller, "'Ich habe die Juden möglichst gemieden': Ein aufschlußreicher Briefwechsel zwischen Heinrich Wiepking und Alwin Seifert," *Garten+Landschaft. Zeitschrift für Landschaftsarchitektur* No. 8 (1995): 4–5.
64. A "political evaluation" by the NSDAP from 1943 states that he did not know any longer whether he left the party in 1921, 1922, or 1924: Gauhauptstellenleiter Theodor Baumann to the NSDAP, Gau office Munich-Upper Bavaria, Gau Personnel Office, 12 May 1943, AGM Akte S 453. Compare this with Seifert's application to the Reich Writers' Chamber, in which he listed his membership as "approximately 1920–1923." Berlin Document Center, Archiv Reichsschrifttumskammer, application of 18 December 1940.
65. Seifert, *Leben*, 34.
66. "Ehrung Münchner Künstler," *Völkischer Beobachter*, 22 April 1938, HAUTUM personnel file Seifert; Circular, 12 August 1940, 2, ASP 117; Anna Bramwell, *Blood and Soil. Richard Walther Darré and Hitler's Green Party* (Bourne End, 1985), 176–177, 256; Gunter Vogt, *Entstehung und Entwicklung des ökologischen Landbaus im deutschsprachigen Raum* (Bad Dürkheim, 2000), 136–42, 145–148; Uwe Werner, *Anthroposophen in der Zeit des Nationalsozialismus (1933–1945)* (Munich, 1999), 268–270; Gestapo Staatspolizeileitstelle Munich to Heydrich, 13 September 1941; Reich Security Main Office to the State Police Office (*Staatspolizeileitstelle*) Munich, November 1941 [no day given], both Bundesarchiv Berlin, R58/6194;

File Memorandum 15 January 1942, BayHStA MK 58597. For a more detailed account of Seifert's career under National Socialism see Thomas Zeller, "Molding the Landscape of Nazi Environmentalism: Alwin Seifert (1890–1972) and the Third Reich," in *How Green Were the Nazis?*, ed. Franz-Josef Brüggemeier, Mark Cioc, and Thomas Zeller, 147–170.
67. Hermann Giesler, *Ein anderer Hitler. Bericht seines Architekten Hermann Giesler. Erlebnisse, Gespräche, Reflexionen*, 4th ed. (Leoni, 1978), 316. This autobiography is unrepentant and self-serving, but the description of Seifert is illuminating nevertheless.
68. An attempt at a conceptual distinction between landscape architecture ("Landschaftsarchitektur"), care of the landscape ("Landschaftspflege"), land cultivation ("Landespflege"), and landscape design ("Landschaftsgestaltung") can be found in Karsten Runge: *Die Entwicklung der Landschaftsplanung in ihrer Konstitutionsphase 1935–1973* (Berlin, 1990), 38. In the period examined by the present study, these terms were but vaguely differentiated and related in substance. Gert Gröning and Joachim Wolschke-Bulmahn, "Einleitung," in Gert Gröning and Joachim Wolschke-Bulmahn, *Grüne Biographien. Biographisches Handbuch zur Landschaftsarchitektur des 20. Jahrhunderts in Deutschland* (Berlin, 1997), 5–8, 5; Ulrich Eisel and Stefanie Schultz, eds., *Geschichte und Struktur der Landschaftsplanung* (Berlin, 1991); Gert Gröning and Joachim Wolschke-Bulmahn, *1887–1987. DGGL. Deutsche Gesellschaft für Gartenkunst und Landschaftspflege e.V. Ein Rückblick auf 100 Jahre DGGL* (Berlin, 1987); Joachim Wolschke-Bulmahn and Gert Gröning, *1913–1988. 75 Jahre Bund Deutscher Landschafts-Architekten BDLA, Teil 1: Zur Entwicklung der Interessenverbände der Gartenarchitekten in der Weimarer Republik und im Nationalsozialismus* (Bonn, 1988).
69. When I speak of professionalization here, it is not in the strict sense of social history, which situates doctors and lawyers prototypically in the professionalization debate, with their state regulation of training and professional licenses. See, pars pro toto, Michael Burrage, "Introduction: The Professions in Sociology and History," in *Professions in Theory and History. Rethinking the Study of the Professions*, ed. Michael Burrage and Rolf Torstendahl (London, Newbury Park, New Delhi, 1990), 1–23; Stefan Körner, *Der Aufbruch der modernen Umweltplanung in der nationalsozialistischen Landespflege* (Berlin, 1995), 8. He describes the congruence of beauty and utility as the mark of landscape planning under National Socialism. Ibid., 9.
70. Heinrich Fr. Wiepking-Jürgensmann, "Die Landesverschönerungskunst im Wandel der letzten 150 Jahre," *Zentralblatt der Bauverwaltung* 60 (1940): 317–320, 320.
71. This tension between artistic and technical elements in the overall picture was also reflected after 1950 in the question where the main emphases should be placed in training the new generation of landscape cultivators. Wiepking demanded the formation of complete personalities, while Seifert emphasized at the same time that the discipline was predominantly technical in nature: Körner, "Aufbruch," 108–109, note 29.

Chapter 4

PLANNING THE AUTOBAHN BEFORE AND AFTER 1933

The failed autobahn project of the interwar period

Is the automobile not such a valuable and promising means of transportation that the attempt to create its own roadways (*Bahnen*) is worth the while? We need the construction of the autobahn, because it offers the opportunity to perform work for the future. We need the courage to make the first attempt. I believe the Hafraba Association has the great and wonderful task of mustering the courage for the first attempt. Should it indeed succeed, it will have achieved something magnificent for Germany's future.[1]

In the interwar period, lobby groups appeared in some European countries and pushed for the construction of traffic lanes for the exclusive use of the automobile. These intersection-free roadways were characterized by divided lanes, traveling and passing lanes, shoulders, and intersection-free on- and off-ramps, the goal being to create an unimpeded route solely for automobiles. While these efforts bore little fruit in Germany before 1933, they have been well studied. Scattered appeals for the construction of what were called "Nur-Autostraßen" (roadways for cars only) culminated in 1926 in the establishment of the Hafraba Association. Its name captured programmatically the desire to see a toll road reserved for automobile traffic—called autobahnen—that ran from the *Ha*nse cities of Lübeck and Hamburg via *Fra*nkfurt to *Ba*sel. The Association's backing came from local politicians and organizations; the founding chairman was Robert Otzen, Professor for Iron and Structural Engineering at the Technical University in Hannover, head of a civil engineering laboratory, and after 1927 head of a roadway research office. The managing director was Willy Hof, General Director of the German Trade Association and a motor sports enthusiast.[2]

Notes for this section begin on page 71.

Given the low level of motorization in Germany, the Association bore the burden of justifying its plans. When the first all-German traffic count was carried out in 1924/1925, "carriage traffic," that is, horse-drawn carriages, held only a slight lead over motorized vehicles. Moreover, there was no such thing as noticeable long-distance traffic involving motor vehicles. A study group dispatched to Germany by General Motors in 1929 returned with the verdict that the German automobile market was eighteen years behind its U.S. counterpart. If road construction was discussed at all in the political arena, it was expansion more than new construction that was desired. As late as 1930, cities and communities were still arguing that the idea of building roadways exclusively for cars could be entertained only after the existing network had been expanded. New construction could be justified "only in cases of extreme exception," as between Cologne and Bonn. This approximately twenty-kilometer long motor vehicle roadway, not a Hafraba project, had been opened in 1932 by the Prussian Rhine province as a local connector; one of its initiators had been Cologne's Lord Mayor Konrad Adenauer. This short segment was seen explicitly as an exception. This reveals just how much automotive traffic was seen as local traffic, and the degree to which efforts were focused on expanding the existing network. This tendency must be seen against the background of the organizationally fractured nature of road construction, which remained a matter of the states also in the Weimar Constitution; in Prussia, responsibility lay with the individual provinces. A German Road Building Association (*Deutscher Straßenbauverband*) was established in 1922 in response to this situation; it was an association of road-building administrations that tried, until its dissolution in 1935, to establish uniform technical standards.[3]

The chief model and stimulus for German lobby groups were the *autostrade* in Italy. The first European implementation of the idea to build intersection-free, two- and four-lane roads as overland connections was not in Germany. The Italian engineer Piero Puricelli had the first known *autostrada* built near Milan in 1924, with a length of 36.5 kilometers; by 1935, the Italian network of privately operated highways was expanded to 478 kilometers. Drivers had to pay a toll. This infrastructure project became part of the Fascist state's propaganda; Mussolini integrated road construction into his self-representation during the first years of his regime. Unlike in Nazi Germany, where the dictator adorned himself with the roads, in Fascist Italy it was Puricelli who became a mythic figure in the public eye; one Hafraba member crowned him the "king of the road." The design of the *autostrada* was based strictly on railway parameters, with almost no attention paid to landscaping and with billboards allowed alongside the roads.[4]

North of the Alps, the Hafraba lobbyists, beginning in October of 1927, focused on a partial section to illustrate how close their plans were to becoming reality. That same year, rough plans had already been presented for the entire stretch (Bremen/Lübeck)-Hamburg-Frankfurt-Basel. The more detailed proposals concerned the section Frankfurt-Darmstadt-Heidelberg, with the route and the number of exits specified. The line also connected Heidelberg and Mannheim, ran past Weinheim, Bensheim, and Darmstadt on the west (coming from the south), and turned in the direction of Wiesbaden at the south-western edge of Frankfurt. The strategy of the Hafraba lobby was to achieve Germany's entry into the autobahn by focusing first on a relatively short section. This, too, failed. Still, design parameters for the route to be constructed were developed until 1931. For the Hafraba with two traveling lanes, the width of the roadway was 20.5 meters, and the greatest allowable gradient was set at 4 percent. These detailed plans were created to provide those trying to obtain parliamentary approval of toll roads with a blueprint that was ready for passage. The upshot was that the Nazi dictatorship later had realistic plans at its disposal.[5]

In the meantime, the Hafraba Association, with support from interested politicians, was pushing in the Reichstag for legal changes in order to obtain permission to impose user fees on roads built for that very purpose, thus making it easier to finance them. A bill proposed in July of 1930 was undone by the dissolution of parliament a short while later; a subsequent motion at the beginning of 1931 met with opposition from the NSDAP and the communist party and never came up for a vote. When Reich Chancellor Heinrich Brüning resigned in 1932, the Hafraba lost its most important political supporter. The wish to legalize privately financed autobahnen was unable to make headway in the rapid turnover of cabinets during the final phase of the Weimar Republic. Opposition from within the government came from the German Reich Railroad (*Deutsche Reichsbahn*), which was eager to prevent any competition in long-distance transportation. But even the Reich Association of the Automobile Industry (*Reichsverband der Automobilindustrie*) expressed concerns. For one, it raised technical objections. The manufacturers were secretly afraid that cars would not be able to withstand the sustained stress of fast overland driving. For another, both the representatives of car makers and the German Automobile Club (*Automobilclub von Deutschland*, AvD) considered the expansion of existing roads a more urgent task than new construction. To this were added troubles within the Hafraba lobby. Faced with the threat of failure, some members left the organization. Frustrated by the sluggish parliamentary process, the chair of the managing board, Robert Otzen, published on his own a memorandum in which he proposed a network of highways for all of Europe, not merely a single road. In the context of ideas of European integration through large-scale technological projects, he praised this network as a path to "pan-European understanding." The remaining members of the managing board, who came from the executive branch, opposed this kind of expansion "without limits"; in response, Otzen resigned from Hafraba's managing board.[6]

During the Great Depression, efforts to build new roads faced even more pressure to justify themselves, as car ownership remained largely reserved for the middle and upper classes. The economist Werner Sombart considered autobahnen "roads for the enjoyment of rich people." Among countries with a comparable level of industrialization, Germany was one of the least motorized. In 1932, there were eight private cars per one-thousand inhabitants, in the United States the figure was 183. Already during the Weimar Republic, a few observers took these figures as indicating that Germany was lagging behind in modernization. But the focus was, if at all, on cars and less on roads. The new construction projects that attracted the most attention were race tracks like the Avus in Berlin (planning began in 1909, and it opened in 1921) and the Nürburgring in the Eifel region (1927), where tens of thousands of spectators experienced cars racing at great speeds on roads built for that very purpose—as Sunday sporting events, not as a form of day-to-day transportation.[7]

Meanwhile, discussions about the design of the Hafraba roads with trees and shrubs remained merely on the level of suggestions prior to the assumption of power by the Nazis. One engineer, who was a member of Hafraba's managing board, called for giving up the usual roadside trees used for urban avenues and fruit trees along the side of the road. Instead, functional bushes should be planted, which would allow an unobstructed view and protect the roads from "careless humans and animals." In collaboration with the garden architect Alexander Schimmelpfennig from Kassel, who later worked on the *Reichsautobahnen*, blueprints were drawn up that envisaged largely dense conifers. Tall-growing trees were to be used as signal trees to announce dangerous curves. Roadside trees were planted on a test track. While Bauhaus architect Ludwig Mies van der Rohe questioned the readability of such botanical signals, garden architects criticized the use of nonnative plants.[8] It is revealing, however, that the Hafraba plans for roadside trees and the test plantings were not mentioned by the landscape architects of the *Reichsautobahn*. It is likely that its builders were aware of these plans, but were intent on emphasizing the novelty of the National Socialists roadways.

The failure of the Hafraba Association under the Weimar Republic is therefore attributable to a combination of uneven public support and legislative and procedural difficulties. The short duration of the presidential cabinets in the final phase of the Weimar Republic was not favorable to the kind of lobbying work done by Hafraba; internal dissension within the Association also played its part. And since not all automobile associations joined the coalition in support of transregional road construction, the effectiveness of such a lobby was that much weaker. It is in this light, also, that one must see the continuity with the autobahn construction by the Nazis. Although the Hafraba Association provided usable technical blueprints, unlike the Weimar plans, the Nazi autobahn was operated as a large-scale network under public oversight, with public financing, and without tolls. There is no question that the idea of an autobahn was present in Germany prior to 1933, was publicly discussed, and had been planned down to the details of landscaping. Many of the job creation proposals during the Great Depression contained references to the building of the autobahn or road building in general. Still, the idea of the autobahn represented more a lobby of associations and prominent citizens than a popular movement. What follows is a look at how a relatively peripheral idea of the interwar period became the central infrastructure project of the Nazis. First it is helpful to examine the regime's transportation policy.

Building the Nazi autobahn

Although the *Reichsautobahnen* are the most prominent example of Nazi transportation policy, they do not embody its entire spectrum. Recent studies emphasize the degree to which the state's direction of transportation was marked by competing authorities and by vague—or from a modern perspective, false—priorities. The most sweeping verdict comes from Christopher Kopper, for whom the regime's transportation policy proceeded as slowly as the famed spring procession in the Luxemburg town of Echternach rather than resembling a purposeful striding into modernity."[9]

On the organizational level, the levels of authority dealing with transportation policy were fractured: the established administration of the Reich Transportation Ministry was confronted by the expansive claims of the newly created institution of the Inspector-General of the German Road System, which appropriated competencies of the states and the Reich Transportation Ministry and in so doing created both horizontal and vertical conflicts. The management of the German Reich Railway formed another power block. Although the general director of the Reich Railway, Julius Dorpmüller, was appointed transportation minister in 1937, the railways suffered from inadequate financing and excessive demands on their capacity.[10]

The regime's goal of modernizing freight traffic was achieved only halfheartedly. The situation of conflict between road and rail traced out since the Weimar Republic remained largely unchanged under National Socialism. The German Reich Railway maintained its position of leadership in long-distance freight hauling. It was protected against nascent private competition by restrictions on concessions for the transport industry and by rate regulations. On the level of organizational politics and transportation infrastructure, the conflict was personified in General Director Dorpmüller and Fritz Todt, the Inspector-General for the German Road System. Both men laid claim to competencies for freight and passenger traffic. Todt's ideas, which tended to be truck-friendly, did not prevail in the Long Distance Freight Law of 1936, for example. The Nazi regime did not live up to its self-proclaimed pretension that it would pursue an active motorization policy also in the area of freight traffic.[11]

The Reich Transportation Ministry remained largely uninvolved in the largest single project of Nazi transportation policy, the building of the autobahnen. The massively publicized construction of the highways did little to restructure freight transport. When it came to motorized individual transportation, a series of tax incentives were put in place. In a speech at the International Automobile and Motorcycle Show in February of 1933, Hitler announced a motorization offensive and called upon industry to develop an affordable car for the masses. On the issue of road construction, he proclaimed: "If one used to try to gauge the level of life of nations by the kilometers of railway tracks, in the future one will have to use the number of kilometers of roads suited for freight traffic." During an internal meeting with the managing director of Hafraba, Hof, it became apparent that Hitler imagined a gigantic road network, while Hof wanted to proceed gradually. Hitler's vision prevailed.[12]

The idea that new roads and a wide diffusion of automobile traffic would go hand in hand was wishful thinking, however. While the autobahn network expanded rapidly, the growth of motorization lagged far behind. Even the Volkswagen project started up on the basis of a design by the engineer Ferdinand Porsche, and with a target price of 900 Reichsmark for the final product, did not change this situation. To be sure, Porsche's blueprint found a strong supporter in Hitler. The dictator was fascinated in equal measure by Henry Ford's mass production of cars in Detroit and by his anti-Semitism. Since the German automobile industry had little interest in the project of an affordable mass car with low profit margins, Hitler charged the German Labor Front, the successor organization to the dissolved labor unions, with producing the Volkswagen. Tens of thousands of "*Volk* comrades" paid monthly contributions in advance in the hope of one day taking delivery of the automobile. But those who saved up their money in installment were disappointed: the Volkswagen plant in Wolfsburg in Lower Saxony, built on the model of Ford's River Rouge plant, produced mainly military vehicles. Nevertheless, the regime was able, through massive propaganda, "to style itself as the initiator and guarantor of mass motorization."[13] The number of automobiles increased under Hitler. In 1935, there were 204.4 vehicles (not counting motorbikes) per 1,000 people in the United States. For Germany, the number stood at 16.1, for France 49.0, for the United Kingdom 45.2, for Denmark 41.6, and for Switzerland 21.7. Only Italy (9.5) and the Soviet Union (1.5) were below Germany. In 1938, as well, the motorization gap between Germany and France and Great Britain was more than ten years, which means that nothing had changed in the ratios in Western Europe from 1933, in spite of the increase in absolute numbers.[14] In the area of individual motorization, the promises had thus not been kept. The situation was very different, though, when it came to roadways.

Nazi transportation policy proved to have the greatest staying power when it came to the building of the *Reichsautobahnen*. Yet a look at the German transportation system of the 1930s shows the full extent of the disconnect between this new offer of mobility and a demand for it by car owners. In the most highly motorized country in the world, the United States, one envious highway engineer proclaimed: "Germany has the roads while we have the traffic." Statistically, four persons in the U.S. shared one automobile in 1938, while the comparable figure in Germany was sixty.[15] When it came to results, National Socialist transportation policy was thus beset by striking contradictions: the largely completed construction of the autobahnen went along with the failure of the mass motorization project of the Volkswagen. While the German Railway, by far the most important transportation carrier, suffered from inadequate investments, excess investments for the autobahnen created a supply for individual transportation that was far ahead of the demand.

When it comes to the autobahnen, there are chiefly three factors that explain this discrepancy: the potential of the highway network for propaganda, which Italian Fascism had already exploited; the groundwork laid by the Hafraba lobby; and the proposals put forth by two engineers and members of the NSDAP—Fritz Todt and Gottfried Feder. The latter point needs elaboration. When Fritz Todt summarized the situation of the roads in the Reich in December of 1932 in his so-called Brown Memorandum (for the color of its jacket), he had already acquired a reputation as an expert on road construction through his work in lower branches of the party. Todt had joined the NSDAP as early as 1922, and he worked as an engineer for the Munich construction company Sager & Woerner. In 1927, Todt authored a preliminary study for a motorway from Munich to Lake Starnberg, a few kilometers outside of the city. Beginning in 1931, Todt was *Oberführer* of the SA. Hitler received Todt's "Brown Memorandum" in April 1933; a few weeks later he also had a memorandum on road construction from the pen of Gottfried Feder on his desk. Feder was the former advisor for the party program of the NSDAP, author of the program "to break the slavery of interest," and a member of the Reichstag beginning in 1924.[16]

Todt's memorandum opened with a harsh critique of the Weimar Republic's road construction policy. Because of "weak technical leadership," an industry with a ruthlessly capitalist attitude, a technically inexperienced national government, and the prevailing financial system, the "assault of the automobile on the highways (*Landstraßen*)" had led to the complete destruction of the existing road surfaces, so Todt's exaggerated verdict. Research on the choice of asphalt, tar, or concrete as the road surface had not produced any results. When it came to the "restoration of the Reich," Todt argued that the expansion and new construction of such "arteries of life" was indispensable. Those arteries served primarily the defense of the country, and after that the transportation of people and goods and thus the "opening up of the entire country and the promotion of culture everywhere." The building of five to six thousand kilometers of roadway should be undertaken by a central office charged with coordinating the oversight function. "A capable expert with a staff of two to three persons is perfectly adequate" for the job. Todt concluded his memorandum with a look at the propagandistic importance of such a project.[17]

Todt's booklet presented itself as a characteristic mixture of professional thinking, technological utopianism, and political assessment. The dubiousness of such a large autobahn network in terms of transportation policy, one of the main obstacles to the realization of the Hafraba project, was not even addressed. Instead, Todt emphasized the possibility of combining the vigorous undertaking in a technical field with public self-representation. Economic arguments about whether such an enormous commitment of resources was efficient were subordinated to a political economy in which the autobahnen were seen as the instrument with the greatest propagandistic yield. An infrastructure project like the autobahn seemed like a way for the new regime to demonstrate its ability to take concrete action. The realization of the project was to be entrusted to engineers in their capacity as experts who could work most effectively outside of the conventional administrative pathways. Still, the notion that a staff of only a handful of people would be able to coordinate the construction of six-thousand kilometers of roads seems half-baked even by National Socialist standards.

What Todt was asking for largely coincided with Feder's documented comments, even though the latter was concerned almost exclusively with the technique of building the roads.[18] The routing and construction of the highways would have to be determined in accordance with "principles completely different" from those governing the construction of railroads and highways. The automobile placed different demands on the road than the train did on the track, and it was also able to climb steeper grades. That is why people who "all their life have built railroads or highways" were unsuited to the job. The roads could be laid out only in the terrain, not in the office on a map. For intersections with railway tracks or other roads, specific types had to be prescribed, and Feder had already finished a design for entrance ramps. The road itself must not have a perfectly straight course, but should "always be slightly curved after a maximum of two kilometers of straight line."

It is revealing that Todt paid little attention to the concrete routing of the highways in his own memorandum, written six months earlier. Feder's substantive demands were aimed at giving the autobahnen a different form, one reflecting a different function from that of the railroads. However, these demands were elaborated only to a small extent. What Todt's and Feder's memoranda shared was the fact that both men highlighted the military significance of a network of long-distance roads.[19]

Competition emerged between the two Nazi engineers for the post of Inspector-General, which Hitler eventually decided in favor of Todt. Feder became state secretary in the Reich Economics Ministry and remained relatively unimportant; Todt, on the other hand, began his rapid ascent in the Nazi hierarchy with the building of the roadways. By the time he died in a plane crash in 1942, he had accumulated so many titles and powers that his successor, Albert Speer, instantly vaulted to the rank of a minister extraordinaire. Todt was the head of the Main Office of Technology of the NSDAP, from June 1933 he was the Inspector-General for the German Road System, and from June 1938, he was the chief engineer of the "Western Wall," the line of fortification in the western part of the Reich, whose construction units were later renamed "Organization Todt," and built war infrastructures all over Europe. From December 1938, he served as general plenipotentiary for regulating the construction industry, from February 1940 as the Göring-appointed general plenipotentiary for the special tasks of the Four Year Plan, from March 1940 as the Reich Minister of Armament and Munitions, and, finally, from July 1941 as the Inspector-General for Water and Energy. Compared to other members of the cadre of Nazi ministers, Todt seemed like an efficient manager and organizer for the *Reichsautobahn* and the Western Wall. This made him into the central figure of the German construction industry. At the same time, though, his attempts to force the companies of the armaments industry into line in his capacity as minister and to coordinate the planning of the energy sector during his brief stint as Inspector-General for

Water and Energy failed.[20] His rise as one of the most important managers in National Socialism and his claim to be the innovator of technology were based on the relatively marginal field of road construction, which he sought to both define and expand. He often operated outside of and in opposition to the existing ministerial bureaucracy and had the legal powers to do so.

The two memoranda by Todt and Feder show that sections of the NSDAP were receptive to the idea of roadways at the beginning of 1933, at the latest. At this time already, the design of the roads was being discussed; Feder wanted it to be explicitly different from that of the railroad and to introduce a new style of road building. This notion of a parallelism between the means of transportation and its pathway, between automobiles and new and different roads for them, was not unique to National Socialism, though the Nazis did articulate it specifically. The hasty push to build the autobahnen was an expression of this idea and the place where conflicts over it were fought out. The institutional framework for the autobahn, to which I will now turn my attention, reveals how rife the project was with potential conflict.

The place of the autobahn in the Nazi dictatorship

The motorization offensive of the Nazi-led government created complex and convoluted legal structures for road building. Following Hitler's speech of February 1933 and internal discussions, the "Law on the Establishment of the Association *Reichsautobahnen*" was passed on 27 June 1933. Two institutions were set up for the planning and construction of these roadways: the Inspector-General for the German Road System, and the Association *Reichsautobahnen* as a branch of the German Reich Railroad. The title "Inspector-General" was borrowed from the Prussian army, where special matters were placed in the hands of such an official. In France, on the other hand, "inspecteurs généraux" functioned as the heads of civil or military offices, including the "École de Ponts et Chaussées," the original school of civil engineering.[21]

The division of labor between Todt's agency and the subsidiary of the German Railroad was arbitrarily defined and led to conflicts down the road. While the Inspector-General was in charge of the route and the design, the actual construction work was the job of the fifteen regional planning offices of the Association *Reichsautobahnen*.[22] The agency of the Inspector-General drew on plans from the Association for the Preparation of the *Reichsautobahn* (*Gesellschaft zur Vorbereitung der Reichsautobahn*, Gezuvor), the successor institution to Hafraba after 1933. Added to this was the fact that by the Law on the Provisional New Regulation of the Road System and Road Administration (issued on 22 March 1934), the Inspector-General's office was given the authority to make classifications for all roads in the Reich and was put in charge of the Reich roads, which meant that it arrogated the authority of the states; the Inspector-General had supervisory power over all roads. This was one of many examples of Nazi centralization of powers.[23]

In 1935, thdue Gezuvor was changed into the Association for the Preparation of Reich Planning and Regional Planning (*Gesellschaft zur Vorbereitung der Reichsplanung und Raumordnung*). Todt's Inspector-General's office resisted attempts by this agency to coordinate road planning and successfully defended its autonomy in road building matters within the chaotic jumble of the Nazi bureaucracy.[24]

This intertwined and confusing organizational structure for the autobahn project was the product of clashes within the new government. Whether the autobahnen made sense or not was a hotly contested question within the cabinet. Reich Railroad General Director Dorpmüller joined the ministries of finance and transportation in opposing the building of the superhighways. Like the Reich Transportation Ministry, he recommended that the existing network of roads be expanded, instead. Hitler, however, forced the Reich Railroad to finance the autobahnen with the vague promise that it would have a monopoly over freight transport on land, a long-held wish of the railroad management. Contrary to the popular perception today, the military dimension of the autobahnen was not the primary motivation behind their construction. It is now generally accepted in the scholarly literature that this view is one of the myths surrounding the roadways. The armed forces did not accord the autobahnen any strategic value for their own war planning and preferred the expansion of existing roads. They rejected autobahnen close to the borders so as not to provide invasion routes for potential enemies and create bombing targets in an air war. Military leaders saw little reason to radically alter their logistics, which centered on railroads. From a purely military standpoint, Germany, with its extensive railway network, was the European country with the least need for an expensive road network. Yet Hitler ignored also the Reichswehr's opposition. Logistically, the Second World War was primarily a railroad war for the German Wehrmacht, along both the eastern and the western fronts, even if the military benefited from the new regime's motorization program by having the option of requisitioning trucks in case of war.[25] Incidentally, the Wehrmacht employed more and more horses instead of trucks and cars as the Second World War wore on, leading one historian to conclude that, by the end of the war, even the most modern elements of the German armed forces ran on oats as much as on gasoline.[26]

As far as the motivation behind the autobahn project is concerned, it seems appropriate to regard Hitler's personal predilection for the automobile as a vehicle that embodied a promise of modernity, and the propaganda potential of the project, as the primary driving force. As Ian Kershaw put it, "Hitler's propaganda instinct, not his economic know-how, led him towards an initiative that both assisted the recovery of the economy (which was beginning to take place anyway) and caught the public imagination."[27]

With Dorpmüller, whom one historian calls a pragmatist obedient to authority, in charge of overseeing the construction project in his capacity as chairman of the executive and administrative boards of the Association *Reichsautobahn*, the Reich Railroad had attained at least formal control over its rival's transportation routes. Moreover, the law of June 1933 did not exclude the possibility that the operator of the roads could levy tolls, but this option was ruled out for good in 1936.[28]

Next to the desire to contain the Reich Railroad as a modal competitor, the government had another reason to be interested in the railway. The basic capital of the Association *Reichsautobahn*, 50 million Reichsmark, came from the Reich Railroad; moreover, it was becoming clear that the Reich Railroad's civil engineers would be indispensable for the rapid realization of the autobahnen. In 1934, 853 civil servants of the railway were reassigned to the autobahnen: the following year the number rose to 1,106. At a deeper level, the dual setup of an Inspector-General and the Association *Reichsautobahnen* was, as Martin Broszat has said, "a typical pattern for the emergence of central organs directly subordinate to the Führer and outside the Reich government." The office of the Inspector-General of the German Road System under Todt, established by decree on 30 November 1933, had quasiministerial powers without the relevant status. It had no general administrative task like a ministry, but merely a very specific charge, in this case the construction and operation of the *Reichsautobahnen*. This situation expressed the priority of Todt's tasks over those of the specialized departments. Broszat has said that Todt's leadership apparatus "was a peculiar mixture of authoritarian and economic management"; it had a hand in the gradual emasculation of the cabinet as a collegial organ and was at the same time the precondition for the rapid construction of the autobahnen. In subsequent years, the effectiveness of this office was increasingly based on the fact that Todt had constant access to Hitler.[29]

The structural problem of having two agencies for one task led to substantive and organizational clashes. To put it bluntly, the Association *Reichsautobahnen* was for Todt an initially useful but later increasingly bothersome institution for accelerating the building activity. After three years of work on the autobahnen, Todt spoke in an internal memo to the Reich Chancellery of a "less than pleasant working relationship" between the office of the Inspector-General and the Association. Dorpmüller, however, was not willing to relinquish his legally guaranteed position. In December 1937, Todt directed another, urgent request to Reich Minister Hans Heinrich Lammers, the chief of the Reich Chancellery, asking that he be given a completely free hand in the face of a "catastrophic exodus of engineers." Civil engineers were evidently abandoning the autobahn project as the economy was recovering, and Todt wanted to use higher pay to persuade them to stay. But it was not until 1 January 1941 that the Association *Reichsautobahnen* was finally incorporated as a department into the agency of the Inspector-General.[30] The last ties that connected the autobahnen to the Reich Railroad were not severed until the majority of routes had been planned and built. These administrative structures will have a bearing on the history of the landscape planning.

Given this administrative chaos, the speed with which the road builders went to work is all the more surprising. It was the Hafraba plans that made this possible; moreover, the regime was interested in quick propaganda successes and therefore pushed the construction with all its might. Hitler broke ground for the section Frankfurt-Darmstadt-Heidelberg as early as 27 September 1933. Before seven-hundred workers and the assembled press, the sweat-drenched dictator filled an entire dumper with dirt and spoke of the "construction of this, the largest road network in the world." A similar ceremony took place on 21 March 1934 in Unterhaching for the section from Munich to the country's border with Austria. That day was declared the beginning of a "labor battle," because work was begun simultaneously at twenty-two construction sites. The choice of the first three autobahn sections was based not on an expected transportation utility in the form of rapid links between important economic centers, but on the greatest possible propaganda effect in connection with how far the planning and design work had already advanced. Thirty years later, one civil engineer recalled that in the beginning, "priority was given to what were in every respect the simplest sections, with no special attention to considerations of transportation policy or even military concerns."[31] Moreover, the section from Munich to the border promised, as we shall see, a considerable propaganda benefit from the easily realized consumption of the landscape along this corridor. As a result, when construction began it produced relatively short autobahn sections, which came together into a connected network only in 1940 (see map 4.1).

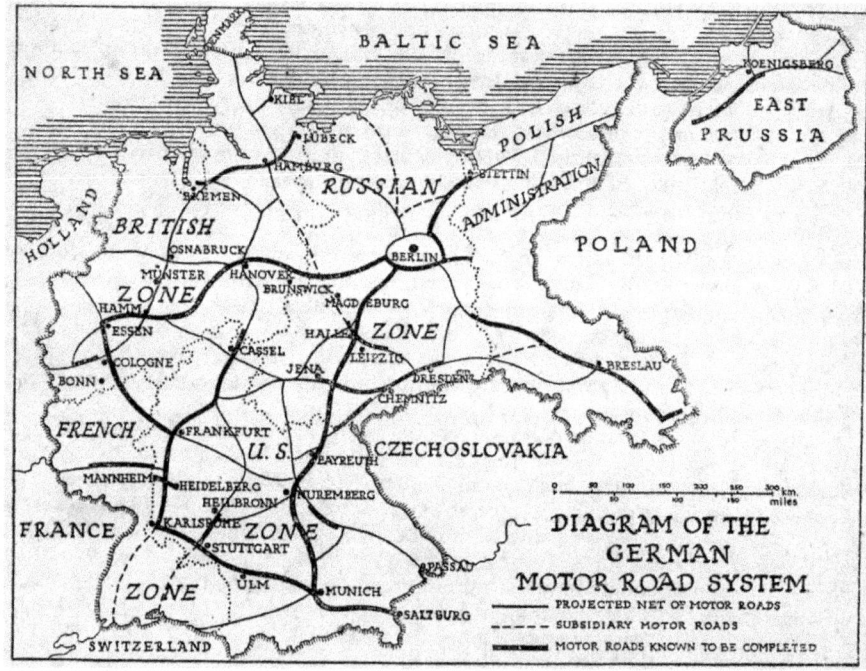

Map 4.1. Diagram of the autobahn system in 1946. During the boom years of the autobahn from 1935 to 1939, some 1,000 kilometers (622 miles) of freeways were built each year. Construction commenced at as many sites as possible in order to achieve the greatest propagandistic return. Only in 1940 did some of the individual stretches form a more coherent network.

Department of Scientific and Industrial Research—Road Research Laboratory, *German Motor Roads 1946. Road Research Technical Paper No. 8. British Intelligence Objectives Sub-Committee Overall Report No. 5* (London: His Majesty's Stationery Office, 1948), p. 3, figure 1.

Hitler, Inspector-General Todt, and Reich Railroad Director Dorpmüller had settled on an annual building pace of 1,000 kilometers of *Reichsautobahnen*. This target figure formed the basis of all planning and presupposed that the excavation work would be about a year ahead of the construction of the road surface. That goal was met until the outbreak of the war. On 1 January 1935, a total of around 1,162 kilometers were under construction; on 19 May of that year, Hitler opened the section Frankfurt-Darmstadt to traffic as the first piece in the network of *Reichsautobahnen*. By 1 January 1937, 1,086 kilometers were already in operation and 1,590 kilometers under construction. A year later, 2,026 kilometers had been opened to traffic and 1,459 kilometers were under construction. The expansion of the "Third Reich" into Austria and Czechoslovakia was reflected in the breaking of ground for the autobahn Salzburg-Vienna on 7 April 1938 by Hitler himself, and on 1 December 1938 by Heß in Eger for a "transit autobahn" from Breslau (Wroclaw) via Brünn (Brno) to Vienna that was never built. A few days before Christmas in 1937 and 1938, the opening of the 2,000th and 3,000th autobahn kilometer, respectively, was celebrated with great pomp. These opening dates reveal the extent to which the roadways were integrated into the Third Reich's calendar of inaugurations, festivals, and myths.

Beginning in May 1938, the pace of construction slowed because of the building of the Western Wall, and it declined further after the attack on Poland. At the end of 1941 and the beginning of 1942, Todt ordered the construction of the roads to be suspended completely. By that time, 3,625 kilometers had been completed, though only 560 since the beginning of the war. Around 800 kilometers were left as unfinished construction sites. With gas shortages and bans on driving during the war, one section near Rosenheim in Bavaria was used as a runway. As they retreated before the advancing Allied troops in the last months of the war, the Wehrmacht blew up numerous bridges—including the Mangfall Bridge in Upper Bavaria and the Lahn Bridge in Hesse, both darlings of Nazi propaganda—and rendered roads unusable.[32]

The popular myth of the *Reichsautobahnen* includes the idea—propagated by Nazi propaganda—that the roadways created jobs that played a decisive role in the economic upswing. Historical scholarship regards it as a certainty that the direct extent of employment from the construction of the autobahn was short-lived and minor. Moreover, after 1936 it lagged behind the emerging economic activity of the armaments industry. What is debated are the extent and effect of employment on the autobahnen and of motorization. While most historians have noted that Germany was merely catching up with other countries, and that this effect was only to a minor degree attributable to the policy of the Hitler regime, Richard Overy has spoken of an active policy of motorization. He estimates that an average of around eighty-thousand people worked on the autobahnen each month. Evidently for reasons of autarchy, in the early years of autobahn construction, machines were hardly used, with the work mostly done by manual labor and light railways.[33]

It would appear that the Reich Labor Service sent few workers to the construction sites (in the spring of 1938 it was merely 122 of more than 95,000), though it did administer the camps along the routes. The vast majority was sent out by the Reich Office for Job Placement and Unemployment Insurance (*Reichsanstalt für Arbeitsvermittlung und Arbeitslosenversicherung*). Because of the great demand for labor beginning in the spring of 1934, professional groups other than construction workers and the unskilled unemployed were also drafted for work on the *Reichsautobahnen*. Because of the poor food and the unusually harsh physical labor, the demands of the work in many cases overtaxed the capacities of the workers. This was especially true for the years 1934 and 1935, when the initial demand that the construction be done with the greatest amount of wage work possible largely ruled out the use of machines; the flipside was that the autobahn workers had to take on the arduous excavation tasks. In fact, during the first few months locomotives were not even used to move the dumpers. The workers with their shovels performed unhealthful tasks such as the extraction of gravel, the removal of humus, the excavation of mountains of earth, and the building of embankments. In 1938, even an article in Todt's laudatory autobahn magazine *Die Straße* described "shovel disease" as the result of arduous spade work combined with inadequate nutrition and workers being unaccustomed to work. The unemployed sent from urban areas to the rural work sites of the *Reichsautobahn* also complained about the poor accommodations. In addition, work on the *Reichsautobahnen* proved to be dangerous. According to a recent study, in the first five years of construction, there was one fatality for every six kilometers of autobahn.[34]

The harsh working conditions, an hourly wage of 53-57 pfennigs, and accommodation far from home in camps did not attract workers; in 1934, the *Reichsstatthalter* (Reich Governor) in Bavaria spoke internally of "extraordinarily depressed" wage conditions. The poor working conditions spawned numerous protests and work stoppages in 1934 and 1935. One of the largest strikes took place in the fall of 1934 on the section Hamburg-Bremen, when 380 workers of the Siemens Bauunion, a construction subsidiary of the Siemens company, walked out. When 141 refused to return to work in spite of heavy pressure, they were placed on a special train under heavy guard and sent to Berlin, where the Gestapo was supposed to take them into "protective custody." A combination of stronger supervision and better-equipped camps was intended to boost the satisfaction of the workers. The German Labor Front subsidiary organization *Kraft durch Freude* organized "leisure activities" in the camps in the form of lectures, concerts, and a separate *Reichsautobahn* theater. As the labor market recovered, those in charge of the construction were plagued by the increasing exodus of workers. The answer was higher wages and greater mechanization. Beginning in 1938, construction of the Western Wall, also supervised by Todt, put additional pressure on the labor market. A shortage of personnel began to slow the pace of construction; between the end of 1938 and the end of 1939, only 238 kilometers were opened to traffic.[35]

Todt believed that one answer to the problem lay in the use of prisoners of war, which the Reich Labor Ministry authorized in the summer of 1940. The Foreign Office also approved the forced labor of ten-thousand prisoners of war. In addition, around four-thousand Jews—primarily from Poland—performed forced labor at the construction of the autobahnen from the end of 1940 to the middle of 1942. The regional planning offices organized these coercive measures and set up new work camps with an especially repressive system. To be sure, as late as March 1939, Todt had opposed the "use of Jews on construction sites of the *Reichsautobahn*." On ideological grounds, the Reich Security Main Office (*Reichssicherheitshauptamt*, RSHA) also expressed an interest in "cleansing" the Reich territory of Jews, though it justified the forced labor at the autobahnen with the strategic value of the section Frankfurt/Oder-Posen. That decision broke an ideological taboo. To implement this policy, fifty forced labor camps were set up on the territory of the *Altreich* (Germany before the annexation of Austria). When construction on the roadways was suspended for good in the spring of 1942, the SS absorbed the forced laborers into its own system of camps.[36]

At this point in the analysis, it makes sense to take a look at the costs of building the autobahnen. As one would expect, no realistic financing plan existed when construction began, nor was the project ever put on sound financial footing. The budget allocations were ignored every year, as officials of the Reich Railroad had to follow Hitler's capricious fancies and his expansion of the scope of the project. A more recent study has put the construction price per kilometer at more than 1.1 million Reichsmark (RM).[37] Earlier studies contend that, in Germany and Austria, a total of around 6.5 billion Reichsmark were spent on building the *Reichsautobahnen*; the average price per kilometer of 900,000 marks exceeded the estimate from 1933 by threefold. Two-thirds of the financing came from the coffers of the Reich Office for Job Placement and Unemployment Insurance, the rest from the regular budget of the Reich through oil tariffs and gasoline and transportation taxes.[38] According to the accounts of the Association *Reichsautobahn*, expenses up to 31 March 1944 amounted to 5.58 billion RM and revenues to 46.8 billion, with capital expenditures amounting to 5.52 billion RM. The largest item, accounting for 30 percent of total costs, was earth and rock moving work; roadway preparation as well as bridges and cutthroughs accounted each for 11 percent of expenditures. 15 percent was spent on the road surface. The number of bridges built or under construction by 1942 is estimated at 9,000; up to September 1939, a number of 7,339 is solidly documented.[39]

As I will examine in connection with the landscaping work, the combination of an expensive construction project, a rapid building pace, and ambitious completion dates exerted strong cost pressure on the officials in charge. The scope of the autobahn project, in terms of both civil engineering and its time frame, exceeded the capacities of the construction industry. This led to a shortage of labor and materials; when demand from the public and private sector began to rise, this situation drove up construction prices. The desire to open autobahnen on schedule, motivated by propaganda reasons, produced other cost overruns. According to a tabulation by the Directorate *Reichsautobahnen*, completion of the first one-thousand kilometers by the projected date in 1936, alone, caused additional costs of 3.1 million RM. Meeting deadlines was of the highest importance at the construction sites: the regime's self-stylization by means of a transportation project with symbolic capital exacted a high cost. That cost had to be paid not only by the Reich treasury, but also by the formerly unemployed, by forced laborers, and by camp inmates from central Europe. This infrastructure project, economically superfluous in this form, sought to demonstrate the dictatorship's greatness and ability to act, but it revealed the racially motivated power fantasies of its builders.[40]

While the working conditions and financial problems were kept mostly hidden from the public during the Nazi period, the system-supporting function of the roads was carried into every last household in Germany with the help of relentless propaganda. The myth of this successful infrastructure project was created in the first place by this coordinated effort. What follows is therefore a look at the content and the media employed by the autobahn propaganda.

Propagandizing the Reichsautobahn

The goal of the autobahnen was to symbolize power and the conquest of space by means of a large-scale technological system and to stabilize the dictatorship. The already mentioned myth of the *Reichsautobahnen* is based in large measure on the ways the roads were depicted during the Nazi period. A more recent study of the *Reichsautobahnen* conceived of itself explicitly as the "history of a fascination," in which the authors confessed that the reality and the effect of the roads were impossible to separate in the historical process and in the collective memory. After all, the autobahn myth is one of the most tenacious left behind by the Third Reich. Not only is the building of the roadways sometimes seen in popular memory as one of the regime's "positive accomplishments" and balanced out—in a peculiar accounting move—against its "dark sides," but it is also appreciated as a supposedly nonpolitical achievement. None of these views do justice to the history of these freeways. Analyzed from a psychoanalytical perspective, the autobahnen appear as the most important building block in a strategy of remembrance by means of which National Socialism could be integrated into a person's own biographical account and self-identity. The picture of the autobahnen as peaceful structures allowed one to mentally split the Nazi dictatorship into a positive, energetic period of the first years, and a dark, criminal period of the Second World War and the Holocaust. In this process, the propaganda-fed notion of the job-creating autobahnen combined, in personal memory, with their aesthetic appeal to form a piece that was superbly suited for this mental split. Such ideas served the moral reconstruction of an immoral period, a process that occurred both on an individual level and on a massive scale after 1945.[41] Of importance to the present context is the degree to which the public representation of the autobahnen in the Third Reich created the basis for this kind of memory. In the same way that the autobahnen were—according to contemporary accounts—embedded within the landscape in exemplary fashion, "Adolf Hitler's Roads" were part of the staged reality of the Führer state, with its publicly conveyed mixture of coercion and enticement.[42]

The construction and operation of the *Reichsautobahnen* were among the events in Nazi Germany that were celebrated with effusive praise and pomp. Hundreds of publications celebrated the roadways as a technological achievement of the highest order and as attractive structures, as an effective means for overcoming unemployment, and thus as a contribution to the creation of a *Volk* community. This view of the autobahnen, which was limited to these three factors, was overarched by the myth of "Adolf Hitler's Roads"—the legend that Hitler himself had drawn up the plans during his imprisonment at Landsberg after the failed Munich putsch of 1923. Todt promoted this falsification of the Hafraba past by asking Julius Streicher, the Gau chief of Nuremberg, to provide details from his own recollection for a piece in Todt's house organ *Die Straße*. The myth that Hitler came up with the idea of the highway network and then gave it to his *Volk* was central to autobahn propaganda. In this way, Hitler and "his" work fused into a single entity, which formed one building block of the Hitler cult. At the same time, the *Reichsautobahn* was depicted as uniquely German, for according to the propaganda, given the dimensions and high degree of organization, these roads were possible only in Germany.[43]

Contemporary propaganda took a wide variety of forms. It used newspapers, books, the theater, movies, radio, public speeches, and even collectible pictures and board games. No fewer than twenty films on the *Reichsautobahn* are documented. Autobahn films for a general public carried titles such as "Bahn Frei!" (Open Road), "Straßen der Zukunft" (Roads of the Future), "Auf Deutschlands neuen Autostraßen" (On Germany's New Highways), "Schnelle Straßen" (Fast Roads) and "Straßen machen Freude" (Roads Are Fun).[44] The titles show that the idea of an unencumbered ride on four-lane roads had to be introduced and explained to the audience. Collectible pictures in cigarette packs, which could be pasted into a Hitler booklet, showed Hitler as the father figure of the roads and the Germans. The accompanying text emphasized how deeply the dictator was supposedly involved in designing the details of the segments and the bridges.[45] The novels and stories took place in various parts of the Reich, but all followed the basic pattern of a conflict between old and young, farmers and engineers, workers and bosses, a conflict that was resolved by the "common work" on the road and by the very magnificence of the project. Titles such as *Granite and Heart* or *The Nibelungen Road* point to how bombastic these efforts were.[46]

Radio, especially, whose modern, unifying technology resembled that of the autobahn, embraced the new network of highways. With ring connections and reports from the construction sites it anticipated the 1,000th kilometer and the 2,000th kilometer. In addition, the *Reichsautobahn* was the topic of shows of dedication and edification. A genre all its own was autobahn painting, for which landscape painters were employed. It was their task to glorify the construction work and the positive changes to the landscape through the highways. In so doing, they were supposed to revive the genre of landscape painting, which was underrepresented in modernity, by giving it a technological orientation. Through exhibits and reproductions in newspapers and magazines, the effect of the paintings radiated far beyond a given highway section into those regions of the Reich that had to wait for the blessings of an autobahn for some time yet.[47]

Precisely the landscape of the *Reichsautobahnen* could be succinctly captured or even projected into the future in the landscape paintings of the autobahn genre. The section of the autobahn near Munich shown in figure 4.1 is depicted not in its construction state, but as what it would look like forty years after its opening. The dominance of the roads over space corresponds with their dominance over time. The regime obviously saw itself in the form of the highways as a type of government that was focused far into the future, one that made possible a harmonious coexistence of nature and technology. The road itself in this painting leads into a far distance; in this vision, the autobahn project as a whole stood for a drive toward a modern, fast, and visually attractive future. In that sense, this painting is part of the promise that the roads would not be imposed upon the German landscape, but merged with it. The network of autobahnen was also found on postcards, stamps, portfolios, dice games, and tear-off calendars. For example, Inspector-General Todt commissioned a silver goods manufacturer in his home town of Pforzheim to make silver cigarette cases, which he presented to trusted engineers at the opening of segments. The lids of the cases showed a map of Germany with the network of the celebrated roads. Landscape advocate Seifert asked a painter in Munich to transfer the network motif onto a tabletop. The complete table was to be made by the State Porcelain Manufacture in Berlin; the precious piece of furniture was intended as a gift to Hitler.[48]

Based on an examination of the autobahn propaganda with a view to how the integration of the roads into the landscape was mentioned and processed, it is possible to say that the propaganda was functionally subdivided: the bombastic radio broadcasts and cigarette picture albums were aimed at what was regarded as an undifferentiated mass of "Volk comrades" and emphasized the job-creating nature of the roads, the rapid pace of construction, and the magnificence of the new roads. Elaborate picture books and art magazines were aimed at the educated middle class, which was supposed to learn to appreciate the creative power of the Third Reich. In the process, the embedding of the roads into the landscape—as a reconciliation of nature and technology—was supposed to appeal to those readers who sympathized with *Heimatschutz* concerns. The emphasis on the roads as a work of art and as successful landscape structures was a direct continuation of the *Heimatschutz* discourse of the interwar period. At the same time, the National Socialist concept of "German Technology" provided a new shorthand for the highways.

Figure 4.2. Fritz Bayerlein: autobahn painting from the 1930s, portraying the road in the 1970s. *Postcard in possession of the author.*

German Technology (Deutsche Technik) and the Reichsautobahn

Contemporary publications praised the autobahnen as the embodiment of a German Technology (*Deutsche Technik*). To put it in strongly oversimplified terms, National Socialist ideologues and propagandists claimed that the dictatorship had developed and applied a new, genuinely National Socialist style of technology. Unlike other nations (e.g., Great Britain, France, or the United States) and in contrast to German styles of technology prior to 1933, National Socialist technology—under the slogan German Technology—was intended to mirror and improve German culture and nature, not destroy them. Technology and values regarded as "German" were now compatible. However, contemporary publications in this area provided more general pronouncements than directives for concrete action.

For engineers as a social group, German Technology promised a substantial boost in status, since they could now be placed on an equal footing with other creators of culture. Many in the profession welcomed this development. At the same time, engineers were to be reeducated in the spirit of German Technology, so that their creations would no longer harm German culture and nature. To that end, Fritz Todt, who saw himself as the leader of the engineers, trained a future elite of educated technicians and engineers, who, at Plassenburg Castle in Franconia, were subjected to ideological training courses with calisthenics and the music of Bach. These new qualities of German Technology should become especially apparent in infrastructure projects; it was Todt's goal to turn the *Reichsautobahnen* into the prime example of his ideology.

This ideological construct possessed vague contours and a specific core; in the debates over the landscape of the autobahnen, German Technology provided the stimulus and framework. *Deutsche Technik* was also the name of the journal published between 1933 and 1943 by the *Kampfbund Deutscher Architekten und Ingenieure* (Fighting Association of German Architects and Engineers), a Nazi organization founded in 1931 by Schultze-Naumburg, among others.[49]

At first, on an organizational level, the coordination (*Gleichschaltung*) efforts of the Nazi state were also extended to the engineering associations. The "reorganization of German technology," initially pursued by Feder, after 1934 by Todt, and not completed until 1937, did not lead the NSDAP to the quick successes it wanted. To be sure, by 1937 the Nazi party had created an organizational monopoly of professional representation in the Main Office for Technology and in the National Socialist League of German Technology (*Nationalsozialistischer Bund Deutscher Technik*, NSBDT). The continuing professional organization Association of German Engineers (*Verein Deutscher Ingenieure*, VDI) was incorporated and "coordinated." The regime's goal of politicizing the engineers corresponded with the hope of the latter for an improvement in their social and political status. Added to this was a long-standing—and under the Nazi banner even more pronounced—loyalty to the state and its organs as the precondition for the ideological accommodation of technology to the Third Reich. On an economic level, the labor market for engineers improved dramatically, after it had suffered severely during the economic crisis. Between the second quarter of 1932 and the third quarter of 1935, unemployment among the members of the Association of German Diploma Engineers (*Verein Deutscher Diplom-Ingenieure*) declined from around 11 percent to below 2.5 percent. At the same time, hundreds of engineers classified as Jewish left Germany for countries like the United States, England, and Palestine.[50] The remaining engineers were to be given an enhanced status as a social group under the banner of German Technology.

Recent research has emphasized the heterogeneous nature of the label German Technology, whose vague goal was a rhetorical enhancement of technology under the Nazi banner. What we are dealing with is a mixture of older views on technology and new ressentiments. Hewing to old dichotomies of "culture" and "civilization," German Technology was seen as a cultural accomplishment and culture-creating factor, not merely as a function of civilization. The cultural significance of German Technology was used especially by Todt as a definitive argument in various contexts. During the interwar period, similar ideas about a normative promotion of technology had been articulated within the "conservative revolution." Writers like Ernst Jünger and Oswald Spengler transformed technology—understood in an all-inclusive way—into something that was historically relevant and newly appreciated, without argumentatively endangering their own conservatism; technology was infused with a soul. The language of this linguistic complex was able to move technology from the sphere of civilization—where reason, intellect, internationalism, materialism, and money ruled—into the realm of culture. The values that held sway there were the likes of community, blood, will, immediacy, productivity, and, finally, race. Among right-wing intellectuals could be found a broad spectrum of enthusiasms for and criticism of technology. The interpretation of these debates remains controversial: while Jeffrey Herf noted the specifically German mixture of rationalism and irrationalism in this "reactionary modernism," historians like Michael Großheim and Thomas Rohkrämer emphasize the relative modernity of the conceptions of technology, landscape, and nature in these discourses.[51] What this historiographic debate still lacks, however, are analyses of specific projects within National Socialism that are based on the sources.

Another approach to this debate is the position of the United States as a rhetorical resource. The waves of "Americanization" in the German economy and society reached a first high point in the 1920s. For the Weimar Republic, one can sum up a heterogeneous debate under the banner of "Americanism" (or better: anti-Americanism). In the process, reactionary critics of culture and "cultural critique from a position beyond progress" (Detlev Peukert) had very different goals in mind when they employed the code word "America" in contemporary discourse. The former lamented the leveling of taste, intellectual shallowness and superficiality, and the threatening loss of humanity; the latter identified as the success of unrestrained capitalism a soulless utilitarian rationalism, which ran counter to the essence of old Europe and especially to German essence. In the process, American technology was often equated with modern technology whose possible adoption was controversial beyond party lines.[52]

It would be of little use, though, to equate the "reactionary modernism" of the interwar period with the debate over German Technology. In an eclecticism that occasions little surprise, the complex of National Socialist ideology incorporated elements from various debates. Creativity and politicization were supposed to raise the social standing of engineers. At the same time, this discourse combined elements of the technocracy movement, which regarded Taylorist business management as the blueprint for political leadership. Needless to say, the contours of German Technology remained fluid; this was not a central, though a compatible, component of Nazi ideology. As a peripheral ideology segment, German Technology was limited in its ability to connect to the ideological core of National Socialism, with its racist-anti-Semitic and anti-Bolshevist ideologems. A pragmatic embrace of this ideological core as well as a move to distance itself from it were two equally conceivable scenarios. The possibilities of borrowing from the playbook of Nazi ideology became especially clear in the critique by German Technology of the capitalist profit motive and its allegedly harmful influence on technology. The profit motive, it was argued, had led to an abuse of technology, turning it into a job-destroying force. According to this interpretation, a different economic system, one committed to the common good and not self-interest, made possible the existence of a technology that was compatible with society. In an aggressive version of that view, engineers laid claim to leadership over the creation and application of technology, and thus over economic decision within businesses, which would have interfered with the decision-making powers of businesspeople and lawyers.[53]

Using this kind of justifying rhetoric, which was compatible with Nazi ideology, it was possible to integrate German Technology into the concept of a *"Volk* community" that claimed to equalize social differences, smooth out distinctions of class and estate, and be racially homogeneous. We can see here how a virulent anticapitalist debate that had been going on for some time could be moved from a peripheral position and placed into a close substantive relationship with core elements of Nazi ideology. Racist patterns of explanation offered the link that connected such a critique of culture with Nazi ideology. In this view of the world, the driving forces of development were above all the racial condition of peoples, their membership in a superior or inferior race, and the degree of their "intermixing." Because technology in the Weimar Republic had been allegedly exposed to strong Jewish influence, it had become materialistic, specialized, selfish, and shortsighted. As far as the propagandists of German Technology were concerned, the point was to cast off this influence, especially since "the German *Volk*" was supposedly an especially inventive one.

This attempted new definition of technology shortly after the Nazi takeover of power has left a clear echo in historical scholarship. While the talk about technology has been examined, scholars have less often looked at the actual form it took—or rather, the connection between the ideology of technology and design. In that sense, this study of the landscape design of the *Reichsautobahnen* is intended to help answer the questions raised above. Taking as the starting point the conversation about the shaping of landscape, my goal is to measure the Nazi ideology of technology against its own exalted claim of being a landscape-friendly technology.[54] The degree to which the differentiation from other countries played a role is revealed by Seifert's remark regarding the 1932 road from Cologne to Bonn: because of its straight line, it was, like all the other non-Nazi autobahnen, "alien to the *Volk*" and had something "American or Russian about it."[55]

In all of this the role of technology in the opposition between technology and nature is especially deserving of study. If technology, as a means in the production process, was elevated into a positive force shaping what was in other countries a soulless national economy, it would also be capable of dissolving the dilemma of a nature-destroying modernity. The treatment of nature in the industrial age had been one of the main points in the critique of culture. The potential for conflict inherent in large-scale technological projects had been obvious since the controversies I have already looked at. Engineers and technicians wanted to give their answer to the cultural critique that equated large-scale technological construction with the destruction of nature. If the progressive destruction of nature was the expression of a false use of technology, the advance of German Technology would have to be able to proceed without such losses caused by modernity. The door was now open for the desired reconciliation of technology and nature.

This reversal of a categorical contradiction was used as a topos and slogan in all the rhetoric about German Technology. The conflict between the two spheres, believed to have been overcome, is evident in the frequently used word "reconciliation"—one can only reconcile what was previously at odds. The leading engineers postulated that such a reorientation was possible only within German Technology. The essence of technology "in the National Socialist conception," they argued, was connected to the "innermost core" of its ideology, "namely to biological, nature-given thought and action, which is now the central focus in all political, *völkisch*, and cultural spheres." Ideas about nature were seen as the yardstick for technological action, and the relative level of the cultural relevance of technology was determined by the contribution it made to a positive alteration of the landscape. Contemporary reflections highlighted the new reality that such a turn toward nature entailed: "The same principles of a profound change in *Weltanschauung*, which have asserted themselves in National Socialist life in the relationship of politics and the economy, have been able to reassert the primacy of nature also in the relationship between nature and humanity, on the one hand, and technology, on the other." According to this way of thinking, technology was "nothing other than applied natural science"; nature was thus assigned the role of "teacher of technicians, of engineers." The Four-Year-Plan, it was said, had further improved the relationship between technology and nature, for this "planned German technology bound to nature was now opening up vast treasures for the *Volk*." Even the construction of the Western Wall could be celebrated as a "magnificent accomplishment."[56] The *Reichsautobahnen* were presented as the most prominent example of such a landscape-compatible technology. What made this especially attractive was that the topic "technology and nature" picked up the thread of an emphatically design-oriented discourse that was based on the writings of Schultze-Naumburg. But it was the anti-Semitic component that tied "landscape and technology" as an ideological satellite more closely to the core of Nazi ideology.[57]

This notion of landscape was thus different from a conservationist, anti-technology critique from the early days of *Heimatschutz* and from the ideas of "blood and soil." In contrast to Rudorff's *Heimatschutz*, the proponents of a German Technology quite matter-of-factly affirmed the use of technology to modernize the economy, precisely because they believed that this modernization could now be done in a way that was compatible with nature. The radical political turnaround under National Socialism was supposed to bring about a radical dissolution of the conflict between technology and nature and the shift of technology into the realm of culture. The difference between the conception of nature in German Technology and in the blood-and-soil ideology lay for one in the pursuit of different goals. Where the latter was solely concerned with the agricultural sector, the former was interested in the use of technology in general, whether in road construction, power plants, or the supply of energy. The emphasis was not on the simplicity of technical systems, but on their adaptation to nature.[58]

In summary, I will emphasize again the signal function of the *Reichsautobahnen* for German Technology. They served as an icon not only of National Socialism as such, but also of German Technology. This conglomeration of ideas had the ideological function of solidifying technology as a cultural force by transcending its mere civilizational function. Or, as Alwin Seifert put it at the opening of the first *Reichsautobahn* section: "To conceive of motor and motor roadway as ends in themselves, that is just barely civilization; to use them as means for a deeper experience and new insight, that alone is culture." From the perspective of its propagandists, German Technology could escape the pressure of the profit motive and its supposedly racial abuse only in the era of National Socialism, since it was now that an ideological advancement went hand in hand with a social advancement of engineers. Technology thus became useful to the "*Volk* community."

The ways in which technology was applied were supposed to be derived from nature itself and its laws, while the function of technology was subordinated to the *Volk* as a whole in the National Socialist sense. The ideologically charged nexus of landscape and technology, the clash of which was to be transformed into a new harmony, tied the autobahnen, for one, into the regime's ideological self-representation. For another, the idea of these roads stood in a tension-filled relationship to their construction.[59] In what follows, I will examine how the vague self-presentation of German Technology was embodied in the planning and construction of the autobahnen. The development of parts of organized *Heimatschutz* into a technology-affirming architectural lobby, the experiences in Laufenburg and on the Neckar River, the biographical constellations in the form of Seifert's career, and the reallocation of massive financial, administrative, and rhetorical resources to the autobahn project by the Nazis shortly after they came to power—all this created the possibility to define the relationship between landscape and technology in a state-organized infrastructure project and to set it into concrete.

Notes

1. The former Reich Interior and Justice Minister Koch-Weser (DDP, later DSP) on 28 April 1930 during a speech in Baden-Baden, quoted in Theodor Krebs, "Hafraba. Die Geschichte des Ringens um die 'utopische' Idee der Autobahn," in Bundesminister für Verkehr Abteilung Straßenbau, *Hafraba. Bundesautobahn Hansestädte-Frankfurt-Basel. Rückblick auf 30 Jahre Autobahnbau* (Wiesbaden and Berlin, 1962), 24.
2. On the degree of motorization at the time see Heidrun Edelmann, *Vom Luxusgut zum Gebrauchsgegenstand. Die Geschichte der Verbreitung von Personenkraftwagen in Deutschland* (Frankfurt/Main, 1989); Angela Zatsch, *Staatsmacht und Motorisierung am Morgen des Automobilzeitalters* (Konstanz, 1993); Kurt Möser, "World War I and the Creation of Desire for Automobiles in Germany," in *Getting and Spending: European and American Consumer Societies in the Twentieth Century*, ed. Susan Strasser, Charles McGovern, and Matthias Judt (Cambridge, 1998): 195–222; Richard J. Overy, "Heralds of Modernity: Cars and Planes from Invention to Necessity," in *Fin de Siècle and its Legacy*, ed. Mikuláš Teich and Roy Porter (Cambridge, 1990), 54–79; Martin Kornrumpf, *HAFRABA e.V. Deutsche Autobahnplanung 1926–1934* (Bonn, 1990). Until 1928, the abbreviation referred to Hamburg-Frankfurt-Basel. For the Association's first bylaws and its entry into the register of associations see IfZ, Fa 84. The invitation for the founding meeting on 22 October 1926 had been issued by the Economic Office of the city of Frankfurt am Main, whose Lord Mayor, Ludwig Landmann (1868–1945), became chairman of the executive board, in accordance with the bylaws. Members were the federal states, cities, traffic associations, chambers of industry and commerce, Hapag and North German Lloyd, IG Farben, the Reich Association of German Retail and Overseas Trade, automobile clubs, and road construction, building materials, and petroleum companies. See Ehrtfried Böhm et al., *Straßenforschung. 50 Jahre Forschungsgesellschaft für das Straßenwesen 1924–1974* (Bonn-Bad Godesberg, 1974), 319. Landmann was Frankfurt's first Jewish lord mayor and was purged from the Hafraba after 1933.
3. Jürgen Schmädicke, "Bessere Straßen braucht das Land. Der deutsche Straßenbau zwischen den Weltkriegen unter den Anforderungen des Lastkraftwagenverkehrs," in Harry Niemann and Armin Hermann, eds., *100 Jahre Lkw. Geschichte und Zukunft des Nutzfahrzeugs* (Stuttgart, 1997), 356–368; Volker Ziegler, "Il progetto autostradale tedesco fra città e territorio, 1925–1955" *Storia urbana* 26, 3 (2002), 85–120; Carl Wienecke, *Entwicklungsgeschichtliche Betrachtung des deutschen Straßenwesens in den Jahren 1871–1945* (Bielefeld, 1956); Michael Stolz, "Am Beginn des modernen Straßenbaus—Sächsische Straßenbaupolitik und -technik zur Zeit der Weimarer Republik," *Bautechnik* 75 (1998): 391–402, on the traffic survey see 394; Alfred Sloan, Jr., *My Years with General Motors* (Garden City, New York, 1972 [orig. 1963]), 380. For anecdotal accounts see Artur Speck, *Via Vita. Lebensgeschichte eines Straßenbauers im Zeitalter des Kraftwagens* (Bad Godesberg, n. d.)
4. Kurt Kaftan, *Der Kampf um die Autobahnen. Geschichte und Entwicklung des Autobahngedankens in Deutschland von 1907–1935 unter Berücksichtigung ähnlicher Pläne und Bestrebungen im übrigen Europa* (Berlin, 1955); Lando Bortolotti and Giuseppe De Luca, *Fascismo e autostrade. Un caso di sintesi: la Firenze-mare* (Milan, 1994), 15–21; Lando Bortolotti, "Les pré-

mieres propositions d'un système européen d'autoroutes, 1926–1937," in *European Networks, 19th–20th Centuries. New Approaches to the Formation of a Transnational Transport and Communication System. Réseaux européens, XIXe-XXe Siècles*, ed. Albert Carreras, Andrea Giuntini, and Michèle Merger (Milan, 1994), 47–59; Ingrid Heckmann-Strohkark, "Der Traum von einer europäischen Gemeinschaft. Die Internationalen Autobahnkongresse 1931 und 1932," in *Die Schweizer Autobahn*, ed. Martin Heller and Andreas Volk (Zurich, 1999), 32–45, 35; Massimo Moraglio, "A Rough Modernization: Landscapes and Highways in Twentieth-Century Italy," in *The World Beyond the Windshield: Roads and Landscapes in the United States and Europe*, ed. Christof Mauch and Thomas Zeller (Athens, Ohio, 2007).

5. Krebs, "Hafraba," 15; Kornrumpf, *Hafraba*, 40; Hans Lorenz, "Trassierung," in *Hafraba*, publ. by the Bundesminister für Verkehr Abteilung Straßenbau, 174–179, here 174–175.

6. Kaftan, *Autobahnen*, 125; Rainer Stommer, ed., *Reichsautobahn. Pyramiden des Dritten Reiches. Analysen zur Ästhetik eines unbewältigten Mythos* (Marburg, 1982) 25; Krebs, "Hafraba," 17–18, 20–22, 24, 26–28; Alfred Gottwaldt, *Julius Dorpmüller, die Reichsbahn und die Autobahn. Verkehrspolitik und das Leben des Verkehrsministers bis 1945* (Berlin, 1995), 37–38.

7. Karl-Heinz Ludwig, *Technik und Ingenieure im Dritten Reich* (Düsseldorf, 1979 [orig. 1974]), 303 (on Sombart); Overy, *Cars*; Detlev J.K. Peukert, *The Weimar Republic: The Crisis of Classical Modernity*, trans. Richard Deveson (New York: Hill and Wang, 1987), 174; Edelmann, *Luxusgut*; Theo Barker, "A German Centenary in 1986, a French in 1995 or the Real Beginnings About 1905?," in *The Economic and Social Effects of the Spread of Motor Vehicles*, ed. Theo Barker (Basingstoke and London, 1987), 1–54; Christiane Eisenberg, *'English Sports' und deutsche Bürger: Eine Gesellschaftsgeschichte* (Paderborn, 1999), 340; Adelheid von Saldern, "Cultural Conflicts, Popular Mass Culture and the Question of Nazi Success: The Eilenriede Motorcycle Races, 1924–1939," *German Studies Review* 15 (1992): 317–338; AVUS erroneously as the "precursor" of the autobahn: Peter Reichel, *Der schöne Schein des Dritten Reiches: Faszination und Gewalt des Faschismus* (Munich and Vienna, 1991), 276–277.

8. Becker (no first name), "Die Möglichkeit der Verwendung von Pflanzungen beim Bau neuzeitlicher Autostraßen," *Verkehrstechnik* 10/50 (1929): 863–867; Ingrid Strohkark, "Die Wahrnehmung von 'Landschaft' und der Bau von Autobahnen in Deutschland, Frankreich und Italien vor 1933" (Dr. Ing. thesis, Hochschule der Künste Berlin, 2001), 181–193. On the relevant proposals from the garden architect Georg Bela Pniower (1896–1960), who did not work on the autobahnen, see ibid., 215–220. Pniower's name is not found in the clashes over the hiring of landscape architects during National Socialism. He was prohibited from pursuing his profession because of the racial criteria of the Nazi regime, and after 1949 became a professor at East Berlin's Humboldt University.

9. Christopher Kopper, "Modernität oder Scheinmodernität nationalsozialistischer Herrschaft. Das Beispiel der Verkehrspolitik," in *Von der Aufgabe der Freiheit. Politische Verantwortung und bürgerliche Gesellschaft im 19. und 20. Jahrhundert. Festschrift für Hans Mommsen*, ed. Christian Jansen, Lutz Niethammer, and Bernd Weisbrod (Berlin, 1995), 399–411, 399–400. For a review of the scholarship see idem, *Handel und Verkehr im 20. Jahrhundert* (Munich, 2002), 91–101.

10. Gottwald, *Dorpmüller*; Klaus Hildebrand, "Die Deutsche Reichsbahn in der nationalsozialistischen Diktatur 1933–1945," in *Die Eisenbahn in Deutschland. Von den Anfängen bis zur Gegenwart*, ed. Lothar Gall and Manfred Pohl (Munich, 1999), 165–243; Alfred C. Mierzejewski, *The Most Valuable Asset of the Reich: A History of the German Railway Company*, vol. 1, 1920–1932 (Chapel Hill and London, 1999), vol. 2, 1933–1945 (Chapel Hill and London, 2000).

11. Frank Lippert, *Lastkraftwagenverkehr und Rationalisierung in der Weimarer Republik. Technische und ökonomische Aspekte fertigungsstruktureller und logistischer Wandlungen in den 1920er Jahren* (Frankfurt/Main, 1995); Peter Borscheid, "Lkw kontra Bahn. Die Modernisierung des Transports durch den Lastkraftwagen in Deutschland bis 1939," in *Die Entwicklung der Motorisierung im Deutschen Reich und den Nachfolgestaaten*, ed. Harry Niemann and Armin Hermann (Stuttgart, 1995), 23–38; Heidi Rohde, *Transportmodernisierung contra Verkehrsbewirtschaftung. Zur staatlichen Verkehrspolitik gegenüber dem Lkw in den 30er Jahren* (Frankfurt/Main, 1999).

12. Quoted in Schütz and Gruber, *Mythos*, 14; "Bericht des Geschäftsführers der Hafraba e.V., Hof, über eine Besprechung mit dem Reichskanzler zur Planung und Finanzierung des Autobahnbaus am 6. April 1933," *Akten der Reichskanzlei Regierung Hitler 1933–1938, Teil I: 1933/34*, vol. 1 (Boppard/Rhein, 1983), 306–311; Friedrich Hartmannsgruber, ""...ungeachtet der noch ungeklärten Finanzierung": Finanzplanung und Kapitalbeschaffung für den Bau der Reichsautobahnen 1933–1945," *Historische Zeitschrift* 278 (2004): 625–681.
13. Heidrun Edelmann, "Der Traum vom Volkswagen," in *Geschichte der Zukunft des Verkehrs. Verkehrskonzepte von der Frühen Neuzeit bis zum 21. Jahrhundert*, ed. Helmuth Trischler and Hans-Liudger Dienel (Frankfurt/Main, 1997), 280–288, 286; Hans Mommsen and Manfred Grieger, *Das Volkswagenwerk und seine Arbeiter im Dritten Reich* (Düsseldorf, 1996); Mark Spoerer, "Die Automobilindustrie im Dritten Reich: Wachstum um jeden Preis?," in *Unternehmen im Nationalsozialismus*, ed. Lothar Gall and Manfred Pohl (Munich, 1998), 61–72.
14. Overy, "Cars, Roads," 73; Edelmann, *Luxusgut*, 193–240; Rainer Flik, "Ford-Legende und Wirklichkeit. Die Motorisierung des Straßenverkehrs in Europa und Übersee im Vergleich bis 1939," *Traverse* 6, Nr. 2 (1999): 125–142; Axel Doßmann, "Wie wir die Autobahnen lieben lernten. Strukturelle Leitbilder und Automobilismus in Deutschland bis in die sechziger Jahre," *Sozialwissenschaftliche Informationen* 25 (1996): 235–242.
15. The statement was made by the highway commissioner of Michigan in 1938, quoted by Bruce E. Seely, "Visions of American Highways, 1900–1980," in Dienel and Trischler, *Geschichte der Zukunft*, 260–279, 269. Barbara Schmucki, *Der Traum vom Verkehrsfluss. Städtische Verkehrsplanung seit 1945 im deutsch-deutschen Vergleich*, vol. 4, Beiträge zur historischen Verkehrsforschung (Frankfurt/New York, 2001), 60.
16. Ludwig, *Technik und Ingenieure*, 73–79, 306; Seidler, *Todt*.
17. Todt said that he had calculated the resulting damage at 1.38 billion Reichsmark, yet it is unclear how he arrived at this number. Fritz Todt, *Straßenbau und Straßenverwaltung*, BAK R 65I/1a, December 1932, 3–4, 33, 35, 45; Ludwig, *Technik und Ingenieure*, 307–310. According to Joachim Radkau (*Technik in Deutschland. Vom 18. Jahrhundert bis zur Gegenwart* [Frankfurt/Main, 1989], 307–308), the engineering sciences in the mid-1920s for the first time addressed the rebuilding of roads, but not their new construction.
18. "Grundsätzliches zur Organisation des deutschen Kraftfahrwesens, insbesondere der Erbauung und des Betriebes von Fernautostrassen," BAP R 43II/503, fols. 53–56. According to another record, the catalogue of demands was used at a meeting of department heads on 14 June 1933 about the road system, ibid., fol. 56. The following quotes are from folios 54 and 56.
19. Although the later opposition of the Reichswehr to the roadways shows how false this expectation was, it is revealing that Todt and Feder were hoping that their plans would seem more attractive if they situated them within a military framework of justification.
20. Seidler, *Todt*, 164, 203–204, 220, 239, 253, 273, 286. On conflicts of interest, ibid., 222.
21. *Reichsgesetzblatt*, Part II, No. 28, 30 June 1933, 509. "Generalinspektion," in *Der Große Brockhaus*, vol. 17, 15th ed. (Leipzig, 1930), 148. Bruno Belhoste, "Un modèle à l'épreuve. L'École polytechnique de 1794 au Second Empire," *La formation polytechnicienne 1794–1994*, ed. Bruno Belhoste, Amy Dahan Dalmedico, and Antoine Picon (Paris, 1994), 9–30; Antoine Picon, *L'Invention de l'ingénieur moderne. L'École des ponts et chausées 1747–1851* (Paris, 1992).
22. Until 1937, the official name of the regional planning office was *Oberste Bauleitung Kraftfahrbahnen* (OBK); after December 1937 it was called *Oberste Bauleitung der Reichsautobahnen* (OBR). Todt wrote that the word "Kraftfahrbahn" (motor roadway) should be "eradicated" also from "official usage." Signage on the roads should say "*Reichsautobahn*," not "*Autobahn*." Todt to Directorate *Reichsautobahnen* and all members of the department, 9 December 1937, BAK R 65I/38.
23. Karl Massar, "Die deutschen Landstraßen," *Die Straße* 2 (1935): 76–80. On the neglect of the building of non-autobahn highways, see Rohde, *Transportmodernisierung*, 155–175, 303–308.
24. Kornrumpf, *Hafraba*; Kaftan, *Autobahnen*, 155 and 160. See Mechtild Rössler, "'Area Research' and 'Spatial Planning' from the Weimar Republic to the German Federal Republic," in *Science, Technology and National Socialism*, ed. Monika Renneberg and Mark Walker (Cam-

bridge, 1994), 126–138; idem,*"Wissenschaft und Lebensraum": Geographische Ostforschung im Nationalsozialismus* (Berlin/Hamburg, 1990); Jürgen Schulz, "Raumwissenschaft und Raumplanung als Rahmen der Entwicklung der Profession und der Hochschuldisziplin der Landschaftsplanung," in *Geschichte und Struktur der Landschaftsplanung,* ed. Ulrich Eisel and Stefanie Schultz (Berlin, 1991), 192–246; Dieter Stockmann, *Strecke 46. Die Reichsautobahn zwischen Spessart und Rhön* (Veitshöchheim, 1999), 28–32.

25. State Chancery of the Free State of Bavaria to the State Economics Ministry, 21 September 1933 (rejection of the segment Stuttgart-Saarbrücken by the military), BayHStA StK 6949 fol. 44346; "Vermerk des Ministerialrats Willuhn über eine Besprechung des Reichskanzlers mit Verkehrsexperten zur Frage des Autobahnbaus am 18. Mai 1933," *Akten der Reichskanzlei Regierung Hitler 1933–1938,* Part I: 1933/34, vol. 1, 463–464; Kopper, "Modernität oder Scheinmodernität," 405; Gottwaldt, *Dorpmüller,* 41; Overy, "Cars," 74 note 20, 81–82, 85–86; Mierzejewski, *Most Valuable Asset,* vol. 2, S. 40–42; Stommer, *Pyramiden;* Schütz and Gruber, *Mythos,* 12; Gottwaldt, *Dorpmüller,* 41. The erroneous view was recently still propounded by Ludolf Herbst, *Das nationalsozialistische Deutschland* (Frankfurt/Main, 1996), 97–98 and Friedrich Kittler, "Auto Bahnen," in *Der Technikdiskurs in der Hitler-Stalin-Ära,* ed. Wolfgang Emmerich and Carl Wege (Stuttgart, 1995), 114–122. Middle ground by Dietmar Klenke, "Autobahnbau in Westfalen von den Anfängen bis zum Höhepunkt der 1970er Jahre—Eine Geschichte der politischen Planung," in *Verkehr und Region im 19. und 20. Jahrhundert. Westfälische Beispiele,* ed. Wilfried Reininghaus and Karl Teppe (Paderborn, 1999), 249–270, 255–257. The question, however, what influence the Reichswehr exerted *after* the decision had been made on the construction of the autobahn and the choice of the routes lies outside the purview of the present study and must be reserved for a systematic examination of the files. According to Kopper, only the wishes of the *Luftgaukommando* to circumvent industrial areas were taken into consideration, while Silverman speaks of a "virtual veto right" by the military: Dan Silverman, *Hitler's Economy. Nazi Work Creation Programs, 1933–1936* (Cambridge, Mass., 1998), 157. Even Todt conceded internally that the Reich Defense Ministry preferred expanding existing roads to building new ones. Inspector-General to the Reich Finance Minister, 13 October 1934, *Akten der Reichskanzlei, Regierung Hitler,* vol. II, 89.
26. R.L. DiNardo, *Mechanized Juggernaut or Military Anachronism? Horses and the German Army of World War II* (New York, 1991), 102.
27. Ian Kershaw, *Hitler 1889–1936* (London, 1998), 450.
28. Schütz and Gruber, *Mythos,* 11, 15; Kopper, "Modernität," 403; Gottwaldt, *Dorpmüller,* 41.
29. Mierzejewski, *Most Valuable Asset,* 42; Gottwaldt, *Dorpmüller,* 41; Kopper, "Modernität," 403 and 405. Gottwaldt surmises that without the railroad engineers, the construction of the autobahnen would have begun "at least a year later." Martin Broszat, *The Hitler State,* trans. John Hiden (London, 1981), 264–267; Seidler, *Todt,* 75, 100. The Inspector-General was apparently the first office of the German Reich that was headed by an engineer and not by a lawyer. However, the engineers based their salary demands on what was standard in the private sector, not in public administration. Ludwig, *Technik und Ingenieure,* 330, 332. In the discussion that follows, and in keeping with the sources, "Inspector-General for the German Road System" will be used for both the Reich office as a whole and for Todt himself. Where this usage might create confusion, I have noted specifically whether I am referring to the office or its head.
30. Gottwaldt, *Dorpmüller,* 42; Ludwig, *Technik und Ingenieure,* 333; Todt, "Vermerk," 2 March 1937, BAP R 43II/505 fols. 55–57; Todt to Lammers, 9 December 1937, BAP R 43II/505 fol. 111–112.
31. Seidler, *Todt,* 103; BAK R 50I/336, fol. 57–58.; Rudolf Dittrich, *Autobahn-Fahrbahndecken 1934–1956. Grundlagen-Herstellung-Beanspruchung-Bewährung* (Bad Godesberg, 1964), 16.
32. Silverman, *Hitler's Economy,* 173; Schütz and Gruber, *Mythos,* 80; Dittrich, *Autobahn-Fahrbahndecken,* 21; BAK R 50I/336, fol. 57–58; Neil Harris, *Building Lives. Constructing Rites and Passages* (New Haven, Conn., and London, 1999); Norbert Frei, *Der Führerstaat. Nati-*

onalsozialistische Herrschaft 1933 bis 1945 (Munich, 1987), 87–88, 100–101; Seidler, *Todt*, 105–106; Stommer, *Reichsautobahn*, 31.

33. Silverman, *Hitler's Economy*, 244, 261 (Table 11). On the debate at this time see 238–246. Cf. Overy, "Cars," 82–83: 83,863 workers (1934), 115,675 (1935), 124,483 (1936), 95,306 (1938), 80,000 (October 1939). Overy's estimate for the global effects from motorization amounts for 1938 to a total of 1.15 million jobs, about one-twelfth of the workforce. On mechanization: Heinz Herbert Cohrs, *Faszination Baumaschinen. Erdbewegung durch fünf Jahrhunderte* (Isernhagen, 1995), 108–109; Francis Pierre, *Faszination Baumaschinen. Straßenbau-Geschichte* (Isernhagen, 1998), 69.

34. Christoph Hölz, "Verkehrsbauten," in *Bauen im Nationalsozialismus. Bayern 1933–1945. Ausstellung des Architekturmuseums der Technischen Universität München und des Münchner Stadtmuseums*, ed. Winfried Nerdinger (Munich, 1993), 54–97. Karl Lärmer, *Autobahnbau in Deutschland. Zu den Hintergründen* (East Berlin, 1975), 60–70; Dittrich, *Autobahn-Fahrbahndecken*, 16, 21; Silverman, *Hitler's Economy*, 147–174; Theodor Bauer, "Die Entstehung und Verhütung der Schipperkrankheit," *Die Straße* 5 (1938): 587–88. The death rates are given in Schütz and Gruber, *Mythos*, 66–87, 72, although they provide no sources for their claim. See also the interviews with former construction workers in the superb documentary film by Hartmut Bitomsky, *Die Reichsautobahn*, Westdeutscher Rundfunk, 1984.

35. Sieber to *Ministerialrat* Sommer, 7 June 1934, BayHStA StK 6950; Schütz and Gruber, *Mythos*, 72, 76–80; Dittrich, *Autobahn-Fahrbahndecken*, 20 (Charts IV and V).

36. See the desire of the Koblenz *Gauleiter* (*Gau* chief) to procure workers for the construction sites in his region. Inspector-General, Koester, to *Gau* Chief Gustav Simon, Koblenz, 30 May 1941, and 5 September 1941, BAK R65 II/117; *Reichsautobahnen*, regional planning office Berlin to Inspector-General, 28 December 1940, BAK R 65 II/10 (self-management of camps for prisoners of war); draft titled "Einsatz von Kriegsgefangenen an den Bauvorhaben der Reichsautobahnen im Bereich der Obersten Bauleitung Berlin," no date, ibid. The draft was filed on 11 March 1942. See also "Geheimerlaß Generalinspektor für das deutsche Straßenwesen," 10 October 1939 (copy), BayHStA OBB 12816 (employment of foreigners); Wolf Gruner, "Juden bauen die 'Straßen des Führers.' Zwangsarbeit und Zwangsarbeiterlager für nichtdeutsche Juden im Altreich 1940 bis 1943/44," *Zeitschrift für Geschichtswissenschaft* 44 (1996): 789–808, quotes 789–790, 793, 807. The directorate *Reichsautobahnen* classified the segments Stettin-Danzig, Frankfurt/Oder-Posen-Litzmannstadt, and Breslau-Cracow as "important to the war." In addition to the mentioned segments, such forced labor camps for Jews, with especially bad conditions, were also established near Trier. "Der Reichstreuhänder für den öffentlichen Dienst: Vorläufige Anordnung über die arbeitsrechtliche Behandlung der Juden," 19 February 1941, BAK R 65 I/52, fol. 4; "RAB Lager Greimerath an *Reichsautobahnen*, Bauabteilung Wittlich," 13 September1941, ibid, fol. 6; "Israelitische Kultusgemeinde Luxemburg an die Leitung der Reichsautobahn Greimerath bei Wittlich Bez. Trier," 11 September 1941, ibid., fol. 7–8 (petition to release a sixteen-year-old boy from the construction site); "Reichsautobahnen, Vorstand der Bauabteilung Wittlich, Aktenvermerk," 5 September 1941, ibid., fol. 9.

37. Hartmannsgruber, "'ungeachtet der noch ungeklärten Finanzierung.'"

38. Stommer, *Reichsautobahn*, 28–29. According to a survey for Office of Military Government in Germany United States (OMGUS) in 1945, the *Reichsautobahnen* took 1.66 billion Reichsmark from budget funds and 2.7 billion Reichsmark from the Reich Employment Fund (*Reichsstock für Arbeitseinsatz*). The second amount was a loan, but only a fraction was repaid. BAK R2 Anhang 30, 5, 7 and 8. A listing of the revenues in Silverman, *Hitler's Economy*, 260 (chart 11).

39. Dittrich, *Autobahn-Fahrbahndecken*, 20 (Chart IV), 23; Stommer, *Reichsautobahn*, 49; Robert Adamek and Fr. Saake, *Die Straßenkosten und ihre Finanzierung* (Bielefeld, 1962).

40. Added cost of 3,147,629 RM: Directorate *Reichsautobahnen*, "Zusammenstellung der Mehrkosten der Baubeschleunigung zur Eröffnung verschiedener Zivilstrecken am 27. September 1936," 8 March 1937, BAK R 65II/15. In this document, the regional planning office Nuremberg justifies the added expense of 1,11 million RM for the quicker construction of

the segment Schleiz-Lanzendorf with the overtime worked, the use of foreign workers, and the transportation of building material from afar because of shortages. On deadline pressure see Manfred Pohl, *Die Strabag 1923 bis 1998* (Munich and Zurich, 1998), 145–166; idem, *Philipp Holzmann. Geschichte eines Bauunternehmens 1849–1999* (Munich, 1999), 210–216.

41. Radkau, *Technik*, 308; Gudrun Brockhaus, *Schauder und Idylle. Faschismus als Erlebnisangebot* (Munich, 1997), 70–72. On "integration into the landscape" see 106, 115–116, whereby the author vacillates between an assessment of the roads as "ultra-modern nature cosmetics" and genuine respect.
42. The propaganda of the first years was closely connected with the establishment of the first concentration camps: Herbst, *Deutschland*, 80–89.
43. A systematic overview in Eberhard Schütz, "'Jene blaßgrauen Bänder.' Die Reichsautobahn in Literatur und anderen Medien des "Dritten Reiches,"" *Internationales Archiv für Sozialgeschichte der deutschen Literatur* 18/2 (1993): 76–120. Todt to Streicher, 25 March 1939, BAK NS 26/1187; Ian Kershaw, *The "Hitler Myth": Image and Reality in the Third Reich* (Oxford, 1987); idem, *Hitler 1889–1936*, 452.
44. Edward Dimendberg, "The Will to Motorization: Cinema, Highways, and Modernity," *October* 73 (Summer 1995): 90–137, 99.
45. Fritz Todt, "Adolf Hitler and His Roads," in *Adolf Hitler: Pictures from the Life of the Führer 1931–1935* (New York and London, 1978), 88–95. The publisher of the original German version was the "Cigaretten-Bilderdienst GmbH."
46. Schütz and Gruber, *Mythos*, 110–112.
47. Schütz, "'Jene blaßgrauen Bänder,'" 117–120, 193; Kurt H. Lang and Rainer Stommer, "'Deutsche Künstler—an die Front des Straßenbaues!' Fallstudie zur nationalsozialistischen Bildgattung 'Autobahnmalerei'" in Stommer, *Reichsautobahn*, 91–110; Claudia Windisch-Hojnacki, "Die Reichsautobahn. Konzeption und Bau der RAB, ihre ästhetischen Aspekte sowie ihre Illustration in Malerei, Literatur, Fotografie und Plastik," PhD dissertation, Bonn 1989, 203; Bitomsky, *Reichsautobahn*.
48. Todt to silver goods manufacturer Gideon Beck, Pforzheim, 17 April 1935; Family Beck to Todt 2 May 1935, BAP 46.01/1556; Seifert to Todt, 11 November 1935, BAP 46.01/862. The file does not reveal whether the table was in fact made.
49. Ludwig, *Technik und Ingenieure*; Thomas P. Hughes, "Ideologie für Ingenieure," *Technikgeschichte* 48 (1981): 308–323; Jeffrey Herf, *Reactionary Modernism. Technology, Culture, and Politics in Weimar and the Third Reich* (Cambridge, 1984); Michael Allen, "The Puzzle of Nazi Modernism: Modern Technology and Ideological Consensus in an SS Factory at Auschwitz," *Technology & Culture* 37 (1996): 527–571, esp. 545–546; Helmut Maier, "Nationalsozialistische Technikideologie und die Politisierung des 'Technikerstandes': Fritz Todt und die Zeitschrift 'Deutsche Technik,'" in *Technische Intelligenz und "Kulturfaktor Technik." Kulturvorstellungen von Technikern und Ingenieuren zwischen Kaiserreich und früher Bundesrepublik Deutschland*, ed. Burkhard Dietz, Michael Fessner, and Helmut Maier (Münster, 1996), 253–268; Heinrich Adolf, "Technikdiskurs und Technikideologie im Nationalsozialismus," *Geschichte in Wissenschaft und Unterricht* 48 (1997): 429–444.
50. Karl-Heinz Ludwig, "Der VDI als Gegenstand der Parteipolitik 1933–1945," in *Technik, Ingenieure und Gesellschaft. Geschichte des Vereins der Deutschen Ingenieure*, ed. idem (Düsseldorf, 1981), 407–427; idem, *Technik und Ingenieure*, 105–160; Wolfgang Mock, *Technische Intelligenz im Exil. Vertreibung und Emigration deutschsprachiger Ingenieure nach Großbritannien 1933 bis 1945* (Düsseldorf, 1986); Konrad H. Jarausch, *The Unfree Professions. German Lawyers, Teachers, and Engineers, 1900–1950* (New York and Oxford, 1990), 131, 133, 250; Museum für Verkehr und Technik, ed., *Ich diente nur der Technik. Sieben Karrieren zwischen 1940 und 1950* (Berlin, 1995).
51. Herf, *Reactionary Modernism*; Michael Großheim, *Ökologie oder Technokratie? Der Konservatismus in der Moderne* (Berlin, 1995); Thomas Rohkrämer, *Eine andere Moderne? Zivilisationskritik, Natur und Technik in Deutschland 1880–1933* (Paderborn, 1999); idem,

"Antimodernism, Reactionary Modernism and National Socialism. Technocratic Tendencies in Germany, 1890–1945," *Contemporary European History* 8 (1999): 29–50. On the technological avant-garde: Georg Bollenbeck, *Tradition, Avantgarde, Reaktion: Deutsche Kontroversen um die kulturelle Moderne 1880–1945* (Frankfurt, 1999). Frank Trommler, "The Avant-Garde and Technology: Toward Technological Fundamentalism in Turn-of-the-Century Europe," *Science in Context* 8 (1995): 397–416.
52. Peukert, *Weimar Republic*, 178–181; Radkau, *Technik*, 229–230; Mary Nolan, *Visions of Modernity: American Business and the Modernization of Germany* (New York, 1994). Mikael Hård, "German Regulation: The Integration of Modern Technology into National Culture," in *The Intellectual Appropriation of Technology. Discourses on Modernity, 1900–1939*, ed. Mikael Hård and Andrew Jamison (Cambridge, Mass., 1998), 33–67; Konrad Jarausch and Hannes Siegerist, eds., *Amerikanisierung und Sowjetisierung in Deutschland 1945–1970* (Frankfurt/ Main and New York, 1997).
53. Maier, "Nationalsozialistische Technikideologie"; Adolf, "Technikdiskurs," 433–436; Thomas Klepsch, *Nationalsozialistische Ideologie. Eine Beschreibung ihrer Struktur vor 1933* (Münster, 1990); Stefan Willeke, *Die Technokratiebewegung in Nordamerika und in Deutschland zwischen den Weltkriegen. Eine vergleichende Analyse* (Frankfurt/Main, 1995). There is a fundamental methodological difference in the way Adolf and Maier approach Nazi ideology: while Adolf is principally interested in the function of ideologemes and takes them seriously as elements of interpretation, Maier often sees relevant statements as "weird remarks" (265), "nonsense" (260), or "irrational standards (*Eckwerte*)" (255), thereby removing them tendentially from a closer analysis.
54. Eric Dorn Brose, "Generic Fascism Revisited: Attitudes Toward Technology in Germany and Italy, 1919–1945," *German Studies Review* 10 (1987): 273–297; Kees Gispen, "National Socialism and the Technological Culture of the Weimar Republic," *Central European History* 25 (1992): 387–406; Allen, "Puzzle"; Frank Trommler, "Amerikas Rolle im Technikverständnis der Diktaturen," in *Der Technikdiskurs in der Hitler-Stalin-Ära*, ed. Wolfgang Emmerich and Carl Wege (Stuttgart, 1995), 159–174. Trommler argues that after the outbreak of the war, the discourse of the philosophical right had little importance. For two opposing positions concerning the modernity of Nazi technology see Jeffrey Herf, "Der nationalsozialistische Technikdiskurs: Die deutschen Eigenheiten des reaktionären Modernismus," in ibid., 72–93; Anson Rabinbach, "Nationalsozialismus und Moderne. Zur Technik-Interpretation im Dritten Reich," in ibid., 94–113.
55. Alwin Seifert, "Baum und Strauch an der Straße," *Die Straße* 1/1 (1934): 19–22, 19.
56. Alf Gießler, "Natur und Technik," *Deutsche Technik* 4 (1936): 7–11; Josef Pöchlinger, "Natur und Technik," *Die Straße* 5 (1938): 738–39.
57. Borrmann, *Schultze-Naumburg*; Rolf Peter Sieferle, *Fortschrittsfeinde? Opposition gegen Technik und Industrie von der Romantik bis zur Gegenwart* (Munich, 1984), 174–181; Ulrich Linse, *Ökopax und Anarchie. Eine Geschichte der ökologischen Bewegungen in Deutschland* (Munich, 1986).
58. The phrase "blood and soil" is linked especially with the ideas of Walter Darré, the minister of agriculture. The more recent scholarship has emphasized the vague nature of this concept and thus seeks to distance itself from the attempts at a linear account, especially by Anna Bramwell, *Blood and Soil. Richard Walter Darré and Hitler's 'Green Party'* (Buckinghamshire, 1985); idem, *Ecology in the 20th Century. A History* (London and New Haven, 1989). For differing accounts, see Mathias Eidenbenz, *"Blut und Boden": Zu Funktion und Genese der Metaphern des Agrarismus und Biologismus in der nationalsozialistischen Bauernpropaganda R. W. Darrés* (Bern, 1993); Sieferle, *Fortschrittsfeinde?*, 193–205; Gerhard, "Breeding Pigs."
59. Alwin Seifert, "Reichsautobahnen und deutsche Landschaft," in Otto Reismann, *Reichsautobahnen vom ersten Spatenstich zur fertigen Fahrbahn* (Berlin, Frankfurt/Main, 1935). This was a brochure for the opening of the first segment Frankfurt-Darmstadt in May 1935. On similarly tense relationships see Helmut Maier, "Weiße Kohle versus Schwarze Kohle. Naturschutz und Ressourcenschonung als Deckmantel nationalsozialistischer Energiepoli-

tik," *WerkstattGeschichte* 3 (1992): 33–38; idem, "Kippenlandschaft, 'Wasserkrafttaumel' und Kahlschlag. Anspruch und Wirklichkeit nationalsozialistischer Naturschutz- und Energiepolitik," in Bayerl, *Umweltgeschichte*, 247–266; idem, "'Unter Wasser und unter die Erde:' Die süddeutschen und alpinen Wasserkraftprojekte des Rheinisch-Westfälischen Elektrizitätswerks (RWE) und der Natur- und Landschaftsschutz während des 'Dritten Reiches,'" in *Die Veränderung der Kulturlandschaft. Nutzungen-Sichtweisen-Planungen*, ed. Günter Bayerl and Torsten Meyer (Münster/New York: Waxmann, 2003), 139–175.

Chapter 5

CONFLICTS OVER THE HARMONIOUS ROAD

The Hitler regime's road-building program was still known only in vague outline, and Fritz Todt had been in office as Inspector-General for only eight weeks, when the man with a fledgling agency received an invitation at the end of August 1933. Because of the importance of the autobahn project "to the reshaping of the appearance of the *Heimat*," the organizing committee of a national Conference on Historic Monument Preservation and *Heimatschutz* in Kassel asked Todt to send a representative to the meeting. Todt replied promptly. Although he would very much like to speak "about the integration of the autobahnen into the landscape while preserving its unique character," he claimed to lack the time. However, the plan was to consult individuals and organizations who were "highly knowledgeable" in this area. For example, planners were thinking about including the horticultural Fürst Pückler Society, whose representatives were attending the meeting. Consequently, there was every reason to believe that the "legitimate interests regarding landscape protection" were being addressed. Thus, the first call to the Nazi regime to pay attention to the landscaping of the autobahnen came from the organized *Heimatschutz* movement. Todt was receptive to its concerns. Although his name is not found in the literature on *Heimatschutz* before the Nazi dictatorship, beginning in 1936 he was chairman of the Society of the Friends of the German *Heimatschutz*.[1]

Against the backdrop of the debates between the wars, this invitation to a meeting of the *Heimatschützer* was by no means a surprise. Through the publications of the *Heimatschützer* and of the Association of German Engineers on a landscape-friendly building style for industry and infrastructure projects, sensitivity to such concerns had become a familiar topic for broad segments of the educated middle class and the engineers. Todt's general sympathy toward the *Heimatschützer* in his statements in 1933 merely confirms this. However, the question is how the National Socialist state used this body of knowledge, whether

---
Notes for this section begin on page 117.

its ideological undergirdings changed, and how the actual design of the roads related to these ideas. The present chapter will therefore analyze the landscape design of the autobahnen under National Socialism. Following a look at the contact that the *Heimatschützer* established with the National Socialist road administration, I will examine the conflicts over the design of the *Reichsautobahnen*. As a more than cursory glance at the actual construction of the roadways reveals, the autobahn, celebrated in propaganda as a roadway in harmony with the landscape, was the product of many clashes on different levels.[2]

Disagreements marked the selection of the landscape architects who were to ensure that the roads would be compatible with the landscape, and controversy marked their position within the administrative structure of the autobahnen. The marginalization of conservation and regional planning was the outward result of these conflicts. Moreover, the shaping of the roads was a constant bone of contention not only organizationally but also substantively, caught as it was within the triangle of the Berlin office of the Inspector-General, the civil engineers on-site, and the landscape architects. I will argue that these conflicts over ideology, personnel, and building practice were not resolved under National Socialism, but were merely covered up by the hectic pace of construction, the propagandistic exploitation of the project, and its quick end. If one can identify any kind of common denominator for the various approaches to the design and building of the autobahnen, it was Todt's predilection for roads that made possible the visual consumption of landscape.

In using the phrase "consumption of landscape," I am borrowing an analytical category from cultural studies, where the gaze and the vista have been seen for some time as new categories of analysis. Some scholars have already proclaimed the "pictorial turn" as a paradigmatic step analogous to the "linguistic turn." In this approach, vision, the seen, and the observer are not regarded as universal categories, but as phenomena that are constructed in specific historical contexts and are therefore malleable. This applies not only to obvious fields such as art history and the history of photography and film, but also to the study of scientifically and technically constructed forms of observation, which are dependent on cultural codes and at the same time shape subsequent perceptual forms of seeing. Studies of the gaze and of perception do not follow a uniform methodology, but reveal a broad spectrum of approaches to the content of meaning. Scholars have noted self-critically that the diversity of concepts and methods is so great that there is not even a clear notion of what constitutes "evidence." The present study is interested in embedding the categories of gaze and vista as emphasized by the historical actors into a larger scholarly context. John Urry's concept of places explored by and prepared for the tourist gaze offers a valuable point of departure.[3]

When it comes to the history of technology, it also makes sense to connect with the notion of "panoramic traveling," which was common long before that of the "pictorial turn." Here, the question is not merely which technical parameters led to what kind of visual experiences. Rather, the point is to examine, first, who defined and laid claim to the authorship of the gaze, and, second, who had the power to choose visual objects and the nature of the gaze. Within the context of the present study, this approach invariably turns such a history of the gaze into a political history of the gaze. Institutions, actors, and ideologies play an important role in this; decisive in the end is the access to and the exercise of power.[4]

Initially, one of the most important institutions for the political shaping of the *Reichsautobahn* landscape was, as we have seen, the organized *Heimatschutz* movement. The Kassel meeting in 1933 took place a few days before the groundbreaking for the freeways and brought about an organizational and substantive reorientation of the *Heimatschutz* organizations under the banner of the Nazi dictatorship. Under the heading "Monument Preservation and *Heimatschutz* in the Rebuilding of the Nation," four working groups and one public event addressed the question of whether and how the old problems of *Heimatschutz* could be solved by the new regime. In the process, it became clear that it was not necessary for National Socialism to draft the *Heimatschützer* into their cause, for the latter saw an opportunity in the ideas and instruments of the new rulers. The hopes that the *Heimatschützer* placed in the new government corresponded to their declining importance during the Weimar Republic.[5]

In addition, organizational competition to the *Deutscher Bund Heimatschutz* arose with the Nazi dictatorship. The *Reichsbund Volkstum und Heimat*, founded in July 1933 and headed by the twenty-four-year-old Werner Haverbeck, claimed the monopoly in the area of what was called "Volkstumsarbeit" (work having to do with the German national character). That same month, Rudolf Heß, in an official party announcement, confirmed to the *Reichsbund* that it was the only organization in this area authorized by the party. The Kassel Conference was already organized within the framework of the first Reich meeting of the *Reichsbund*. At this meeting, the older *Deutscher Bund Heimatschutz* and its fourteen regional organizations laid the groundwork for a merger with the *Reichsbund*, which was accomplished on 5 October 1933. The *Reichsbund* incorporated conservationists into a Reich Special Office for Conservation (*Reichsfachamt Naturschutz*) and the *Heimatschützer* into a Reich Special Office *Heimatschutz* (*Reichsfachamt Heimatschutz*). The former executive director of the *Deutscher Bund Heimatschutz* and author of books on the built environment, Werner Lindner, became head of the latter.[6]

At the Kassel meeting, the four working groups dealt with "Education for Monument Preservation and *Heimatschutz*," "Construction," "Regional planning, urban building, settlement," and "Monument preservation." In the second working group, Lindner presented a major report titled "Relationships with the economy," while "Architect Seifert, Munich," gave one of the ten short reports in this section. The president of the Association of German Architects, Eugen Hönig, had asked Seifert to give a talk in Kassel on the theme "*Heimatschutz* and free-lance architecture."

In this presentation, Seifert examined the work of the *Heimatschutz* and of its construction consultation offices in relationship to self-employed architects. *Heimatschutz*, he stated, was not in any way driven by "outmoded Romanticism" and "sentimental flower painting," but by the quest for "timeless, magnificently simple basic forms" of architecture. *Heimatschutz* would be a necessary evil as long as architects were motivated by ego-gratification rather than subordination to a higher goal. As soon as there was respect for what had grown and evolved over time and architects were conscious of their responsibility "before history and the *Volk*," one could close all consultation offices of the *Heimatschutz*, he noted provocatively. Seifert later recalled that the meeting had degenerated into "pure whining," but that he, optimist that he was, put forth the demand in the end that all publicly created strips of wasteland along traffic corridors should be reforested with deciduous trees in keeping with the local landscape. This would allow adjoining agricultural steppelands (*Kultursteppe*) to recover. This petition, however, is not found in the official publication of the meeting.[7]

Seifert elaborated his talk at the conference into a one-page memo and sent it, two months after the meeting, to Todt, who—though interested—had not attended; he did not know the man. Seifert's later remarkable rise to prominence on environmental issues under National Socialism began with a simple letter in which he introduced himself to the chief engineer of the autobahn project with proposals for its landscape design. In this unsolicited letter, the Munich architect did not use his contacts to Heß, but the name of a shared acquaintance in administration.

The conference in Kassel had evidently given a boost to Seifert and his cause: in the new Reich, he wrote to a colleague, it would be possible to do more for architects "if we regard ourselves as bearers of culture [*Kulturträger*]—and also act accordingly." It is revealing how the ideological dichotomy between culture and civilization could be minted into the small coinage of a gain in social status for a professional group and potential jobs for Seifert. In a situation of economic crisis, Seifert approached the new regime with a *Heimatschutz* motivation. His note about the "Tasks of the Public Authorities in the Shaping of the Landscape" contained, in a nutshell, the ideological foundations, the patterns of justification, and the key concepts of his later activity.[8]

In the brief memorandum to Todt, Seifert combined ecological with aesthetic arguments; both seem to have been equal driving forces. For example, Seifert believed that a great nonmaterial value—the *Heimat*—was strongly threatened by the economic activities of civilization. The conflict between these two worlds could be seen in agriculture. Prompted by "a science that was materialistic in attitude and by short-sighted self-interests," German farmers had, in one generation, largely moved toward cutting down hedges and field copses. Not only did this constitute a loss of "German cultural landscape," it also impaired the hydrological balance of the soil and thus the climate; the soil was getting depleted, plant growth was declining, birds and small animals were disappearing, and pests were getting out of control. In addition, the landscape was in danger of becoming impoverished in beauty and harmony, a "steppeficiation ["Versteppung"] of the German land and thus the loss of the sustaining, balancing, uplifting power of the *Heimat*." To convince the farmers once more that hedgerows were necessary in the "household of nature," the state had to set a good example and henceforth plant all embankments along traffic corridors. One possibility was to plant native shrubs, "adhering closely to the traditional landscape picture." Or, "in conscious artistic contrast to the landscape picture," one could put in place monumental rows of trees of up to four and eight rows, as in France. The expenses would be minor, relative to the construction costs, "but the benefit for the land and the *Volk* could not even be estimated in numbers."[9]

This suggestion had a twofold thrust. First, Seifert argued within the contexts of ecological effects, which made a connection between economy and the balance of nature plausible. The idea of a nature in which the smallest of interventions could have a pronounced effect formed the backdrop when the cutting of field copses was described as a potential threat to plant growth. Here Seifert was in line with contemporary ecological ideas that stressed interconnections. Second, this argument was linked with a warning against an impending loss of beauty, and in this way Seifert could lay claim to cultural capital. Apart from its perfectly placed function as a conservative code word, aesthetics, the "power of *Heimat*," was thus endowed with a society-stabilizing effect.

Seifert's criticism remained limited to agriculture and excluded both industry and private consumers. Recognized problems should be solved by the state; this fixation was probably the reason why Seifert limited himself to public transportation construction, especially since he was addressing the chief engineer of a roadway project. The contemplative-reactive stance of the early *Heimatschutz* now seemed to have been replaced once and for all with a creative will and ecologically grounded motivation. This attitude was more pragmatic than that of the initial *Heimatschutz*, but it still operated with the concept of beauty. It is also noteworthy that Seifert's proposal addressed various, mutually exclusive design options—the artistic accentuation of traffic corridors with broad tree-lined avenues as well as plantings of native flora. It seems reasonable to see the effect of Schultze-Naumburg's writings in all of this. Seifert was very familiar with them and could assume that Todt was, as well. As we shall see, as the debates over the roads' incorporation into the landscape unfolded, these design ideas were increasingly narrowed down.

Incidentally, Seifert's proposal was not new: as a member of the Bavarian State Association for *Heimatschutz*, he had already placed a similar demand before the *Bund Naturschutz* in May 1932. At that time, too, he had invoked aesthetic reasons and the threat of steppefication. Against the opposition of hydraulic engineers, Seifert had asked Werner Linder from the *Bund Heimatschutz* for help and had not pursued his demand further until the Nazi state offered a potential sphere of activity in the form of the autobahnen.[10]

The chief engineer of the *Reichsautobahnen* was receptive to Seifert's letter. Todt responded on 23 November 1933: "The question regarding the landscape design of the autobahnen is one of the most important." He asked Seifert to inspect the segment of the superhighway from Munich to Holzkirchen in the Hofoldinger Forest, which had already been cleared of trees over a stretch of twenty kilometers. If Seifert's memoirs can be believed, Todt came to see him shortly thereafter at home, "on a Saturday at noon," ten minutes after a phone call. The two men agreed in their dislike of side ditches along the autobahnen, of the sort that were customary until then along roads. They were to be replaced by flat embankments. Without addressing Seifert's ecological justification or detailed suggestions, Todt encouraged him to draft an expert memorandum.[11]

And in fact, a week later, following an inspection on foot, Seifert composed a "Proposal for the landscape incorporation of the section from kilometer 8 to kilometer 24 of the highway Munich-border," his first commissioned work for Todt. A little more than a week later, the *Reichsbund Volkstum und Heimat* applauded Todt for asking Seifert to do this work and described him as one "of the best and most circumspect collaborators on *Heimatschutz.*" Seifert, it went on, knew "how to effectively represent the interests of care for the *Heimat* [*Heimatpflege*] while remaining receptive to the technical necessities of this large-scale planning." Seifert would undoubtedly be able to name additional consultants of this kind. Todt immediately asked the leadership of the *Reichsbund* to pass these names on to him. However, his invitation contained an important caveat:

> I ask you, however, to make sure that no narrow-minded landscape dreamers are named. These autobahnen have to fulfill very specific purposes in terms of transportation policy, which require that certain conditions with regard to the alignment and the design are met. The gentlemen in question must be able to give sufficient weight to these technical problems to be appointed collaborators, so that our autobahnen will be given a landscape character that is in accordance with the German essence.[12]

By couching the task ahead in these terms, Todt strengthened the role of technology from the outset and anticipated later fault lines of conflict. In a posthumous tribute, Todt was quoted as saying that the conservation movement alone was too negative; on the other hand, the striving for "landscape-bound work" was by no means "stagecoach romanticism," for a healthy landscape influenced a healthy *Volk.*[13]

The personal conflict between technicians and landscape designers had its counterpart in the substantive conflict between "narrow-minded landscape dreamers" and technical issues regarding the alignment, issues that were evidently not negotiable. By referring to transportation policy, Inspector-General Todt placed this clash within the framework of the ruling ideology. With their written praise for Todt, Lindner and Haverbeck from the *Reichsbund Volkstum und Heimat* had anticipated Todt's decision about appointing a landscape consultant—whether intentionally, in order to strengthen Seifert's position, or unknowingly, is not clear. It is also impossible to determine whether Seifert was Todt's only candidate as landscape consultant: a limited selection process on the part of Todt in January 1934 mentioned by Seifert in his autobiography cannot be confirmed on the basis of the existing documents, yet is likely to have taken place. We do know, however, that Seifert, following a talk about landscape integration to the executive boards of thirteen regional planning offices on 18 January 1934, was offered informal employment in Todt's organization. Todt wrote that henceforth he would consult Seifert "as an advisor on the question of the landscape design of the *Reichsautobahnen* and of the general road network." Seifert was hired, not as a regular employee, but as an expert on a honorarium basis.[14]

In his response, the forty-three-year-old Seifert wrote, with an exaggeration he would repeat on other occasions, that he was very excited about the possibility "of placing the fruits of all my life's work up to this point in the service of the German *Heimat*." Two months later, Seifert solicited assurances about this position with Todt by informing him of an offer to design gardens for all future settlements of the German Labor Front. He therefore needed to know how involved he would be in Todt's roads: "Doing the gardens is simpler and more convenient, but others can do that just as well. I would prefer the work on the roads, which I also consider more important over the long term."[15] He stayed involved with the roads.

In summary, I should emphasize the role of the established *Heimatschutz* as a place of contact between Todt's agency and underemployed garden architects like Seifert. The appreciation of landscape-sensitive construction that was contained within the notion of German Technology corresponded with a general and vague readiness on the part of Todt to involve consultants with *Heimatschutz* experience in the planning for the autobahnen, provided they affirmed the primacy of technology. In the process, the second generation of the *Heimatschutz* in the 1930s was in part ideologically compatible with German Technology and thus ensured that the basic orientation would be a conservative construction policy. For ambitious men like Seifert, the institution of the *Heimatschutz* was a forum in which to raise professional demands and a vehicle to improve their own economic lot.

Finding a niche for landscape architects

Seifert's first contact to Todt and thus the link of the *Heimatschutz* to the road building administration was loose and noncommittal. However, the way in which landscape architects and civil engineers collaborated was of fundamental importance to the success or failure of the landscape-friendly roads so often and noisily invoked at the time. It is therefore worthwhile to look at the landscape advocates as a group. Special focus will rest on the structural conditions of their work, the beginning institutionalization, and the differentiation into regional subunits in charge of the construction of the *Reichsautobahn*. The backdrop to these observations is the deeper understanding of how power functioned in the Nazi regime.

For more than two decades now, a growing number of historians have discovered that centralized power did not exist in Hitler Germany to the degree that a simplistic view of totalitarianism would suggest. Rather, the dictatorship's power to act was divided up among numerous power centers that were often at odds.[16] One of these power conglomerates was Todt's constantly growing sphere of influence. But considerable power gradients and imbalances can be detected also within the internal structure of Nazi road building. This situation shaped the work of the landscape consultants. On the most basic level it should be noted that Inspector-General Todt integrated landscape consultation into the organizational scheme of the regional planning offices that were set up by June of 1934: every regional planning office was supposed to have an expert consultant assigned to it. Selecting these consultants was one of the first and most important tasks that fell to Seifert, whose work for Todt was characterized "by personal contacts," that is, by his nonbinding activity as an advisor.[17] Seifert was to have full discretion in picking the various consultants. He passed on his suggestions to the office of the Inspector-General in Berlin, from where the individual consultants then received their official letter of confirmation. Interested garden architects therefore applied directly to Seifert, or he contacted them by mail. It would appear that the Munich architect was answerable only to himself in making his selections. Even the Berlin garden architect Hermann Mattern, who was at times skeptical toward Seifert's design ideas, later recalled that Seifert had brought him "to the autobahn as a consultant" in 1936—not some construction office and not Inspector-General Todt.[18]

Seifert produced expert opinions for the section from Munich to the border with Austria and later collaborated on the planning and construction of the German Alpine Road, a tourist route along the northern edge of the Alps in Bavaria, from Lindau to Berchtesgaden. At the same time he functioned as the spokesman for the landscape advocates (*Landschaftsanwälte*), as the consultants on landscape issues were called from the beginning of 1934. Seifert laid claim to being the creator of this descriptive title. The idea came to him, we are told, during an undated lecture before the *Deutscher Werkbund* chapter in Königsberg. The suggestive use of the legal term *Anwalt* (attorney) was meant to exemplify that the consultants acted as representatives of the landscape and its interests vis-à-vis the road builders.[19] One of Todt's engineers justified the title in retrospect this way: "The name is apt: a spokesman for mute but life-filled nature before the felling of especially stately trees or before decisions on radical change and replanting that were not considered symbiotically."[20]

Landscape advocate was thus the description of an activity as well as a status description with the regional planning offices. The landscape advocates were supposed to draft expert opinions about the routing of the autobahn and draw up planting plans; they were supposed to join in the debate, persuade others, and represent their cause. If pursued with enough rhetorical skill and persuasiveness, their consulting work could end up with construction engineers adopting the arguments of the landscape advocates as their own. The consultants' options for exerting influence were limited from the very outset to their purely consultative function. Their potential power to push through their position emerged on two levels: first, on the level of the regional planning offices, where they had to hold their own in the daily clash of arguments; second, with Todt himself, who, advised by Seifert, could take on concerns about landscape protection and passed relevant directives about the route and design of the *Reichsautobahnen*, directives that were binding for the engineers on the ground. The status of the landscape advocates was by no means secure, but rather the result of constant negotiations. The development of an intense group feeling among the landscape advocates was probably also a reaction to these structural uncertainties.

The first question, however, is what sort of individuals became members of this group and what kind of influence Seifert, the Inspector-General's agency, and the NSDAP had. Decisions about the selection of the consultants were made within these three power centers. Seifert's autobiographical account of a selection process in which he first placed "fine men of reputation and renown" with the autobahn and later removed the Nazi party's favorite candidates from their posts is not tenable given the archival material in Seifert's own papers; instead, we are dealing with an example of self-generated mythologizing during the process of autobiographical reconstruction. The fact is that the building of "Adolf Hitler's Roads" involved from the beginning landscape advocates whom Seifert regarded as unqualified candidates of the NSDAP. Moreover, he suffered a few defeats with the very first selection.

A closer look at this personnel policy is worthwhile for two other reasons. First, it shows how far the influence of the Nazi regime extended and how broad Seifert's decision-making freedom really was; second, the makeup of the group of landscape advocates predetermined their concrete work to a considerable degree. One thing that was beyond dispute is that the group was entirely male, which was clearly seen by all involved as perfectly self-evident.[21]

In his search for "fine men," Seifert initially fell back on colleagues whom he had come to know either in an association of garden architects or as practicing biodynamic gardeners. His knew his three closest collaborators from the Association of German Garden Architects (*Verband Deutscher Gartenarchitekten*), where Seifert had been a member since 1929. In 1934, Seifert explicitly vouched for the garden architects Carl Siegloch (consultant to the regional planning office Stuttgart), Wilhelm Hirsch (regional planning office Frankfurt), and Max K. Schwarz (regional planning office Altona near Hamburg) to the directorate of the *Reichsautobahnen*. Hirsch was the managing director of the association; Schwarz was the head of the "Horticulture and Settlement School" in the artist colony of Worpswede near Bremen, a training institute for biodynamic agriculture. When the association was "coordinated" and membership in the Reich Chamber of Visual Art was made a prerequisite for garden architects to practice their profession, Seifert protected longtime colleagues and thereby exerted considerable influence on this process of negative professionalization. Siegloch and Schwarz were members of the Anthroposophical Society. The landscape advocates Werner Bauch (regional planning office Dresden and Nuremberg) and Camillo Schneider (regional planning office Hannover) were also organized Anthroposophists. Of the total of twenty-two landscape consultants, just under one-fifth were thus members of the Anthroposophical Society, and according to an unverifiable statement by Seifert's wife Maria during her husband's de-Nazification process, "even more ... were adherents of biodynamic agriculture."[22]

The landscape advocates Guido Erxleben (regional planning office Essen) and Wilhelm Hübotter (regional planning office Hannover) were members of the Association of German Garden Designers (*Verband Deutscher Gartengestalter*), another garden design club. Camillo Schneider was coeditor of the eminent horticultural journal *Die Gartenschönheit* ("The Beauty of Gardens") and had known Seifert since 1928. The close circle around Seifert, his "old friends," thus accounted for at least six of the twenty-two landscape advocates in 1935. If we count Seifert himself and the Munich garden architect Ludwig Schnizlein chosen by him, eight positions were held by members of his circle of friends. These men worked primarily on the autobahnen in southern, northern, and western Germany, while other landscape advocates not selected by Seifert tended to be active in central and eastern Germany. Moreover, the Seifert candidates worked on those autobahn segments that were opened first (with the exception of the route Königsberg-Elbing).[23]

Seifert's personal circle was evidently not large enough, however, to make a sufficient number of appointments. Apparently as a result of the competition over the post of the top landscape advisor, the Inspector-General's office had already installed two landscape advocates—the garden architects Gustav Allinger (regional planning office Stettin) and Hinrich Meyer-Jungclaussen (regional planning office Halle). Seifert coopted his two colleagues by asking them for the names of other qualified garden architects. "I think I am fairly familiar with [garden designers] who are artistically suitable," he wrote to Allinger. Seifert had thus absorbed the competitors who had lost out to him into his group while at the same time expanding his regionally limited knowledge about others in the profession: "I don't know ... the people up there [in northern Germany]," he had lamented to his friend Schwarz. Allinger and Meyer-Jungclaussen responded to his request, as did the Reich Association of German Horticulture (*Reichsverband des Deutschen Gartenbaus*). Allinger's list included Hirsch and Siegloch, two names from Seifert's circle of friends. Two other candidates, who were evidently being promoted by the NSDAP, were Oswald Langerhans and Reinhold Hoemann, who eventually became landscape advocates with the regional planning office Hannover and the regional planning office Cologne.[24]

Unless candidates had powerful backers, Seifert based his decisions on the professional reputation of the applicants. Six landscape advocates were appointed as the result of competitions where Seifert and the Inspector-General's office solicited sample expert opinions: Kurt Schütze (regional planning office Breslau), Rudolf Ungewitter (regional planning office Berlin), Hans Kayser (regional planning office Frankfurt/Main), and Rudolf Wilhelm Gräbner and Max Müller (both regional planning office Nuremberg). Meritocratic criteria were thus applied to a limited extent, even if the choice of applicants invited to participate in the competition was based on Seifert's contacts within a small professional community.[25]

In four cases we have documentation of how the NSDAP influenced the filling of individual positions. "We were put under strong political pressure," Seifert wrote in April 1934 to his confidant Erxleben. While he had successfully rebuffed these pressures, he intended to keep the party candidate Reinhold Hoemann (regional planning office Cologne), whose work was useful. Erxleben now had to share his area with Hoemann. The latter even found his way into Seifert's circle of friends, and in 1937 he was among those landscape advocates who were informed "in strictest confidence" about Seifert's quarrels with Todt.[26]

The attempt to influence the appointment to the post of landscape advocate to the regional planning office in Königsberg in East Prussia produced exactly the opposite result. When Seifert asked the head of the regional planning office to advertise a competition among East Prussian garden designers, he was told curtly that the agency had already signed a contract with an architect by the name of Hans Gerlach, who had commenced working. Seifert's position was evidently not powerful enough to allow him to alter a decision by one of the heads of a regional planning office. He therefore shifted to professional criticism. Almost a year later, Seifert informed the directorate of the *Reichsautobahnen* that the planting plans provided by Gerlach were "unusable." He pushed for Gerlach's dismissal, but he did not get his wish until 1938. Gerlach's successor was, untypically, not a freelance garden architect, but the director of the Gardener's Teaching Institute in Tapiau, Bruno Hildebrand. The landscape consultation for this segment completely escaped Seifert's influence during its planning and construction.[27]

When Seifert picked a landscape advocate for the regional planning office Dresden he encountered not a curt dismissal by a regional planning office as in the case of Königsberg, but interference by the NSDAP. Allinger and the Reich Association of Horticulture had recommended the garden architect Wilhelm Röhnick for the post. During the appointment process, the regional office (*Gauleitung*) of the NSDAP contacted Seifert directly. Röhnick, he was told, had not been admitted into the party because of a previous membership in a lodge, and he was also described as politically unreliable by "our officials." The letter continued, in an awkward formulation: "We want to prevent at all costs that, as in earlier times, the gentlemen of the reaction and the lodge no longer step into prime positions in their professions." The party had two counterproposals for the post. Seifert sought backing from Todt, but the latter was not willing to stick out his neck for a Freemason, because "landscape design, especially, is something that provokes a lot of criticism." Seifert took Todt's advice and asked Röhnick to respond to the charges. A competition among five Dresden garden designers was unsatisfactory; three of the four proposals had been "quite unusable." When Röhnick admitted to his lodge membership, his references to Nazi-compatible fellow Masons like the fathers of Leo Schlageter, an early Nazi who was executed by the French for resistance during the Ruhr occupation in 1923, and of Horst Wessel, the alleged author of the eponymous Nazi song, and to his professional qualifications were of little avail. Werner Bauch, who was selected by Seifert for Dresden evidently as a result of the competition and who had no party backing, and Max Lange, one of the NSDAP's candidates, became landscape advocates for the regional planning office Dresden, even though Seifert asserted that the latter lacked "artistic talent." This compromise reflects the extent of the direct influence exerted by the National Socialists. What Seifert construed as professionalism was subject to competing views by local chief administrators and the NSDAP; against his wishes, Seifert did not attain complete authority over the selection of the landscape consultants to the *Reichsautobahn*. The intransigence of one head of a regional planning office was enough to reveal the limits of his authority. In response, Seifert took pains to establish professionalism as a counterargument and strengthen his position by doing so. It is revealing that he tried to make Todt his ally within the complex organization of the Nazi autobahn construction, though the latter did not support his effort to foist a candidate on the regional planning office in Dresden.[28]

Although Seifert, thanks to his key post within the organizational structure dealing with landscape design along the *Reichsautobahn*, was able to install a few colleagues in the new positions, he lacked comprehensive authority on matters of personnel. His attempt to exert influence in the selection of landscape advocates through the office of the Inspector-General failed. Competency, in other words, was newly negotiated from the very beginning. Membership in a Freemason lodge was a cause for exclusion that could not be undone.[29]

This is true even though Seifert did have some success in the case of the Berlin garden architect Hermann Mattern. The influence exerted by the NSDAP and its various organizations was more convoluted and the political pressure more subtle than it had been with Röhnick. The obstacles in the path of Mattern's career were his embrace of Bauhaus modernity and the "cosmopolitanism" of the so-called "Bornim Circle," to which Mattern had belonged as a garden architect before 1933. The name refers to, first, the garden design office and nursery of Karl Foerster in the Potsdam suburb of Bornim, and, second, the circle of architects and artists who gathered there. The company "Foerster & Co." in Bornim had been in business since 1928, and Mattern and Herta Hammerbacher were its associates. After 1945, both held chairs at the Technical University in West Berlin. Like Hammerbacher, Mattern, an enthusiastic *Wandervogel*, was trained as a horticulturalist. He saw his influences in German expressionism and the artist colony Worpswede, and he was a guest student at the Bauhaus in Dessau. After working briefly with Leberecht Migge, Mattern—as Foerster's partner—designed gardens with modernist architects like Hans Poelzig, Hans Scharoun, and Martin Wagner. Regular guests at Foerster's place in Potsdam were the artist Käthe Kollwitz, the pianist and composer Wilhelm Kempff, and the architect Richard Neutra. Mattern's garden concept, which became known under the catchword "world garden," was characterized by a high degree of functionality; the unity of house, garden, and landscape; and artistic expressiveness. He used existing landscape features undogmatically and planted "native" (*bodenständige*) plants as well as those not originally native to a given piece of soil. As late as 1939 he implemented these ideas about landscape gardens at the Reich Garden Show in Stuttgart.[30]

Mattern's employment in the construction of the *Reichsautobahnen* was evidently as much in his interest as in Seifert's. Following a meeting, Mattern reassured Seifert: "I would like to emphasize that I bring the necessary respect to working on such things already ideologically (as a *Wandervogel*)." The decision whether or not he was qualified was something he left to Seifert. The latter quickly agreed to let him work in the region of this first choice, around Kassel, where he had grown up. As soon as the sections were ready for construction, Seifert declared, he would begin with his work. But the problems had only just begun. "By accident," Seifert wrote to Mattern suggestively after two months, "your appointment as landscape advocate to the regional planning office Kassel, requested by me on 21 June 34, was not passed on by the Inspector-General." The situation was difficult, he continued, because the NSDAP's *Gau* administration of Kurhessen had "very emphatically" proposed an architect by name of Fritz Stück. At this juncture, Seifert arranged a competition between Mattern, Stück, and a third candidate, Schimmelpfennig, who had been involved in the Hafraba planning for the landscaping of the superhighways.[31] Seifert was clearly aware that meritocratic criteria alone were not sufficient to have a candidate appointed. After examining the submitted samples, Seifert concluded that Stück's and Mattern's work "was virtually equal in quality." In the meantime, he had contacted the *Gau* Administration Kassel again and had been told that it was very committed to providing Stück a livelihood. Given this clear signal, Seifert proposed a compromise: Stück would become landscape advocate in Kassel, and Mattern in Berlin. This was done.[32]

In accounts after the war, which should be seen as tactically motivated, Seifert and Mattern embellished their roles. Mattern, in his whitewash statement at Seifert's de-Nazification procedure, maintained that Seifert had repeatedly defended him against political attacks, "all the way up to Dr. Todt." Seifert himself later summarized his personnel policy in the Mattern case as follows: "It was enough for Todt that I personally vouched for him [Mattern]." Mattern did in fact work for the most part unimpeded as landscape advocate for the regional planning office Berlin, but that by no means implied that his position was secure. He tells us that "as a pacifist and socialist," he was officially under political surveillance until the fall of 1933. Following that surveillance, various party offices offered different assessments of the man. In 1936, the NSDAP Gau Administration Potsdam described him as an "idealist in the area of aesthetics" in a declaration for the General Building Inspector for Berlin, Albert Speer, whose residential garden Mattern designed. There was "hardly any doubt that he feels and affirms the greatness, power, and strength of the Third Reich, for the simple reason alone that this Reich is about to realize his aesthetic ideals."[33]

Through Seifert, Mattern was given commissions from one of the power centers of the Third Reich, the road building sector under Todt. His jobs from the German Labor Front became uncertain after a gardener informed against him. An internal letter declared that since the Foerster business in Bornim had been "organized in a purely Communist fashion" and Mattern had belonged to the German

Communist Party at "least in spirit," he was not to receive any further commissions. In a letter to Speer, Mattern asserted that he had enjoyed working with the German Labor Front, however: "It is not in my nature to pretend some kind of devotion and to allow myself to be dragged along." Although it was internally said that Speer was assuming responsibility for assignments to Mattern, in December 1937, German Labor Front State Secretary Julius Schulte-Frohlinde informed the garden architect that he would not receive any further commissions. Later, however, Speer supported Mattern through the Organization Todt.[34]

Mattern's precarious position did not escape the notice of Heinrich Wiepking-Jürgensmann, the only holder of a chair in landscape architecture in Germany. Next to Seifert, Wiepking was the most prominent landscape architect in Nazi Germany; he designed the greenspace for the Olympic stadium in Berlin and was in charge of the landscape plans in the "General Plan East," which covered large parts of eastern Europe. He and Seifert competed for leadership in the area of landscape architecture under National Socialism. These politically relevant animosities between the two men reached far back: in 1931, Seifert had blocked Wiepking's admission into the Association of German Garden Architects. Wiepking was shut out of the National Socialist autobahnen as the office of the Inspector-General rejected his application with flimsy arguments. It is likely that Seifert wanted to exclude his rival from the outset. Subsequently there emerged two circles of landscape architects that competed against each other for state commissions in the Third Reich: Seifert's group at the autobahnen and Wiepking's alliances with the architects who were working on the plans to transform Berlin for the Olympic Games in 1936, and with the SS for its plans of conquest in eastern Europe after 1940.[35]

Wiepking sought to turn Mattern's past, which was open to a wide range of interpretations, into political capital, publicly criticizing the fact that the modernist architect Hans Scharoun had designed Mattern's house. In the course of this controversy, Wiepking allegedly threatened to smear his name as a "communist and Bolshevist artist." In response, Seifert escalated the clash to the point of a "challenge to a duel that was to be fought out after the war." This masculine ritual was not carried out, however: both Wiepking and Seifert died of natural causes. The office of the Inspector-General, meanwhile, stood by Mattern. An official with the agency warned Seifert in early 1941 that trouble was brewing for Mattern, which allowed the latter, with backing from Todt, to defend his position in a meeting with the NSDAP District Leader in Potsdam. Seifert applauded: "I am delighted that you cleared up the matter so quickly with the district leader. It is indeed best to seize the bull by the horns right away."[36]

To stick with the metaphor: this time, Seifert and Mattern had defeated the bull. Seifert's advocacy for a Berlin colleague who was tainted by a whiff of Communism, and Mattern's self-confidence and considerable skill in dealing with those in power evidently worked hand in hand to achieve this victory. The polycratic structure of Nazi rule thus offered, at the margins of its largest propaganda project, a niche for an architect who was politically suspect, and who in turn traced out the whole range of a contradictory life between his supposed closeness to Communism and his design for Albert Speer's residential garden. It is noteworthy that Mattern sought and found an ideological bond with Seifert through his *Wandervogel* association, a bond that bridged political differences. It should also be noted that even Todt, as late as 1941, rebuffed objections from party offices when the status of this particular landscape architect was at risk. Coalitions of interest could thus override the potential for ideological conflict. Seven years after the beginning of construction on the *Reichsautobahnen*, Mattern was able to establish himself as an expert who stood above politics, and as such he could be protected within the Nazi system of rule even by the "old fighter" Todt. As we shall see later, Mattern was not among those landscape architects who drew criticism from the Inspector-General for their "community garden (*kleingärtnerisch*)" work. Instead, he was able to adjust to the new standards of landscape architecture and pulled off the process of self-discipline and simultaneous rise in status that I will discuss further on. This relative success, however, cannot be separated from the defeats suffered by a personnel policy that pretended to be meritocratic.

One of those defeats was undoubtedly the appointment of the landscape architect Stück, whom the NSDAP successfully hoisted into Mattern's post in Kassel. Seifert described him as an "utterly incompetent man ... who has cost us a lot of money, trouble, and almost lawsuits." Stück was eventually let go. Seifert played a crucial role in his firing, and Stück's peculiar behavior helped. The office of the Inspector-General informed Stück as early as September 1935 that he might lose his job. What was lacking, the office charged, was a trusting collaboration between him and the regional planning office in Kassel. Todt himself, "on the basis of a presentation from an older party comrade in Nuremberg," had Seifert spend a day with Stück so he could evaluate his work.[37]

The NSDAP Office for Technology, which had helped to elevate Stück into his position, reported to Seifert about difficulties he was having with the regional planning office. Stück was evidently being prevented from visiting the autobahn line; this changed only after Berlin intervened. The general inspection noted that the officials in Kassel were generally not convinced of the need for landscape consultation and were put off by Stück's difficult personality; the man often made "the gentlemen of the regional planning office, who were strongly focused on the here-and-now, lose their composure." His suggestions were largely ignored.[38] A sharp letter from the *Gau* office for technology six months later went so far as to assert that the regional planning office was systematically working against the landscape advocate and against Todt in his capacity as Inspector-General. One planner had allegedly mocked Todt as "lawn commissioner." The outraged head of the *Gau* office reported to the Inspector-General that the officials in Kassel believed that the landscape advocate existed merely "to put a bandage on the wounds that the autobahn was inflicting on the landscape, whereas according to your own words, the position is significantly broader."[39] The Office for Technology, which was subordinated to Todt within the party hierarchy, thus sought to forge an alliance with him to support one of the party's candidates and oppose the civil engineers of the Kassel planning office. In the case of Stück, Todt proved himself a defender of the party's interests, especially since Stück could be presented as someone who was fighting against the intransigence of the local civil engineers, and therefore as a representative of the building style preferred by Todt. This interweaving of factual arguments with those invoking the interests of the party proved convincing with the top Nazi engineer.

In the meantime, the tensions between Stück and the construction officials continued to grow. Todt intervened in the matter in person and gave Stück two months' reprieve in the summer of 1936, even though the regional planning office was ready to dismiss him; on 1 January 1937, the office finally fired its landscape advocate. Stück blamed this on an act of revenge and a "despicable smear campaign" by his designated successor, Schimmelpfennig, who had informed against him. He asked Todt for a meeting face-to-face and sent him a bombastic poem—dedicated to Todt "in sincere appreciation"—full of self-pity and entitled "To myself" (*Mir selbst*). Together with the NSDAP, Todt continued to advocate for the fired landscape advocate. Eventually, Stück, who described himself as an architect and cultural historian, was allowed to devote his energy to a well-paid "Study on the best possible way to take into account old Germanic cult sites along the line of the *Reichsautobahn* Kassel-Siegen-Cologne"—a sinecure, without a doubt. The section was not completed by 1945.[40]

This incident had more than anecdotal character. It shows how, in addition to a successful self-presentation as an expert willing to collaborate (as in the case of Mattern), a landscape advocate's party membership could—in Stück's case—mobilize considerable activities on his behalf, all the way up the ladder to Todt himself. Evidently the combination of an allegedly uncooperative local planning office and the interests of a party office in employing a member generated this strong support for him. However, it was not enough to ensure Stück's continued employment. Instead, he ended up writing expert opinions that were irrelevant to the construction process.

The NSDAP thus intervened in the selection process of landscape advocates with varying degrees of vigor. In the case of Hoemann the pressure can be rated as mild, in the case of Gerlach it added to intransigent construction officials, and in the case of Stück it was direct to the point of blunt demands. Mattern, for whom it no longer mattered at all what political role he had actually played before 1933 (reputation was enough), was able to prevail by pushing back. The two last-named cases are so much a mirror image of each other that one can hardly look at them in isolation. However, before moving to a concluding examination, I will shed some light on the end of Gustav Allinger's work as a landscape advocate. Here, ideological views about "correct" planting became the sharp weapons of disagreement.

Allinger's dismissal went back to an initiative by the highest-ranking landscape advocate, Seifert. As we have already seen, Allinger, a garden architect from Berlin, had been put in charge of the segments of the regional planning office

Stettin. According to Mattern, Allinger's appointment was the result of a diktat by the NSDAP, though Seifert attacked him largely with professional arguments. Allinger himself was the cause behind the clash over his person. He was stripped of his office as president of the German Society for Horticulture after he had "removed" the membership files from the society's premises shortly before Christmas 1934 and tried to subordinate the organization to the NSDAP's Office for the Cultivation of Art (*Amt für Kunstpflege*). Seifert was asked to respond to what had transpired and spoke of how Allinger had demanded a special position for himself within the corps of landscape advocates. He accused him of "doing his own thing and pursuing separate goals" and complained that he had not joined the working community of the landscape advocates. "He shows in every individual action and in every opinion that he is neither a National Socialist nor a gardener." Seifert no doubt employed this fusion of professional and party-related elements assuming that they would have their strongest effect this way. Whenever he wanted to disavow a rival in power struggles, Seifert used the same rhetorical strategy as party offices; in this way, the categories of "expert" and "party member" merged into one. It was Seifert's way of trying to secure patronage.[41]

At the same time, Seifert was able, through this controversy, to strengthen his position among the other landscape advocates. After Allinger's lawyer threatened to pursue a lawsuit, one of Seifert's closest collaborators, the Stuttgart garden designer Siegloch, backed him up. He advised Seifert not to take Allinger's threats seriously, "all the more so since you can count on the fact that all of us, many of whom are indebted to you for their current livelihood, are absolutely solidly behind you, possibly with one or two exceptions, and will stand up for you to the last." The economic importance of employment on the *Reichsautobahnen* reduced the risks that landscape architects faced in their precarious status as self-employed professionals, a circumstance reflected in declarations of loyalty of this kind. Seifert thereupon wrote to Allinger to say that he had been completely isolated since the spring. Seifert concluded his letter with threatening words: "If you think that you must cause me new difficulties on account of this, do not be surprised if I have no further desire to continue to hold on to you against those forces who no longer wish to see you as a collaborator on the great work of the Führer."[42]

Seifert transmitted the entire correspondence to Todt's deputy Eduard Schönleben in Berlin and suggested implicitly that Allinger not be considered for any new assignments. The comments that the officials of the Inspector-General made about the quarrel are revealing. While the civil engineer Xaver Dorsch agreed with Seifert, he noted that Allinger's work was no worse than that of Camillo Schneider, one of the landscape advocates in Hannover. Dorsch (1899–1976) had been a member of the NSDAP since the early 1920s and noted with self-confidence: "Mr. Seifert should be *very* careful about making declarations about whether someone is or is not a Nat.[ional]-Soc.[ialist]." The gap that existed between what Seifert and the Berlin officials considered good landscape design is revealed by a comment from the civil engineer Hans Lorenz: "If one applied to all landscape advocates the same strict criterion that Mr. Seifert is applying to

Mr. Allinger, *a large part* of the landscape advocates would have to be recalled. Though not in terms of biology, in terms of *design*, Mr. Allinger does not need to hide from Mr. Seifert." The uniformity of the landscape design which Seifert and the other landscape advocates desired should thus also be seen as a reaction to how controversial this design was among the top engineers in the office of the Inspector-General. The remark that Allinger was neither a National Socialist nor a gardener, intended by Seifert to deliver the final persuasive blow, carried no weight for the simple reason that Seifert himself was not yet a member of the party. In this respect, politics was far more than personnel policy.[43]

Allinger's work had already aroused Todt's displeasure. At the end of 1935, the Inspector-General criticized the landscape advocate for having used three times as many plants along the segment to Stettin as should "really be sufficient." Allinger did so much planting, Todt polemicized, that this road segment could be used as a nursery. Seifert, however, did not criticize how much Allinger had planted, but what he had planted. Allinger, Seifert asserted, had planted Douglas firs and larch trees in the forests of the March of Brandenburg. To Seifert, this was a flagrant violation of the law of nativeness. He accused Allinger of wanting to place "the pseudo-Romanticism of the city park of yesterday over the vital laws [*Lebensgesetze*] of the German landscape." Seifert maintained that his native-oriented proposals were aimed at "restoring primal German landscape in all its diversity," something to which all landscape advocates had pledged themselves, with only one exception—Allinger. The latter did not wish to be tied down to taking his cues "all too strongly" from scientific considerations. The Berlin landscape architect certainly believed that a few exceptions could be made on a case-by-case basis on "practical and aesthetic grounds." Following a meeting in the offices of the Inspector-General, Allinger was eventually urged to reduce the plant volume by 20 percent and to avoid nonnative species. Finally, in 1938 he was dismissed and his position was filled by Hermann Göritz, whom Seifert recommended. After the chief landscape advocate had thus pushed out three party candidates over the years, he tried to solidify the ideological homogeneity of the group by establishing the nativeness of the plantings as the indispensable principle.[44]

Before taking a closer look at the landscape advocates as a group, I will summarize personnel policy, which was guided by Seifert, Todt, and the NSDAP in varying ways. Eight of the initially appointed landscape advocates came from Seifert's circle of close friends. Five others had obtained their appointments without any visible group membership. Of the four candidates who had joined the corps of landscape advocates through pressure by the Nazi party, three were gone again by 1938, at the latest—while one gained entry into Seifert's circle. The rest of the group was composed of former rivals of Seifert's and young compromise candidates. The majority of the landscape advocates in Seifert's closer circle were men in their forties, the two exceptions being Camillo Schneider and Reinhold Hoemann, who were 58 and 64, respectively, when construction began. Seifert's ideal scenario in which every regional planning office would have one consultant could not be realized. Some offices had two consultants assigned to them; in

Berlin there were even three. Conversely, two landscape advocates worked for more than one regional planning office.[45]

The fact that the landscape advocates were overwhelmingly garden architects strengthened their sense of group cohesion; their professional identity was one of the ways they could set themselves apart from other groups while collaborating on the propagandistically supercharged autobahn project. Seifert tried to emphasize the expert status of his fellow landscape advocates in the face of the party's attempt to exert influence on their selection, though in other cases he did not shy away from intermingling professionalism and party patronage. One should also ask whom Seifert did not wish to have in his cadre of consultants. Apart from party candidates he disliked, he expressed his opposition to Leberecht Migge, whom he described pejoratively as "*the* intellectual" among the German garden architects. Migge had made a name for himself in the 1920s with plans for urban gardens for workers, and advocated a functionalist garden concept, which he subordinated to social needs. Seifert wrote to Todt that Migge stood for a "technologization of the garden that was utterly alien to nature." He also noted that he was politically the most left of all garden architects. With his garden concepts he did not fit in with the Seifert group, which had been committed to nativeness by their leader. As we have seen, Seifert's rival Wiepking-Jürgensmann was also excluded from working on the *Reichsautobahnen*. Lastly, it was easy for Seifert to ignore the wishes of the Reich Food Estate, which tried to inject itself into the selection process for landscape advocates. The Reich Food Estate was home to "coordinated" horticultural organizations, and they recommended their members; these candidates, however, did not get anywhere.[46]

The men around Seifert were more than simply, as he wrote in 1934, "guided by the ardent desire ... to leave a more beautiful Germany to our grandchildren." A significant number of them came from the Youth Movement, were part of an economically precarious profession, were—in conjunction with their professional sensitivity to the soil and the land—at least open to biodynamic agriculture (and the closer they were to Seifert, the more open they were), were largely in agreement with National Socialist ideas about reconstruction and beauty, and were guided by a landscape design impulse in accordance with the second generation of *Heimatschutz*. Contrary to the assumption voiced in the scholarship, these were not conservationists or idealists, but professional garden architects who took a positive stance toward the reshaping of landscape out of professional as well as ideological motives, provided it was tied in with their ideas about nativeness and aesthetics. German Technology offered them ideological points of contact, and the *Reichsautobahnen* offered them an opportunity for work. The selection process for the landscape architects reveals, first of all, the high degree of attention that the road building bureaucracy, all the way up to Todt himself, devoted to the individuals who were to work on "Adolf Hitler's Roads" as landscape consultants. The result of the selection can be understood as a twofold process of disciplining: it was important to Todt's agency and to Todt himself that the candidates fit ideologically into Nazi Germany. Contrary to a meritocratic attitude on Todt's part that Franz Seidler assumes, in the present case we can note a policy that was clearly driven by party interests. It was Seifert's function to bind his professional colleagues to himself through their selection and to create a network of loyalties. As we have seen, their status as professional experts was from the outset contested and had to be renegotiated time and again.[47] The polycratic model of Nazi rule is thus very well suited to an analysis of the fractured lines of authority governing the appointment of landscape advocates. This raises the question, then, of how the landscape consultants, once they were appointed, fared within the National Socialist power structure and what results their work had.

Searching for a job description

When the landscape advocates were appointed, their tasks were by no means clearly circumscribed. Although Seifert had pointed the way with his proposals for the planting of the section Munich-Holzkirchen and his notion of nativeness he articulated in them, exactly how much latitude the landscape advocates had with the regional planning offices is something they had to carve out themselves, in a few cases against considerable resistance. A clue about their position comes from their salary, which was long a contentious issue. As the network of the *Reichsautobahnen* grew, so did the number of joint meetings; the landscape advocates saw themselves increasingly as a group and maintained a loose correspondence with regular circulars. Thus, within the large organizational system of the *Reichsautobahn* there developed a subsystem, whose three above-mentioned aspects—salary, position, and group formation—will be examined in greater detail. These processes took place against the background of the breakneck pace and size of the construction project.

The first conflict over the status of the landscape advocates was triggered by the question of compensation. To be sure, Seifert claimed that the work of the landscape architects would help save on construction costs. This was based on the assumption that the routes suggested by the consultants could be built more cheaply than what the engineers had in mind. Yet the plantings and the fees for the consultants were the most visible items when the regional planning offices and the Directorate above them sought to reduce costs. For unlike the office of the Inspector-General for the German Roads, this part of the autobahn bureaucracy was integrated into the administrative network of the German Railroad, with auditors and the audit office as controlling authorities. Since the autobahn project was given top priority, these traditional institutions could no longer question the necessity of the construction itself, hence they shifted their attention to demanding that it be done in a more cost-effective way.[48]

How the landscape consultants would be compensated was initially an open question. Analogous to Seifert's status, they were not to be employed by the regional planning offices, but would receive consulting contracts as garden architects. Not until 1937 were two landscape advocates hired as employees, as an exception. Whether the consultants would submit invoices for the work they did or would receive a flat fee as compensation was decided in 1934. Seifert had initially advocated flat fees, but then requested an hourly fee of eight Reichsmark for the landscape advocates, and ten Reichsmark for himself, because of his "undoubted added value." The first fee rate in May of 1934 was lower, however—seven marks per hour, and high enough to arouse the suspicion of parts of the road building bureaucracy. As early as July 1934, Seifert warned his collaborators that the Directorate *Reichsautobahnen* had the impression that "the landscape advocates are seeing their new task as a good cow for milking."[49]

In the summer of 1934, the Directorate *Reichsautobahnen* temporarily and arbitrarily set a flat fee of four-hundred Reichsmark per month, which corresponded to an assumed workload of eight days. However, the administration gave this arrangement up again and on 1 October, it reduced the hourly fee to six marks. Todt showed himself to be sympathetic and noncommittal. In the clash with the Directorate *Reichsautobahnen*, he described the landscape advocates "as truly cheap workers in relation to the rest of the project." The Directorate saw the matter differently. From October 1934 to April 1935—that is, over a period of seven months—it paid out 67,515 Reichsmark to the landscape advocates as honoraria and reimbursements for expenses. In the five months from May to September 1935 it paid nearly the same amount, 65,685 Reichsmark. In the eyes of the Directorate, the landscape advocates "were far from paying sufficient heed to the urgent recommendation that they be moderate in their monetary demands," and it therefore asked Seifert for further suggestions for savings. In view of the first cost accounting, Seifert had already reported that the monthly honorarium for the "hardest working and most valuable" landscape advocates was between 300 and 450 Reichsmark; all the more apparent was the abuse of trust by Stück (Kassel) and Gerlach (Königsberg), who were submitting excessive demands. Nevertheless, costs continued to mount and totaled 53,838 Reichsmark in only three months between January and March 1936.

Out of self-interest, the bureaucracy of the Reich Railroad pursued the goal of keeping the expenses for road construction that had been foisted upon it as low as possible. From its perspective, the expense items for the landscape architects were not intrinsically necessary, and it therefore saw them as a runaway trend in expenses that had to be stopped.[50] To that end, Director Karl Rudolphi from the Association *Reichsautobahnen* called a meeting for 29 May 1936—without Seifert, but including one deputy from the Reich Audit Office and two representatives from the Inspector-General. The assembled officials identified three possible paths to rein in costs: first, a return to flat fees, though in individual cases these were unfair; second, lowering the hourly rates, though this would hit those consultants hard who were already working cost-efficiently; and third, "continuing the substantive development of the landscape tasks." What that meant was to train civil engineers more thoroughly in the goal of landscape integration, which would thus make the landscape advocates and their expenses unnecessary in many cases: "Thus the improved performance by the engineer can reduce the costs of landscape consultation and limit it to those cases in which the engineer's training is not adequate." At the same time, the civil engineers had to realize that the "landscape concerns" were a demand not only of the Inspector-General, but also of the Directorate. One convoluted statement reveals how little regard the civil service engineers had for the guidelines for landscape integration issued by Todt's agency: "Some of the negligence still palpable today comes from the opinion that the non-observance of the suggestions from the Inspector-General did not matter in the evaluation of personnel by one's own superior office."[51]

The career civil servants of the Reich Railroad thus realized that in the intertwined dual construction of the *Reichsautobahnen*, the Inspector-General for the German Roads, who was in charge of the design, had only very indirect possibilities of sanctioning the regional planning offices within the Directorate *Reichsautobahnen*, the Reich Railroad institution in charge of the actual construction. To that extent, the directives from the Inspector-General on landscape integration and the suggestions by the landscape advocates were not central for the work of the regional planning offices. Even more, the fact that the local civil engineers came from the Reich Railroad organization created no incentives of any kind to incorporate such considerations into their work. What mattered most to their careers was the evaluation by their Reich Railroad superiors, to whom Todt's ideas, however, tended to be rather alien.

Following the meeting, the Directorate *Reichsautobahnen* resorted to a draconian punishment. It unilaterally cancelled the compensation contract for the landscape advocates as of 1 July 1936 and reduced the hourly rate to four Reichsmark. In addition, it asked the regional planning offices for suggestions for savings and pointed out that the garden designers would remain merely consultants, and that the construction offices would make the final decision in every case on substantive questions. The agency of the Inspector-General had not approved this cut in compensation at the meeting, but it did not object now, since it was meant to be only temporary. The Inspector-General's office noted that the cut should be seen "for the time being in the legal sense" as a termination.[52]

This was tantamount to a radical curtailment in the authority of the landscape advocates. Seifert was by no means willing to accept the cut and suggested to deputy Schönleben from the Inspector-General's office that the work of the landscape advocates be divided into three areas: general consultations, production of planting plans, and the technical implementation of the planting. This would allow him to stop the abuse of the relationship of trust that "incompetent and materialistic garden designers" had been guilty of. In his communications with the Directorate *Reichsautobahnen*, Seifert argued very formally with the fee regulations of the Reich Chamber of the Fine Arts, which did not permit such a low honorarium.

In the middle of July, the Directorate presented a proposal that dispensed with any hourly compensation and called for separate expense agreements for each individual task. Speaking to one landscape advocate, Seifert saw this—no doubt correctly—as an attempt to eliminate the consultants altogether. He was afraid that individual assignments at the discretion of the regional planning offices would have subjected them to the whims of the construction officials. That was also the thrust of an attempt by the regional planning office Halle to have planting plans prepared by technicians in its employ, as a way of demonstrating that the landscape advocates were superfluous. It is very clear that the Directorate *Reichsautobahnen* preferred to consult the landscape advocates on a case-by-case basis, if at all, instead of integrating them into the administrative structure of the project.[53]

Seifert now tried to secure the status of the landscape advocates by going through Todt. In a letter to the Inspector-General, he vowed that he would never accept such a proposal and threatened that especially the most capable garden designers would turn to more lucrative jobs under such regulation. Just how much the positions had hardened is revealed by his remark that any solution agreeable to the Association *Reichsautobahnen* had to be wrong, because it sprang from the "spirit of yesterday."[54] The Directorate *Reichsautobahnen* and the landscape advocates were thus locked in a state of mutual rejection, which Seifert could only overcome by going to Todt.

During a "thorough" talk on 31 July 1936, the Inspector-General's office and Seifert managed to have hourly fees restored, though only at the rate of five Reichsmark. Newly appointed garden designers would receive merely four Reichsmark per hour for the first year of their work, 3.5 Reichsmark if they were younger than thirty. These rates remained in place until the end of the construction of the *Reichsautobahnen*; in 1942, a request for raises by Seifert was turned down as "not war-essential."[55]

The issue of compensation for the landscape advocates provides a clear view of the institutional barriers to landscape design that were built into the system of road construction. The directorate of the Association *Reichsautobahnen*, a subordinate agency of the Reich Railroad, became the focal point for the collective dislike that the regional planning offices felt toward the consultants, their proposals, and the costs of their work. The trickery and threats of the autobahn administration, as well as the sudden cancellation of the contracts, reflected the degree of discontent that found its bureaucratic expression in these actions. The landscape advocates, for their part, supported their position solely with the goodwill of Todt and his agency, which vacillated in its intensity. In contrast to the influence Todt exerted—in favor of the landscape advocates—in some cases when it came to the selection of personnel, he devoted relatively little energy to the question of their pay. This is all the more remarkable considering that Todt, through a decree from Hitler in January 1935, had acquired substantial influence over the Reich Railroad agency, without stripping Dorpmüller formally of his power. When it came to the compensation for the landscape consultants, he decided to spend little political capital. In the process, the Directorate *Reichsautobahnen* eventually brought matters to a head in 1936 when it simply cancelled the contracts with the landscape advocates.[56]

The result of this almost antagonistic clash of two positions, the five Reichsmark compromise, meant a deterioration in the economic situation of the landscape advocates. Consequently, work on the *Reichsautobahnen* provided the landscape advocates with a livelihood that was only temporary and always dependent on the relationship to the regional planning offices. Even if the landscape advocates enjoyed the propagandistic support of the Third Reich, its treasury was reluctant to spend much on them. The explanation for this lies, first, in the interwoven organization charged with building the highways, in which the substantive demands for the incorporation of the landscape put forth by one institution (Inspector-General's Office) had a very difficult time penetrating into the other institution (the regional planning offices in the Directorate *Reichsautobahnen*). Second, the established Reich Railroad bureaucracy conveyed clear incentives to the construction offices to carry out the building project more cheaply. The latter could satisfy these appeals to greater thriftiness by, among other things, dispensing with the landscaping work that could potentially be declared superfluous. Finally, these structural problems coincided with personal factors, which I will examine in the following section.

Pitting landscape architects against civil engineers

The status of the landscape advocates as consultants went hand in hand with the attitudes of the civil engineers, which—depending on the specific construction office—ranged from goodwill and the willingness to let them be, to incomprehension, all the way to intransigent opposition toward the tasks of the landscape advocates. What has come down to us are chiefly numerous complaints from the consultants; in those cases, Seifert, as the highest authority and through his direct access to Todt, was supposed to make things better for the landscape advocates. In the same way in which Todt derived much of his power from his constant access to Hitler, Seifert built his own position on the fact that Todt was usually receptive to what he had to say. Reports to Seifert about obstructions were most frequent when construction began and the potential for conflict between civil engineers and landscape architects was at its greatest.[57]

Characteristic for this phase is the complaint that Camillo Schneider, landscape advocate with the regional planning office Hannover, sent to Seifert in the summer of 1934. The powers of the landscape designers with the regional planning office were unclear, Schneider noted. Todt should settle this matter with Director Rudolphi. "Actually, this should have been done from the very beginning, for in its absence there was surely some arbitrariness in certain respects." The regional planning offices did not know what to do with the landscape advocates. However, as we have seen, the "quick, thorough decision" that Schneider asked for on the payment question did not come.[58]

In addition, the landscape advocates on the ground suffered from the bureaucratic dualism I described above. They had been selected via Seifert by the

Inspector-General for the German Roads, who then asked the Directorate of the Association *Reichsautobahnen* to appoint the individual landscape advocates to the various construction offices. The strained relationship between the two institutions manifested itself in distrust on the part of the Directorate *Reichsautobahnen* toward the landscape advocates. A year after the beginning of construction work, the Directorate instructed the regional planning offices to supervise the consultants stringently to make sure they made full use of their time. In a letter of complaint to Rudolphi, Seifert explained that this regulation had embarrassed some of the civil engineers, since the landscape advocates were not young people who still needed supervision. One landscape advocate thus identified the tensions between the two agencies as the cause for the discord. It was "really quite stupid in this day and age" if Reich Railroad Director Dorpmüller "worked against Todt with all means, and whatever else is happening behind the scenes." In the case of the regional planning office Hannover, its head, in a meeting with the landscape advocate at the end of 1934, bluntly dismissed what he called "gardening work" as "entirely insignificant vis-à-vis the technical construction work." Because of a general cutback in construction funds, savings had to be made especially in the former.[59]

What is remarkable about this quote is not so much the striking devaluation of landscaping work, but that it was set against the construction work. In doing so, the civil engineers laid claim to an inner core of their work that they would not let outsiders like the landscape advocates interfere with. If landscape integration was a new design style, it touched on engineering matters. After all, it was these issues that were supposed to be changed. In the face of all of this, the head engineer in Hannover insisted on his power to decide what was what—German Technology be damned.

Landscape advocate Meyer-Jungclaussen reported on intense clashes with the regional planning office Halle. After complaining about his bad situation to Seifert for two years, he eventually expressed little hope that things would improve—unless Seifert or the Inspector-General came to his aid. From Munich came Seifert's angry response, which is very revealing about the status of the landscape advocates: it remained Inspector-General Todt's position that "every landscape advocate has to create his own position vis-à-vis the regional planning office; under the given circumstances that is certainly the right thing, and most have also succeeded in doing so." That he, Meyer-Jungclaussen, had failed, Seifert reprimanded him, was solely due to his fussiness and arrogance. Moreover, the Directorate *Reichsautobahnen* wanted to use the regional planning office Halle to show how one could get by without landscape advocates.[60]

Seifert put forth similar arguments in a different case: when the Stuttgart landscape advocate Siegloch had his commission revoked, Seifert wrote to him that the mutual stubbornness by the regional planning office and Siegloch himself was the reason why the office had always consulted him only "when absolutely necessary." That is why he was going to appoint a more flexible successor. Siegloch responded by saying that what Seifert considered stubbornness was to him concern for the landscape.[61]

At first, the regional planning offices in Hannover and Altona allowed the landscape advocates to visit the routes only when asked to do so by the construction officials. Following a meeting between Seifert and the Directorate *Reichsautobahnen*, these invitations were no longer necessary and the situation for the landscape advocates in the north was calmer, for a time. Schwarz (regional planning office Altona) believed that in spite of a difficult beginning, he would prevail, and that simply took time. The consultant Schneider noted with a mixture of defiance and resignation: "So far things are going well with the autobahnbahn [*sic*]. One finds a way to prevail. The regional planning offices are becoming increasingly bureaucratic." Schneider did not stop to marvel at the red tape of the Reich Railroad. And even though his ideas met with a good deal of interest, after working nearly two years as a landscape advocate he concluded: "In time you get hardened, you only regret how much energy you have to waste on things that could be so easily done differently, but for the ominous 'auditing office' that everyone is afraid of."[62] He was alluding to the established procedure for auditing accounts within the Reich Railroad.

Schneider left the regional planning office Hannover disgruntled and wrote Seifert a heated letter about his departure: "I know full well the blunders I made, but I don't know if the office of the IG [Inspector-General] clearly sees how our concerns were sabotaged etc. especially in Hannover. And Hannover is not an isolated case, but typical." Thus if the second-oldest landscape consultant is to be believed, the hostile attitude of the construction officials expressed itself in a systematic policy of obstructionism toward the landscape advocates.[63]

The same conclusion was reached by Otto Kurz, landscape advocate for the section Ulm-Augsburg, which was overseen by the regional planning office in Munich. His frustration was so intense that he summarized his four years of experience with the civil engineers in a fifty-eight-page report. Kurz prefaced his demands with some fundamental thoughts about the shaping of the German landscape. *Volkstum* and landscape, he believed, were analogous to blood and soil, the "foundations of the life of our *Volk*." Keeping the landscape "pure and clean" was thus equally as important as a corresponding racial policy. His report culminated in a call to reorganize the way landscape consulting was being done. In the beginning, the uncertain status of the landscape advocates had been quite appropriate, he acknowledged, but today "the much too loose connection that our activity has with the actual construction work, and thus the nonobligatory nature of our consultative position," was no longer useful. Like Schneider, Kurz, too, perceived a system behind the attempt by the civil engineers "to rid themselves of the inconvenient warners sooner or later" with the help of the bureaucratic routine. The engineers, he maintained, accepted those demands that were not too arduous to carry out—like the shaping of the terrain and the removal and storage of the topsoil for later plantings. However, the regional planning office trivialized those tasks that should be done by the landscape advocates—Kurz was thinking of the alignment and the plantings. The landscape advocates thus had nothing to show for their work, and soon after, the bureaucracy would be able to drive them out. "The first consistent case of this kind" had already happened. Kurz was referring to the near-dismissal of landscape advocate Schwarz at the end of 1939, which Todt had reversed through personal intervention.[64]

For Kurz, the result of the attitude of the officials he had described was lazy compromises on a daily basis. Instead of shared work "on a great goal," antagonistic parties had formed. Kurz concluded:

> It was only this emphasis on the nonbinding status of the landscape advocates that gave rise to the demeaning and fruitless horse-trading, which would perforce reduce the landscape advocate to a more or less witty chatterbox, while the decisions about his professional tasks are left to the whims of non-experts.

Kurz suggested establishing—analogous to the organization of the construction offices—vertical structures with gardeners, chief gardeners, and the landscape advocate at the top, and to include the latter in the planning process at an earlier stage. Contrary to the picture of a successful integration into the landscape that was disseminated by propaganda, the work of the landscape advocates was dominated by complaints about their powerlessness, and they saw in this the manifestation of organizational shortcomings. Frustration over the authority of the landscape architects, which was vaguely defined and had to be constantly renegotiated, meant, for one, that the line separating experts and laymen was never precisely drawn. The consultants had little success in asserting their competency in landscape matters against the academically and bureaucratically secured competency of the civil engineers when it came to traffic routes.[65]

Even the fearless Seifert ran into trouble with the regional planning office in Munich, part of whose section he was overseeing. In 1936, Todt's chief consultant wrote to Berlin that an *Oberbaurat* was boycotting everything having to do with landscape integration. "Something has to change," he demanded and showed signs of frustration, though he covered them up with auto-suggestive appeals for a "struggle for a better construction attitude" and loyalty to Todt, lest "those who live in the past" be allowed to triumph. In 1938, Seifert's contact with the regional planning office was limited to the exchange of letters. The joint hikes along the route before the drawing of the blueprints, described as the ideal scenario, thus remained a demand that was usually not met.[66]

Under these circumstances, only those consultants were able to prevail who stood out by virtue of their demeanor, personality, and persistence. However, these factors were limited by the "understanding and goodwill" of the officials. Seifert conceded as much in his autobiography: "Each autobahn section was given its special appearance, which reflected the peculiarities (*Eigenart*) of the respective landscape advocate and those of the office overseeing the construction." The free-floating status of the landscape advocates as mere consultants, which was originally intended to guarantee their independence, thus worked against them if and when the regional planning offices regarded them as a nuisance. Such an attitude on the part of client was new to the landscape advocates;

as garden architects they had received commissions for gardens and parks from interested private and public clients. Now they were confronted by a group of civil engineers who were at best well-meaning, tended to be uninterested, and were at times hostile. Given the pace and scale of autobahn construction in Nazi Germany, the landscape advocates were thus in danger of being marginalized.[67]

It would appear that Todt very much wanted this situation, and it seems plausible to see this policy as a laissez-faire approach grounded in Social Darwinism in which the best would prevail. Such an attitude not only puts a question mark behind the characterization of Todt as a modern manager, it also points to larger power-political contexts in science and technology under the Nazi regime, which Herbert Mehrtens has described as "anarchic technocracy." Todt's response to the quarrels over competency between consultants and engineers was sporadic intervention and a general lack of interest in making structural improvements. Within the organizational duality for the autobahn, the landscape advocates had to earn Todt's support on their own, as it were; their self-mobilization was rewarded. In this regard, Todt appears as a hesitant sponsor of a landscape-oriented construction, someone who preferred personal clientele relationships.[68]

In response to a weak institutional grounding within the road building bureaucracy, the landscape advocates strengthened the cohesion of their group through two instruments: regular meetings and internal communication. From the beginning of their work on the *Reichsautobahnen*, they came together under Seifert's chairmanship for working meetings (which they were paid to attend, incidentally). At these meetings, Seifert explained the latest guidelines on plantings and routing, the consultants reported to each other on their practical experiences, and new autobahn sections were inspected. The first meeting in Munich in June 1934 was followed by at least ten others. With the exception of the crisis year 1937, when Seifert suspended his collaboration with Todt for more than half a year, the landscape advocates met about once a year with a growing number of guests in attendance. The group dynamic within this circle can certainly be seen as clique-formation. Seifert's leadership claim remained uncontested in all of this; his personal contacts to Todt helped the garden designers to obtain commissions for the *Reichsautobahn* and with the Organization Todt. In addition, in 1935 Todt had a working group for landscape design set up within the Research Association for the German Road System, and apart from spokesman Seifert it included Ungewitter, Schwarz, Erxleben, and Hübotter.[69]

Outside of the meetings, communication was continued with circulars beginning in 1939. The loose group centered on Seifert became known as the "Working Circle of Landscape Advocates" and continued in existence in the Federal Republic of Germany after the war. Before 1945, it encompassed up to forty, exclusively male landscape advocates, garden architects, and scattered conservationists. No doubt, this working circle, with its compatible ideology, regular meetings, and many friendly visits between members, had something fraternal about it. Especially against the backdrop of the Nazi dictatorship and the bureaucratic muddle of the autobahn construction, such a group became both a place of refuge and a basis for action. The emerging group dynamic was given a formal foundation with the circulars, which were edited by Seifert's friend and landscape advocate Wilhelm Hirsch. Revealingly enough, the external occasion was the German attack on Poland on 1 September 1939. Exactly one week after the first shots were fired, Seifert informed the landscape advocates: "The proven camaraderie among the landscape advocates shall be cultivated even more during the war." Hirsch would therefore collect and pass on reports from "comrades in the field." The spokesman of the landscape advocates closed the letter with "Until we meet again joyfully following the victorious conclusion of the war!"

It is one of the internal contradictions of this group that Seifert, in spite of such certainty of victory, included a passage from a letter in which the wife of a Belgian garden designer thanked him for the friendly reception at the last garden congress. Hirsch's call to join in, with the wish that "the war will be brought to a good end as soon as possible," was less brisk than Seifert's. The next day, Seifert informed everyone that all the landscape advocates who had not been called up for military service should continue their work on the *Reichsautobahnen* "unchanged."[70] Of the nineteen landscape advocates on the autobahn and other roads, four had been drafted, and they recounted their military experiences. The East Prussian landscape advocate Hildebrand praised the "unique community of like-minded people." On the first Christmas in wartime, and on all subsequent ones, Hirsch included a blue candle—apparently borrowed from the blue flower of Romanticism—in the circular for each landscape advocate so that they could think of each other. "We want to be comrades not only of work, but comrades of life who help each other in times of professional and personal need." Henceforth, the landscape advocates reported to each other the progress of their work and recommended new books.[71]

During the first months of the war, the military element in the speech of those consultants who had already been fighting battles with the civil engineers gained the upper hand. At Christmas 1939, Seifert, who had not been called up, wrote to "My comrades!" in the form of an annual roll call: "A great year is coming to an end, an even greater one begins. Next Christmas will find us once again in the midst of fruitful construction work." The Inspector-General was happy with the work of the landscape advocates and pleased about the tight-knit camaraderie. For the time after the war, Seifert prophesied a "wealth of the most pleasant work"; even then, of course, it went without saying that the most important thing was remaining loyal to Todt. What becomes clear here is the dual loyalty of the landscape architects toward Seifert and Todt, which was based on patronage relationships.[72]

The hectographed circulars, with a few pages of personal information and reports from the Wehrmacht or the Organization Todt, recommendations on fruit cultivation and the home garden, and thoughts about the reorganization of conservation, reflected the interests and ideas of the landscape advocates along with their changing attitudes about war and nature. Prescribed euphoria soon gave way to growing skepticism and a rediscovery of nature as a counterworld to the reality of the war. And there was surely some escapism in the plans for the future, first for the next generation of landscape designers, and second, for the circular, which was supposed to be expanded into a magazine, "as a unifying organ for all forces shaping the earth: roads, water, energy, garden, landscape, land amelioration etc."[73]

Appeals to help bombed-out comrades were found alongside calls for more involvement. While the landscape advocates in Wehrmacht or Organization Todt uniforms repeatedly expressed their joy over the circular and eagerly penned reports, those who remained at home were far less enthusiastic about writing. A total of twenty-nine circulars have survived. Reflecting the availability of paper during the war, the number of editions dropped from eight in 1940 to four three years later. The last circular, dated 11 December 1944, had only three pages and contained, apart from Hirsch's introductory words, a letter from the now seventy-four-year-old landscape advocate Hoemann from the Rhineland. Following a peace for Germany won through military struggle, Hoemann was expecting and hoping for a Spartan isolation, since the "'civilization' of the enemy countries with their luxury and claim to a comfortable life … would kill us more surely than this men-murdering war." At that time the landscape advocates would then have the task "of building up our German landscape as German cultural landscape in a German way, free from all foreign additions." "German to the core" (*kerndeutsch*) was the key idea, "the cultural landscape [shall be] German to the core in all its details, in forest and field, in meadow and garden, in all its bodies of water, in mountain and valley."[74]

*

The selection, compensation, and organizational position of the landscape advocates stand in stark contradiction to the account of harmonious collaboration in the area of landscape design that is found in contemporary propaganda and in some of the scholarly literature. Seifert had to make concessions already on the appointment of landscape architects, forced to yield to the veto of the NSDAP as well as Todt's inconsistent intervention. Furthermore, the result of placing the *Reichsautobahn* project within the established administration of the German Reich Railroad had the result that pre-Nazi priorities like cost-consciousness and efficiency were more important to some civil engineers than new design criteria based on the advice of the landscape advocates. It also meant that within the dualistic structure of the autobahn project, the landscape consultants were dependent on the influence of Todt's agency if they wanted to attain a secure status with the local construction offices. However, Todt, like Seifert, was willing to go to bat only for those consultants who had already proven themselves in daily clashes with the engineers. In summary, one can thus say that the desired status as experts was something that the landscape advocates had to constantly renegotiate; authority was attained through a political coalition whose parameters are best described as a patronage relationship. Finally, it should be emphasized that the existing sources reveal little about the reasons behind the partial opposition of the civil engineers. Seifert, in particular, distorted the relationship between the two groups at times to the point of caricature with a simplistic friend-foe thinking, depicting the engineers as stubbornly attached to the old ways. However, the examination so far has revealed the structural absence of incentives for the engineers assigned to the project by the Reich Railroad to incorporate the suggestions of the landscape advocates consistently into their planning. The lack of civic freedoms under the dictatorship meant that the conflicts were always very much constrained in the breadth of the discussion and the depth of the arguments: for example, there is no evidence of openly expressed doubts about whether "Adolf Hitler's Roads" made sense in the first place, given the low level of motorization in society. The debate, which took place within narrow parameters, was limited largely to the nonpublic arena and was chiefly carried on by experts.[75] In this process, conservation and regional planning were systematically pushed aside.

Marginalizing conservation and spatial planning on the Autobahn

When Alwin Seifert, who had assumed his consulting work for Todt in Berlin, returned to Munich, he was confronted by bitter complaints from the conservationists among his friends. As he later recounted in his autobiography, they charged that "these technicians had already despoiled so much lovely landscape, and I was now helping them to destroy more on a very large scale." Seifert answered them with the image of a train in motion: one could just let it pass by, or one could jump on and find the brake. With his response to their fundamental criticism he showed that he did not reject modernity and technology outright, but sought to shape it according to ideological and professional preferences.[76]

One of the biggest priorities for conservationists, beginning in the 1920s, had been a nature protection law for the Reich, though they did not get one. That is why Walther Schoenichen, after 1922 the director of the State Office of Nature Protection, and with him many conservationists, were placing great hopes in the assumption of power by the Nazis; in 1935, the State Office was absorbed into the Reich Office for Nature Protection. Substantively, Schoenichen continued the approach of the 1920s by making Ernst Rudorff's concept of nature—now expanded with a design component—into the basis of his thinking: "*Heimatschutz* in the Rudorffian sense and landscape design in the spirit of the new times" were the goals whose outlines had been becoming clearer for a number of years and to which conservationists were getting closer through the Nazis' assumption of power. Schoenichen mentioned road building as one area in which landscape cultivation had to be taken into consideration.[77]

To realize these demands, Schoenichen offered his services to "Chief Engineer Todt" in December 1933 and sent him an article in the journal *Naturschutz* (Conservation) on "long-distance roads and their effects on the landscape." In addition, he signed up Todt as a subscriber to the magazine. More surprising than Schoenichen's letter is Todt's reaction. The letter bears the inscription "file without response." Todt evidently believed that the consulting system he had set up was a sufficient answer to Schoenichen's concerns, making a response seem unnecessary.[78] At least Todt passed on to Seifert a memorandum entitled "The Hafraba in the area of Frankfurt am Main" that had been sent to him. The garden architect Carl Heicke had written it in December of 1933 for the Working Association for Nature and Landscape Protection Frankfurt and Environs (*Arbeitsgemeinschaft für Natur- und Landschaftsschutz Frankfurt und Umgebung*), an umbrella organization with twenty-five groups and supposedly twenty-five-thousand members, and he sent it to both Todt and Seifert. Heicke detailed the poor response the Frankfurt conservationists had received. Following a meeting with Hafraba director Willy Hof in October 1932, the Working Association had been deliberately kept from any further contact with him. The beginning of construction in the fall of 1933 had also caught the Hesse conservationists by surprise, as a result of which Heicke complained "emphatically about the marginalization we have suffered." From the perspective of the conservationists, the reaction to their demands before and after 1933 was a slight.[79] Heicke's substantive demands were not so different from those of Seifert. The alignment, he argued, must not be adopted from that of the railroad under any circumstances, German rather than foreign flora should be used, the embankments should be gently rounded, and advertising along the autobahn should be prohibited as "excrescences of vile commercialism and materialism." Only the planting of allotment gardens on the embankments departed from Seifert's ideas. Seifert therefore expressed to Heicke his full agreement, though he noted that the route had already been laid out. To Todt he wrote that the only reason Heicke had not been brought in was his advanced age.[80]

These few occurrences just about cover the contacts of the conservation movement with the agency of the Inspector-General. The result was that state-organized conservation was of no consequence at the highest level of the autobahn construction. Individual landscape advocates were at liberty, however, to make use of local conservation commissioners to present their concerns on issues where their interests overlapped. From the perspective of the landscape consultants, conservationists were helpers—on account of their status and their education. To the professional garden architects, they were mere laymen.

The majority of the conservationists (most of whom held unpaid positions) were teachers and thus civil servants. German teachers participated in the conservation movement in two ways: first, the educators made up a large portion of the membership; second, by virtue of their profession, they were important multipliers for the movement. A survey in 1936 found that about 57 percent of the district commissioners for conservation in the German Reich were teachers; only 15 percent were not civil servants. The ratio was much higher in Prussia than in the other states. The landscape advocates of the *Reichsautobahn* tried to undercut these volunteer conservationists with the promise that the architects could provide professional consultation by trained experts.[81]

Nevertheless, there was occasional cooperation with the institutionalized conservation movement. For example, the head of the State Office for Conservation and *Landespflege* in Württemberg, Hans Schwenkel, participated in the planning of the *Reichsautobahnen*. Schwenkel sent a courtesy letter to Seifert along with an offer of help. Seifert advised Schwenkel to approach the landscape advocate Siegloch directly. The latter wrote to Seifert that as a longtime member of the *Bund für Heimatschutz*, he had contacted Schwenkel only a few days after his appointment as landscape advocate, and the two had already walked some of the routes.[82]

Schwenkel proved remarkably accommodating on the routing for the autobahn. For example, in a letter to the Ministry of Culture of Württemberg, he approved plans for the ascent into the Swabian Jura. Even though he realized that forestry would be seriously affected, the roads, he declared, were more important. Schwenkel accorded them monumental quality: "In a work that is being built for millennia, however, one must accept this damage, which is, after all, temporary." On the section Stuttgart-Heilbronn, he argued—against Siegloch—for the construction of a bridge instead of an embankment to cross a valley near Höpfigheim. The Directorate *Reichsautobahnen* pegged the additional costs for the bridge solution at 400,000 Reichsmark and expected that it would add at least a year to the construction schedule. For that reason, the Directorate asked the Inspector-General to reject a bridge in case the Ministry of Culture of Württemberg, Schwenkel's superior agency, submitted such a request. The clinching argument came last: the embankment was already under construction. This example makes it abundantly clear how little factual influence the established conservation movement had on the autobahn.[83]

This observation is not contradicted by the fact that Schwenkel developed a fairly close relationship with the landscape advocates and attended two of their meetings: when Siegloch clashed with the regional planning office, he was on his own. Siegloch and Schwenkel discussed basic issues, but the day-to-day conflicts with the regional planning office Siegloch had to fight alone. Schwenkel himself concluded in 1950 that it was in part due to the "partial failure" of the official conservation establishment on the question of landscape design that it had been "nearly completely sidelined" in the construction of the autobahnen.[84]

The landscape advocate Max Schwarz (regional planning office Altona) took a prime issue of conservation into his own hands by defending the hedgerows in Schleswig-Holstein (which were called "Knicks") against being cleared to create more arable land. This consolidation of arable land had already prompted Ernst Rudorff's criticism of agriculture a generation before the construction of the autobahn. Unlike Rudorff, Schwarz advanced both ecological and aesthetic reasons for opposing the cutting of the hedgerows. The concrete occasion was the building of the *Reichsautobahn* Hamburg-Lübeck, as part of which the land amelioration office Lübeck wanted to pursue "a sweeping consolidation of arable land deep into the landscape" in the area of the construction section

Bad Oldesloe "at the expense of the *Reichsautobahn*." According to Schwarz, the agency wanted to clear the hedges simply because its cleanup plans—which he considered purely mechanical—called for it. However, without hedges, the landscape was in danger of steppifying within five to ten years. During an on-site meeting with representatives of the farmers, Schwarz described the importance of the hedgerows. He went beyond a purely agricultural justification and asked his listeners to consider that an alteration in the "character of a landscape" also reshaped "the character of the people who grow up there"—in this case, the change would go against the goals of National Socialism.[85]

When this argument, too, failed to be persuasive, his urgent demand that the cutting of the hedgerows be halted reached the Reich Food Estate via Seifert and Todt. While the agency acknowledged that the *Knicks* had "a certain importance for the water and climate balance," it pointed to difficulties at harvest time. In view of the "battle for food," it argued, only economic arguments could be accepted. Moreover, wasteland areas were being reforested at a growing rate, which means that the climate function of the hedgerows was receding. Schwarz, however, had not seen any evidence of reforestation during his extensive travels in Schleswig-Holstein. The controversy over the hedgerows ebbed, and the cutting evidently continued. Although Todt had invested the issue with some urgency, he did not prevail against the Reich Food Estate, where economic considerations held sway.[86]

Two examples of where conservationism was successful shall round out the picture. Still in the planning phase, Schoenichen, as head of the Reich Office for Nature Protection, prevented a monumental autobahn bridge from being built across a valley in the so-called Franconian Switzerland region in northern Bavaria, bordered by Bamberg, Bayreuth, and Nuremberg. The Kleinziegenfeld Valley had been "discovered" by the educated urban bourgeoisie in the eighteenth century as a Romantic landscape. Since 1937 there had been talk about a supplementary section to the *Reichsautobahnen* from Bamberg to Lanzendorf, which would have connected Kulmbach, where Todt held his engineering classes on Plassenburg Castle, with the network of highways. A bridge would have spanned the valley as part of this section. Local conservationists appealed to the Reich Office for Nature Protection for help. During a meeting of the Research Society for the Road System at the Plassenburg, Schoenichen visited the valley in November 1937, and in a report to Reich Forestry Minister Hermann Göring he asked that it be left untouched. A change in the plans was in fact agreed upon during a meeting at the agency of the Inspector-General. The arguments by the local conservationists that the bridge would destroy the solitude of the valley were countered by one department head from the regional planning office, who claimed that an "imposing bridge of natural stone" would probably enhance the beauty of the landscape. In any event, the section was never built; the local landscape advocate did not play any part in the entire affair.[87]

By contrast, the District Office for Conservation in the area of the settlement association (*Siedlungsverband*) of the Ruhr coal district spoke of "close and lively cooperation" with the landscape advocate of the autobahn. The route selection for Duisburg had been controversial for a long time: the original Hafraba planning did not provide for a connection of this city to its Rhine harbor, which the city administration attributed to the influence of the northern Hanse cities. Following a press campaign in the summer of 1933, Todt finally agreed to connect Duisburg to a new section from Frankfurt to Emmerich. The route proposed by the Inspector-General's office cut through the city's forest and would have required the zoo to be moved. The city, however, preferred a solution in greater proximity to the city. The engineers rejected this option by pointing to the higher costs, as construction would have affected the water and electricity grids. After being threatened with the State Police, the city administration gave in, though the location of the section within the city forests was evidently moved.

The Duisburg conservationists were happy that the autobahn was not cutting the city forest in half, but was traversing it with the "least possible interference." The demands from the Settlement Association and the city of Duisburg had supposedly helped to bring about this alteration in the plans. The conservationists had early on expressed their wishes for the landscaping of the *Reichsautobahnen* and had included lists of native (*bodenständige*) plants for the Ruhr region, where original plant communities hardly existed after decades of vigorous industrialization. In view of the local conflict, the collaboration between landscape advocate Erxleben and the District Office for Conservation was in the beginning certainly closer than elsewhere; Erxleben had won a political ally on the issue of the city forest. Later however, "intolerable tensions" arose between conservationists and the landscape advocate.[88]

In the Prussian Rhine province, local conservationists were incensed at plans to run the autobahn as close as possible to the Siebengebirge mountain range in order to open up this landscape to motorists. Here, too, the quarrel revolved around a bridge, which was not built under National Socialism. Important for the present context is the amazement of the conservationists at the professionally and artistically motivated approach of the landscape advocates, for whom regional traditions of protection were less important than overarching considerations of beauty and design.[89]

These examples on the local level show the differing degrees to which official conservation was involved in the planning of the *Reichsautobahnen*. The Reich Office for Conservation was from the outset excluded from any systematic participation. From the perspective of the landscape advocates, interventions by individual conservationists were sometimes welcome, although they were always relegated to a helper status. In the case of the section Hamburg-Lübeck, the initiatives by the local landscape advocate against the cutting of hedgerows failed. The only recorded case of effective intervention by the Reich Office for Conservation against the bridge in Franconian Switzerland required the mobilization of precious political resources in the form of intervention by Göring. As for Duisburg, this was a one-time cooperation as a result of a temporary coalition of interests, which did not last long. The case of the planned bridges in Franconian Switzerland and in the Rhineland reveals the ideological constellations in the relationship between conservationists, civil engineers, and landscape architects: while conservationists regarded bridges as intolerable interference in the landscape, engineers were convinced that these structures could have a positive aesthetic effect. The landscape advocates found themselves between these two positions: while they sought solutions that mediated between the two camps, they tended to see solvable design issues instead of fundamental conflicts.

In summary, one can say that the participation by conservationists was minor, that the construction planning remained in the hands of the Inspector-General's office, and that if anyone had influence with that agency, it was almost exclusively landscape advocates. To be sure, Seifert's later statement that he had "no knowledge" of any participation by the conservation movement in the construction of the *Reichsautobahnen* seems exaggerated, given the examples I have described. However, it certainly reflects the tendency to marginalize conservation when it came to the building of the highways. As an alternative to what the landscape advocates regarded as conservation organizations that were outdated, run by laypeople, and inadequate in their staffing, they offered a professional approach with certain competencies for themselves. The Inspector-General's office encouraged them by excluding conservation from the construction of the *Reichsautobahn* as much as possible. As the following section will show, this policy of exclusion on the part of Todt's agency also took legal forms.[90] First, however, I will look at the importance that was given to regional planning.

As I have shown earlier, the Gezuvor and, after 1935, its successor organization, the Reich Office for Reich and Regional Planning, presented a rough plan for the routing of a section between individual cities. The office of the Inspector-General, however, reserved the right to make the final decision, and considerations of regional planners were not systematically taken into account in the construction of the *Reichsautobahnen*. That much was also conceded by the author of an article in the professional journal *Raumforschung und Raumordung* (Spatial Research and Regional Planning) in 1937. He noted that "in view of the profound reciprocal influences between traffic and area policies, the wishes that regional planning makes of traffic planning must be taken into consideration more strongly than has been the case so far." This demand fell on deaf ears, however. At best, the young agency of regional planning participated in the decisions about the autobahnen in an advisory capacity. Final decision-making remained with the office of the Inspector-General, which operated without the collegial participation of other ministries. For example, the head of the Reich Office for Area Planning, Hanns Kerrl, could only express his regret that the decision about the *Reichsautobahn* in the eastern part of the Ruhrgebiet had already been made without his input.

However, when it came to planning in the conquered countries of eastern Europe, a new type of planning seems to have prevailed. A few weeks after the attack on Poland, the office of the Inspector-General asked the Reich Office for Area Planning to a meeting about an autobahn section Posen-Lodz-Warsaw-Minsk, without the landscape advocates.[91]

The fragmentation of the National Socialist system that dealt with the built environment in the broadest sense is revealed by the various degrees of influence that the landscape advocates had within different institutions and bureaucracies. To be sure, the landscape architects had little interest in conservation in the narrower sense of the phrase. The office of the Inspector-General, however, sought to implement its ideas about the technological landscape also over the wishes of the conservation bureaucracy.

Legalizing the exclusion of conservation

In the scholarly literature on the environmental history of National Socialism, the Reich Nature Protection Law (*Reichsnaturschutzgesetz*) of 1935 holds a special place. Given the fact that the conservation movement tried in vain to get such a law passed during the Weimar Republic, it has occasionally been seen as a success. The Reich Nature Protection Law for the first time put conservation on a uniform legal footing throughout the Reich. The conceptual, legal, and organizational possibilities of the conservationists were expanded along the lines they had wished for during the Weimar Republic. The actual implementation of the law, however, was a profound disappointment to conservationists. Recent scholarship has pointed out that the effect of the law was only short-term, and that it was more of a Pyrrhic victory. The discussion that follows will examine the extent to which this law influenced the activities of the Inspector-General on the legal level and which counterreactions this provoked within Todt's agency.[92]

The Reich Nature Protection Law was passed after some turf battles. The main participants were Hermann Göring, Reich Forestry Minister and Prussian Minister President; Bernhard Rust, Reich Minister of Science, Education, and Popular Culture; and the Reich Ministry of Justice. Göring emerged the victor. The debate about the law also attracted the interest of the Inspector-General. During the preparatory phase of the law, one official noted that, "strange to say," a Reich nature protection law was being worked on in the Justice Ministry. "Considerable conflicts over competence" were evident at an initial meeting at which the Inspector-General's office had also been represented. The office of the Inspector-General was not involved in the subsequent drafting of the law, but it countered with its own draft law worked out by Seifert and the forester Erhard Hausendorff, who promoted what is today called ecoforestry. The plan was to place a thirty-meter-wide protective strip of land on both sides of the autobahn under the legal authority of the Inspector-General's office. This land was to be planted in accordance with the ideas of the landscape advocates, that is to say, with native plants.[93]

Following passage of the Reich Nature Protection Law, and in view of its expanded powers with respect to nature protection, the Inspector-General's office sought to widen its sphere of competency. The goal was "to declare the visual field (*Gesichtskreis*) of the autobahnen a protected nature area (*Naturschongebiet*) in contrast to the actual nature preserves." In a move that did not use this specific term but was fraught with the potential for legal conflict, the Inspector-General's office, in the "Decree on Road Building in the Open Landscape" of 19 November 1936, and the "Decree on Protective Forests along the *Reichsautobahnen*" of 17 March 1937, laid claim to its own legal preserves so as to place groves and natural monuments in the landscape along the *Reichsautobahn* under its own authority. The plan was for the office of the Inspector-General to have sole decision-making authority about features along the roads that were worthy of protection.[94]

As was to be expected, conservationists were outraged. Schoenichen saw the rights of nature protection eroding under the scope of the law. Through the decree on road construction, he argued, conservation had, for all intents and purposes, relinquished the rights it had been given by the Reich Nature Protection Law. Moreover, the decree on protective woodlands excluded conservationists from establishing and caring for the plantings. But this was precisely an area in which they were very knowledgeable, he claimed. For him, it was more than doubtful whether "the landscape advocates of the Inspector-General, whose training is, after all, more on the artistic side," could do this equally as well. Schoenichen summarized his thoughts in a rather resigned tone: "On the whole, I believe that I am supposed to glean from the two decrees that the Herr Inspector-General of the Roads wants to free himself as best he can from the regulations of the Nature Protection Law, and, in any case, that he wants to reserve the decision as much as possible for himself and his staff."[95]

This was a pretty accurate description of the intention of the Inspector-General's office. After conservationists had up to that time collaborated only in sporadic fashion, they were now to be stripped of the legal basis for doing so. The Württemberg conservationist Schwenkel summarized the situation very clearly. He called the agreement a "terrible defeat for conservation," which he could not understand, given Todt's attitude.[96] The *Reichsautobahnen* were to be given a special status within Nazi Germany both legally as well as in terms of their relationship to the landscape, a status that expanded the range of tasks of the landscape advocates. The institutional interests of the Inspector-General's office in expanding its administrative competencies, and the professional interests of the landscape architects in expanding their professional competencies came as a shock to the conservationists. The landscape advocates claimed that they were engaged in positive landscape design, while the conservationists were interested merely in conserving outdated states of nature. The engineers' claim to social status benefited from the fact that the landscape advocates were certifying that technology could be friendly to the landscape, and in that regard the landscape advocates entered into a coalition with the engineers within the framework of German Technology. However, this did not rule out significant substantive differences between landscape architects and civil engineers when it came to existing competencies, even as they joined forces in fighting for future competencies against other government offices, like the Reich Office for Conservation.

In the event, though, the hopes of the landscape advocates to use the decree to create forests suited to local conditions along the autobahnen were hardly fulfilled. In 1944, Seifert conceded that the efforts had not progressed much beyond early stages here and there. The reason, he maintained, was the obstructionism by lawyers and "all sorts of opposition" within the organization of the autobahnen. He had been promised, however, that after the war the strips of protective forest would be expanded to a width of one-thousand meters. Another effort that failed was a topsoil decree for the entire Reich, which stipulated that on all construction projects, the layer of humus should be removed at the beginning and specially stored to be reused for plantings.[97]

Looking at the results, the approach of the Inspector-General's office seems like an attempt to acquire a special zone within legally regulated nature protection and subsequently to solidify it, after such a zone had already for the most part been achieved in the day-to-day reality of the autobahn construction. As a result, nature protection lost legal authority outside of its already weak areas. Alongside the Reich Labor Service, the construction of the *Reichsautobahnen* had a strongly transformative effect on the landscape in Nazi Germany; in both areas, the responsible actors sought to become quasi-autonomous. Todt's expansive course was manifested on the outside in decrees. The following chapter will shed some light on the internal conflicts.[98]

Notes

1. Conference on Historic Monument Preservation and *Heimatschutz*, executive committee to Todt, 31 August 1933, BAP 46.01/1486; Todt to Conference on Historic Monument Preservation and *Heimatschutz*, 1 September 1933, ibid.; Helmut Fischer, *Deutscher Heimatbund. 90 Jahre für Umwelt und Naturschutz. Geschichte eines Programms* (Bonn, 1994), 40–41. The representative of the Fürst Pückler Society was most likely the landscape architect Meyer-Jungclaussen, whose essays on the landscaping of roads the Society published as pamphlets: Hinrich Meyer-Jungclaussen, "Landstraße und Landschaftsbild," *Verkehrstechnik* 36/4 (September, 1931): 147–150; idem, *Landstraße und Landschaftsbild*, Flugschrift der Fürst Pückler-Gesellschaft 2 (Muskau: Fürst Pückler-Gesellschaft, 1931). The Society had been founded in 1930 to foster the memory of Prince Hermann von Pückler-Muskau (1785–1871), who published his classic landscaping treatise *Remarks on Landscape Gardening* ("Andeutungen über Landschaftsgärtnerei") in 1834. Alfred Richard Meyer, "Die Fürst-Pückler-Gesellschaft," *Zeitschrift für Bücherfreunde* 37, no. IV (1933): 69–72.
2. One thing that was evidently noncontroversial was the prohibition of advertising along the roads. This was something that *Heimatschüzer* had demanded already during the interwar period, by pointing to among other things, the commercialized *autostrada*. The laws governing the *Reichsautobahnen* contained such prohibitions against billboards from the very outset. Hans Ulrich Schaefer, *Die Gesetze der Reichsautobahnen mit einschlägigen Vorschriften und Verweisungen* (Berlin, 1937).
3. Martin Jay, "Vision in Context: Reflections and Refractions," in *Vision in Context. Historical and Contemporary Perspectives on Sight*, Teresa Brennan and Martin Jay, ed. (New York and

London, 1996), 3–12, 10–11; Jonathan Crary, *Techniques of the Observer: On Vision and Modernity in the Nineteenth Century* (Cambridge, Mass., 1990); Urry, *Consuming Places*.

4. Schivelbusch, *Railway Journey*; Stilgoe, *Metropolitan Corridor*; König, *Bahnen und Berge*.
5. Andreas Knaut, *Zurück zur Natur! Die Wurzeln der Ökologiebewegung* (Greven, 1993); Rollins, *Greener Vision*; Klueting, *Antimodernismus und Reform*; Karl Ditt, "'Mit Westfalengruß und Heil Hitler.' Die westfälische Heimatbewegung 1918–1945," in ibid., 191–215.
6. Reinhard Bollmus, *Das Amt Rosenberg und seine Gegner. Zum Machtkampf im nationalsozialistischen Herschaftssystem* (Stuttgart, 1970), 47–50; Linse, *Ökopax und Anarchie*, 35–36 and 170, note 53. Raymond H. Dominick, *The Environmental Movement in Germany. Prophets and Pioneers, 1871–1980* (Louisville, Kentucky, 1993), 102–103. "An unsere Mitglieder!," *Bayerischer Heimatschutz* 29 (1933): 1; "Aus dem Jahresbericht des Bayerischen Landesvereins für Heimatschutz," *Bayerischer Heimatschutz* 30 (1934): 82–83.
7. *Denkmalpflege und Heimatschutz im Wiederaufbau der Nation. Tag für Denkmalpflege und Heimatschutz im Rahmen des Ersten Reichstreffens des Reichsbundes Volkstum und Heimat Kassel 1933* (Berlin, 1934), 84–89, 84, 89. See also the short program of the meeting in BAP 46.01/1486. Seifert to Lindner, 1 August 1933, Seifert Papers (Seifert-Nachlaß am Lehrstuhl für Landschaftsarchitektur und Entwerfen der Technischen Universität München-Weihenstephan [hereafter SN]) 5; Seifert to Hönig, 22 August 1933, ibid.; Seifert to Day for the Cultivation of Monuments and *Heimatschutz*, 25 August 1933; Seifert to Hönig, 11 October 1933, ibid. In this last letter, Seifert asked the architects' league to subsidize his talk, given his "rather constrained economic situation." In his autobiography, Seifert wrote that he had been sent to Kassel by the building committee of the Bavarian State Association for *Heimatschutz* "in order to represent certain interests of the Alpine regions, which were very different from those of other landscapes." This statement is not borne out by the sources. Seifert, *Leben*, 35. Regarding the petition, we can assume that Seifert's motion did not receive majority backing and was therefore not listed in the official publication of the meeting. Had it received such backing, the perennially confident Seifert would likely have informed Todt of this, especially since it would have provided an additional boost to his concerns. Seifert to Hönig, 11 October 1933, SN 5.
8. Seifert to Todt, 18 November 1933, BAP 46.01/1487.
9. Seifert, "Aufgaben der öffentlichen Hand zur Landschaftsgestaltung," 18 November 1933, BAP 46.01/1487. In Seifert's autobiography, these demands were reduced to that of a native reforestation (i.e., one that was rooted in the local soil and landscape). Seifert, *Leben*, 36.
10. Seifert to Lindner, 23 May 1932, SN 5; Lindner to Seifert, 11 June 1932, ibid.; Seifert to Lindner, 16 October 1932, ibid.
11. Todt to Seifert, 23 November 1933, Deutsches Museum Munich, Archives (hereafter DM) NL 133/56 (copy in BAK NS 26/1188). Nearly six years later, Todt wrote that he had previously audited a lecture by Seifert at the Technical University in Munich and had been won over by Seifert's personality. Todt to Seifert, 3 May 1940, BAK NS 26/1188. See Seifert, *Leben*, 38.
12. "Vorschlag zur landschaftlichen Eingliederung," DM NL 133/56. See Alwin Seifert, "Die landschaftliche Eingliederung der Strecke [München-Holzkirchen]," *Die Straße* 2 (1935): 446–450. The author claimed that he was "surely the first to have used" the concept of "landscape integration" (*landschaftliche Eingliederung*) in this article. Seifert, *Leben*, 41. Reichsbund Volkstum und Heimat, Reich leadership, Lindner and Haverbeck, to Todt, 8 December 1933, BAP 46.01/1487. Todt to Reichsbund Volkstum und Heimat, Reich leadership, 11 December 1933, ibid.
13. Eduard Schönleben, *Fritz Todt. Der Mensch, der Ingenieur, der Nationalsozialist* (Oldenburg, 1943), 76, 80.
14. The garden architects Gustav Allinger, Hinrich Meyer-Jungclaussen, and Rudolf Ungewitter, the city garden inspector of Mannheim, Joseph Pertl, and one unidentified farming war buddy of Todt's were apparently in the running for the position: Seifert, *Leben*, 42–46; Seifert to Mrass, 9 April 1967, SN 200; Todt to Seifert, 18 January 1934, BAP 46.01/1487; Seifert to Todt, 20 January 1934, ibid.

15. Seifert to Todt, 7 March 1934, BAP 46.01/1487.
16. Ian Kershaw, *The Nazi Dictatorship: Problems and Perspectives of Interpretation*, 4th ed. (London, 2000), 84–92.
17. Todt to Seifert, 18 January 1934, BAP 46.01/1487. The placement of these consultants reveals the interwoven organizational scheme in the construction of the *Reichsautobahnen*: the OBK (Oberste Bauleitung Kraftfahrbahnen, or regional planning offices) were subordinated offices of the Society *Reichsautobahnen* and thus of the Reich Railroad, while the landscape advocates were appointed by the office of the Inspector-General.
18. *Hermann Mattern 1902–1971. Gärten, Gartenlandschaften, Häuser. Ausstellung der Akademie der Künste und der Technischen Universität Berlin vom 17. Oktober bis 17. November 1982* (Berlin, 1982), 7. However, this account can also be seen as part to Mattern's attempt to distance himself from National Socialism.
19. Seifert, *Leben*, 47.
20. "Erinnerungen an Leben und Werk von Dr.-Ing. Fritz Todt von Dr.-Ing. E.h. Richard Auberlen," IfZ, Ms 392, 11.
21. Seifert, *Leben*, 47–48.
22. "Vergütung für die Sachverständigen für landschaftliche Beratung (Gartengestalter) für die Monate Mai-September 1935," SN 116. "Aufstellung für die Monate Oktober 1934 bis April 1935," SN 117; Association of German Garden Architects, "An die Vereinsmitglieder," 29 July 1929, SN 215; Association of German Garden Architects, Hirsch to Seifert, 14 February 1929, ibid.; Association of German Garden Architects, "An die Verbandsmitglieder," 3 November 1931, ibid.; "An alle Mitglieder der Sondergruppe Deutsche Gartenarchitekten," n.d., ibid.; Joachim Wolschke-Bulmahn and Gert Gröning, *1913–1988. 75 Jahre Bund Deutscher Landschafts-Architekten BDLA, Teil 1: Zur Entwicklung der Interessenverbände der Gartenarchitekten in der Weimarer Republik und im Nationalsozialismus* (Bonn, 1988), 27–28, 59–77. The Association of German Garden Architects is described here as elitist. Joachim Wolschke-Bulmahn, "Biodynamischer Gartenbau, Landschaftsarchitektur und Nationalsozialismus," *Das Gartenamt* 42 (1993): 590–595, 638–642; Seifert to Directorate *Reichsautobahnen*, 10 February 1934, SN 204; Hirsch to Seifert, 27 December 1933, SN 130; "Bezeugung Maria Seifert," 18 September 1946, AGM Akte VII 3702 Prof. Alwin Seifert; Claudia Vierle, *Camillo Schneider. Dendrologe und Gartenbauschriftsteller. Eine Studie zu seinem Leben und Werk* (Berlin, 1998), 53–91.
23. Wolschke-Bulmahn and Gröning, *75 Jahre BDLA*, 52, list 32 landscape advocates for 1940, of whom twelve were former members of the Association of German Garden Designers and two were members of the Association of German Garden Architects. Camillo Schneider, "Eidesstattliche Erklärung," 27 January 1947, AGM VII 3702 Prof. Alwin Seifert; Seifert to Schneider, 22 December 1935, SN 146; On Königsberg: Otto Reismann, *Deutschlands Autobahnen. Adolf Hitlers Straßen* (Bayreuth, 1937), 81.
24. Seifert to Allinger, 26 January 1934, SN 123. Not eligible were "opportunists who only now have discovered their bond to the soil [*Schollenverbundenheit*]." Allinger to Seifert, 2 February 1934, ibid.; Meyer-Jungclaussen to Seifert, 18 February 1934, ibid.; Seifert to Schwarz, 29 January 1934, SN 150; Reich Association of German Horticulture, "Der Sonderbeauftragte für die Bearbeitung sämtlicher Gartenbaufragen und die Eingliederung der innerhalb des Gartenbauwesens bestehenden Verbände und Vereine, Boettner," to Seifert, 7 Ostermond [April] 1934, SN 123; Seifert to Hübotter, 20 March 1934, SN 215.
25. Seifert to regional planning office Breslau, 24 March 1934, SN 148; Inspector-General's office to Schütze, 30 May 1934, ibid.
26. Seifert to Erxleben, 13 April 1934, SN 126; Seifert to Schwarz, 29 January 1934, SN 150; Seifert to Schwarz, 18 February 1934, ibid.; Allinger to Seifert, 2 February 1934, SN 123; Seifert to Hirsch, 19 June 1937, SN 116. Seifert's confidants were Hirsch, Siegloch, Heiler, Erxleben, Schwarz, Hübotter, Langerhans, Bauch, and Hoemann.
27. Seifert to regional planning office Königsberg, *Reichsbahnoberrat* Lewerenz, 12 July 1934, SN 165; Lewerenz to Seifert, 20 July 1934, ibid.; "Erklärung Hermann Mattern," 19 September

1946, AGM VII 3702 Prof. Alwin Seifert; Seifert to Directorate of the Society *Reichsautobahnen*, 8 July 1935, SN 204; Seifert to Garden Director Königsberg, 16 September 1935, SN 165.

28. Allinger to Seifert, 2 February 1934, SN 123; Boettner to Seifert, 7 April 1934, ibid.; Wolschke-Bulmahn and Gröning, *75 Jahre BDLA*, 21; NSDAP *Gau* administration Saxony, Personnel Office, to Seifert, 24 Ernting [August] 1934, BAP 46.01/1487; Todt to Seifert, 28 August 1933 (copy), BAK NS 26/1188. Todt's biographer Seidler points to this letter—completely erroneously—as an example for Todt's personnel policy uninfluenced by party interests. Seifert to Todt, 31 August 1934 (stamp of date of receipt 26 September 1934), BAP 46.01/1487. The letter has the handwritten addition by Eduard Schönleben, "Röhnick rejected for good as a Freemason! 7.10. Sch."; Röhnick to Seifert, 3 September 1934, BAP 46.01/1487.

29. Because of this defeat, when it came time to search for a successor to a landscape advocate to the regional planning office Königsberg, Seifert did not even propose the garden architect Stabe from Preußisch-Eylau, since he was also handicapped by membership in a lodge. Seifert to Schönleben, 15 September 1935, BAP 46.01/864; Seifert to Schwarz, 17 August 1935, SN 150.

30. Seifert, *Leben*, 49; Grit Hottenträger, "New Flowers—New Gardens. Residential Gardens Designed by Karl Foerster, Hermann Mattern and Herta Hammerbacher (1928–c. 1943)," *Journal of Garden History* 12 (1992): 207–227; Vroni Heinrich-Hampf, "Über Gartenidylle und Gartenarchitektur im Dritten Reich," in *Faschistische Architekturen. Planen und Bauen in Europa 1930 bis 1945*, ed. Hartmut Frank (Hamburg, 1985), 271–281; "Hermann Mattern," *Garten und Landschaft* 82 (1972): 350.

31. Mattern to Seifert, 4 June 1934, SN 142; Seifert to Mattern, 11 June 1934, ibid.; Seifert to Mattern, 13 August 1934, ibid.; Stück to Seifert, 3 August 1934, SN 155. Although he was not a party member, Stück enjoyed "the full confidence" of the *Gau* administration. Directorate of the Reichsautobahnen to Seifert, 2 August 1934, ibid.; Gau Administration Kurhessen, Office for Technology to the Directorate *Reichsautobahnen*, 28 July 1934 (copy), ibid.; Seifert to Mattern and Stück, 14 September 1934, ibid.

32. Seifert to Mattern, 23 October 1934, SN 142. Stück was also supported within the "staff of the Deputy of the Führer," that is to say, by one of Heß's staff, as a "tried-and-true National Socialist fighter:" Inspector-General's office to Seifert, 6 June 1934, BAP 46.01/1487; Seifert to Karl Gerland, Commissioner on the Staff of the Deputy of the Führer, 18 November 1934, SN 155.

33. Seifert, *Leben*, 49; "Erklärung Hermann Mattern," 19 September 1946, AGM Akte VII 3702 Prof. Alwin Seifert; NSDAP Gau Administration Kurmark District Administration Potsdam, 1 April 1936, BAP 46.06/221; Heinrich-Hampf, "Gartenidylle," 279. The author says, incorrectly, that there was little personal liking between Seifert and Mattern; mutual visits suggest the opposite. Seifert to Mattern, 13 October 1943; Seifert to Mattern, 27 March 1944; Seifert to Mattern, 19 May 1944, SN 142.

34. Chief Gardener Creplin, Nonanes Post Neubabelsberg, 22 May 1936, BAP 46.06/221; German Labor Front, Central Office, to Treasury, German Labor Front Building Assessment Division, 17 December 1936, ibid.; Mattern to Speer, 12 July 1937, ibid.; Schulte-Frohlinde to [German Labor Front -]Treasury, Section Construction, 12 November 1937, ibid.; Schulte-Frohlinde to Mattern, 6 December 1937, ibid. When Speer was head of the Organization Todt, Mattern worked on providing the OT with vegetables and for the organization's agricultural farms. Mattern to Seifert, 7 January 1943, SN 142; Mattern to Seifert, 11 August 1943, ibid.

35. Inspector-General, Schönleben, to Wiepking-Jürgensmann, 6 March 1934, BAP 46.01/1486; Todt to Wiepking-Jürgensmann, 2 December 1941, AGM Wiepking; Seifert to Wiepking, 31 October 1939, ibid.; Wiepking-Jürgensmann to Seifert, 13 November 1939, ibid.; Seifert to Hirsch, 11 June 1931, SN 215; Association of German Garden Architects, Hirsch to Seifert, 15 June 1931, ibid.; Hübotter to Seifert, 16 June 1931, ibid.; Seifert to Hübotter, 7 July 1931, ibid.; Thomas Zeller, "'Ich habe die Juden möglichst gemieden,'" *Garten + Landschaft. Zeitschrift für Landschaftsarchitektur* No. 8 (1995): 4–5; Gröning and Wolschke-Bulmahn, *Liebe zur Landschaft. Teil III*; Mechtild Rössler and Sabine Schleiermacher, *Der Generalplan Ost. Aspekte der nationalsozialistischen Planungs- und Vernichtungspolitik* (Berlin, 1993).

36. Seifert to Wiepking, 24 September 1939, AGM Wiepking; Seifert to Wiepking, 18 November 1939, ibid.; Schnell [on private stationery] to Seifert, 14 January 1941, ibid.; Declaration Maria Seifert, 18 September 1946, AGM VII 3702 Prof. Alwin Seifert; Mattern to Seifert, 11 January 1941, SN 142; Seifert to Mattern, 15 January 1941, ibid.
37. Seifert to Wiepking, 24 September 1939, AGM, Akte Wiepking; Inspector-General, Schönleben, to Frist [sic] Stück, 10 September 1935, SN 155; Todt to Seifert, 18 September 1934, ibid.
38. NSDAP Office for Technology to Seifert, 24 September 1935, SN 155. The same letter went to Todt, who passed it on to Seifert. Todt to Seifert, 3 October 1935, ibid.; File note Lorenz, 4 November 1935, BAP 46.01/860.
39. NSDAP *Gau* Administration Kurhessen, Office for Technology, Head of the *Gau* Office, Haselmann, to Todt, 10 July 1936, BAP 46.01/860; Stück to Office for Technology, 6 November 1936, BAP 46.01/865.
40. Todt to Directorate Reichsautobahnen, 18 July 1936, BAP 46.01/865 (copy in SN 155); File note Schönleben 14 December 1936, BAP 46.01/865; Stück to Todt, 5 February 1937, ibid.; Report about the meeting with architect Fritz Stück on 16 February 1937, 17 February 1937, ibid.; NSDAP Gau Administration Kurhessen, Gauinspector Adam, to Todt, 5 April 1937, BAP 46.01/860; Notes of the meeting at the Gau Administration Kassel (secret!), 29 April 1937, ibid.; Todt to Schönleben and Köster, 2 July 1937, ibid.; Todt to Hermann Stück, Opel Works, 13 August 1937, ibid.; file note Schönleben 24 July 1937, ibid.; Stück, Memorandum [undated] about the incorporation of scenic terraces and hiking paths along the section Göttingen-Kassel, BAP 46.01/867. The second stanza of Stück's poem reads: "Wo du wandertest auf Bergen, wiesest steilen Hochziel-Pfad:/ ward den kümmerlichsten Schergen freie Bahn für niedre Tat./ Wo Du gabst mit vollen Händen, wo Du über engsten Zaun/ wiesest zu der Zeiten Wenden, ward verspottet Dein Vertraun;/ ward geschändet Blut und Boden, Deiner Heimat Heiligtum:/ Schwätzer, Hetzer und Heloten ernten Ansehn, Amt und Ruhm" (Where you wandered in the mountains, showing the path to lofty goals / there the most miserable henchmen had a clear road for a dastardly deed. / Where you gave most generously, where you pointed over the narrowest fence / to the turning of the times, your trust was mocked / blood and soil, your *Heimat's* sacred shrine, was violated: / braggers, demagogues, and helots harvested renown, office, and fame").
41. Declaration Hermann Mattern, 19 September 1946, AGM VII 3702 Prof. Alwin Seifert; German Society for Horticulture to Seifert (copy), 11 January 1935, BAP 46.01/864; Seifert to German Society for Horticulture (copy), 17 January 1935, ibid.
42. Siegloch to Seifert, 17 January 1936, SN 153. The words "with 1 or 2 exceptions" were crossed out in the version received by Seifert. Walter Schwarz, attorney and notary, to Seifert, 29 May 1936, SN 123; Seifert to Allinger, 3 June 1936, ibid. (copy in BAP 46.01/864).
43. Handwritten remarks on: Seifert to Schönleben, 30 June 1936, BAP 46.01/864. Emphases original. On Dorsch's early membership: Ludwig, *Technik und Ingenieure*, 65; Franz W. Seidler, *Die Organisation Todt. Bauen für Staat und Wehrmacht 1938–1945* (Koblenz, 1987), 17.
44. Todt to Allinger, 21 December 1935 (copy); Todt to Seifert, 21 December 1935; Seifert to Allinger, 27 December 1935; v. Kruedener to Seifert, 18 January 1936; Allinger to Seifert, 9 January 1936; Inspector-General, Schönleben, to Allinger; Notes concerning the planting of the *Reichsautobahn* segment Berlin-Joachimsthal, 21 January 1936 (all SN 123); Inspector-General for the German Roads, Schönleben, to Seifert, 23 August 1938, SN 116; Inspector-General to a) the Directorate of the *Reichsautobahnen* b) the chief road-building agencies of the *Länder* and the Prussian provinces, 23 August 1938 (copy), ibid. and BAK R 65 III/vorl. 10. On that day, Allinger, Max Lange (regional planning office Dresden), Rudolf Ungewitter (regional planning office Berlin), and the briefly employed landscape advocates Julius Kynast (regional planning office Dresden) and Albert Lilienfein (regional planning office Stuttgart) were terminated.
45. Seifert to Schneider, 24 April 1941, SN 146; Circular of 15 April 1940, SN 118; Seifert, *Leben*, 47.
46. Seifert to Todt, 16 July 1934, BAP 46.01/1487; Birgitta Ringbeck, "Architektur und Städtebau unter dem Einfluß der Heimatschutzbewegung," in Klueting, *Antimodernismus*, 216–287;

Fachbereich Stadt- und Landschaftsplanung der Gesamthochschule Kassel, ed., *Leberecht Migge 1881–1935. Gartenkultur des 20. Jahrhunderts* (Kassel, 1981), esp. the essay by Günther Uhlig, "Siedlungskonzepte Migges und ihre reformpolitische Bedeutung," ibid., 96–101; Schwarz to Seifert, 9 November 1934, SN 150; Reich Food Estate, The Reich Farm Leader, Administrative Office, Main Section II, to Todt, 22 February 1934, BAP 46.01/1486; *Landesbauernschaft* Baden to Seifert, 28 February 1934, SN 207; State Expert Group Garden, Park, and Cemetery Design (*Landesfachgruppe Garten-, Park- und Friedhofsgestaltung*) of the *Landesbauernschaft* Silesia in the Reich Food Estate to Seifert, 17 April 1934, ibid.; Seifert to *Landesbauernschaft* Silesia, 22 April 1934, ibid.; Seifert to *Landesbauernschaft* Baden, 18 September 1934, ibid.; Seifert to *Landesbauernschaft* Baden, 9 October 1934, ibid.; Reich Food Estate, The Reich Commissioner for Regulating the Sales of Garden Products, to Seifert, 17 December 1934, SN 155. The garden architect Pniower, who in 1931 had advocated the planting of roadways, was also not involved in the autobahnen. Wolschke-Bulmahn suspects there were political and racial reasons behind it. Joachim Wolschke-Bulmahn, "Political Landscapes and Technology: Nazi Germany and the Landscape Design of the *Reichsautobahnen* (Reich Motor Highways)," *Council of Educators in Landscape Architecture (CELA) Annual Conference Papers* VII (1995): 157–170, 159. See chapter 4, section *The failed autobahn project of the interwar period*.

47. Seifert to Directorate *Reichsautobahnen*, Rudolphi, 2 November 1934, SN 204; Klenke, "Autobahnbau und Naturschutz," 476.

48. Seifert to Directorate *Reichsautobahnen*, Director Hof, 23 February 1934, SN 204; Directorate *Reichsautobahnen* to the heads of the regional planning offices, 7 December 1934, BAK R 65II/16 (criticism of the price per kilometer of 750,000 Reichsmark).

49. The men hired were Otto Rindt (regional planning office Halle) and Kern (regional planning office Kassel). Inspector-General, Schönleben, to Directorate *Reichsautobahnen*, 21 January 1937, SN 116; Seifert to Directorate *Reichsautobahnen*, 10 February 1934 und 23 February 1934, SN 204; Directorate *Reichsautobahnen* to all regional planning offices, 16 May 1934, ibid.; Seifert to the landscape advocates, 7 July 1934, SN 116.

50. Directorate *Reichsautobahnen* to Inspector-General, 16 July 1934 (copy), SN 116; Inspector-General, Schönleben, to Directorate *Reichsautobahnen*, 13 August 1934, ibid.; Inspector-General, Circular No. 134, 4 September 1934, ibid.; Directorate *Reichsautobahnen* to all regional planning offices, 21 December 1934; Seifert to Schönleben, 31 August 1934 ([added by hand] "Todt Herrn Rudolfi" [sic], n.d.), BAP 46.01/1487; Directorate *Reichsautobahnen* to Inspector-General for the German Roads, 5 December 1935, SN 116; Payment to the experts for landscape consultation (garden designers) for the months May-September 1935, ibid.; Payment to the experts for landscape consultation (garden designers) 22 June 1936, SN 117; Directorate *Reichsautobahnen* to Inspector-General for the German Roads, 5 December 1935 (addendum to Seifert) SN 116; Seifert to Directorate *Reichsautobahnen*, 8 July 1935, SN 204; Directorate *Reichsautobahnen* to Inspector-General, 5 December 1934, SN 116.

51. Inspector-General file note, re: Expenses for landscape consultation of the *Reichsautobahn*, 5 June 1936, SN 116. Schönleben considered this third way the best. Inspector-General, Schönleben, to Seifert, 14 June 1936, ibid.

52. Directorate *Reichsautobahnen* to all regional planning offices (telegram letter), 30 May 1936, SN 116; Inspector-General, Schönleben, to Seifert, 6 June 1936, ibid.; Directorate *Reichsautobahnen* to all regional planning offices, 6 June 1936, ibid.

53. Seifert to Inspector-General, Schönleben, 17 June 1936, SN 116; Seifert to Directorate of the Society *Reichsautobahnen*, 26 June 1936, ibid.; Seifert to the landscape advocates, 9 June 1936, ibid.; Inspector-General, Schönleben, to Seifert, 18 July 1936, ibid.; Directorate *Reichsautobahnen* to Inspector-General, 14 July 1936 (copy), ibid.; Seifert to Meyer-Jungclaussen, 18 August 1936, SN 138.

54. Seifert to Todt, 24 July 1936, SN 116.

55. Seifert to Reich Chamber of the Visual Arts, 4 August 1936, SN 116; President of the Reich Chamber of the Fine Arts to the Inspector-General for German Roads, 3 September 1936,

ibid.; Seifert to the Inspector-General for German Roads, 5 August 1936, ibid.; Seifert to the landscape advocates, 18 August 1936, ibid.; Schönleben to Directorate *Reichsautobahnen*, 9 October 1936, ibid.; Seifert to Schönleben, n.d. (copy), in Circular, 8 September 1941, addendum 7, fol. 13, SN 118; Inspector-General, Schulze-Fielitz, to Seifert, 4 May 1942, AGM File "Landscape Advocates Beginning Dec. 1941."
56. Note, Ministerial Councilor Willuhn, 3 November 1934, *Akten der Reichskanzlei*, vol. II 1934/35, Part II, Munich 1999, 146–148. On Hitler's decree ibid., 148, note 5.
57. It was not necessary, Seifert wrote to one landscape advocate, to send him all reports, "except in cases where you cannot get anywhere with the regional planning office." Seifert to Stück, 13 December 1934, SN 155.
58. Schneider to Seifert, 30 June 1934, SN 146; Schneider to Seifert, 12 July 1934, ibid.; Schneider to Seifert, 17 July 1934, ibid.
59. Seifert to Rudolphi, 2 November 1934, SN 204; Schneider to Seifert, 13 November 1934, SN 146; Schneider to Todt via Seifert, 15 December 1934, SN 146.
60. Meyer-Jungclaussen to Seifert, 3 June 1934, 11 July 1936, and 16 August 1936, SN 138; Seifert to Meyer-Jungclaussen, 17 July 1936 and 18 August 1936, ibid. In the fall of 1936, he was facing his imminent dismissal: Meyer-Jungclaussen to Schönleben, 1 November 1936, BAP 46.01/863.
61. Seifert to Siegloch, 11 May 1938, SN 153; Siegloch to Seifert, 25 June 1938 and 15 September 1934, ibid.
62. Schwarz to Seifert, 20 December 1934, SN 150; Schneider to Seifert, 15 December 1934, 22 December 1934, 11 May 1935, 22 August 1935, 13 October 1935, and 17 December 1935, SN 146; Seifert to Schneider, 22 January 1935, ibid.
63. Schneider to Seifert, 28 May 1937 and 18 March 1938, SN 146.
64. Otto Kurz, "Landscape design on the Reichsautobahn. Redacted as a report on the activity as landscape advocate of the Reichsautobahn section Augsburg-Ulm in the years 1936–1939, with general observations and conclusions, which lead to programmatic demands for the future of landscape design beyond the framework of the Reichsautobahn," SN 508/5, 4, 5, 17; *Reichsautobahnen* regional planning office Hamburg to Schwarz, 27 December 1939 (copy), SN 117; Todt to the heads of the regional planning offices, 5 January 1940 (copy), ibid.; Seifert to Schönleben, 23 January 1940, ibid.
65. Kurz, "Bericht," SN 508/5, 29, 18, 21–23.
66. Seifert to Inspector-General, Schönleben, 6 May 1936, BAP 46.01/862; Seifert to Todt, 15 August 1938, ibid.
67. Seifert had to put an end even to trivial things: it was only at the end of 1935 that the landscape advocates were released from the obligation to submit two prints of every photograph they took along the segment to the regional planning office. Directorate *Reichsautobahnen* to the regional planning offices, 16 November 1935 (copy), SN 116; Kurz, "Bericht," SN 508/5, 18; Seifert, *Leben*, 89. It is revealing how Seifert adopted the key concept of nativist landscape thinking—"Eigenart"—to describe a human conflict.
68. Herbert Mehrtens, "Kollaborationsverhältnisse: Natur- und Technikwissenschaften im NS-Staat und ihre Historie," in *Medizin, Naturwissenschaft, Technik und Nationalsozialismus. Kontinuitäten und Diskontinuitäten*, ed. Christoph Meinel and Peter Voswinckel (Stuttgart, 1994), 13–32, 26. The social Darwinist interpretation has been successfully applied to Hitler in the scholarship: Kershaw, *Nazi Dictatorship*, 84.
69. The following working meetings are documented: 16–18 June 1934 in Munich with a subsequent mountain excursion (Seifert to Siegloch, 6 June 1934, SN 153), 29/30 October 1934 in Heidelberg (Seifert to the landscape advocates, 21 October 1934, SN 116), 1–3 July 1935 in Munich (Seifert to Inspector-General, Huber, 11 June 1935, SN 51), 24–26 February 1936 in Munich (Invitation to the meeting, SN 51), 9–12 October 1936 in Bad Segeberg (Schönleben to Society *Reichsautobahn*, 9 October 1936, SN 116), 20 August 1938 in Essen, following the International Congress of Garden Designers (Seifert to Schönleben, 5 August 1938, SN 116),

15–17 September 1938 at the Technical University in Munich (Meeting of the landscape consultants for the *Reichsautobahnen*, Reich, and State Roads, SN 116), 27/28 July 1939 in Stuttgart (Seifert to the landscape advocates, 23 June 1939, SN 116), 10/11 September 1940 in the maintenance facility by the Rauz Alp on the Arlberg Mountain in Austria (Program of Meeting SN 54), 31 January –2 February 1942 in Munich (Program of the Meeting SN 55), und Fall 1942 at Plassenburg Castle, the "Reich School of German Technology" (Seifert to Mrass, 9 April 1967, SN 200). Ludwig, *Technik und Ingenieure*, 172; Guse, "Spirit of the Plassenburg"; Todt to Seifert, 18 January 1935 und 11 February 1935, SN 212; Seifert to Todt, 6 February 1935, ibid.; Seifert to Research Society for Roads (Forschungsgesellschaft für das Straßenwesen), 1 April 1935, ibid.; Ehrtfried Böhm et al., *Straßenforschung. 50 Jahre Forschungsgesellschaft für das Straßenwesen 1924–1974* (Bonn-Bad Godesberg, 1974), 64, 335, 341.

70. Walter Mrass, *Die Organisation des staatlichen Naturschutzes und der Landschaftspflege im Deutschen Reich und in der Bundesrepublik Deutschland seit 1935, gemessen to den Aufgabenstellungen einer modernen Industriegesellschaft* (Stuttgart, 1970), 17; Seifert to the landscape advocates, 8 September 1939 and 9 September 1939, SN 116; Hirsch to the landscape advocates, 8 September 1939, ibid.
71. Hirsch, "Liebe Kameraden!," 5 October 1939, SN 116; Hirsch, "Liebe Kameraden," Third Sunday of Advent 1939, ibid.
72. Seifert, "Meine Kameraden!," 22 December 1939, SN 116.
73. Wilhelm Hübotter, Circular, 8 December 1941, fol. 4, SN 119.
74. Circular, June 1942, SN 118; Circular, 30 October 1943, SN 119; Circular, 11 December 1944, ibid.
75. For an example of such a conflict-oriented environmental history see Ulrich Linse et al., *Von der Bittschrift zur Platzbesetzung. Konflikte um technische Großprojekte. Laufen, Walchensee, Wyhl, Wackersdorf* (Berlin and Bonn, 1988). Schütz and Gruber mention an internal clash between Todt and Georg Halter, Professor of Highway Construction and Railroads at the Technical University in Munich, who spoke critically about the autobahn and was silenced by Todt: Schütz and Gruber, *Mythos*, 20–22.
76. Seifert, *Leben*, 46; Wettengel, "Staat und Naturschutz," 365–367.
77. Karl Ditt, "Nature Conservation in England and Germany, 1900–1970: Forerunners of Environmental Protection?," *Contemporary European History* 5 (1996): 1–28; Williams, "Chords of the German Soul;" Matthew Jefferies, "Heimatschutz: Environmental Activism in Wilhelmine Germany," in *Green Thought in German Culture. Historical and Contemporary Perspectives*, ed. Colin Riordan (Cardiff, 1997), 43–54; Rollins, *Greener Vision*; Wettengel, "Staat und Naturschutz," 372–380.
78. Schoenichen to Todt, 29 December 1933, BAP 46.01/1486. The handwritten note is dated 30 January. Upon his request, Schoenichen later received memoranda on landscape design. Schoenichen to Inspector-General, 21 March 1936, BAP 46.01/137/2, fol. 126.
79. Carl Heicke, "Die Hafraba im Gebiet von Frankfurt am Main," BAP 46.01/1487. Another copy in SN 130; Heicke to Seifert, 4 January 1934, ibid.
80. Heicke, "Hafraba," 4, 5, and 10; Seifert to Todt, 24 January 1934, BAP 46.01/1487; Seifert to Heicke, 29 January 1934, SN 130. Heicke and Seifert knew each other from the Association of German Landscape Designers.
81. Wettengel, "Staat und Naturschutz," 371; Mrass, *Organisation des staatlichen Naturschutzes*, 40, note 101; Gerhard Trommer, *Natur im Kopf. Die Geschichte ökologisch bedeutsamer Naturvorstellungen in deutschen Bildungskonzepten*, 2nd ed. (Weinheim, 1993).
82. On Schwenkel's accommodation to National Socialism see Gert Gröning and Joachim Wolschke, "Naturschutz und Ökologie im Nationalsozialismus," *Die alte Stadt* 10 (1983): 1–17, 4–5; Schwenkel to Seifert, 26 March 1934, SN 153; Seifert to Schwenkel, 28 March 1934, ibid.; NSDAP Gau Württemberg-Hohenzollern, *Gau* Culture Warden, to Seifert, 16 April 1934, SN 153; Seifert to NSDAP Gau Württemberg-Hohenzollern, 13 April 1934, ibid.; Siegloch to Seifert, 28 April 1934, ibid.; Seifert to Siegloch, 2 May 1934, ibid.

83. Schwenkel to Ministry of Culture of Württemberg, 12 July 1934 (copy), SN 153; Directorate *Reichsautobahnen* to Inspector-General for German Roads, 21 January 1938, BAK R 65II/136.
84. Seifert to Schwenkel, 5 August 1940, 22 August 1940, and 20 January 1942, SN 208; Siegloch to Seifert, 25 February 1935, 6 March 1935, and 16 March 1935, SN 153; Seifert to Inspector-General, Schönleben, 24 May 1939, ibid.; Mrass, *Organisation*, 17.
85. Schwarz to regional planning office Altona, 23 October 1935 (copy), BAP 46.01/861; Seifert to Schwarz, BAP 46.01/864.
86. Reich Food Estate, Reich Farmers' Leader, to Todt, 4 February 1936 (copy), SN 150; Todt to Schwarz, 15 February 1936, ibid.; Schwarz to Todt, 20 February 1936, ibid.
87. Josef Urban, "Die geplante Reichsautobahnbrücke über das Kleinziegenfelder Tal. Zur Geschichte des Natur- und Landschaftsschutzes im Landkreis Lichtenfels," *Vom Main zum Jura* 3 (1986): 59–87, 76; Thomas Adam, "Parallele Wege. Geschichtsvereinigungen und Naturschutzbewegung in Deutschland," *Geschichte in Wissenschaft und Unterricht* 48 (1997): 413–428. Unsuccessful admonitions of the landscape advocate are chronicled in Franz Semlinger, *Die Autobahn von Hienberg bis Nürnberg. Bau und Bedeutung 1934 bis heute* (Neunkirchen am Sand, 1998), 155–157.
88. District Office for Nature Protection in the region of the Settlement Association Ruhr coal district in Essen. Annual report for fiscal year 1934/35, 8 May 1935, BAK R41/74 fol. 70–71; District Office for Nature Protection, Wishes of the District Office for the landscaping of the *Reichsautobahnen* that traverse the region of our Office, 14 May 1934, SN 126; Erxleben to Seifert, 22 May 1934 and 22 February 1935, ibid.; Erxleben to regional planning office Essen (copy), 26 July 1935, ibid.; Erxleben to Seifert, 26 July 1935, ibid.; Seifert to Schwenkel, 20 January 1942, SN 208.
89. Thomas M. Lekan, "Regionalism and the Politics of Landscape Preservation in the Third Reich," *Environmental History* 4 (1999): 384–404; idem, *Imagining the Nation*, ch. 5. The autobahn project as a whole was clearly characterized by centralized plans, often without any regard for local situations. For one example, where a route cut through the middle of a village, see Helmut Meißner, "Das Leiden eines Dorfes unter dem Großprojekt eines Diktators: Der Bau der Reichsautobahn Berlin–München vor 60 Jahren mitten durch den Ort Lanzendorf," *Geschichte am Obermain* 21 (1997/98): 103–122.
90. Mrass, *Organisation des staatlichen Naturschutzes*, 17. On bridges see British Intelligence Sub-Committee, *German Autobahn Bridges* (London, n.d.); Rainer Stommer, "Triumph der Technik. Autobahnbrücken zwischen Ingenieuraufgabe und Kulturdenkmal," in Stommer, *Reichsautobahn*, 49–76, Hartmut Frank, "Bridges: Paul Bonatz's Search for a Contemporary Monumental Style," in *The Nazification of Art. Art, Design, Music, Architecture and Film in the Third Reich*, ed. Brandon Taylor and Wilfried van der Will (Winchester, 1990), 144–157.
91. Kopper, *Modernität*; Marcel Herzberg, *Raumordnung im nationalsozialistischen Deutschland* (Dortmund, 1997); Rudolf Hoffmann, "Neue verkehrs- und raumpolitische Entwicklungen," *Raumforschung und Raumordnung* no. 11 (1937): 455–462, 461; idem, "Aktive Verkehrs- und Raumpolitik," *Raumforschung und Raumordnung* no. 4 (1937): 148–156; File note Kerrl, Oct. 1937, and Expert Opinion Land Planning Association (*Landesplanungsgemeinschaft*) Rheinland, BAK R 113/1619; Inspector-General, Schönleben, to Reich Office for Area Planning, 9 Oct. 1939, BAK R 113/1621.
92. Michael Prinz, "Die soziale Funktion moderner Elemente in der Gesellschaftspolitik des Nationalsozialismus," in *Nationalsozialismus und Modernisierung*, ed. Michael Prinz and Rainer Zitelmann (Darmstadt, 1991), 297–327, here 315 (older view); Wettengel, "Staat und Naturschutz," 382–387; Konrad Ott et al., "Über die Anfänge des Naturschutzgedankens in Deutschland und den USA im 19. Jahrhundert," in *Naturnutzung und Naturschutz in der europäischen Rechts- und Verwaltungsgeschichte*, ed. Erk Volkmar Heyen (Baden-Baden, 1999), 1–56; Karl Ditt, "The Perception and Conservation of Nature in the Third Reich," *Planning Perspectives* 15 (2000): 161–187; Williams, "Chords," 377–378; Charles Closmann, "Legaliz-

ing a *Volksgemeinschaft*: Nazi Germany's Reich Nature Protection Law of 1935," in *How Green Were the Nazis?*, 18–42.
93. File note Schönleben, 12 April 1935, BAP 46.01/2070.
94. Inspector-General, file note re: landscape design, 23 December 1935 [author not identifiable], BAP 46.01/861. Emphasis original.
95. Schoenichen to Reich Forestry Minister, 14 April 1937, BAK B 245/170, fols. 395–401, 397, 400–401.
96. Schwenkel to Seifert (confidential!), 18 February 1937, SN 208.
97. Seifert to Master Forester Graser, Weimar, 31 March 1944, AGM Waldbau after 1943; Seifert, *Leben*, 68–70; "Merkblatt II vom 12. Januar 1935 Betr. Mutterbodenbewirtschaftung beim Bau der Reichsautobahnen," *Die Straße* 2 (1935): 62.
98. Manfred Seifert, *Kulturarbeit im Reichsarbeitsdienst. Theorie und Praxis nationalsozialistischer Kulturpflege im Kontext historisch-politischer, organisatorischer und ideologischer Einflüsse* (Münster and New York, 1996).

Chapter 6

THE MYTH OF THE GREEN AUTOBAHN

Road alignment as a subject of controversy

Herr Alwin Seifert planted little trees from a true miracle tree./His curly head started wobbling, thus "nature" became his occupation./A mountain rose, the road it forked, with a gentle declination / Todt yelled when he beheld the marvel: "You all belong to Dachau, yes / had I to see a road like this, I'd start to rebuild it. / The curves they are much too crooked, it's not crooked, it's stupid! / The roadway is confusing, no reasonable person can drive it." / So we listened to his words and gave the line a gentle bend. / And thus the first autobahn arrived safely in Munich's hall."[1]

The grim humor of this awkward poem conveys an impression of how heated the controversies over the roads in Nazi Germany could be behind the scenes. This chapter will examine the role and extent of these controversies. The plotting of the roads in the landscape, referred to by civil engineers as alignment, had been a topic of publications on conservation and landscape issues long before the building of the *Reichsautobahnen*. The sinuous line that, as we have seen, Schultze-Naumburg preferred for roads outside the flat countryside was more difficult for landscape architects to push through than the ideological intermingling of *Heimatschutz* and National Socialism would have led one to expect.[2] In contrast to such architectural ideals, nineteenth-century straight and level railroad tracks were anchored in the awareness of the garden architects as a visible example of geometric traffic routes. William George Hoskins and Wolfgang Schivelbusch have described the routing of the railroad as a "geometrization of the landscape": cuts, tunnels, and embankments were to allow for the straightest possible lines.

Notes for this section begin on page 172.

Especially in Great Britain, pioneers of the railroad pushed for routes with few inclines so as not to overstrain the weak engines. That goal was achieved through massive excavation work. The experience of a journey in compartments moving horizontally has come to be referred to (using Schivelbusch's phrase) as "panoramic travel": the foreground of the landscape flying by at great speed became a blur, while the eye focused on the background. The other reaction was boredom, which was relieved with new kinds of travel literature.[3]

When the second modern network of long-distance routes was built in the form of the autobahnen, the railroads presented the negative design foil, as it were. "The routing has to be designed differently for the automobile than for the railroad. The railroad is a medium for mass transit (also for masses of people). The roadway is a medium for individual transport. The train is usually a foreign body in the landscape. The motor roadway is and remains a road, and the road is part and parcel of the landscape. The German landscape is full of character. The motor roadway, too, must be given German character." With these words Todt had outlined his aesthetic credo at the presentation of the autobahn network in January 1934 to Hitler. The contrast between the railroad as leveling mass transportation and the automobile as a vehicle of social separation had already marked the bourgeois auto literature at the turn of the century, which equated the individuality of transport with the individuality of the person. Todt was trying to translate the "attraction of the independent journey at a person's whim" into an attractiveness of the roadways built specifically for the car. Moreover, in a nationalized context, landscape offered itself as a nexus between the driver and the environment. Individual traffic allowed for active traveling; motorists could recapture the foreground that was lost in railroad travel. "The panoramatic experience on the train was replaced by the 'feasibility' of the experience of landscape," as one historian observed with respect to the automobilists of the early twentieth century. They praised the car as a return to a landscape individually appropriated, as a self-guided experience of nature.[4]

Some twenty years later, in the Germany of the 1930s, the relationship with the automobile was increasingly redefined. Use of a private car no longer fulfilled only purposes of luxury, adventure, and sport, but was increasingly subordinated to other purposes as a mere transportation device. The car and its use became increasingly quotidian—after all, the motorization offensive launched by the Nazi regime was aimed precisely at making private motor vehicles commonplace. The subsequent failure of this project made little difference to the perception of this profound change in those years. Concomitantly, mass use raised questions of safety. While the early phase in the appropriation of the automobile had been characterized by a preference for unpredictability and risk, automotive safety and accident avoidance became relatively more important in this decade—namely in the interplay of motor vehicle and road.[5] One observer noted how the new roads were devoid of the distractions of the old ones, thus making them safer:

The old highway offered so much diversion: there were villages, cities, sharp curves, wild ascents, switchbacks, the alternation of good and not-so-good roads, bicyclists, horse-drawn carts, herds of sheep—all things that may have sometimes been enjoyable for the sporty, 'proper' gentleman driver, but which were and no doubt still are interfering obstacles for the professional driver.[6]

Restrictions on access to driving through driver's licenses and traffic education were intended to enhance safety, as were the separation of types of traffic in the cities and the dedication of roads exclusively to cars on the autobahnen.[7] One autobahn propagandist already articulated the functioning of the road, its availability at all times, and its potential for speeding up travel as a civic claim: "The automobile is a *means of transportation*. When I get into my compact car in Heppenheim a.[n] d.[er] B.[ergstraße] [a town near Heidelberg], I want to be in Berlin at five in the evening, and along the way I want to have breakfast in Fulda and lunch in Naumburg. That is my perfectly good right. Our German cars can accomplish that today. Germany has become *automobile-friendly*. We have an *Inspector-General* who is providing us with *good roads*. But what is the reason if I am not in Berlin on time at five in the evening? It is only *road closings* and *detours*."[8]

Individual consumption and emphasis on personal will gave rise to an attitude of entitlement vis-à-vis the state, whose duties evidently included providing an uninterrupted and safe infrastructure of roads. Certain technical parameters, such as a route that had the fewest possible curves or was "sinuous," could thus be presented in the rhetorical clashes as either promoting or detracting from safety. All these factors resonated when Todt postulated the "German character" of the roads. It was not clear, though, what kind of technical parameters this entailed; in this regard, Todt offered no definitions, only ideologically underpinned encouragement. The details of road design were a bone of contention between engineers and landscape architects, and it is to these clashes over the alignment of the roads that I will turn next.

In looking at this controversy, it is necessary to distinguish between the engineers of the Inspector-General's office and those of the regional planning offices, whose differing professional and ideological agendas were examined above. The landscape advocates, on their part, had a predilection for sinuous routes, that is, roads that ran through the landscape in sweeping curves. The basic assumption is that we are dealing with a process of negotiation between the two groups of experts, the civil engineers and the landscape architects. The arguments that were traded back and forth in the process can be separated into aesthetic and functional ones, though at the time they were often mixed together.

As we have seen, the detailed plans produced by the lobbying work of the Hafraba Association served as the basis for the initial road planning in building the *Reichsautobahnen*. Those plans envisaged straightaways four or five kilometers long, connected with circular arcs and short transition curves, following standard designs for railway tracks. As the regime was eager to show some quick successes, these sections were realized first in their existing form. After the Berlin office had made decisions about the rough plans, these were sent to the respective regional planning offices to be transformed into construction-ready blueprints. In the process, the civil engineers of the German Railroad preferred, as a design tool, the Hafraba model of long straightaways with short transition curves. One engineer who came out of the road administration recalled in his autobiography that his colleagues rejected other forms as "interruption."[9]

In the beginning, the fast construction pace did not change these attitudes in any way. It would appear that the routing of the very first sections was drawn up without consulting the landscape advocates. In an essay about this work, the landscape advocate for the first section Frankfurt-Darmstadt, Hirsch, said nothing about having influenced the routing. Instead, he spoke of having improved the "wounded edges of the forests" with plantings, and having accommodated embankments and cuts into the landscape through gentle transitions: "And so pictures and spaces gradually took shape—time and again, the work was improved as it unfolded." His words point to occasional opportunities for improvement against a backdrop of unchangeable, fundamental parameters when it came to routing. Figure 6.1 shows an aerial view of this straight autobahn section with a short transition curve.[10]

Figure 6.1 One of the most hotly debated questions regarding the design of the autobahn was whether it should be built with long straightaways or in sinous, sweeping curves. While the propaganda claimed that the roads were integrated into the landscape following the latter pattern, most of the early autobahn stretches resembled this picture: Long straight sections were connected with short curves. The aerial view shows the autobahn from Frankfurt/Main to Darmstadt.
Otto Reismann, *Deutschlands Autobahnen—Adolf Hitlers Straßen* (Bayreuth: Gauverlag Bayerische Ostmark, 1937), 144.

Apart from the dictatorship's desire to open partial sections as quickly as possible, another factor contributed to making the succession of straightaways and circulars the predominant form that the *Reichsautobahnen* assumed in the initial phase. As a result of the institutional integration of the Inspector-General's office and the Association *Reichsautobahnen* with the German Railroad, the majority of the staff on the regional planning offices came from the personnel of the German Railroad. Of the fifteen regional planning offices that existed on the territory of the Reich in 1935, thirteen were headed by engineers with the titles *Reichsbahnoberräte* or directors with the Reich Railroad; two of the heads were *Oberbauräte*, thus indicating a non-railway career.[11]

Given their training and professional background, the railway engineers tended to design the road similar to a railroad, aiming for long, straight sections whenever topographically possible. During the first years of construction, the Reich Railroad engineers received support from Todt himself in their use of long straightaways—in spite of his rhetoric, which was generally directed against the railroad. The question of whether the roads should be laid out as straight as possible or with a sinuous line was hotly debated between landscape advocates and the Inspector-General. At stake in the issue for the consultants was their participation in the power to define the design of the autobahnen; one of them emphasized that "our most important work on the autobahn is tracing out the route, since a route that is alien to the landscape can never be corrected with plantings after the fact." Another landscape advocate seconded that view, arguing that it was absolutely necessary for the individual consultants to be able to contribute their suggestions on the routing as early as possible. Seifert had demanded in June 1934 that the landscape architects traverse the segment with the civil engineer in charge on foot, and that they decide with him where in the landscape the autobahn should be laid out, where bridges and embankments should be built, and where rest areas and gas stations should be located.[12]

In the face of the impending loss of influence, Seifert therefore worked that much harder against the long straightaway as a routing element. He considered it an abomination: in his eyes, the straight *Reichsautobahn* route was simply not appropriate to the landscape. The straightaway was not of the earth, but something from outer space. Old roads with long straightaways were either "constructed along the sightlines of that age-old cultic placement that once covered all of central Europe," or they were un-German (*volksfremd*) structures imposed from the outside. The more a road's sinuous curves were nestled into the millennia-old bends of the landscape, the more it was in tune with the landscape, and the smaller was the necessary excavating work and the required number of embankments and dams. For each technical task, and thus also for the routing of the *Reichsautobahn*, there was an "entirely perfect, indeed, an elegant solution" that was determined by laws. Those laws, however, could only be intuited "in a kind of nature perception that can express itself only as a feeling." Seifert's virulent antirationalism was clearly on display here. Since it was clear to him that the design characteristics of the roads must be derived from their surrounding landscape, the option of straight roads was out of the question. Such roads were alien to nature, an argument whose fundamentalness was beyond challenge.

The categorical imperative of this view prompted an equally categorical response from Todt.[13] In the debate with the Inspector-General, the argument shifted to seemingly anthropological terrain. Both Seifert and Todt were competing over the "nature" of man as it expressed itself in the operation of a car. Seifert, at any rate, could claim functionality on his side when he wrote to Todt that long straightaways were not suitable to man, "for reasons having to do with human nature." Monotonousness quickly made people tired, which is why the danger of deadly accidents was great on routes with few curves. Seifert therefore proposed to build the autobahn with sweeping curves. Todt did not want to open the door to such changes in 1935 and resorted in turn to comparisons from the animal world: "After all, the motor vehicle is not a rabbit or a deer that jumps around the terrain in winding and twisting lines, but is a technological artifact that was created by man and demands a suitable driving surface," he wrote to Seifert. At nighttime and in foggy conditions, it was difficult for drivers to get their bearings on long, sweeping curves. The Inspector-General continued the nature analogies and compared the "fast motor vehicles to the water strider or other skipping insects who cover smaller partial sections in straight lines and then change their direction from point to point." Seifert responded in the context of this naturalization that "no life form" could propel itself in a straight line. This merely confirmed his view that the straight line was of cosmic origin and not of this earth.[14]

As we have seen, Seifert's passionate opposition to the straight line was based on his aesthetic preferences. In his rhetorical competition with Todt over the question of what accorded best with a road's "German character" he enlisted analogies from nature, which were evidently supposed to be applied directly to the driver of a car. His characterization of the straight line as extraterrestrial had to meet with dissent from Todt, who held a doctorate in engineering. He rejected Seifert's expansive holism and sought instead to define the "nature" of the motorist.[15]

What the two men shared, however, was general suppositions about driving that they derived from various sources: Seifert from "cosmic" ideas, Todt from no less fundamental propositions of experience that were evidently based on his own or observed driving and were covered with a mantle of general validity that was not questioned. The question of whether long straightaways were particularly safe or unsafe was controversial also among engineers. For the most part, however, safety or the lack thereof was postulated rather than proved. Seifert could thus leap into an opening when he combined design and safety into a single argument in favor of his sinuous layout. Incidentally, the effect of long straightaways on traffic safety remained a contested issue for some time: in the United States, the New Jersey Turnpike that was opened in 1951 was built as straight as possible to reduce the number of accidents. Today, however, it is precisely the straightest sections of the U.S. interstate network that are considered the most accident-prone.[16]

In the correspondence with Todt about concrete segments, Seifert transformed these fundamental arguments of *Weltanschauung* into observations about spatial effect and safety. On the Lauterbach-Odelzhausen stretch of the autobahn connecting Munich and Augsburg, a long straightaway of up to eight kilometers "was entirely appropriate to this level landscape." However, because of the meager plantings provided for in the plans, it would take seventy to eighty years before the desired spatial impression was created. But it alone made possible a "certain feeling of security and thus good driving"; without that feeling, it would require constant attention to stay on the straight roadway. Seifert went on to transfer this level of unverifiable feeling to the only slightly more secure category of safety. What remained unmentioned in the background was the notion of a pleasurable trip on the autobahnen with little traffic. Carefree locomotion via the automobile implied here as the goal was more in the category of a bourgeois pleasure outing than purposeful transportation. If constant attention was described as something to be avoided, it meant that the density of traffic had to be simultaneously very low.[17]

The uncertainty over the "appropriate" routing thus reflected the uncertainty over the purpose of the *Reichsautobahnen*. A mixture of various elements was chosen for the autobahn as well as for its technical parameters. Characteristic for this mix of contradictions is a decree of September 1935 from the office of the Inspector-General to the Directorate *Reichsautobahnen*. While it described severely straight segments as undesirable because they were tiring, their upper limit was set at four kilometers, which was still far more than the landscape advocates deemed appropriate.[18]

On the question of straight or "sinuous" roads, the interests and the possibilities of exerting influence were thus variously distributed. Whereas the engineers of the regional planning offices sought to reduce the technical parameters to the simplest possible link of longer straightaways and short circular arcs, and wished to stick to this given the pace of construction, the attitude within the superordinated office of the Inspector-General was not uniform. While Todt initially defended straightaways against the landscape advocates, his deputy Schönleben sought to at least restrict them in official guidelines beginning in 1935, at the latest. The landscape architects, meanwhile, were interested in curvy roads, which they sought to push through with nonnegotiable aesthetic criteria. They underpinned their primarily aesthetically motivated thinking with safety arguments only when their initial attempts were thwarted by the maze of the organization.

In this quarrel, which was carried on in part via private correspondence and in part via articles and essays, Todt retained the power to define what was an appropriate road. The first sections of the *Reichsautobahnen* were built following the pattern straightaway-circular arc-straightaway, which Seifert mockingly referred to as "zigzag," and still today they stand as lapidary witnesses to the early thinking that created these roads. Although Seifert's vigorous campaign for a sinuous line was published in Todt's house organ *Die Straße*, the Inspector-General did not exert corresponding pressure on the regional planning offices. Instead, the office of the Inspector-General issued general appeals to the civil engineers to see the routing as a "creative act." The job of laying out the road was the "most wonderful and rewarding" task for a highway engineer. In fact, civil engineers were largely given a free hand in this call for creativity: it was impossible to specify routing elements such as the radius of the curvature or of the transition curve in every case; rather, laying out the road presupposed less a knowledge of technical parameters than a feel for the landscape and respect for nature.

At first glance, such a published directive reveals the complexity of the hectic construction phase in the beginning. While Todt long felt that straightaways were appropriate to human nature, his deputy called for a less formulaic approach to the routing of the roads. However, one must bear in mind that a process of feeling nature might very well end up with a straight road. While Todt's views described a general goal, the publications in *Die Straße* explained a method that would establish design as a creative act. In reality, though, the solutions to the routing were often subject to other criteria: because the high pace of construction was maintained, engineers fell back on existing plans.[19]

That the designs for the roads were supposed to be simultaneously subjected to at least the beginnings of a standardized approach with the help of guidelines further reveals the heterogeneous nature of the methodological canon. Geometric routing principles for the *Reichsautobahnen* were published in May 1934, spring 1936, early 1937, and even as late as 1943, following the cessation of construction work. However, they did not recommend specific lengths for straightaways, but stipulated the minimum radius for circular arcs. The minimum radius of two-thousand meters in the very first plans (evidently adopted from the Hafraba blueprints) was differentiated in May 1934, depending on the topographical conditions. Up to two-thousand meters was stipulated for level segments, up to one-thousand meters for "segments that had to accommodate the terrain of the landscape or a densely built-up area," and up to one-thousand meters for mountainous roads. In this last category, the threshold was lowered further to six-hundred meters, and it could even go as low as four- hundred meters. How nonobligatory such publications were is revealed not only by construction practice, but also by Schönleben's above-quoted call for the greatest possible creativity.[20]

Very informative sources exist on the extent of the first *Reichsautobahnen*, which were planned and built with long straightaways. A publication by the German Federal Ministry of Transportation in the mid-1970s spoke of "around two-thousand kilometers of well laid-out autobahnen" prior to 1945. If we compare this to a total length of 3,625 kilometers reported by the Nazi government for Germany and Austria, it would mean that about one-thousand-six-hundred kilometers were not "well laid-out," meaning that they were built according to the *Reichsbahn* model. If we add the eight-hundred kilometers of unfinished projects left behind as construction sites in 1942, the total length of autobahnen that were aesthetically unsatisfying rises to about two-thousand-four-hundred kilometers. One could object that these figures are estimates and were made after the fact. In a contemporaneous letter to a *Gau* chief, Seifert explained in more detail that "the first sections of the *Reichsautobahn* were laid out essentially after railroad ideas."

In 1943, that is, one year after the end of construction work, he listed specifically the sections Frankfurt-Darmstadt, Berlin-Stettin, Berlin-Magdeburg, Hamburg-Bremen, Munich-Mangfall Bridge, and Breslau-Liegnitz. That would add up to merely 476 kilometers of railroad-like sections. At the same time, Seifert noted that the curvy form of the road did not become fully established until 1939. Since three-thousand kilometers of autobahn were open to traffic by the end of 1938, we can assume that somewhere between five-hundred and three-thousand kilometers of the *Reichsautobahnen* had been built contrary to the design that the landscape advocates and parts of Todt's agency had in mind.[21]

A report from the regional planning office in Berlin in 1939 reveals just how much the curvy lines were initially scorned. The report apologetically listed the reasons why a "partial curving of the route through the terrain was unavoidable" on the Reppen segment of the road from Frankfurt/Oder to Posen. In the beginning, the road builders certainly did allow approaches to a "sinuous" routing on individual road segments, but they wanted to make sure that the highway kept the upper hand over the landscape. An excessive adaptation of the gradient was inconsistent with the width of the autobahn, noted deputy Schönleben from the office of the Inspector-General in an internal directive. The 24-meter-wide roads had a "certain momentum of aesthetic inertia" that permitted only minor bends in the horizontal and vertical. If this law is ignored, the autobahn will look "crooked or bent. ... The autobahn should not do violence to the landscape, but in my view, majesty cannot tolerate being subject or secondary to the landscape in all things." Tests on partial segments from Hamburg to Bremen, which had avoided a frequent change in the gradient and alleviated cuts into the landscape with flattened embankments, turned out to be also "economically very favorable."[22]

Following this turbulent phase of experimentation on the ground, the sinuous forms in the layout of the routes prevailed after 1939, at the latest. The primary reasons were the greater aesthetic landscape effect of the curves, and an unexpectedly large number of serious accidents on the *Reichsautobahnen*, which builders hoped to counteract with curves. It was only the combination of both arguments—presumed safety and a more effective staging of the landscape—that led to success from the perspective of the landscape advocates. The aesthetic argument allowed them to connect to the trend toward panoramic exploration, which the integration of the roads into the landscape would help to achieve; the second argument made their demands part of the discourse about safety.

As we have seen, the pace of construction on the *Reichsautobahnen* slowed down after the attack on Poland. In this phase, the civil engineers rethought the application of the technical parameters against the backdrop of the sections that had already been built. One staff member in the office of the Inspector-General had pointed to the "need for an aesthetic of routing" as early as 1938. Based on the geometric forms of the route, the "flow of parallel lines," the goal was to achieve a harmonious alternation of straightaways and "various, widely arched curves": "The structure of the flow of the line is harmonious when the changes in the alternating elements take place continuously with respect to both their *form* and their *size*." The article asked engineers to weigh technical and natural considerations under the overarching perspective of continuousness. Todt was receptive to this criticism using engineering arguments. In a speech he gave at an architects' meeting on the Plassenburg in August 1940, he redefined his autobahn policy against the backdrop of the war. The Inspector-General spoke of making the flow of the roads "even more fluid":

> I still regard it as a drawback of our alignment that such a road ensemble is generally composed of straightaways, curves, and circular arcs. The more one drives on finished roads, the more one has the wish to enter more gently into the transitions, and maybe to get away after all from the previous instruments of the ruler and the circular arc, and to achieve an even greater adaptation to nature.[23]

In their postwar planning for the autobahn during the Nazi years, engineers spoke of a building style that avoided a "narrow-minded adherence" to the movement of the terrain in the routing, while at the same time seeking to accommodate itself to the landscape. One author insisted that the road should not be subordinated completely to the landscape, depicting the autobahn instead as the representative of a new aesthetic: "For all the integration into the landscape one must not forget that the autobahn always deserves to be emphasized for its own sake. It must not be hidden within the landscape, but should stamp its special mark upon the landscape. It should not fracture the landscape, but instead emphasize even more the unique character of the landscape through its skillfull alignment; only then will driving the autobahn become what it should be, the joint experience of autobahn and landscape."[24]

Evidently these qualities applied only to roads in Germany, however. Todt declared that he could not imagine "that we should make a big effort" to cultivate the "remnants of landscape beauty" in conquered Poland. There one should place "somewhat stronger" emphasis on the military character of the road. Something similar applied to Belgium: on its completely level terrain an autobahn should head toward the channel coast "in a relatively straightforward course" and the cities should be linked to it via connectors. The integration of the roads into the landscape, an attempt that was charged with nationalistic feelings, thus ended at the borders of Germany (and Austria). It was regarded as an additional effort, one that the conquered countries were not worthy of. At the same time, these demands reveal just how much the autobahn described as landscape-friendly was a prewar phenomenon that seemed increasingly obsolete in connection with the National Socialist wars of conquest.[25]

It would appear, therefore, that the change in thinking about the layout of the roads was the result of the construction-free phase after 1939 and the growing realization among some engineers, based on their own experiences, that movement with a constant change of direction offered a more pleasant driving experience than movement along a perfectly straight road.

The seemingly technical detail of whether the routing of the *Reichsautobahnen* should be straight or sinuous was the topic of heated discussions. The debate dealt with the nature of driving and of the—exclusively male—driver, as well as with the nature of the road and the landscape. Engineers from the office of the Inspector-General and the landscape advocates sought to define these elements in contrary ways; the civil engineers of the regional planning offices remained largely silent during these debates. The arguments put forth by the engineers and the landscape advocates arrived at opposite conclusions: the former that it was in the motorist's nature to prefer straight roads, the latter that he preferred curvy roads. The argument that one style or another was safer also remained on the level of mere assertion. In the meantime, a large portion of the sections was built with the use of long straightaways. As the layout of the autobahnen shows, the landscape architects were not able, because of their insecure status, to acquire early and systematic influence over the planning. In 1935, the office of the Inspector-General fixed the maximum length of a straightaway at four kilometers and tried, as the supervising agency, to regain the power to make the final determinations. In 1938, doubts about the aesthetic effect of long straightaways were voiced for the first time by engineers; however, it was only as the construction of the autobahnen was winding down that a comprehensive rethinking of this design element took place. One added aspect was that the adaptation to the contours of the terrain promised to lower construction costs. In the process, engineers and landscape architects tried to expand their specific professional oversight to encompass the relationship between road and landscape. The civil engineers were keen to emphasize the preeminence of the road and to highlight its attractiveness, not that of the landscape by itself.

Characteristic of this controversy is also the degree to which "the driver" functioned as refuge and target category. Both groups were able to avoid addressing their own professional, ideological, and hierarchical differences by invoking the presumed interests of "the" motorist. The masculinity of this rhetorical figure remained a self-evident a priori condition of this discourse. As the autobahnen became older, the driver became less amorphous: the participants in the debate seem to have condensed their own experiences on the road into the figure of the motorist.

What both groups shared, however, was that the experience of road and landscape was formulated as the goal of driving the *Reichsautobahnen*, though the emphasis was placed differently. The new view of the landscape acquired from the autobahn functioned as the ideological link connecting various justificatory contexts. The aim was a specific constitution, a visual consumption of the landscape. A closer examination of various descriptions of autobahn sections shows that the gaze upon the landscape from the moving car was singled out as the intentional product of the construction of these roadways. The technical means to make this vista possible were ascents over mountains and hills: they made it possible to open up panoramas that would have remained closed on a journey over the autobahn in the valleys.

"One drives faster than I can write": visual consumption on the Reichsautobahnen

The panoramic exploration of the Irschenberg Mountain on the road from Munich to Salzburg is a good test case for examining these questions and with them the political meaning of the gaze that was raised at the beginning of chapter five (for a contemporaneous Irschenberg scene, see figure 6.2). A route in the valley instead of over the mountain would have been easier to build, though it would not have offered a vista of the Alps. This mountain became central to the landscape conception of the *Reichsautobahn* when a picture of it won first prize in a photography contest. In an essay, Schönleben spoke about this route having "fateful significance." Todt himself, we are told, laid out the road; following a hike on the mountain "with a few engineer and skiing friends," he chose the route across the Irschenberg. The mountain was presented to the heads of the regional planning offices as an example: "No other route offered the possibility of composing the landscape experience of the route with such variety and intensification as here."[26]

Figure 6.2. The showcase segment of the Nazi autobahn was the Irschenberg mountain on the route from Munich to Salzburg. Instead of traversing the valley, planners decided that the freeway would climb over this foothill of the Alps. A rest stop was built on top of the mountain, enabling views of the Alps towards the south. Such alignments turned landscapes into objects of visual consumption. They also necessitated relatively steep inclines, which made the roads less useful for trucks and more hazardous for every user in the winter. Today, the Irschenberg is known as a site of recurring traffic jams.
Ullsteinbild/The Granger Collection, New York

While these hints at the creative activity of a composer point to the cultural import of the road's routing, the latter becomes even clearer in a description of the segment by Todt. The 125-kilometer-long stretch from Munich to the Austrian border began with an exit avenue bordered by linden trees, at the end of which, "as the title of the entire segment, so to speak," there was a "comprehensive vista of the Upper Bavarian Alps," which "towered with imposing height above the approaching forest belt." At three to four kilometers, this segment was long enough to allow even a fast driver to take in the "magnificent vista. ... Any planting that could obstruct this sweeping view has been omitted on this stretch. One drives faster than I can write."[27]

After passing through the Hofoldinger forest over a length of twenty kilometers, a forest that "received" the motorist (in Todt's words) and made him forget the walls of the big city, the road went across the Mangfall Bridge. A mere two-hundred meters later, behind the first transected moraine hill, there opened up "a splendid view of the mountains at Bayrischzell and Schliersee." The route along the Seehamer Lake was described as an "entertaining interruption," until a gradient of six percent led up to the ridge of the Irschenberg. "Over a length of three kilometers (km 42–45), one enjoys from this height an encompassing panoramic view of the mountains." Todt described the descent into the moraine landscape by talking about the topographical details along the autobahn. After the Inn Bridge, a moraine depression seemed particularly favorable for the line of the road, because it skirted a massif: "The craggy Kampenwand mountain is only six kilometers away." Thereafter, an easy ascent allowed for the "landscape surprise of the entire segment," namely the "unexpected view down to Lake Chiemsee." Todt's dramatic description was specific to the visual revelation of the *Reichsautobahnen*:

> The sudden change in vista, next to the mountains on the right the large, expansive surface of the Chiemsee ahead and to the left of the road, has surprised and captivated everyone who has come to this spot. Anyone who has a proper feel for this landscape as a motorist turns off the motor and silently glides down the three-kilometer-long slope to the southern shore of the lake, where a bathing beach, parking places, or the *Fischerwirt* [inn] invite you to stay and rest.

The routing directly along the shore of the lake was recommended as an opportunity to park the car. In 1938, the largest rest house of the Nazi autobahn was opened at this location. Hitler gave his own input on the design and made sure he had a separate bay-window corner with a view of the lake. Beginning in 1940, the fifty-three rooms were used by the Wehrmacht; after 1945, the U.S. Army turned it into part of a recreation center.[28]

A few more kilometers farther along the Alps, engineers developed an elevation of around six-hundred meters, which now offered "magnificent views away from the mountains to the north and northeast into the high plain." On clear days one could see all the way to the Bavarian Forest, Todt exaggerated. More important was for him, however, that this change in the direction of the gaze imparted to the route "an entirely different landscape character." Eventually the road turned back toward the mountains on the way to the Austrian border.[29]

Picking up on this very point, landscape advocate Seifert, in his comments on the route, praised the fact that in designing the descent into the Salzburg plain, the engineers had, among the thirteen available options, intuitively found the one that made "the impossible possible: to resume once again the sequence of landscape beauty that becomes more intense from Munich to the Chiemsee and, in a sense, to continue it on another level, in the view from the mountains onto the endless high plain, which only the likes of Adalbert Stifter would be able to adequately depict." In relatively sober prose, the head of the regional planning office Munich described as the main criterion for the bridges of the *Reichsautobahn* that they should preserve "as much as possible the clear view for the user."[30]

With emphatic deliberateness, engineers and landscape advocates jointly sought to construct an exciting journey for the motorist along this showpiece of the *Reichsautobahn*. The authorship of the gaze thus remained clearly with the builders of such a route, though they made it so suggestive to the motorists on the autobahn that one can refer to it as a panoramic production. Although this panorama was explored by the drivers individually, the orientation of the gaze was standardized by the layout of the route. Moreover, the emphasis on the succession, surprise, and intensification of varied, non-tiring gazes from the moving vehicle characterizes the experience of the autobahn sought after by the builders as visual consumption. The presented genres, such as Alpine peaks, lakes, and more Alpine peaks, constituted landscape as a nonutilitarian gaze upon noneconomic objects. Panoramas outside the urban sphere were opened up and presented; that included landscapes as much as cultural monuments in a process whose main features Rudy Koshar has described as a growing aestheticization and consumer friendliness.[31]

The manner of presentation was especially intensified through the speed of the movement in the automobile and can be described as consumption not only metaphorically. What was at stake, after all, was an offering of mass culture that had been deliberately arranged for urban, well-to-do consumers, and which offered the user ways of presenting oneself and one's family. Delight in novelty and pleasure in variety were likewise constitutive. Small-scale vistas rushing by were not suitable for leaving behind lasting, visual, "automobilized gazes" (Burckhardt). That is why it was emphasized that the mountain ridge of the Irschenberg offered a view of the Alps over a distance of three kilometers, and that the the road ran along the southern shore of the Chiemsee for four kilometers. Only extended visualization allowed the impressions to unfold their desired effect; and only in this way could the transitions come as genuine surprises. We are dealing with something far more than the mere transfer of elements of landscape architecture in the eighteenth-century English style, in which the impression of a surprising view was described as the "ha-ha effect." The autobahn strove to stage the landscape beyond the road: that is what it was claiming to do and the effect it was hoping to achieve. At the same time, the road was understood as a technological structure. Finally, there was the rapid locomotion of the motorist. These three factors make clear that we are dealing not with the continuation of a traditional aesthetic, but with a consumption-oriented refocusing of the gaze in the twentieth century.[32] With this visual appropriation of the landscape, the German autobahnen took on one of the technological characteristics of the parkways in the United States. These recreational roads, built only for automobile traffic and not for trucks, had realized such visualization concepts. Todt's agency had the relevant technical literature translated.[33]

The panoramic production of the *Reichsautobahnen* can be demonstrated on numerous other segments. Although the route Munich-Salzburg was the only one that could provide views of the Alps, the highlands in other parts of Germany offered enough potential for the technological appropriation of panoramas. In the process, the Alpine route was seen as a model for other segments. Even the first Nazi autobahn segment Frankfurt-Heidelberg/Mannheim, which was laid out largely in a straight line and had far fewer opportunities for a sequence of heightened landscapes, was lauded for its "varied, unimpeded views" out of the forest. In another case, the gradient that engineers accepted in return for a better vista was 7 percent. And for the climb of the autobahn Stuttgart-Munich into the Swabian Jura, the Inspector-General explicitly authorized a gradient of no less than 8 percent along with a curve radius of two-hundred meters. The construction of tunnels was discussed, but rejected because they offered much poorer options for panoramic views: "Even perfectly designed structures would have, by their size, invariably robbed the splendid landscape completely of its original character. The view of the singular scenery would have remained closed to drivers and travelers by the rapid succession of tunnels." It was understood that the steep gradients in general would make driving on the *Reichsautobahnen* at times difficult for trucks, but this critique was answered by noting that motors were expected to become more "mountain happy." One author boldly and incorrectly predicted that cars would be "insensitive to gradients."[34] During construction of the *Reichsautobahnen* in Hesse, one service area was built deliberately at the highest point of the autobahn in this region so as to make possible long-distance vistas. Near Kassel, engineers even put a freeway interchange on a hilltop; to this day, drivers have to negotiate a height difference of eighty meters to get from one autobahn to another.[35]

There was a tense relationship between this visual consumerism and the postulated safety of the roads; still today, gradients and curves impede the flow of traffic, especially during bad weather. (The Irschenberg is infamous for its traffic jams in the winter.) However, the landscape character of the roads was able to take precedence over such concerns. In planning the autobahn from Salzburg to Vienna, Todt explicitly weighed traffic safety and the enjoyment of the landscape against each other. Following a flight over the route, he noted that a close approximation of the autobahn to the mountains "greatly diminished" the transport utility of the route during the five or six months of winter. However, in the Salzkammergut region just east of Salzburg Todt accepted this trade-off for more panoramic vistas: "We have decided to subordinate the principle of unconditional winter fitness to the desire to see as much as possible of the Salzkammergut lakes." This setting of priorities was to apply to the entire route Salzburg-Vienna, so as to convey to the motorist "the full landscape beauty of the German *Ostmark*." The opposition between aesthetics and safety, each of which demanded different design features from the autobahn, had thus been decided in favor of visual consumption. For Todt and the office of the Inspector-General, this quality of the route was, in doubtful cases and especially in southern Germany and Austria, more important than the mere transportation function of the road. The motorist who was the target of these ideas was clearly sitting behind the wheel of a car, not a truck.[36]

That Todt had a soft spot for vistas is also revealed by an anecdote outside of the autobahnen: when enormous hydropower plants and power lines were built in the Alps as part of the expansion of the electricity industry, one of the overland lines almost impaired the view from one of the Inspector-General's vacation homes. Following Todt's intervention, the power line was moved, not the house.[37]

The flora of the Nazi autobahn: contesting native plants

In contrast to the clashes over the alignment of the roads, one would have presumed that the planting of the median and the sides of the autobahn would have fallen more clearly into the task area of the landscape advocates. However, even in this area, the extent and pattern of the integration into the landscape were a bone of contention between architects and engineers. What is more, one can detect conflicts in the generation of knowledge about what, where, and how much should be planted. In what follows, I will take a closer look at this question.

At the very outset of his work, Seifert had described the furnishing of the roads with trees and shrubs as the second great task of the landscape consultants, alongside the influence on the routing. "Two options: either the landscape rules or the road rules," Seifert had noted succinctly about this issue during his introductory presentation to Todt in January 1934. Roadside trees had been, since the eighteenth century, a design tool in the planning of urban avenues and tree-flanked roads in the countryside. One example known throughout Europe was Napoleon's national roads (*routes nationales*). As we saw above, Seifert mentioned an avenue-like design when he first established contact with Todt, but he did not bring the idea up again later. With its dead-straight line and the dense, regular planting of trees, the conventional avenue possessed in the eyes of the designers of the *Reichsautobahn* an obvious artificial character, one that ran counter to their goal of a naturalized technology.[38]

In his presentation, Seifert avoided listing the aesthetic effect of a planted autobahn as a motivation. Instead, he addressed its functional importance. First off, planting was favorable for the roadbed, since it would otherwise dry out. Moreover, the planting of trees and shrubs was to be "the beginning of the restoration of the natural balance in the cultural landscape (bird protection, protection against soil depletion, the preservation of dew and carbon dioxide in the soil, climate improvement)." Seifert evidently expected that such functional arguments would carry greater weight with the engineers. Leaving aside the purely tactical approach, we also find reflected here not only a view of the natural environment that is interested in causal contexts, but also the blending of static conceptions of ecology with nationalistic motivations into a policy of ecological restoration.

Before the work of the landscape architects on the *Reichsautobahnen* began, the planting was functionally differentiated. To be sure, in one of his essays aimed at a broader audience, Seifert had postulated that "a road must have trees if it is to be a German road."[39] However, when working with the civil engineers, the landscape architects differentiated according to the specific location of the autobahn in a forest, in well-structured agrarian landscapes, or in areas of monocultures, referred to derisively as "cultural steppe" (*Kultursteppe*). "In the *Kultursteppe*, the road must set the tone," Seifert had noted in his Berlin presentation. In the "treeless and shrubless deserts of rye, potatoes, and beets," exemplified by the agrarian regions of central and northwestern Germany, which attained the highest degrees of agricultural efficiency, it was appropriate to present the autobahnen as "master of the steppe." For Seifert this was not a concession to an aesthetically superior technological structure, but the consequence of the blandness of the landscape. Tall trees should emphasize the road artistically, and they also accomplished the practical goal of shading the roads. In this context of use, one could not dispense with "foreign" plants, that is, plants that were not native to the location. Specifically, Seifert mentioned the locust tree for dry soils, the red oak for wet east German sandy soils, and Canadian poplars for locations where not enough native black poplars could be found.[40]

Native plantings were explicitly called for, however, for autobahnen in forests. "Seen as an organism," Seifert argued, most of the forests were sick. Seifert blamed this situation on a forestry that was interested in the greatest possible yield and therefore preferred monocultures. It was therefore wrong to draw conclusions from the existing plants as to the species that were suitable for the autobahn. Instead, the landscape advocates should determine "what the composition of the forest would be if man had not been interfering in its life with an ignorant hand for a century; what is native (*bodenständig*) must be sought out and turned into the foundation of all new work." Native plantings required no care and were healthy, since they grew by themselves, after all, provided human influence did not prevent them from spreading. In his introductory presentation, Seifert had elaborated further on this functional argument and had already addressed the burden from automobile exhausts. Only "what is *bodenständig* (and not simply indigenous)" was resistant to the stress from dryness, wind gusts, wakes, and "poison gas." Instead of the monotonous fir forests on the gravel soil of the Alpine foothills, to name just one example, the goal was to restore forests of oak, linden, yoke elm, and maple.[41]

Nativeness would become the key concept for the planting of the Nazi autobahn. It became the topic of intense clashes between landscape advocates and the office of the Inspector-General. In what follows, the insistence on the use of native plants will be seen as an instrument of ideological self-assertion. This ideology was very much in flux, and Seifert and the other landscape architects employed it in various phases with different degrees of intensity and a different thrust. Examining this clash will allow us to draw inferences about the ideas of nature and landscape held by the actors involved.

To begin with, Seifert combined a personal mission with the principle of nativeness. He referred to his reflections on garden architecture he had published in the interwar period: "When I laid out the foundations of a native garden art five years ago in a larger essay, it met with virtually no resonance. The victory of the National Socialist *Weltanschauung* has strongly boosted the value of what is native and species-specific (*arteigen*); in garden design, too, nativeness is now garnering respect, and here I will leave open the question of how much should be attributed to honest conviction, and how much to clever sailing with the wind," Seifert observed in 1935 with typical self-conceit and a characteristic linkage of nativeness with elements of Nazi ideology. This ideological linkage has already been discussed in the scholarly literature. Here I will examine the question of whether—and if so, how—these bold pronouncements were realized and how the justifying rhetoric changed.[42]

To be sure, in calling for nativeness, Seifert was neither the only one nor the first to do so. However, Todt's chief landscape architect helped this principle to achieve prominence in a large-scale technological project. Since the turn of the century, garden architects had been trying to establish their emerging discipline on a scientific foundation. In the process of emancipating their discipline from building architecture and the profession of gardener, some garden and landscape architects articulated the principle of native plantings for their gardens and parks.

The form and content of this principle corresponded with a change in scientific methodology in classifying biology interested in the interrelationship of systems, that is, ecology. In studying plant communities, researchers in this field increasingly preferred a concept linked with the notions of succession and climax. The descriptive biologists studied communities of life in a given context, such as a specific piece of forest, and directed their attention at both the causal relationship between environmental conditions and plant coverage, and the relationships between individual species. The functional connection between specific plants assumed an increasingly changed character in the eyes of researchers in the last third of the nineteenth century, namely that of an inner, mutual necessity. Like the collaboration of individual members in an organism, the plant community could function only when each member was present and functioning.[43]

Added to this was the basic assumption of succession, the temporal change in vegetation in the same location. The nineteenth century saw a growing number of studies about this sequence; according to Ludwig Trepl, the "organism" established itself as the guiding metaphor. Succession was understood as the historical replacement of one group of plants by a higher group. These sequences of successive living communities serve as the foundation for an order of vegetation. In this way, various plant communities could be distinguished hierarchically. The last link in such a sequence was regularly a stable community. Its stability was derived precisely from the fact that environmental conditions and vegetation were in balance if they corresponded to each other. Such "final communities" were called climax.

This perspective was radicalized by the superorganism theory of the American biologist Frederick Clement.[44] Central to this theory was the idea that the climax formation itself was now seen as an organ with a life cycle. Here is Clement's description: "The unit of vegetation, the climax vegetation is an organic entity. As an organism, the formation arises, grows, matures, and dies. [...] The climax formation is the adult organism, the fully developed community, of which all initial and medial stages are but stages of development."[45]

This plant community moves inexorably toward its predetermined, automatic fate. Predetermination became implicitly the guiding image. The parallel between this approach and the view of history of a writer like Oswald Spengler is evident. Applied to nature, this view could only mean implementing the conservative utopia of the subordination of human life to life's habitat as "a purposely functioning organ from which it receives its meaning, in the first place." This organic metaphor of accommodation reverberated also in the concept of landscape integration (*landschaftliche Eingliederung*), which Seifert claimed to have coined himself.[46] This new understanding of these plant communities showed its effects especially in intensified research into so-called plant sociology (*Pflanzensoziologie*, or phytosociology). This subdiscipline of biology encompassed and described plant communities and could thus offer clues to plant ensembles that were "natural" to a given location, that is, they occurred without human influence. The first European schools for phytosociologists formed in Zurich and Montpellier in the wake of publications by the Danish biologist Eugenius Warming and his German colleague Andreas Franz Wilhelm Schimper. In 1904, English researchers established the first association with a similar orientation. In the 1920s, vegetation analysis established itself among Swedish ecologists in Uppsala. At the same time, Josias Braun-Blanquet (1884–1980), the most important phytosociologist outside the English-speaking realm, worked at the "Station internationale de Géobotanique méditerranéenne et alpine" in Montpellier. In contrast to Clement's extreme theory of the superorganism, phytosociologists of the Braun-Blanquet school were content to study the composition, environment, and structure of the plant communities. One of these students was the later collaborator on the *Reichsautobahnen*, Reinhold Tüxen (1899–1980), widely regarded as the founding person of German phytosociology. The institutional anchoring of the discipline at the universities was weak in Germany in the 1920s.[47]

The name given to phtyosociology (also referred to as vegetation science) suggested similarities with human sociology. To be sure, one certainly could not speak of a "close parallelism" between phytosociology and, for example, the sociology of Auguste Comte, wrote Braun-Blanquet. However, there were points of contact between the two sciences: "They do not deal with the life expressions of individual organisms as such, but with groups of organisms or societies that react more or less in the same direction and are connected through the interactions of the individual members." What united the two was the overarching view with a functional orientation. Moreover, on the level of underlying ideology, both were marked by the notion of stable and healthy community. In other words, instability or "retrogression" were the result of human activity and could be recognized by phytosociologists. This doctrine of stability had profound consequences for the human image of nature. Conceptualizing nature as a constant, firmly established unity allowed for the emergence of the popular notion of the "balance of nature" that was upset by human interference. It is hard to overestimate the importance of this notion, since it was the explicit or implicit motivation for many conservationists and environmentalists and to some extent still is today. Against these pictures of stasis and the endpoints of natural "development," current ecology sets the concept of a dynamic nature characterized by constant change.[48]

For the landscape architects of the *Reichsautobahn*, the application of insights from phtyosociology amounted to an infusion of new scientific understanding. From phytosociology, with its epistemological interest in observation, classification, and collecting, they expected concrete directives for the planting of gardens and parks. What we are dealing with is a process of transfer and translation. The results of such studies were indications about which ensemble of plants was "appropriate" (*standortgerecht*) to a given location. In what follows, I will compare how a part of the landscape architects understood and used these "laws of nature" in their conventional work, and how this procedure changed during the work on the autobahnen.

In the first decade of the twentieth century, the garden architect Willy Lange (1864–1941) understood ecology as the "doctrine of the relationships between location and the household of plants," and he described it explicitly as the preforming foundation for architectural design: "From the physiognomy of plants we deduce the location appropriate to them, and we avoid combining plants in the garden that do not belong together also aesthetically, because nature, judging from their physiognomy, would never have created them at the same location. The law of nature becomes the law of art." Drawing on these widely held views, Seifert formulated his credo of nativeness in 1929 in harmony with economic efficiency for gardens. What still predominated in this article was the importance of nativeness as an optional, noncompulsory design element of a garden architecture that had a *Heimatschutz* orientation.[49]

The rhetoric justifying nativeness was that much bolder in Seifert's publications after 1933. The move from fenced gardens to open space, from garden art to landscape design, and an interval of five years were the external indications. On the ideological level, Seifert strove to coordinate his views with National Socialist core beliefs; professionally he had developed from a lecturer at the Technical University in Munich to an advisor to the new state's prestige project. Although Seifert radicalized his views as a whole, he did make a distinction between private gardens and landscapes designed for the public. For gardens, designers had some latitude; when it came to landscapes, he denied that there was any room for discussion on matters of design. Nativeness became the determinant for the landscape and the people who lived in it. When doing plantings, the landscape advocate must "accommodate himself to the same law that has created the face of the landscape in many thousand years of growth." The absence of the "foreign plants" lilac, laburnum, jasmine, roses bred for urban parks, Douglas firs, and rhododendron was "not blind chance, but fate, inner necessity. And we know that we were not born into this harsher land by chance, but out of necessity, as fate. But no fate can be resolved any other way except by affirming it. We shall not shirk it, we will not embellish, instead we will affirm this land, just the way it was created, and we will preserve it exactly this way."[50]

Seifert placed the responsibility for this principle's ability to assert itself on powers above the individual. The time for these ideas has simply come, he wrote and described himself, with feigned modesty, as the mere herald of an idea that has attained "the dominance for which its was predestined." As already noted, the principles of nativeness that were published in 1939 differentiated rigorously between gardens and landscape. The garden was defined as a place of uncommon plants, whether native or not. In a garden, every plant that attained the full measure of its beauty and was in artistic and biological harmony with its immediate and wider environment was native. When it came to the circumscribed garden, freedom and license in design were permissible.[51]

The situation of independence and adherence to regularity was very different in the landscape. As the "eternal *Heimat* of the Germans," it had to be handed down from generation to generation "unadulterated and pure in its special characteristics in each instance." This is where the wishes and pleasure of the individual ceased to matter, "here the legacy of the *Volk* needs to be preserved. In the landscape we are even more strict than the nature protection law, which prohibits the planting of foreign plants. Not only must that which is alien to the Reich be kept out; even what is merely foreign to the landscape has lost its right here." The absoluteness of his claim corresponded to the importance of the loaded concepts of "*Volk*" and "legacy." Seifert sought to secure the relevance of the concern of nativeness by linking it with core elements of Nazi ideology. In the process, his demands became increasingly shrill:

> We like blackthorn and hawthorn, European euonymus (*Pfaffenhütchen*) and hazel shrubs, wild pears, linden trees and wild cherry along the edge of the forest better than all red oaks and Douglas firs of the world, and most of all: they are closer to our heart! With unrelenting tenacity and unshakeable optimism, we shall bring about that the forest borders along the *Reichsautobahnen* will be such genuine and rich forest borders in 30 years; alongside the greatest technological project of all times, the original landscape will once again have its home.[52]

Until such time, however, Seifert had unsheathed the rhetorical sword: "We declare picea pungens glauca [Colorado blue spruce] enemy of the state No. 1, and we prophecy to all those nursery people who continue to support it that the nobler the blue of their plants is, the more money they will lose with them." For his chromatics went like this: "We shall leave the blue spruce to all those countries in which the landscape is gray or yellow or red, and not green, as ours is everywhere." He declared war on all garden directors and city gardeners who were planting pinus montana (mountain pine). For it was "a sin against the nobility of our mountains" to create such distorted pictures.

For Seifert, this demand contained a thrust that was directed against civilization: he was concerned with nothing less than putting an end to "a century of aberration between nature and technology." Materialistic self-interest had caused parts of the German landscape to waste away to a "cultivated steppe" (*Kultursteppe*). Foresters and garden architects had become unfaithful to their habitat through unnatural monocultures. Seifert believed that the German quality of the landscape was under assault from rapid industrialization, if it had not already been lost. The restoration of original plant ensembles thus became an attempt to return German landscape to its presumed right. In this way, the *Reichsautobahnen*, in particular, were supposed to provide a model for restoring the landscape. In the eyes of some of its builders, the most extensive construction project under National Socialism was supposed to reverse the damage caused by civilization by carrying the new mindset vividly and concretely out into the land. This contradiction between the obviously massive intervention into nature by an infrastructure project and the claim to be restoring nature could be resolved only by having propaganda transfigure the roads into the bearers of culture. Seifert's reaction was all the more furious when an intransigent regional planning office ignored suggestions from himself and the affiliated landscape advocate and built a rest place on its own with a "virtually childish dilettantism." He scolded, "the arrangement of the paths and small flower beds, the plantings and the seats at the rest place at the Drackenstein slope [on the segment Ulm-Stuttgart] corresponds more or less to what the Smoke and Savings Club Harmony might have done in 1910 on its Sunday recreational plot, but not with the obligatory stance of Adolf Hitler's Roads."[53]

These mocking attacks from the pen of the leading landscape architect of the *Reichsautobahn* exemplify how radical the rhetoric of this group became by 1939. They pointed to an inherent design and identity problem for the architects: the creative act of selecting the plants and distributing them over the space of the *Reichsautobahn* was embedded within the field of tension between artistic expression and conservative accommodation to the laws of nature. Although the planting was the task of each individual landscape advocate, what form it took was to be deduced from the landscape in question, from the timeless law "to which all artistic license has to subordinate itself." The charge of the landscape consultants lay in recognizing the original core of the landscape underneath the layer of vegetation that had grown up with civilization. A desirable possibility had thus turned into a compulsory law: Seifert presented nativeness in an increasingly radicalized form as the nonnegotiable design criterion for the planting of the *Reichsautobahn*.

For Seifert and the landscape advocates, this rhetoric took on the function of proving themselves to be necessary within the uncertain structure in charge of building the autobahn. Ideologically it was easy to connect nativeness readily with race and soil; in this sense it was to support the professional goals of the landscape architects, whose status had been, at the very least, vaguely defined. The patterns of ecological justification that Seifert had invoked when he began his work gave way to a rhetoric of exclusion that was underpinned with nationalistic sentiments. The intensity of the debate increased.

This radically revisionist eloquence collided during the actual construction process with skepticism on the part of the civil engineers—and especially Todt—about the principle of nativeness and the financial parameters of the project. No doubt this also had something to do with the fact that it would be obvious to every driver how and what had been planted. Even the unswervingly optimistic Seifert called the plantings on the *Reichsautobahnen* "a somewhat tragic chapter." This tragedy, however, lacked a dramatic turning point.[54]

Todt's general critique of his landscape advocates was that they were planting too many trees and shrubs on the roadside and in the median strip. His criticism was more than just words, for he cut back the extent of the plantings. "Time and again, Todt threatened especially my best helpers that he would cancel their contract, because they were planting more than he believed was necessary," Seifert recalled in his autobiography. Behind such discussions stood not only the issue of the amount of roadside greenery; from the outset, Todt pursued a different plant concept than the landscape advocates. He expressed his views as a reaction to plantings that were planned or had already been carried out. What becomes clear is that the agency of the Inspector-General wanted to see the experience of a trip on the autobahn heightened by the right kind of plantings. The goal was to accentuate views through and into the landscape, while the speed of the trip was another factor. Todt systematically thinned out the group of landscape advocates, because their planting proposals exceeded his budget and his idea. "The expansively planned and built *Reichsautobahn* also requires expansive planting. I have been preaching this since the first day, and over the course of the year 1938 I will get rid of those landscape advocates who can think only in allotment garden terms along the *Reichsautobahnen*," he threatened.[55]

It was against this backdrop of constant uncertainty, which was linked to the question of compensation for the landscape architects that remained unclear for a long time, that the consultants drew up planting plans for the individual segments. Crucial design criteria such as the density of planting on the median strip were initially not defined. Shrubs seemed a good choice to provide a shield against headlight glare. After Todt and Seifert visited the still unopened first *Reichsautobahn* segment Frankfurt-Darmstadt in January of 1935, the Inspector-General specified that "it was not necessary to plant remotely as much" as had been assumed. The distances between the bushes on the median strip could be between fifty and one-hundred meters. The landscape advocates had come out in favor of a denser planting. Following the inspection of other segments, Todt complained in

December 1935 that on the median strip, four times the amount "of what would be sufficient for a proper planting" was being planted. A loose planting was sufficient for driving safety; the character of a strip of grass was to predominate.[56]

In the summer of 1936, Seifert pointed out that the ratio of planted to growing plants had to be 5:1. The occasion for this observation had been a drive along the segment Berlin-Magdeburg. However, Seifert could not get the office of the Inspector-General to see it his way. This is clear from the marginal comments to Seifert's letter to Berlin by *Ministerialrat* Hans Lorenz. More than thirty years later, Seifert still remembered the "misfortune" that Lorenz had brought upon the landscape advocates. The reason behind it was evidently the competitive relationship between Lorenz and Seifert. As we have seen, Lorenz was the only civil engineer who took over the tasks of a landscape advocate for the road Nuremberg-Leipzig along the segment Lanzendorf-Bayreuth-Nuremberg.[57]

Where Seifert had written in reference to the density of plants, "Nature begins even more densely," Lorenz added dryly, "but with seeds, not nursery products." Where Seifert had written about the segments of landscape advocate Schneider that four times the amount of planting was the minimum, Lorenz added: "I told him he shouldn't plant so much." In the meantime, Todt had found other occasions to complain about excessively dense plantings. During an inspection drive with the heads of all the regional planning offices along seven segments in the fall of 1936, Todt concluded that too much planting was being done. The result of his displeasure was a circular to all landscape advocates and the regional planning offices, which Todt asked Lorenz to write with the following directive: "It would be best to compose the circular in such a way that, for all its unmistakable clarity, it does not call forth among the engineers a certain *Schadenfreude* about the landscape advocates, but raises the sense of responsibility of both groups."[58]

The letter noted the following as the primary goal of the landscape design: "During the rapid drive over the motor roadways, the impressions of the landscape are determined chiefly by the large spaces of the landscape and by the succession of these spaces." A careful examination of local conditions would almost always show that plantings were needed only on one-tenth to one-twentieth of the segment. The letter also went on to say: "The reason—apart from saving on avoidable costs—why the greatest restraint is called for with artificial planting is that even the greatest artists cannot fully succeed in creating a planting that is capable of simulating natural growth." The landscape advocates were therefore admonished not to try to create a landscape on a small scale, but to serve "the great doings of nature." Still, Todt's exhortations did not eliminate the divergent views about the plantings.

In November 1936, all landscape advocates were summoned to Berlin; the reason, in Seifert's words, was to "bring them to heel and to permit them no more than a moderate embellishment of the autobahn." According to Seifert's account, the meeting would have erupted into scandal but for the speech by the Rhineland landscape advocate Hoemann, "our white-bearded senior" and an imposing figure. With strong words he supposedly declared that he felt committed only to his *Heimat*, the Bergisches Land, a region along the east bank of the Rhine, through which "the autobahn had been chopped." His contribution to the debate was effective: the landscape advocates kept their jobs, "but the trust was gone and with it the joy."[59]

Leaving aside the anecdotal account, this meeting was indicative of the prevailing tensions. The amount of plantings had been controversial since 1934. Todt believed they were overdone by a factor of four or five. Apart from the obvious financial considerations—fewer plants meant fewer expenses for nursery goods, garden contractors, and maintenance and upkeep—Todt voiced his concerns that a densely planted autobahn would leave the motorist with a visual impression that did not support the speed and expansiveness of the drive. During his inspection visits, he often had individual plantings removed and tried to discipline the landscape advocates with admonishments and threats. When that failed, he issued new, temporary directives following the meeting in Berlin. Now the primary task of the plantings was to invigorate the motorist through a succession of views and vistas. Integrating the roads completely into the landscape through plantings was listed only as the second task. The planting was to take place over a number of years. Through plantings, a landscape-sensitive routing, and road profiles related to the landscape's form, the road as a whole would become "the crown of the landscape it opened up."[60]

As an obvious element of the integration of the roads into the landscape, the number of trees and shrubs planted was criticized by the civil engineers of the agency of the Inspector-General. Added to this was the fact that the type of plantings, that is to say, the nativeness postulated by the landscape advocates, remained controversial. Although the office of the Inspector-General gave some commissions to plant sociologists beginning in 1935, Todt remained fundamentally skeptical:

> It would be theory if the relatively sparse plantings of the median strip and the strips along the side of the road were based exclusively on what was native here in the post-glacial period, with the intention of reshaping the sylvan flora in keeping with its location.

Against the strict application of the principle of nativeness, Todt posited that the soil and groundwater conditions, and especially the soil climate, on the autobahn were substantially different from its surrounding area. Moreover, the surrounding soil had often been changed from its primeval conditions, "frequently through centuries of improper cultivation." As a result, it would often take a fairly long development until the *bodenständig* woody plants could flourish again. Hence, expert opinions based on phytosociology could be applied only "with a sensible consideration of what the landscape had actually become and with preference given to so-called pioneering species [such as fast-growing willows and birch]."[61]

While Todt thus did accept the argument of "improper cultivation" (*Fehlkultur*), in opposition to Seifert's express radicalism, he ordered a gradual introduction of *bodenständig* plants. For one, Todt saw the autobahn on a larger scale as an autonomous artifact within the environment, with its own climatic conditions and laws. For another, his pragmatic position was also based on the skepticism about cost voiced by the *Reichsautobahn* bureaucracy, which is why he recommended pioneering species as simple and cost-effective plants that were more likely to flourish. Even the nationalistic underpinning of the theory did not lead to its immediate acceptance.

The landscape advocates gradually weakened the Inspector-General's doubts about nativeness. Beginning in the third year of construction, Todt's agency gave financial support to phtyosociology studies and to studies dealing with the subsoil of the roads. However, the differences between the Inspector-General and the landscape consultants meant that each group preferred one of two different institutions. On one side was a Research Office for Bioengineering (*Ingenieurbiologie*), which the forestry director Arthur von Kruedener had set up in Munich, on orders from Todt. The bioengineers sought a reconciliation of technology and nature that was compatible with engineering; in practical terms they worked up proposals for embankments that were supposed to be more lasting than methods that were more alienated from nature. Today, bioengineering is a method of design and construction using manmade structures in combination with vegetation for erosion control and habitat restoration. As Kruedener put it: "Mobilizing the living force of nature is biological engineering."[62]

The landscape advocates, however, preferred the Hannover plant sociologist Tüxen, whose sociological experimental garden the local landscape advocate Hübotter had come to know. Since 1926, Hannover had been home to the Provincial Office for the Natural Monument Preservation; beginning in 1930, it awarded phytosociological contracts to find areas worth protecting. In 1931, the College of Veterinary Medicine in Hannover established a "Section for Theoretical and Applied Phytosociology" headed by Tüxen. Seifert wrote in his memoirs that he had overcome "strong resistance" in order to enlist Tüxen as a collaborator. At a meeting of the landscape advocates in June 1935, "the entire group knelt on the ground in a still natural, small forest of oak and yoke elm, eagerly botanizing under Tüxen's guidance; I called out to them Goethe's words after the cannonade at Valmy: 'From this place and from this day forward begins a new era in the history of world, and you can say that you were part of it!' I proved to be right in this exclamation." Pompously, Seifert wrote as his own historian with the sort of literary references used by the educated bourgeoisie.[63]

Following the historical greatness of that moment in the forest near Holzkirchen, what transpired between Tüxen and von Kruedener were quite ordinary and, as far as the climate of the autobahn construction is concerned, very revealing quarrels over competency, since the areas of activity had not been demarcated with sufficient precision. Todt continued his policy of competing institutions and individuals for similar tasks; to this were added very different levels of support: "Kruedener and his people received excellent financial support—we had to scrape by." Seifert felt that there was "virtually nothing" the landscape advocates were able to learn from von Kruedener.[64]

Tüxen established a close professional relationship with the landscape advocates of the *Reichsautobahn* and especially with Seifert. He wrote in a thank-you note: "I believe that our meeting was the kind of decisive step for my life for which I was previously indebted only twice to friends, the last of whom was Braun-Blanquet nine years ago."[65] In October 1935, Tüxen received a commission from the office of the Inspector-General to create a vegetation map for segments of the *Reichsautobahnen*. In this case, the lobbying effort by the landscape advocates had established a starting point. However, since there was an internal rivalry with von Kruedener's institute of bioengineering, the areas of work were initially divided up geographically: segments in southern Germany were taken on by von Kruedener, those in the north by Tüxen.[66] Substantively, Tüxen formulated that the vegetation maps had the purpose to determine, for the planting of the median strip and the sides of the *Reichsautobahnen*, mixtures of wood that are appropriate for a given location, that is, suitable to the climate and soil. The map was to be done "according to the methods of phytosociology …: all forests will be depicted in their *natural* condition, all other plant communities in their current condition." The landscape advocates also received lists of the species of wood that are naturally occurring in the forest communities, with regard to their relative proportions, and likewise for the grasses and types of clover that make up the meadows.[67]

Subsequently, the Inspector-General informed Tüxen and his collaborators which segments they were supposed to inspect with the landscape advocates. However, the lines of competency between Tüxen and von Kruedener were unclear; in 1938, the working areas of Tüxen and Kruedener were reallocated once again. While Tüxen was now in charge of creating maps based on phytosociology for each area touched by the autobahn, von Kruedener was responsible for providing advice on silviculture and geology.[68]

There is no question that this move broadened the argumentative basis for landscape consultation to the *Reichsautobahnen*. In conflicts with the civil engineers, the landscape advocates could now invoke expert knowledge from a third party, using it to determine the nature of the new plantings. The academically generated knowledge suited the aesthetically motivated demands of the architects and their desire to receive professional recognition. But while the architects welcomed this new impetus for their work, the office of the Inspector-General rejected the literal application of the results of Tüxen's research. This can be seen from the example of the so-called Olympic road through Forstenried Park in Munich. The road was part of the segment from Munich to Garmisch, which was expanded for the Winter Olympics 1936 and then again in 1939/40.

Here Seifert suddenly appeared as an offender against trees. An irate telegram reached Todt in January 1940 in Berlin: "Magnificent avenue of chestnuts Olympstr. Forstenried Park is being destroyed right now by Doctor Seiffert [*sic*] outrage in the population enormous urgently request countermeasure, help, and protection for Germany's most beautiful tree-lined avenue." The breathless outcry was signed by Christian Weber, one of Hitler's closest cronies and a profiteer who was locally known as the "bigwig king" (*Bonzenkönig*). Todt responded the same day, also by telegram. The intention was not to cut down the chestnut avenue in Forstenried Park; instead, "the crippled and sick trees" were to be removed and replacement trees planted. Nevertheless, the "measure" was halted.[69]

Internally, Todt conceded that the avenue was being cut down as not native to the location and passed on the pressure. All landscape advocates and regional planning offices received a circular in which he protested against the strict application of the "Tüxen theory," that is, the views of the consulting phytosociologist:

> A chestnut in bloom delights the eye of many thousands, even if it is in the wrong place in Forstenried Park according to Tüxen's theory—in the same way that in urban parks a bed of tulips or some other bed of greenhouse plants delights many more people than a newly created, so-called native planting that, according to the Tüxen theory, is in line with the plant community of the wilderness 4,000 years ago. Every theory becomes extreme as soon as it is pushed too narrowly and one-sidedly.

Seifert responded that only dead or sick trees had been cut down. What kind they were had played no role. Quite independent of phytosociological and other theories, he had merely pursued an artistic goal: "I do believe that I have earned the kind of reputation as a protector of tree and bush that one should assume sound reasons if I myself suggest the removal of trees." Tüxen himself informed Todt that there was no "Tüxen theory," only a theory of Braun-Blanquet. In his defense he said that he himself was merely an observer, and what he wanted was not to restore some kind of old wilderness, but to establish plant communities that were "today natural or possible."

Restoration had clearly been put on the defensive on the autobahnen. The cutting of existing trees in a city park symbolized for Todt that his landscape architects were in certain ways divorced from reality. As the top manager of the autobahn project, Todt rejected the goal and extent of the ecological restoration that his consultants had in mind.

In the meantime, phytosociology was in demand not only on the autobahn: Tüxen's research office in Hannover attracted other commissions from the Nazi state and created vegetation maps for the grounds of the Nazi party congresses in Nuremberg and the site of the later extermination camp in Auschwitz.[70]

In sum, we can say that the landscape advocates saw the application of native principles as an opportunity to establish and expand the design features that were derived from garden architecture. Their professional prestige could only gain from the ecologically generated knowledge. In a process of translating the findings of phytosociology, which were the product of a different epistemological interest, they sought to articulate precise directives for concrete action. The descriptive and classificatory approach of these directives was distilled into planting plans, by means of which they were seeking to restore landscapes that were deemed German. Since they rejected the prevailing land use as materialistic, they wanted to change the cultivation of the land by changing the landscape forms. The quest for a primal condition of natural balance in a healthy landscape, stable and untouched by human hand, drove them to engage in what the engineers at times referred to as a naïve and unrealistic revisionism.

At the same time, a chronological perspective is called for: the demands of the landscape advocates became increasingly radical in the course of the clashes over the integration of the roads into the landscape. In one sense we can see this as an attempt at establishing greater internal discipline. Given the uncertain status conditions and the external framework that had to be continuously renegotiated, the shared commitment to native plantings created a greater degree of internal homogeneity. Yet this sense of togetherness did have authoritarian qualities, in that Seifert saw himself as the leader of the landscape advocates and used these methodological questions to bind the other architects more closely to himself. Vis-à-vis the office of the Inspector-General, nativeness as linked with phytosociology promised a boost in reputation from a greater scientific character. In spite of continuing skepticism, the landscape consultants persuaded the agency to ask the plant sociologist Tüxen to draw up vegetation maps.

If we look at the actual result, the scientific accompaniment to the plantings along the *Reichsautobahn* was characterized more by arbitrariness and contingency than by systematic surveying and broad application. Moreover, it is quite apparent that the increasingly radical language about nativeness went hand in hand with the growth of status anxieties among the landscape architects. Initially, Seifert had justified foreign woody plants for the "cultivated steppe" (*Kultursteppe*) on biological grounds, but at the end of the 1930s, he declared war on all such plants. At the same time, there was growing pressure from the office of the Inspector-General, which combined doubts about the gain in knowledge from the methods of nativeness with criticism of the volume of plantings. While I do not wish to suggest a simplistic parallelism here, it is worth noting that these two processes occurred in such chronological proximity. The growing tendency to underpin the rhetoric of nativeness with reverential invocations of "legacy" and "*Volk*" can be interpreted as an effort to reconnect a marginal theme more closely to core areas of National Socialist ideology. This development also reflects the vanished stylistic pluralism of the early years of the Nazi construction of the autobahn, when the design of the roads within the landscape was made up of and negotiated from various elements. In the background stood divergent pictures of landscape put forth by civil engineers and landscape architects. While the office of the Inspector-General understood landscape as a component of a new, speed-charged experience of a trip by motorcar and envisaged correspondingly sparse plantings, the landscape advocates tried to engage in ecological restoration under their aesthetic control. In these conflicts, "technology" had played a subliminal role as a category and an object of contention. After 1936, these conflicts grew even more intense.

An ideology disintegrates: technology in the crisis of 1937

I have already shown that the relationships between the agency of the Inspector-General, the executing officials of the regional planning offices, and the landscape advocates on the whole grew worse up to 1937 by looking at the contentious issues of routing and plantings. The greatest crisis, however, occurred in 1937, when Seifert suspended his work for the *Reichsautobahnen* for nine months. In a vivid description he attributed this to personal factors. In what follows, however, I will examine the structural problems and predetermined fracture points in the collaboration between engineers and architects by looking at the crisis of 1937.

In that year, the first thousand kilometers of autobahn were already in operation, with 1,590 kilometers under construction at the beginning of the year and 1,459 at the end. While work was pushing ahead at a rapid pace, the spokesman of the landscape advocates remained at home in Munich. During a stay in Berlin that summer, "I strolled as a free man across Paris Square [right next to Brandenburg Gate] with the beautiful daughter of an old friend from Steglitz on my arm; cheerfully we looked up to the windows of the Inspector-General for the German Roads, behind which people were working with dead seriousness."[71] The tireless worker had turned into a mocking observer. According to his autobiography, oak trees had helped Seifert to adopt the life of a flaneur. On the showpiece segment of the *Reichsautobahn* network from Munich to the Austrian border, Seifert, in the spring of 1937 as the landscape advocate in charge, had young oaks planted along the road and in the median strip close to the town of Prien and south of the Chiemsee Lake to close gaps in the existing tree cover. The oak in the median strip aroused Todt's wrath, and the Inspector-General ordered that the segment east of the town of Siegsdorf should be planted, not by Seifert, but by civil servants from the Munich construction office. Seifert, for his part, then stopped his work on the western segment. Now he was watching "as the signalman's romanticism spreads," Seifert wrote to a colleague derisively, an allusion to the railway background of the civil servants. His action was meant as a note of protest and triggered an exchange of letters, in which Todt and his advisor articulated their positions in the sharpest terms. Both men vented their accumulated anger over the form their collaboration had taken until then, and their exchange throws a spotlight on the relationship between nature and technology in German road construction at the time.[72]

The clash took place on two levels. For one, Todt took umbrage at Seifert's general remarks about technology, whose role he, Todt, wished to see enhanced in the National Socialist state. For another, what was being negotiated was the status of the landscape advocates and their leeway for action with the individual regional planning offices, and thus the integration of the roadways into the landscape as a reality. Already two years after Seifert had begun his work, Todt had reprimanded him for criticizing mistakes by engineers in public. He reminded Seifert that his was a dependent and advisory relationship: "After all, you didn't come to me to call my attention to mistakes in technology, but I sought out a helper who would support my thinking and I found my way to you." The following lines reveal something about Todt's view of himself as a leading figure in technology and a political fighter: "Through me, technology has called upon you to be her ally. And so I would like you now to be a faithful ally and not to malign your brother-in-arms." This warning had put Seifert in his place and had made the differences in power between patron and client unmistakably clear; the substantive differences between the Inspector-General and the landscape advocate remained, however.[73]

The occasion for the scandal of 1937, when Seifert was simultaneously suspended from his work and left voluntarily in protest, was what the landscape advocates felt to be unsatisfactory collaboration with the regional planning offices. Todt, too, spoke of a "critical point" in the work of the landscape advocates, "not least because the view on planting of some landscape advocates stands in direct contradiction with the way in which the Inspector-General wants the autobahn to be planted." To be sure, Todt credited the advisors with having taught the engineers how to see, especially since the railroad people had lacked an understanding of landscape-sensitive construction. However, some of the landscape advocates had turned into "dogmatists of a rigid approach." To them, the planting itself was more important than the planting of the autobahn.[74]

By contrast, distinct from these landscape advocates were consultants like Werner Bauch in the area of the regional planning office Dresden, who had "struggled through to an expansive planting, to an embrace of these great roads." Todt praised the fact that Bauch was pushing back the edge of the forest to between twenty and forty meters beyond the road and was thus creating "the necessary space," while other landscape advocates in principle had the edge of the forest begin directly at the road (figure 6.3). Moreover, the crisis was further exacerbated by the fact that younger engineers were coming up who could decide for themselves where to plant and where not. Todt described it as "gratifying that the creative engineer does not like to hand his road over to the landscape advocate for planting, but that he likes to decide for himself where to plant." Seifert should welcome this development, for the original intent of both men had been to teach engineers to engage in landscape-sensitive construction, not to train landscape advocates. Todt was planning to "part with some gentlemen" to allow the engineers to apply their new insights themselves. The remaining landscape advocates, however, would have to reduce their planting by between a third and a half. "In fact, it will be necessary to have *de*-planting plans follow the planting plans, in order to remove what is excessive, what merely brings unrest to the swift and great line of our road." For Seifert, therefore, what was at stake in this clash was the scale and nature of the work of the landscape advocates. The lines of conflict had shifted. Initially, the landscape architects had been lined up against the local construction offices and were able to obtain sporadic, though unsystematic, help from the officials of the agency of the Inspector-General. Now, however, the head of the agency regarded them increasingly as potentially superfluous and was threatening to terminate the employment of some of them. He didn't have to fire them, since they merely had consulting contracts. As the course of the conflict reveals, the landscape advocates, on the other hand, were indeed eager to obtain, via their function as consultants on the autobahnen, a professional position for themselves and their work.

Figure 6.3. Often, the autobahn traversed forests, which created particular design challenges for landscape architects and civil engineers. Some preferred a road that was as close to the trees as possible. Fritz Todt, however, the chief autobahn engineer, recommended more clearcutting in order to give drivers a feeling of open space on a fast journey.
Otto Reismann, *Deutschlands Autobahnen—Adolf Hitlers Straßen* (Bayreuth: Gauverlag Bayerische Ostmark, 1937), 194.

In his response, Seifert spoke of the "unclear and demeaning situation" of the landscape advocates. He reminded Todt of his own words that he, Seifert, was to be the technician's conscience, and once in a while that conscience should be allowed to trouble him. He then went on to reproach Todt: "You want to have the magnitude and splendor of the motor roadways clearly expressed, and you would rather take a one hundred meter-wide strip of land for that purpose than the 35 or 40 we have." By contrast, Seifert and his older collaborators were out to serve the landscape and to be "advocates of our *Heimat*." That is why they felt that steep roadside embankments were raw wounds in the landscape as long as they were not grown over with native shrubbery. Seifert countered Todt's embrace of expansiveness and his promotion of the driving experience by criticizing the behavior of the gentleman motorist: "The emphasis on the magnificence and size of the new roads, if translated onto thousands of kilometers, will lead to a desolateness, though it will not be experienced that way by the person who sits at the wheel of his car only as long as he enjoys it and then has his driver take over." Seifert here addressed the link between roads and car ownership. He picked up two core adjectives of Nazi rhetoric when he criticized that Todt's effort could also not be correct in "*völkisch* and social" terms. The great monuments of the "Third Reich" all had to fit into "an overarching whole." But if "the motor roadways are to be oriented chiefly to His Majesty the Motorist, this will tear open a new chasm in the *Volk* between him and the six non-motorists that will still be there even after motorization has been implemented. And the motor roadways are, after all, not being built with the gas pennies of the motorists, but with the fields of the farmer that will be lost forever." Seifert highlighted in detail the importance of the integration of the roads into the landscape and described himself as one of the top five or six German garden designers. Should the "signalman's sentimentality and the landscape distortion" of the Munich segment continue the way it has, he would like a declaration that he had nothing to do with it.

In an afterthought, Seifert admitted that he was not a pleasant or easygoing person: "But my goal is not to have an easy time with the people who are the leaders of today, instead I want to be able to justify myself in what I did and did not do to those who will come after us ... It always went without saying for me to stand by you and your work. But above everything stands loyalty to the *Heimat*." With this letter, Seifert had accumulated as many ideological attributions as possible for the work of the landscape architects, which he evidently regarded as its greatest political capital. By combining an oath of loyalty to the greatness of the "Third Reich" with a profession—seemingly above politics—of *Heimat*, he removed the tasks on the roads of the political dimension they had at the time and placed them into a larger context of meaning. That context was explicitly historical: "In fifty years, nobody will ask any more who did the work, what it cost and how long it took, but only whether it is right." [75] The criticism of the limited use of the roads by a few car owners points to the rhetorical target figure of the motorist, who possessed a different profile for Seifert than he did for Todt: the notion of a motorist who is driving for pleasure with his chauffeur clashed with Todt's implicit notion of a broadly conceived mass of motorists. This discourse was shaped by the uncertainty over mass motorization.

Todt struck a conciliatory tone in his reply. He was sorry that the conflict had arisen. The cause, however, was not that he was seeking to lay claim to the roadside whose width was antisocial. Rather, a large number of landscape advocates, in spite of his admonitions, continued to see the autobahn as an allotment garden instead of as a "large landscape space." The second reason for the quarrel was that "you have too often insulted the engineer and technology in a hurtful way." Seifert's attitude, Todt charged, was brusque and accusatory, and his criticism assumed the "tone of hurtful reproach." What was needed, Todt admonished, was not self-righteousness, but persuasion. "Truly," Todt recapitulated, "I gave the landscape advocates a rare freedom, which in about half of them led to fruitful collaboration. But one must not constantly insult the comrades in the common task." Finally, Todt, with conciliatory intent, suggested that they remember what they had in common and offered to talk things over in his Bavarian vacation house during his vacation.[76]

Seifert was not willing to take the accusation that he was maligning technology lying down. This had "long since ceased to be true." He had not voiced such general criticism in his comments and reports. At the same time, he conceded that the "gruff way" for which Todt was reproaching him had been necessary. Finally, he lamented a loss of trust. For the time being, however, no meeting came about. Seifert bided his time, once he sensed—as he later wrote—that he was slowly gaining ground by staying away. Following a talk in December 1937, Seifert resumed his work, "with more trust than before, but with hardly less friction." Seifert offered various accounts of how the reconciliation came about. In his memoirs he wrote that he had informed Todt unceremoniously that he would continue working. In a later letter he recalled that Todt "quite soundly capitulated in December, whereby I naturally offered him every possible way out."[77]

Whatever the formalities of the meeting may have been: this conflict, fought out with personal bitterness, throws a telling spotlight on the power structures between architect and engineer. The Inspector-General determined the parameters of his collaboration with Seifert and retained for himself the power to define central concepts. That this relationship was akin to feudal dependency is revealed by a remark from Todt to a third party: he was keeping Seifert "as my conscience vis-à-vis my house technicians."[78]

The differences in the concepts of Todt and his advisors became especially apparent in the question of the plantings, the most visible part of the landscape integration of the roads. While the Inspector-General shied away from high costs for shrubs and trees and did not wish to see the staged effect of the road, along with the road itself, buried beneath arboreal greenery, Seifert and the other landscape advocates sought to implement ideas about native planting on a large scale. In addition, their attitude and their desire to plant more were an expression of their skepticism toward the idea of a 24-meter-wide autobahn without green integration. One obvious way to describe this conflict is as a clash of aesthetics.

While Todt sought to heighten the experience of driving the autobahn through the alignment, and thus to embed the roads into a new relationship of space and time, the landscape architects were more interested in regionally distinct roads, which, through their plantings, would make possible a restoration of static German landscapes. Ideological points of contact could be found in the function of these roads within Nazi propaganda and in the conservatism of the landscape advocates. Where they pursued an integration into the larger totality and a subordination to nature, Todt tended to be captivated more by the dynamism of motorized travel, which permitted new possibilities of perception, and wanted to produce it as something fascinating and exciting. Visual consumption is what the road builders had to offer. In a picture book to commemorate the first anniversary of Todt's death, entitled *The Experience of the Reichsautobahnen*, breathless prose invoked this new gaze that would be cast by the masses under the impression of speed:

> Run, my car, run! Like lightning the autobahn now flashes far through the valley from this height here. It was not allowed to tune into the melody of the landscape in any other way! But how, I ask myself and cover it with my hand as I drive, would I have laid it out? Exactly like this? I am unsure to nod affirmatively. It is the visual triumph of joint human-divine creation; the spark, the thought, the idea itself has become stone here and we are whizzing along on it, we greet you, hills, we greet you, steepled city, you, villages in the green, you, stream, and you, the sky above! Germany, here it lies wonderfully laid out, only a piece of it, onward, today we don't want to enjoy it in the small and cozy, it shall fly to our heart ever larger, ever more varied, so that we shall know how rich we are and how much of it we still need to conquer for ourselves. Today we are after the melody of its togetherness, not so much the diversity of its dialects in which it becomes song and resounds as it is sung. Across the *Gaue* it carries us onward, without borders, over time itself.[79]

With descriptions like these, the architectural style of the landscape consultants, which drew on local and regional traditions, was overarched by a homogenized driving experience, one that was more akin to flying than driving. In these accounts, speed itself became the intoxicating goal; the description is reminiscent of aerial pictures and their "moment of dequalifying the existing landscape." By rendering the largely unattainable transport medium of the airplane at least a potential possibility in the form of the fast drive on the autobahn, the sought-after modernity of the roads could be doubly charged by the landscape and by its rapid disappearance.[80]

However, this new spatial sensation of driving, so lauded for its speed, was the result of a myriad of conflicts over the routing of the roads in the landscape, over their plantings, and over institutional positions during their construction. The way in which they were carried through the landscape was embedded in a contradictory mixture of stylistic elements, functional attributions, and ideological foundations. Between the architects, installed as experts for the landscape, and the civil engineers—of both the office of the Inspector-General and the construction offices—, a conflict was fought out, one that Todt himself had triggered and in which he intervened in a moderating role. In the final analysis, though, he always retained the right to make definitions for himself by seeking to implement his own aesthetic ideas autocratically. From the perspective of the landscape advocates, work on the landscape integration of the roads had to remain unsatisfactory in the end, because they were suffering from an uncertain status assignment, had to continuously renegotiate their maneuvering room, and were able to achieve only scattered success. In the meantime, their rhetoric and their efforts to embed their concerns within the reality of Nazi rule grew increasingly radical. Before embarking on an excursus about the importance of landscape architects outside of the autobahn construction, I will conclude this section with an examination of the financing of the roads as a regulative force.

The value and cost of landscaping

Overall, criteria of profitability stood in the background in the construction of the *Reichsautobahn*, especially as far as the general decision to build it was concerned. What was at play here were less economic arguments than motives such as prestige and propaganda. Likewise, the decision not to charge motorists a toll was not motivated by profitability. However, the picture of an autobahn bureaucracy that was happily working away is not accurate. Especially as far as the work of the landscape advocates was concerned, the Directorate *Reichsautobahnen* was from the very beginning of the planning work out to lower the costs of their activities. The agency was made up of civil servants from the Reich Railroad, who intended to treat the construction of the *Reichsautobahnen* in accounting terms no differently from the construction of a railroad.[81]

I have already described the insistent and successful attempts to reduce the compensation for the landscape advocates. The cost argument came into play also in decisions by the Inspector-General concerning the building of an embankment instead of a bridge, or the plantings that were seen as too thick. In 1936, Todt stipulated explicitly:

> On the question of whether, in consideration of the landscape's appearance, a bridge or an embankment should be chosen to traverse a valley, the results of the calculations are initially decisive in drawing up a design, that is, the *cheaper* method is to be chosen, and preference shall be given to the method more favorable to the landscape only if the costs are the same or insignificantly higher.[82]

What was considered "insignificant" were additional costs of no more than 5 percent of the costs for the structure. In the same decree, Todt stipulated the following: "A perfect adaptation of the roads to the terrain, which also includes leaving out all unnecessary separating ditches, is usually tantamount to a reduction in the total movement of earth. Landscape consulting, exercised sensibly and on time, must therefore pay for itself with a reduction in costs." This prescribed rather than described the economy of landscape integration. It was a reasonable presumption that it would result in a lower volume of earth to be moved. However, the constant attempts to save money soon created a pattern of cost-cutting that I will call the "money trap."

The reason was that the costs for building the *Reichsautobahnen* rose along with the pace of construction. The capacities of the construction industry were overextended, workers were increasingly hard to find, especially by the mid-1930s, and, most of all, the pressure of deadlines raised prices. The cost factor came into play most strongly from 1937 on, when, as part of the Four-Year Plan, bridges of natural stone were declared to be the ideal form, only to become economically unsustainable a year later. Bridges stood at the beginning of planning and were (and are) constructed as the first components of the route. In many places, as we have seen, the work of the landscape advocates was limited to the subsequent planting of nearly finished segments.[83] At that point, however, the funds were often already allocated, namely for construction of the segments and bridges. There was a tendency for actual costs to be higher than initially calculated: construction companies sent higher invoices; the terrain was less accessible than assumed, which necessitated labor-intensive excavations or the unplanned hiring of outside companies to blast marshlands; or the actual construction took longer than planned and had to be accelerated with additional personnel or through overtime right up to the inauguration date.

The budgets for planting the road shrank accordingly. In the end, these tasks were left with the least amount of money; the money trap closed. Thus, some of the planting as part of the landscape integration fell victim largely to self-created cost pressures. We are left with the question of how much the office of the Inspector-General actually intended to spend on landscape integration, and how much it did spend. In a 1934 letter to a landscape advocate, Seifert wrote that at the beginning of the construction work, Todt had reckoned 1 percent of construction expenses to pay for the work of the landscape advocates and the planting: "I don't know what it looks like today." Though there were no precise directives about how much was to be spent on the landscape advocates and their work, the expenses settled down at a relatively low level compared to the overall expenditures. An internal report from the office of the Inspector-General after three years of building activity provided a meticulous list of the added costs for the work of the landscape advocates. Based on documentation from the regional planning offices, costs were summarized for the following activities: compost preparation; topsoil storage for the plantings; planting of the median strip, the embankments, and the ramps, as well as of additionally acquired areas of terrain; procurement of grass, acquisition of meadows or sowing; purchase of land along the autobahn; and expenses for compensating the landscape designers. The report concluded that a total of 808,500 Reichsmark had been spent on this expense item by the end of 1936, which came to about 800 Reichsmark per kilometer.[84]

By way of comparison: the additional costs merely for ensuring that the segments would be completed on time for the planned opening date of 27 September 1936 came to 3.147 million Reichsmark. On that day, the first one thousand kilometers of the *Reichsautobahn* were "ceremoniously handed over" to the accompaniment of noisy propaganda. But back to the kilometer prices. The average of 900,000 Reichsmark per kilometer given in the examined sources exceeded the original estimate of 1933 three-fold. Appeals to save "by every means" could not prevent this rapid rise. If we posit that the figures by the directorate of the *Reichsautobahn* in 1937 are accurate, that the expenses for the landscape integration remained at the same level, and we ignore inflation, the numbers show that 800 of the 900,000 Reichsmark per kilometer were spent on integrating the roads into the landscape. That would amount to merely 0.09 percent of construction costs. A recent article even speaks of a price per kilometer of 1.1 million Reichsmark, which would reduce the share spent on landscape integration to 0.07 percent. Even at a price per kilometer of 750,000 at the end of 1934, the share devoted to landscape work, 0.1 percent, was still negligible.[85]

Upon closer examination, the financial support given to landscape integration leads to two conclusions. First, the propaganda about landscape integration and the willingness of the autobahn bureaucracy to spend money on it were inversely proportional: the louder the propaganda, the fewer resources were expended on landscaping. Second, on a deeper level, the interest in landscape was often limited to care and maintenance after the fact. Within the framework of this logic, the support given to landscape design was meager, especially since visual consumption on the roads could be achieved also with less elaborate and less costly landscape integration.

The landscape advocates seek power beyond the autobahn

The group formation of the landscape advocates has been seen as a response to the uncertain status they occupied in the construction of the autobahn. This section will examine the extent to which the landscape architects tried to expand their radius of professional work in the Third Reich and what strategies they pursued in the process. One important current in these efforts was aimed at replacing the established institutions of conservation with new bureaucracies that included the landscape advocates. As a result of the quarrels over competency between road builders and conservationists following passage of the Reich Nature Protection Law of 1935, the office of the Inspector-General for the German Roads had carved out for itself a preserve within the sphere of state-run conservation. The landscape advocates appointed by the Inspector-General subsequently sought, with growing self-confidence, to expand their sphere of action. In the process, they had a growing number of run-ins with the official conservationists. Their plans for a reorganization were aimed at creating a different hierarchy for landscape design alongside the state-run conservation.

The occasion for what was initially an internal discussion among the landscape advocates was a suggestion from one of their own, Max Schwarz (Worpswede), in the January circular in 1940. Schwarz criticized the conservation establishment, charging that while it did support the "preservation of the appearance of the landscape, ... it is failing utterly in putting forth proposals for a landscape that is to be newly designed." Given the growing agricultural land developments, regroupings, and cultivation of wasteland, this was more important, however, than mere conservation activities. He suggested that the nature protection officials could certainly continue to work in an honorary capacity, but the "regular appointment of an experienced landscape advocate" was necessary for design work. Every planning agency would then have to inspect the prospective construction site with the landscape advocate before the project phase and then decide with him on further consultation or planning. This kind of reorganization was also important "especially for the great settlement work in the East." With the military expansion of the Nazi state into central and eastern Europe, the landscape advocates smelled a professional opportunity, which they regarded—following the example of the autobahnen—as the successor to conservation.[86]

Hirsch's demand received backing from the landscape advocate Bauch (regional planning office Dresden), who regarded the "merely museum-like" attitude of nature protection as wrong for the "continued building, deliberate and healthy, of the German cultural landscape." Bauch believed that it was necessary to consolidate the circle of the landscape advocates, to whom he referred as a "shock troop." Even nature protectors got involved in the debate: the conservation commissioner in the province of Hannover, Gert Kragh, was a student of Tüxen's and emphasized the unity of conservation and landscape design. Hermann Schurhammer, a construction official in Baden who joined the landscape advocates late and was the only engineer among them, joined Schwarz's suggestions and called for a legal basis to strip conservationists of the jurisdiction over new construction.[87]

As early as 1939, the landscape advocate Josef Leibig (Düsseldorf) had negotiated a separation of competencies with the conservation commissioner in Prussia's Rhine province. According to the terms of this agreement, the conservationist was in charge of preservation and protection, the landscape advocate for building up and shaping the landscape. "Interventions in the landscape" were to be reviewed by both men. Because the landscape advocates saw ever-new areas for their work in Reich waterways and hydrological engineering, they called for a uniform regulation "throughout the entire Reich." At a working meeting of the *Deutscher Heimatbund* at Sternberg Castle in Westphalia in July 1941, the demands of the landscape advocates openly clashed for the first time with the ideas of the conservationists. The latter, as one landscape advocate put it, did not want to saw off the branch on which they were sitting by letting go of landscape design. A suggestion by the landscape-minded architect Erich Kühn at the meeting, however, was aimed at an institutionalized landscape cultivation in the various provinces with a "Reich landscape advocate" at the top. This would have meant the adoption of the organizational scheme of the autobahn construction. Kühn also used the terms from this area, though he said that he did so without thinking about the persons of the autobahn construction. Moreover, he headed a committee with conservationists and landscape advocates that was set up at the Sternberg meeting, but it could not agree on the organizational plans.[88]

One landscape advocate, Josef Leibig, expressed his support for the Kühn solution in the circular, as long as Seifert would join the Reich Office for Nature Protection as an advisor; Max Schwarx rejected it as excessively bureaucratic. Only one of Seifert's collaborators, Ludwig Roemer, recommended objectivity and professionalism, not the demarcation of spheres of interest. In a meeting at the Reich Forestry Office, Seifert declared his willingness to support the organization of landscape cultivation for the entire Reich, but the legal groundwork for it was subsequently never done.[89]

One participant in this muddle that led to nothing in the end was the Württemberg State Commissioner for Conservation, Schwenkel. He had been working since April 1940 in a secondary capacity as consultant for landscape cultivation in the Chief Office for Nature Protection in Berlin. In letters to the landscape advocates he affected the tone of a subordinate—at the latest after Seifert had made it clear to him how much greater his accomplishments were compared to those of Schwenkel. Seifert boasted to two confidants among the landscape advocates that there was "no reason to thank conservation for what we have worked for." The conservationists had "truly no part" in the success of the work of the landscape advocates.[90]

At the end of 1942, landscape advocate Hirsch summarized the quarrels as follows: "We are now at war. The settling of such questions at a time like this is really not acceptable." But the fact that other landscape advocates fought over them so intensively shows how eager they were to defend the territories they had begun to inhabit and to acquire new ones. In substantive terms this seems the beginning of an institutionalized break with a conservationist atttitude of nature protection. The exaggerations of the Seifert group that only they were capable of doing landscape design could be seen as professionally motivated; the thinking of the landscape advocates in terms of what was their own preserve was carried on here. A unifying effect came also from the racist underpinning of the ideas on conservation and landscape design. In 1940, Schwenkel saw a need to act, for when it came to hydrology as well as external advertising, "the new, truly German ideas of landscape design must prevail over the still very strong, liberal-American—if not to say, Jewish—forces."[91]

With statements like these the landscape advocates sought to achieve influence over the great landscape-altering projects of the Nazi regime. In spite of the substantive differences over the ideological foundation of the landscaping of the autobahnen, they were able to present themselves as being closer to the regime than the conservationists. In the background was competition with the Berlin landscape architect Wiepking-Jürgensmann, whom the SS involved as a landscape consultant for its "General Plan East," very much to Seifert's displeasure.[92]

Thanks to personal alliances with Todt, individual landscape advocates attained positions of wide-ranging power, which were evidently greater than those of the established nature protection. In 1941, when the Reich Chancellery, some of the ministries, and the Reich Office for Nature Protection deliberated about a moratorium on the draining of wetlands (which never got anywhere), it became clear that Seifert's network of informal relationships had replaced the state-organized nature protection as far as the "closer relationships to higher offices" were concerned. During hydropower projects in the Alps, Seifert presented himself as Todt's protégé and was able to influence the planning.[93]

In the present context it is not possible to take a closer look at the debate over a "steppefication" of Germany that Seifert triggered in 1936. In this debate he attacked the work of hydrological engineers: there was a danger that the groundwater level could sink from river regulations and the growing number of hydropower plants, which increased the threat of soil erosion. Typically enough, he combined these functional arguments with aesthetic ones and drew vociferous disagreement from hydraulic engineers and Minister of Agriculture Darré. The debate over "steppefication" dealt with larger ecological interconnections than was the case with the autobahnen; as an outsider, Seifert could engage in it with great vigor. In the end, however, this polemic, too, despite attracting a lot of attention, had no tangible result in the Nazi state.[94]

*

Landscaping the *Reichsautobahnen* turned out to be more problematic than it seems at first glance. Hitler's highways presented themselves as a contradictory mix of stylistic elements, functional attributions, and ideological aspects. In what follows, I will summarize and explain them.

To begin with, the claims put forth by "German Technology" were reflected in the structure and its propaganda. After 1933, the idea of the autobahnen was disconnected from its prehistory as a project floated by prominent citizens and integrated into the representation of the Nazi regime as a means of mass motorization. "German Technology," as an allegedly German *Sonderweg* into technological modernity, promised an all-encompassing industrial modernization without negative side effects including stopping the loss of traditional cultural landscapes. The *Reichsautobahnen* were to offer visible proof that the creation of such an infrastructure could be accomplished without destroying the landscape. As we have seen, the two groups in question, the landscape advocates and civil engineers, had sufficient ideological overlap for them to present "German Technology" jointly as a showpiece. However, the ideological hodgepodge of "German Technology" offered few concrete directives. The rhetoric of building and designing the project united both groups, which were clearly at odds over the meaning of even such central categories as "landscape" and "technology," as the quarrels between Seifert and Todt revealed. Landscape could be understood as a malleable background for the driving experience, or as the starting point for a restoration of prehuman landscapes. The ideology of the roads was not fixed from the beginning; for a long time it was defined and redefined and became clearer only as construction proceeded. In addition, engineers and architects were hoping for a gain in status and improvement in their professional standing from the overarching ideology in the new regime. While civil engineers were eager to proclaim technology a cultural factor, former garden architects welcomed the opportunity to translate their notions of landscape architecture to a building project.

At the same time, the autobahn bureaucracy began to transform itself into an almost autonomous institution. It is true that in the beginning, this development was confronted by the interlocked organization of the Inspector-General's office, some leading engineers, and the *Reichsautobahn* enterprise with civil engineers from the Reich Railroad in charge of carrying out the project. But the agency of the Inspector-General clearly proved to be the most potent of these power blocks. The process of the autobahn got under way, and every year about a thousand kilometers of the superhighways were built. The landscape architects tried to use the anarchic aspects of the situation to their advantage by seeking to carve out their own position of power. Although they were successful with the help of individual personal alliances, they soon realized that their status was shaky and that they were unable to establish any continuity to their work. In this situation, their rhetoric grew harsher and was articulated with increasingly strident nationalistic and racist undertones. Clearly, this was a strategy—conscious or not—to save their own work from becoming marginalized, and to establish points of connection with the racial dogmas that were at the center of Nazi ideology. In this context, ideology and technological knowledge were not fixed and temporarily overlapping spheres, but were fluid and mutually interdependent. In this respect, the level of discourse on the roads and the history of the process of building them most definitely cannot be separated. The landscape advocates did not go to work on the autobahnen as an ideologically and professionally solidified group; instead, they constituted themselves on both levels only through their participation in the turbulent process itself.

Seifert was already unable to enforce his meritocratic ideas fully when he selected the landscape consultants, and had to tolerate candidates picked by the NSDAP to be landscape advocates. On the other hand, a potential critic of the regime like the architect Mattern was tolerated on "Adolf Hitler's Roads," provided he placed his creative potential in service to the project. He was able to accommodate himself to the new standards of landscape architecture decreed by Todt, and he went through the process of self-disciplining with a simultaneous boost in status. This pattern is in line with what happened in other cultural areas of the Nazi state.[95]

The work of the landscape advocates for the regional planning offices was marked by a precarious independence grounded in their status as consultants and by structural powerlessness. This already became clear in the issue of compensation. Even if the landscape advocates enjoyed the propaganda support of the Third Reich, the Nazi state was reluctant to open its treasury to them. As a result, the landscape integration depended to a large extent on the personality of each individual landscape advocate, his assertiveness in a masculine climate of competition, and the contacts he cultivated with the local civil engineers. Individual consultants could bolster their position at best through Seifert and his access to Todt. This, in turn, reflected the basis of Todt's power, which was derived from the fact that he was directly subordinate to Hitler. For their part, the landscape advocates formed into a group seeking homogeneity. Outside of the *Reichsautobahn* construction they were able to expand on scattered connections to other projects. All in all, the collaboration of consultants and engineers, especially in the case of Seifert and Todt, can be described as a quasi-feudal patronage relationship defined from the top down, in which Todt decided about competing approaches at his own discretion. The discussed conflicts in a "state of collective hysteria" were built into the confusing autobahn bureaucracy from the beginning, were wanted by Todt, and were consciously directed.[96]

As for the attitude of the civil engineers, one must begin by distinguishing between the engineers doing the actual construction in the regional planning offices, and the supervising engineers in the office of the Inspector-General. For some in the latter group, the landscape advocates functioned as a conscience that was supposed to help in overcoming an outdated attitude toward nature. But when the landscape architects demanded a share of the power to define suitable road designs, even Todt himself reverted back to his autocratic status as the final expert. That applies at least to the early phase of the project, when long segments were built after the railway pattern of straightaway-circular arcs-straightaway around which the Hafraba planners had designed the roads. The *New York Times* exaggerated only slightly when, in 1937, it called the autobahn "the railroad man's idea of the way highways should be built."[97] As it is, during the first two years of construction one can note a mixture of stylistic pluralism and uncertainty over function. A gas station by Mies van der Rohe was built in the same network of roads as concrete bridges that stonemasons made to look like natural stone. Then, by the middle of the 1930s, a building style emerged that can be seen as in part a German adaptation of the American parkways. The roads were designed around the visual consumption of landscapes. With the help of modern road building techniques, the experience of the car as a domesticated adventure machine could lead to views and vistas that made possible entertaining moments of surprise and eventful outings for the sake of driving. As a result of this staging of an exciting drive, which is what Todt explicitly favored, roads were ideally routed over mountains instead of through valleys so they could fulfill this function of visual consumption. The low density of traffic and the fact that the car was still an exclusive mode of transportation were prerequisites for this visual appropriation of landscape. Fast trips through expansive space created these kinds of panoramas, which were widely celebrated in propaganda. Observers with fewer preconceptions experienced the roads as welcome escapist routes, as was the case with Victor Klemperer, the Dresden professor who became a victim of the regime's racial politics. A British writer found them to be boring, mechanistic, and—in the final analysis—inhuman transportation routes, which reduced the driver to a cog in the machinery of modern mass production, while the pines appeared like a solid mass of verdure.[98]

These roads of visual exploration, however, were by no means a straight technology transfer of the American parkways. Unlike the parkways, which led from the cities to recreational areas, the *Reichsautobahnen* were also open to commercial traffic. But the steep ascents were not suited to trucks, and in this way the fitness of the roads for winter driving was consciously reduced. The function and design of the roads began to clash. This conflict was not resolved under National Socialism; instead, it was merely papered over, initially by propaganda and later by the obvious failure at motorizing German society.

The landscape advocates had no alternative vision to hold up to this concept. They formulated their demand for sinuous roads instead of mostly straight ones as the only concept that was close to nature; this rigid attitude encountered opposition from both the local civil engineers and the engineers in Todt's agency. A rethinking took place only after initial experiences had been made with long straightaways as a design element. They were judged to be less safe than curvy routes, an assessment that was justified with anthropological arguments and personal anecdotal experience. By the time Todt gave a speech in 1940 in which he argued for roads that adhered more strongly to the contours of the landscape, there were already mathematical reasons for why curvy segments should be part of the route, as the next chapter will show.

The push toward a more radical rhetoric on the part of the landscape advocates was most evident when it came to the planting of the *Reichsautobahnen*. The landscape consultants wanted to plant more and differently than did the civil engineers. Their plea that the plants used be native to restore the "original" landscapes following the criteria of contemporary ecology was expressed in an increasingly unyielding and racist manner. It met with indifferent acceptance if it did not interfere with the visual consumption (as in the case of the general support given to Tüxen's office in Hannover), or with rejection if—in Todt's eyes—it was too radical in regarding an existing chestnut avenue as in need of repair. As the Inspector-General saw it, the mediating approach of bioengineering was better suited at finding zones of transition between landscape and technology than was phytosociology pursued with a restorationist agenda. Added to this was that in the eyes of the officials of the Inspector-General's agency, a small number of bushes and trees were sufficient to stage the driving experience. Within the anarchic power and organizational structure of road building, the "scientification" of the work of cultivating the landscape by means of a systematic mapping of the vegetation failed to produce the potent legitimizing effect the landscape advocates had hoped for.

Some corrections to the ideas that have been articulated so far in the historical scholarship about landscape and autobahn under National Socialism are therefore called for. We are not dealing with a mere adaptation of traditional design features of park architecture, as Schütz has maintained. Instead, the highly conflictual process was embedded within the professional self-discovery of landscape architects in the twentieth century, which included precisely the abandonment of garden and park architecture as a way of achieving an elevation in status. It is also not possible to separate the hesitant academicization of this profession from the ideology of those who pursued and sponsored it, as Rollins has done in his search for ecological successes. On the other side of the interpretive spectrum, it should be noted that, contrary to the assumptions of Gröning and Wolschke-Bulmahn, the ideological coalition between landscape architects and the Nazi system was certainly not without ruptures. In fact, the collaborative relationships were marked by constant friction; the increasing radicalization and racist underpinning of the concerns of the landscape architects must be understood within the context of structural powerlessness. Contextualizing this development promises to yield more differentiated insights into the environmental history of this regime.[99] Moreover, the attempted and halfhearted ecological restoration on the *Reichsautobahnen* is a striking example that the restoration of ecosystems is never a politically innocent process, but always serves certain interests and generates meanings.[100]

This study has also shown the need to examine in detail the respective actors and constellations of actors. Contrary to a widely accepted belief, the role of conservation was marginal in the construction of the autobahn; this was the deliberate outcome of the policy of the landscape advocates and the office of the Inspector-General, who, starting from the roads, sought to create factual and legal zones of redesigned landscape where conservation and conservationists were excluded. Against Seidler's interpretation one should note that Todt can by no means be seen as a well-meaning supporter of the landscape architects; instead, he instigated the conflicts over ideology and design with a mixture of laissez-faire and the constant threat to intervene and settled them autocratically as an expression of his position of power.[101]

The supposed ecological sensitivity of National Socialism postulated by various authors such as Schama and Prinz is thus an open question rather than an established fact—at least as far as the example of the autobahnen is concerned. The mixture of stylistic elements, functional attributions, and changing ideology is too contradictory for us to say that the Nazi autobahnen had, on balance, a clearly ecological orientation. If the contradictory parameters can be brought under one heading at all, it would be that of visual consumption, which made the roads—created with strong external and internal pressure—into signs for the consumption-focused reorientation of traffic. The question about the modernity of National Socialism, which was so intensely debated in the 1990s, would thus have to be answered with reference to the paradox of the premature roads and their simultaneous ecologization, which was both abreast of the times and timid. The mere invocation of "blood and soil" is today no longer sufficient to explain the contradictory environmental efforts of the Nazi regime. There is no need to go as far as Peter Fritzsche has, who already described the "spirit of renovation" as modern. But a part of the hectic activity surrounding the autobahnen was in fact the attempt—which failed in the end—to renovate Germany's landscape.[102] The aestheticization of many areas of life in the Third Reich naturally included the autobahnen, yet this process did not rise above that of "lovely make-believe"; in the end, the conflicts over the proper aestheticization remained unresolved.[103] Hence, the green autobahn of the National Socialists is a myth that should be treated as such.

Notes

1. The original reads: "Herr Alwin Seifert pflanzte Bäumchen aus einem wahren Wunderbäumchen./Der Lockenkopf kam ihm ins Wackeln, so muß't er in 'Natur' nun fackeln./Ein Berg erstand, die Straße zweigte, wobei sie sich ein wenig neigte./Todt schrie, als er das Wunder sah: 'Ihr g'hört nach Dachau alle ja/müsst' eine solche Straß' ich schauen, begänne ich sie umzubauen./Die Kurven sind ja viel zu krumm, das ist nicht krumm, das ist ja dumm!/ Unübersichtlich ist die Bahn, die kein Vernünft'ger fahren kann.'/So haben wir zur Acht gezogen, die Linienführung sanft gebogen./So kam die erste Autobahn in Münchens Halle glücklich an." Farewell evening for the staff of the exhibits "The Road" and "Road Building Exhibit Munich 1934" on 24 November 1934, 8–9, SN 56. The exhibit was shown in Munich from June to September 1934.
2. Stephen Bending, "The Improvement of Arthur Young. Agricultural Technology and the Production of Landscape in Eighteenth Century England," in Nye, *Landscape*, 241–253; W[illiam] G[eorge] Hoskins, *The Making of the English Landscape. With an Introduction and Commentary by Christopher Taylor* (London, 1988), 161–62; Schiegerl and Stiegler, "Gärten Seiferts," 27; Schultze-Naumburg, *Die Gestaltung der Landschaft durch den Menschen* (Munich, 1928), 27.
3. Hoskins, *English Landscape*, 254–269; Schivelbusch, *Railway Journey*; for a more recent, relativizing view: James Winter, *Secure from Rash Assault. Sustaining the Victorian Environment* (Berkeley, 1999), 112–119. See Wolfgang Kos, *Über den Semmering. Kulturgeschichte einer künstlichen Landschaft* (Vienna, 1984).
4. Todt on 18 January 1934, BAK R 43 II/403, quoted in Christoph Hölz, "Verkehrsbauten," in *Bauen im Nationalsozialismus. Bayern 1933–1945. Ausstellung des Architekturmuseums der Technischen Universität München und des Münchner Stadtmuseums*, ed. Winfried Nerdinger (Munich, 1993), 54–97, 56; Wolfgang Sachs, *Die Liebe zum Automobil. Ein Rückblick in die Geschichte unserer Wünsche* (Reinbek, 1984), 115; Gijs Mom, "Das 'Scheitern' des frühen Elektromobils (1895–1925). Versuch einer Neubewertung," *Technikgeschichte* 64 (1997): 269–285, 275; Warren James Belasco, *Americans on the Road. From Autocamp to Motel, 1910–1945* (Baltimore and London. 1997 [orig. 1979]), 24.
5. Günter Bayerl, "Die Erfindung des Autofahrens: Technik als Repräsentation, Abenteuer und Sport," in *Sozialgeschichte der Technik. Festschrift für Ulrich Troitzsch*, ed. Günter Bayerl and Wolfhard Weber (Münster, 1998), 317–329, 328–29; Carolyn Höfig, "Engineered Like No Other. German Society and the Automobile," in *Breakdown, Breakup, Breakthrough: Germany's Difficult Passage to Modernity*, ed. Carl F. Lankowski (New York, 1999), 155–174; Harry Niemann, " Zum Interaktionsverhältnis Mensch-Technik innerhalb der Rahmenbedingungen von Schulung und Verrechtlichung in den Anfangsjahren des Automobilismus," in *Die Entwicklung der Motorisierung im Deutschen Reich und den Nachfolgestaaten*, ed. Harry Niemann and Armin Hermann (Stuttgart, 1995), 104–106; Barbara Schmucki, "'Verkehrsnot in unseren Städten!' Leitbilder in der Verkehrsplanung Ost- und Westdeutschlands (1945–1990)," *Technikgeschichte* 63 (1996): 321–342; Doßmann, "*Autobahnen;*" Möser, "World War I."
6. Oskar Weller, "Das Fahren auf den Autobahnen," *Die Straße* 2 (1935): 188–189.

7. According to Fack, until 1945 traffic education was largely reactive: Dietmar Fack, *Automobil, Verkehr und Erziehung: Motorisierung zwischen Beschleunigung und Anpassung 1885–1945* (Opladen, 2000), 463.
8. Kurt Becker and Walter Ostwald, "Was der Kraftfahrer am Straßenbau nicht versteht," *Die Straße* 2 (1935): 157–160, 157. Emphasis original.
9. Hermann H. Gläser, *Via Strata. Roman der Straße. Die durchaus persönlich gesehene Geschichte des Straßenbaus von den Anfängen bis zur Autobahn* (Wiesbaden and Berlin, 1987), 121.
10. Wilhelm Hirsch, "Die Einpassung der Strecke [Frankfurt-Darmstadt] in die Landschaft," *Die Straße* 2 (1935): 320–321, quote 320.
11. Dittrich, "Autobahn-Fahrbahndecken," 13.
12. Hübotter to Seifert, n.d. [presumably 1938], SN 51; Schwarz to Seifert, 9 October 1938, ibid.; Seifert to Todt, 27 June 1934, DM NL 133/56.
13. Alwin Seifert, "Natur und Technik im deutschen Straßenbau," in idem, *Im Zeitalter*, 9–23, 18; idem, "Die landschaftliche Eingliederung der Straße," *Die Straße* 2 (1935): 446–450, 446.
14. Seifert, *Leben*, 57; Todt to Seifert, 26 June 1935, BAK NS 26/1188; Alwin Seifert, "Schlängelung?," in idem, *Im Zeitalter*, 114–117, 114.
15. See Anne Harrington, *Reenchanted Science. Holism in German Culture from Wilhelm II to Hitler* (Princeton, 1996).
16. Conflicting opinions: Weller, "Fahren," 189; Georg Eichler, "Trassierung der Automobilstraße," *Hafraba* 1/3 (1928): 3–6 (calls long straightaways as sleep-inducing); Inspector-General for the German Roads, Guidelines for the Design Work for autobahnen, 12 December 1933, quoted in Paul Hafen, *Das Schrifttum über die deutschen Autobahnen* (Bonn, 1956), 94 (straightaways are not sleep-inducing). Looking back in 1962, Lorenz saw "the historical appreciation for the straightaway" predominate over "the curve, which was in ill-repute as being dangerous." Hans Lorenz, "Trassierung," in Bundesminister für Verkehr Abteilung Straßenbau, ed., *Hafraba. Bundesautobahn Hansestädte-Frankfurt-Basel. Rückblick auf 30 Jahre Autobahnbau* (Wiesbaden and Berlin, 1962), 174–179, here 178; Angus Kress Gillespie and Michael Aaron Rockland, *Looking for America on the New Jersey Turnpike* (New Brunswick, N.J., 1992), 104; Phil Patton, *Open Road. A Celebration of the American Highway* (New York, 1986), 132–133.
17. Seifert to Todt, 5 August 1935, DM NL 133/57.
18. Schönleben to Directorate *Reichsautobahnen*, 25 September 1935, BAK R 65I/92, fol. 138.
19. Seifert, *Leben*, 58; Lorenz, "Trassierung," 178; Klaus Schefold and Alois Neher, eds., *50 Jahre Autobahnen in Baden-Württemberg. Eine Dokumentation im Auftrage des Autobahnamtes Baden-Württemberg* (Stuttgart, n. d. [1986]), 19; Eduard Schönleben, "Linienführung und Ausgestaltung neuzeitlicher Autostraßen," *Die Straße* 2 (1935): 148–153, 148.
20. Dittrich, "Autobahn-Fahrbahndecken," 15.
21. Wilhelm Heubling, "Straße und Umwelt," in Herbert Kühn, ed., *Strassenforschung. 50 Jahre Forschungsgesellschaft für das Straßenwesen 1924–1974* (Bonn-Bad Godesberg, 1974), 253–264, 256; Seifert to the Gau chief in Lower Silesia, 24 February 1943, SN 148. The Gau chief had complained about the "poor design" of the *Reichsautobahn* in Lower Silesia, in response to which Seifert explained how the sinuous line had come about.
22. Regional planning office Berlin, Explanatory Report, 28 December 1939, BAK R 65II/22; Schönleben, Departmental Decree re. Routing, 31 January 1936, BAK R 65I/93.
23. Fritz Heller, "Gedanken zur Ästhetik der Linien- und Gradientenführung," *Die Straße* 5 (1938): 12–15, 13 (emphasis original); Speech of Reich Minister Dr. Todt at the Meeting of Architects of the Inspector-General of German Roads at the Plassenburg, 9, 31 August 1940, BAK NS 26/1188; Seifert, *Leben*, 58.
24. Hugo Koester, "Erfahrungen beim Trassieren von Reichsautobahnen," in *Trassierungsgrundlagen der Reichsautobahn*, ed. Hans Lorenz (Berlin, 1943), 18–34, 18; Alwin Seifert, "Gedanken zur Linienführung der Reichsautobahnen," in ibid., 34–36 (on the "monotonousness" of older autobahn segments).

25. Speech of Reich Minister Todt, 8–9, BAK NS 26/1188
26. Eduard Schönleben, "Der Irschenberg," *Die Baukunst*. [supplement to] *Kunst im Deutschen Reich* (January 1942): 61; Hölz, "Verkehrsbauten," 58. Given what we know from the files, the propaganda claim that Hitler himself had chosen the route over the Irschenberg must be consigned to the realm of speculation. Fritz Todt, "Adolf Hitler and His Roads," in *Adolf Hitler: Pictures from the Life of the Führer 1931–1935* (New York and London, 1978), 88–95, 93. The files that I consulted yielded no evidence for or against Hitler's involvement in this case. Hitler, however, did get involved when the autobahn approached Bayreuth, the site of the Richard Wagner opera festivals. In the spring of 1935, the dictator ordered all construction to be stopped since the road threatened to impair the landscape. Some road structures were torn down after his intervention. Hitler allegedly held a meeting at "Haus Wahnfried" on the autobahn with Bayreuth's Lord Mayor and remarked that the preservation of the landscape was more important than the driver. Todt used the opportunity to remind the engineers to be aware of their responsibility and to search for the culturally and aesthetically optimal solution. Seifert to Todt, 12 March 1935, BAK NS 26/1188; Todt to Society Reichsautobahnen for distribution to all regional planning offices, 16 March 1935, ibid.
27. Fritz Todt, "Der landschaftliche Charakter der Autobahn München-Landesgrenze," *Die Straße* 2 (1935), 67–68. The following quotes are also taken from this essay.
28. Hölz, "Verkehrsbauten"; Klaus Kratzsch, "Reichsautobahn und Denkmalpflege. Das Rasthaus am Chiemsee—ein aktueller Fall," *Deutsche Kunst und Denkmalpflege* 47/1 (1989): 23–26.
29. As an additional embellishment, Todt noted that after the expansion of the Ludwig bridge and Rosenheimer Street, the 4.5-kilometer long stretch from City Hall at Marienplatz in Munich could easily be traversed "in five minutes." Karl Fiehler, "Der Anschluß Münchens an das Reichsautobahnnetz," *Die Straße* 2 (1935): 450–454.
30. Alwin Seifert, "Die landschaftliche Eingliederung der Strecke," *Die Straße* 2 (1935): 446–450, 446–467; Friedrich Doll, "Vom Bau der Reichsautobahn München-Landesgrenze," *Die Straße* 2 (1935): 153–157, 156. In a different article he reported that "only" 4,789 meters of the segment had inclines in excess of 5 percent, and "only" 5,869 had gradients of more than 5 percent, over a total length of 125 kilometers: "Technische Aufgaben beim Bau der Reichsautobahnstrecke München-Landesgrenze," *Die Straße* 2 (1935): 432–440, 433.
31. Rudy Koshar, *Germany's Transient Paths. Preservation and National Memory in the Twentieth Century* (Chapel Hill and London, 1998), 175. On consumption and tourism see Hasso Spode, "'Der deutsche Arbeiter reist.' Massentourismus im Dritten Reich," in *Sozialgeschichte der Freizeit. Untersuchungen zum Wandel der Alltagskultur in Deutschland*, ed. Gerhard Huck (Wuppertal, 1982), 281–306; Christine Keitz, *Reisen als Leitbild. Die Entstehung des modernen Massentourismus in Deutschland* (Munich, 1997); Shelley Baranowski, *Strength Through Joy: Consumerism and Mass Tourism in the Third Reich* (Cambridge, 2004), esp. chapter 4.
32. John Brewer, "Was können wir aus der Geschichte der frühen Neuzeit für die moderne Konsumgeschichte lernen?," in *Europäische Konsumgeschichte. Zur Gesellschafts- und Kulturgeschichte des Konsums (18. bis 20. Jahrhundert)*, ed. Hannes Siegrist, Hartmut Kaelble, and Jürgen Kocka (Frankfurt and New York, 1997), 51–74, 70–73; Alon Confino and Rudy Koshar. "Régimes of Consumer Culture: New Narratives in Twentieth-Century German History," *German History* 19 (2001): 135–161; Martin Burckhardt, *Metamorphosen von Raum und Zeit. Eine Geschichte der Wahrnehmung* (Frankfurt and New York, 1994), 192; Daniel Speich, "Wissenschaftlicher und touristischer Blick. Zur Geschichte der 'Aussicht' im 19. Jahrhundert," *Traverse* 3 (1999): 83–99; Schütz and Gruber, *Mythos*, 129 (erroneously on the Ha-ha effect).
33. Franz Kögler, "Straßen, Straßenbau und Verkehr in den USA. Bericht über eine Studienreise im Juli 1936," BAK R 65II/13; Wilbur H. Simonson and R.E. Royall, *Landschaftsgestaltung an der Straße (in USA). Roadside improvement* (Berlin, 1935); Wolfgang Singer, "Parkstraßen in den Vereinigten Staaten," *Die Straße* 2 (1935): 175–177; Bruno Wehner, "Die landschaftliche Ausgestaltung der nordamerikanischen Park- und Verkehrsstraßen," *Die Straße* 3 (1936): 599–601; William Brewster Snow, ed., *The Highway and the Landscape* (New Brunswick, N.J.,

1959); Bruce Radde, *The Merritt Parkway* (New Haven, Conn., 1993); John Dixon Hunt, "Arrêts de hasard sur l'autoroute," in *Autoroute et Paysages*, ed. Christian Leyrit and Bernard Lassus (Paris, 1994), 85–99; Timothy F. Davis, "Mount Vernon Memorial Highway: Changing Conceptions of an American Commemorative Landscape," in *Places of Commemoration. Search for Identity and Landscape Design*, ed. Joachim Wolschke-Bulmahn (Washington, D.C., 2001), 123–177; David Louter, "Glaciers and Gasoline: The Making of a Windshield Wilderness, 1900–1915," in *Seeing and Being Seen: Tourism in the American West*, ed. David Wrobel (Lawrence, Kan., 2001), 240–270; Justin Reich, "Re-Creating the Wilderness: Shaping Narratives and Landscapes in Shenandoah National Park," *Environmental History* 6 (2001): 95–117; Paul Sutter, *Driven Wild: How the Fight Against Automobiles Launched the Modern Wilderness Movement* (Seattle, 2002).

34. Alfred Pückel, "Die Reichsautobahn Frankfurt a.M.-Mannheim-Heidelberg," *Die Straße* 2 (1935): 306–312, 306; Regional planning office Frankfurt/Main, Justification for the elevation of the partial segment from km 83 to 95 of the Reichsautobahn Saarbrücken-Mannheim, June 1937, BAK R 65II/110; Eugen Kern, "Der Albaufstieg im Zuge der Reichsautobahn Stuttgart-Ulm," *Die Straße* 2 (1935): 474–480, 474; *Aichelberg. A 8 Karlsruhe-München* (Stuttgart, no date [around 1988]); Walter Ostwald, "Steigung und Gefälle auf der Reichsautobahn. Praktische Auswirkungen für den Fahrbetrieb," *Die Straße* 5 (1938): 114–115; Hans Rausch, "Über den Einfluß des Geländes auf die Netzbildung und Linienführung der Reichsautobahnen in Norddeutschland," dissertation, Technical College, Danzig, 1942, 63.
35. Richard Vahrenkamp, "Der Autobahnbau 1933 bis 1939 und das hessische Autobahnnetz," *Zeitschrift des Vereins für hessische Geschichte und Landeskunde* 109 (2004): 225–266, 259–260.
36. Todt to Directorate *Reichsautobahnen* and regional planning offices Vienna, Linz, and Munich, 3 April 1939, BAK NS 26/1187; Todt to regional planning office Munich, 9 May 1939, BAK NS 26/1187; Ludwig, *Technik und Ingenieure*, 342; Fritz Todt, "Reichsautobahn Salzburg-Linz-Wien," *Die Straße* 5 (1938): 408–410, 410. With a greater emphasis on safety: Becker, "Ästhetik der Linienführung der Autobahn," *Die Autobahn* 7 (1934): 128–130.
37. Maier, "Unter Wasser," 162.
38. Presentation to Todt, Berlin, 16 January 1934, DM NL 133/56, 1; Troitzsch, *Technikgeschichtliche Entwicklung*, 130; Irene Markowitz, "Ausblicke in die Landschaft," in *'Landschaft' und Landschaften im 18. Jahrhundert*, ed. Heike Wunderlich (Heidelberg, 1995), 121–155; Uwe Müller, *Infrastrukturpolitik in der Industrialisierung. Der Chausseebau in der preußischen Provinz Sachsen und dem Herzogtum Braunschweig vom Ende des 18. Jahrhunderts bis in die siebziger Jahre des 19. Jahrhunderts* (Berlin, 2000), 318.
39. Alwin Seifert, "Natur und Technik im deutschen Straßenbau," in idem, *Im Zeitalter des Lebendigen*, 9–23, 20. Schütz and Gruber, *Mythos*, 131, draw the overly general conclusion that on the autobahnen, Germany was to be experienced by car as a "rural forest land."
40. Presentation to Todt, 2; Alwin Seifert, "Die landschaftliche Eingliederung der Reichsautobahnen" (manuscript), n.d. [1934], DM NL 133/56 (1934), quotes 8.
41. Presentation to Todt, 1; "Die landschaftliche Eingliederung," 1, 6; Heinrich Rubner, *Deutsche Forstgeschichte 1933–1945. Forstwirtschaft, Jagd und Umwelt im NS-Staat*, 2nd ed. (St. Katharinen, 1997).
42. Alwin Seifert, "Landschaftsgebundene Straßenbepflanzung—auch in England," *Die Straße* 2 (1935): 184; Gert Gröning and JoachimWolschke-Bulmahn, "Some Notes on the Mania for Native Plants in Germany," *Landscape Journal* 11 (1992): 116–126, overestimate, on the basis of published sources, the importance attached to *Bodenständigkeit*.
43. Ludwig Trepl, *Geschichte der Ökologie. Vom 17. Jahrhundert bis zur Gegenwart* (Frankfurt/Main 1987), 145–149.
44. Ronald C. Tobey, *Saving the Prairies. The Life Cycle of the Founding School of American Plant Ecology, 1895–1955* (Berkeley, 1981); Michael G. Barbour, "Ecological Fragmentation in the Fifties," in Cronon, *Uncommon Ground*, 233–255.

45. Quoted in Donald Worster, *Nature's Economy. A History of Ecological Ideas* (Cambridge, 1985), 211.
46. Trepl, *Geschichte*, 146; Sandra D. Mitchell, "The Superorganism Metaphor: Then and Now," in *Biology as Society. Society as Biology: Metaphors*, ed. Sabine Maasen, Everett Mendelsohn, and Peter Weingart (Dordrecht, 1995), 231–247.
47. Worster, *Nature's Economy*, 205; Joachim Wolschke and Gert Gröning, "Regionalistische Freiraumgestaltung als Ausdruck autoritären Gesellschaftsverständnisses? Ein historischer Versuch," *Kritische Berichte* 1/12 (1984): 5–47, 10–11; Thomas Söderqvist, *The Ecologists. From Merry Naturalists to Saviours of the Nation. A Sociologically Informed Narrative Survey of the Ecologization of Sweden 1895–1975* (Stockholm, 1986), 82; Jean-Paul Deléage, *Histoire de L'Ecologie. Une Science de L'Homme et de la Nature* (Paris, 1992), 88–91; Barbour, "Ecological Fragmentation," 512; J.J. Moore, "The Braun-Blanquet System: A Reassessment," *Journal of Ecology* 50 (1962): 761–769; Eugene Cittadino, *Nature as the Laboratory. Darwinian Plant Ecology in the German Empire, 1880–1900* (Cambridge, 1990), 146–157; Seifert, *Leben*, 71.
48. J[osias] Braun-Blanquet, *Pflanzensoziologie. Grundzüge der Vegetationskunde* (Vienna, 1951), 1; idem, "Die Pflanzensoziologie in Forschung und Lehre," *Der Biologe* 1 (1931/32): 175–180; A.G. Tansley, "The Use and Abuse of Vegetational Concepts and Terms," *Ecology* 16 (1935): 284–307; William Cronon, "Introduction: In Search of Nature," in Cronon, *Uncommon Ground*, 23–56, 24–25; Küster, *Landschaft*, 13; Thomas Potthast, *Die Evolution und der Naturschutz. Zum Verhältnis von Evolutionsbiologie, Ökologie und Naturethik* (Frankfurt/New York, 1999).
49. Wolschke and Gröning, "Freiraumgestaltung"; Willy Lange, *Gartengestaltung der Neuzeit*, 6th ed. (Leipzig, 1928, 1st ed. 1907), 12; Alwin Seifert, "Gedanken über bodenständige Gartenkunst," *Gartenkunst* 42 (1929): 118–123, 131–132, 175–178, 191–195, quotes 186, 192; Paul Schultze-Naumburg, *Kulturarbeiten*, vol. 7 (Munich, 1916). Schütz and Gruber, *Mythos*, 127, describe Seifert erroneously as a student of Lange's. On the popularity of native plants in landscape architecture in the U.S. see Wolschke-Bulmahn, "Political Landscapes," 167.
50. Alwin Seifert, "Natur und Technik im deutschen Straßenbau," in idem, *Im Zeitalter des Lebendigen*, 9–23, 22–23.
51. Alwin Seifert, *Von bodenständiger Gartenkunst, Sonderdruck aus "Die Gartenschönheit,"* no. 1–2 (1939), 1–5, 1, 5, SN 511.
52. Seifert, *Von bodenständiger Gartenkunst*, 3. There also the following quotes.
53. Seifert, "Natur und Technik;" Seifert to Allinger, 27 December 1935, SN 123; Seifert to Inspector-General, Schönleben, 24 May 1939, SN 153.
54. Seifert, *Leben*, 75.
55. Ibid., 88; Todt to Erxleben, 2 February 1938 (copy), SN 126; Erxleben to Todt, 4 February 1938, ibid.; Erxleben to Seifert, 8 February 1938, ibid.; Seifert to Erxleben, 12 February 1938, ibid.
56. Seifert to the landscape advocates, 22 January 1935, SN 116; Todt to all landscape advocates, 17 December 1935, ibid.
57. Seifert to Mrass, 9 April 1967, SN 200. Lorenz became Chief Construction Overseer (*Oberster Bauleiter*) for the so-called transit autobahn (*Durchgangsautobahn*) through the "Protectorate" with his seat in Mährisch-Trübau. Inspector-General, Schönleben to Directorate *Reichsautobahnen*, 22 February 1937, BAP 46.01/864. For Lorenz's postwar role, see the section "The postwar trust in numbers" in the following chapter.
58. Seifert to Schwarz, 28 October 1936, ibid.; Seifert to Schneider, 25 June 1936, SN 146; Seifert to Inspector-General, Lorenz, 30 June 1936, BAP 46.01/862; Lorenz, Draft, 23 October 1936, BAP 46.01/864. There also the following quotes.
59. Seifert, *Leben*, 86–87; Inspector-General, Schönleben to the landscape advocates, 6 November 1936, SN 116; Seifert to Mrass, 9 April 1967, SN 200.
60. Preliminary guidelines about the planting of the motor roadways on the basis of the meeting with the Inspector-General on 11 November 1936, SN 116.

61. Todt to all landscape advocates, 17 December 1935, SN 116. Pioneering species, as opposed to climax species, were regarded as simple, hardy plants that would eventually be outcompeted by more complex flora resulting in the climax community. Apparently, Todt was familiar enough with the phytosociological vocabulary, but did not care for the climax. His concern was fast-growing, durable groundcover.
62. Arthur Freiherr von Kruedener, *Ingenieurbiologie* (Munich and Basel, 1951), 10; idem, *Forstliche Standortanzeiger. Auslese zum Gebrauch im Walde*, 4th ed. (Radebeul/Berlin, 1955 [orig. 1940]); Wolf Begemann and Hugo Meinhard Schiechtl, *Ingenieurbiologie. Handbuch zum naturnahen Wasser- und Erdbau* (Wiesbaden and Berlin, 1986).
63. Seifert, *Leben*, 71–72. According to Kruedener, "Forstliche Standortanzeiger," 5, Tüxen was also a student of v. Kruedener's. Reinhold Tüxen, "Die Pflanzensoziologie in ihren Beziehungen zu den Nachbarwissenschaften," *Der Biologe* 1 (1931/32): 180–187; *Aus der Arbeitsstelle für theoretische und angewandte Pflanzensoziologie der Tierärztl. Hochschule Hannover. Ein Tätigkeitsbericht von Reinhold Tüxen, Sonderabdruck aus dem 92. und 93. Jahresbericht der Naturhistorischen Gesellschaft zu Hannover* (Hannover, 1942), 65–66, SN 173. On Seifert's contact with Tüxen: Seifert to Tüxen, 28 January 1935 und 21 June 1935, SN 171; Tüxen to Seifert, 6 February 1935, and 3 May 1935, ibid.
64. Seifert to Mrass, 9 April 1967, SN 200; Seifert to *Forstmeister* Graser, 31 March 1944, AGM Waldbau ab 1941.
65. Tüxen to Seifert, 28 July 1935, SN 171.
66. Inspector-General, Schönleben to Tüxen, 21 October 1935, SN 171; Todt to Seifert, 19 June 1935, ibid.
67. Tüxen, "Vorschläge zur Durchführung der Vegetationskartierung an den deutschen Reichsautobahnen," 2 July 1935, SN 171; emphasis original.
68. Seifert to Tüxen, 11 July 1936, SN 171. Conflicts: Tüxen to Seifert, 18 February 1937, SN 172; Tüxen to Seifert, 19 February 1937, ibid.; Seifert to Tüxen, 27 February 1937, ibid.; Seifert to the landscape advocates, 28 December 1938, SN 116; Tüxen to Seifert, 6 December 1938, SN 172.
69. Hölz, "Verkehrsbauten," 78; Weber to Todt, 25 January 1940, BAP 46.01/140; Reinhard Bauer and Ernst Piper, *München. Die Geschichte einer Stadt* (Munich and Zurich, 1993), 335; Todt to Weber, 25 January 1940, BAP 46.01/170.
70. Todt, Circular, 27 January 1940, BAK NS 26/1188; Seifert to Todt, 17 February 1940, SN 117; Tüxen to Todt, 6 March 1940, BAP 46.01/140; "Die Bedeutung der Pflanzensoziologie für die Landeskultur. Vortrag, gehalten auf der Konferenz der preußischen Landforstmeister in Berlin 1937 von Dozent Dr. Reinhold Tüxen, Hannover," 16, SN 172; "Arbeitsstelle Tätigkeitsbericht," 78–79, SN 173. On Auschwitz as a place of experimentation see Sybille Steinbacher, *"Musterstadt" Auschwitz. Germanisierungspolitik und Judenmord in Oberschlesien* (Munich, 2000), esp. 246–247.
71. Seifert, *Leben*, 88.
72. Ibid., 87. The precise reason is not reported. If one looks at the later controversy, it is likely that the trees bothered Todt because of their future height and the resulting impairment of the vistas. Seifert to Schneider, 2 June 1937, SN 146.
73. Todt to Seifert, 21 January 1936, DM NL 133/57, 1–2.
74. Todt to Seifert, 9 June 1937, DM NL 133/57 (copy in BAK NS 26/1188). The following quotes are also from here. Emphasis original.
75. Seifert to Todt, 19 June 1937, DM NL 133/57. Seifert circulated a carbon copy of the "crucial" letter to eight of his closest co-workers. Seifert to Hirsch, 19 June 1937, SN 116. A carbon copy of the letter can be found ibid., a copy in BAK NS 26/1188.
76. Todt to Seifert, 20 July 1937, DM NL 133/57.
77. Seifert to Todt, 31 July 1937, ibid.; Seifert, *Leben*, 88; Seifert to Mrass, 9 April 1967, SN 200. Nothing can be found to substantiate the two versions reported by Seifert.
78. Todt to Lord Mayor Kurz, Pforzheim, 16 October 1935, BAP 46.01/135.

79. Herybert Menzel, in *Das Erlebnis der Reichsautobahnen. Ein Bildwerk von Hermann Harz mit einer Einführung von Herybert Menzel*, publ. by the Reichsministerium Speer (Munich, n.d. [1943]), no pagination.
80. Christoph Asendorf, *Super Constellation—Flugzeug und Raumrevolution. Die Wirkung der Luftfahrt auf Kunst und Kultur der Moderne* (Vienna and New York, 1997), 36; Erhard Schütz, "'... Eine glückliche Zeitlosigkeit...' Zeitreise zu den 'Straßen des Führers,'" in *Reisekultur in Deutschland. Von der Weimarer Republik zum "Dritten Reich,"* ed. Peter J. Brenner (Tübingen, 1997), 73–99, 91–94; Robert Wohl, *A Passion for Wings. Aviation and the Western Imagination, 1908–1918* (New Haven and London, 1994); Peter Fritzsche, *A Nation of Fliers: German Aviation and the Popular Imagination* (Cambridge, Mass., 1992); Edward Dimendberg, "The Will to Motorisation—Cinema and the Autobahn," in *Speed-Visions of an Accelerated Age*, ed. Jeremy Millar and Michiel Schwarz (London, 1998), 56–72.
81. Seidler, *Todt*, 134; Hans Ulrich Schaefer, *Die Gesetze der Reichsautobahnen mit einschlägigen Vorschriften und Verweisungen* (Berlin, 1937), 15–16; Angela Schumacher, "'Vor uns die endlosen Straßen, vor uns die lockende, erregende Ferne...' Vom Tanken und Rasten auf Entdeckerfahrt durch neue Lande," in Stommer, *Reichsautobahn*, 81.
82. "Auszug Nr. 2 aus Erlaß des Herrn Generalinspektor vom 28. Februar 1936 betr. Wirtschaftlichkeit der Bauausführung," 19 March 1936, BAK R 65II/14 (emphasis original). There also the following quote.
83. Stommer, *Triumph*, 72.
84. Seifert to Schwarz, 26 November 1934, SN 150; Directorate *Reichsautobahn*, draft of letter to all regional planning offices, 5 December 1936, BAK R 65II/14; "Kosten der technisch nicht notwendigen Pflanzungen und Begrünungen," 16 April 1937, ibid.
85. "Zusammenstellung der Mehrkosten der Baubeschleunigung zur Eröffnung verschiedener Zivilstrecken am 27. September 1936, aufgestellt Berlin, 8.3.1937," BAK R 65II/15; Reismann, *Deutschlands Autobahnen*, 81; Hölz, "Verkehrsbauten," 56; Directorate Reichsautobahnen, Rudolphi, to all regional planning offices, 31 October 1934, BAK R 65II/16; Hartmannsgruber, "'...ungeachtet'".
86. Circular, 30 January 1940, 4–5, SN 117. Beginning in 1940, Schwarz participated in the general building plan for Hamburg as a landscape planner. Werner Durth and Niels Gutschow, *Träume in Trümmern. Planungen zum Wiederaufbau zerstörter Städte im Westen Deutschlands 1940–1950*, vol. 2: Städte, (Braunschweig and Wiesbaden, 1988), 607–608. Wilhelm Hübotter received commissions for Hamburg and Hannover, ibid., 1037.
87. Circular, 3 March 1940, fol. 3, 10–11, 13–15, SN 117.
88. Ibid., 11; Circular 8 December 1941, fol. 1, SN 119; Guido Erxleben, "Naturschutz und Landschaftsgestaltung, Anhang 7 zum Rundbrief vom September 1942," 4, SN 118; Mrass, "Organisation des staatlichen Naturschutzes," 19–20. After the war, Kühn was professor of architecture at the Technical University Aachen. *Stadt und Landschaft. Raum und Zeit. Festschrift für Erich Kühn zur Vollendung seines 65. Lebensjahres*, ed. Alfred C. Boettger et al. (Cologne, 1969.)
89. "Kritische Betrachtungen zu den Rundbriefen, Anhang 9 zum Rundbrief Dezember 1942," SN 118, S. 1–7; Mrass, "Organisation des staatlichen Naturschutzes," 20.
90. Schwenkel to Seifert, 9 July 1940, SN 208; Seifert to Schwenkel, 17 July 1940 and 22 July 1942, ibid.; Schwenkel to Hirsch, 9 November 1942, ibid.; Seifert to Hirsch und Erxleben, 23 July 1940, ibid.
91. Schwenkel to Seifert, 9 July 1940, SN 208.
92. Gröning and Wolschke-Bulmahn, *Liebe zur Landschaft III*; Klaus Fehn, "Rückblick auf die 'nationalsozialistische Kulturlandschaft' unter besonderer Berücksichtigung des völkisch-rassistischen Mißbrauchs von Kulturlandschaftspflege," *Informationen zur Raumentwicklung* 5/6 (1999): 279–290.
93. Klose to Emeis, Flensburg, B 245/232, fol. 47; Maier, "'Unter Wasser und unter die Erde,'" 139–175.

94. Details on this debate in Thomas Zeller, "Molding the Landscape of Nazi Environmentalism: Alwin Seifert and the Third Reich," *How Green Were the Nazis?*, 147–170. For sources, see *Die Versteppung Deutschlands? (Kulturwasserbau und Heimatschutz). Sonderdruck mit Aufsätzen aus der Zeitschrift "Deutsche Technik"* (Leipzig, n.d. [1938]); Darré to Todt, BAP 46.01/864; Todt to Darré, 27 February 1937, ibid.
95. John Heskett, "Design in Inter-War Germany," in *Designing Modernity. The Arts of Reform and Persuasion 1885–1945. Selections from the Wolfsonian*, ed. Wendy Kaplan (New York, 1995), 257–285, 271–272.
96. Walter Zschokke, "Technische Bauten und der gelungene Versuch ihrer Aussöhnung mit der Landschaft," in *Moderne Architektur in Deutschland 1900 bis 1950. Reform und Tradition*, ed. Vittorio Magnago and Romana Schneider (Stuttgart, 1992), 221–243, 242.
97. Albion Ross, "Super-Highways for the Reich," *The New York Times*, 14 February 1937, 173.
98. Elaine S. Hochman, *Architects of Fortune: Mies van der Rohe and the Third Reich* (New York, 1989), 226–228; Victor Klemperer, *Ich will Zeugnis ablegen bis zum letzten. Tagebücher 1933–1941* (Berlin 5th ed. 1996), 310–311, 329, 368, 370–371. British visitors who saw the autobahnen vacillated between admiration and rejection of their monotonousness: Stephen Henry Roberts, *The House that Hitler Built* (New York and London, 1938), 235–240, 240; Matless, *Landscape*, 59–61; Angela Schwarz, *Die Reise ins Dritte Reich. Britische Augenzeugen im nationalsozialistischen Deutschland (1933–39)* (Göttingen and Zurich, 1993), 219–223; idem, "Der Hitler-Mythos aus zeitgenössischer Sicht: Stephen Roberts: 'The House that Hitler Built,'" *Archiv für Kulturgeschichte* 73 (1991): 469–481.
99. Schütz and Gruber, Mythos, 122–135; Schütz, "Glückliche Zeitlosigkeit," 85–88; Rollins, "Whose Landscape"; Gröning and Wolschke-Bulmahn, *Grüne Biographien;* eidem, *Liebe zur Landschaft.*
100. Andrew Light and Eric S. Higgs, "The Politics of Ecological Restoration," *Environmental Ethics* 18 (1996): 227–47.
101. Klenke, "Autobahnbau und Naturschutz," 481; Seidler, *Todt*. For the latter point, see Klenke, "Autobahnbau und Naturschutz," note 64.
102. Schama, *Landscape and Memory*, 119; Prinz, "Soziale Funktion"; for important differentiations see Peter Fritzsche, "Nazi Modern," *Modernism/modernity* 3 (1996): 1–21; Paul Betts, "The New Fascination with Fascism: The Case of Nazi Modernism," *Journal of Contemporary History* 37 (2002): 541–558; Kaspar Maase, *Grenzenloses Vergnügen. Der Aufstieg der Massenkultur 1850–1970* (Frankfurt/Main, 1997), 201–205, 233. Oliver Geden, *Rechte Ökologie. Umweltschutz zwischen Emanzipation und Faschismus* (Berlin, 1995), 27–28. Now outdated are Marie-Luise Heuser, "Was grün begann endete blutigrot. Von der Naturromantik zu den Reagrarisierungs- und Entvölkerungsplänen der SA und SS," in *Industrialismus und Ökoromantik. Geschichte und Perspektiven der Ökologisierung*, ed. Dieter Hassenpflug (Wiesbaden, 1991), 43–64 and Janet Biehl and Peter Staudenmaier, *Ecofascism: Lessons from the German Experience* (Edinburgh and San Francisco, 1995).
103. Anson Rabinbach, "The Aesthetics of Production in the Third Reich," *Journal of Contemporary History* 11 (1976): 43–74; Peter Reichel, *Der schöne Schein des Dritten Reiches: Faszination und Gewalt des Faschismus* (Munich, 1991).

Chapter 7

REINTERPRETATIONS:
THE WEST GERMAN AUTOBAHN, 1949 TO 1970

The social and cultural meaning of the German autobahnen changed profoundly after 1945 in the Federal Republic of Germany. Within a few short years, they were reinterpreted from the emblem of a dictatorship into a transportation system that was classified in a functional and rational way. As was the case in the earlier attempts to define these roads, road-building engineers and landscape architects were involved in this process with different ideological and professional goals. The altered state of the general political framework of a parliamentary democracy shifted the parameters of this debate. Moreover, toward the end of the period under discussion, the circle of participants expanded: increasingly, motorists sought to participate in these processes rather than being the objects of experts' professional decisions. This chapter will examine what role the relationship between landscape and road played in this. Along the way, the built environment of "Adolf Hitler's Roads" was seen—more implicitly than explicitly but no less centrally—as a negative template for the West German autobahn. The ideological ballast of this key National Socialist infrastructure project was as overwhelming as its public discussion was subdued. Although the autobahnen were not depoliticized—their scope and financing were too controversial politically for that to happen—the knowledge and the technology of designing autobahnen took on a new social and political meaning. To that extent the present chapter will also look at the relationship of landscape design to the broader political and social change, with special attention to the continuities and discontinuities between National Socialism and the Federal Republic. Such a study will allow us to draw conclusions about the role of technology in dictatorship and democracy, and about the political and rhetorical strategies pursued by various social groups such as civil engineers, landscape architects, and, to an increasing degree, nonexperts

Notes for this section begin on page 224.

like motorists.[1] To do this, it will be helpful to take a look first at how transportation was defined and politically directed in the Federal Republic.

Autobahnen and the politics of the Bonn Republic

So far, this study has dealt with the construction of the autobahnen under National Socialism as the most prominent example of transportation policy before 1945. Although the transportation policy of the Federal Republic between 1949 and 1970 sought to promote the state-run railroad as well as individual transportation, the result was a strong surge for the automobile, which became the normal mode of motorized transportation from the middle of the 1960s. To what extent this process was promoted by government policies is still debated among historians.[2]

It is also important to realize that transportation policy was made not only in the ministry of transportation, but also in ministries and agencies dealing with taxes, regional planning, and technical regulations.[3] Only after 1973 did the politics in Bonn seek to get a handle on the interactions and long-term lines of development in the transportation sector by means of a methodologically overlapping *Bundesverkehrswegeplan* (Federal Transportation Route Plan). Rather than simply planning for each transport mode—waterways, roads, rails, and air—separately, the new comprehensive plan sought to combine transportation infrastructure into a whole. The introduction of this type of planning can be understood as both an admission that planning focused purely on individual transportation carriers had failed, and an attempt at a reorganization of planning, an attempt that, after all, characterized also other areas of West German politics in the late 1960s and 1970s.[4] For the period under discussion here, one can note—at the threat of oversimplification—that political decision-makers sought to impose ideas of restriction and order on the transportation sector, hoping that this would improve the common good. Far into the 1970s, the federal government's directives on transportation policy reveal less a confidence in a free-market system in which all transportation branches compete in a transportation market, than a conception of a comprehensive transportation activity directed from above. As Dietmar Klenke argues, "It was not the free-market principle of achieving the optimum of resource allocation and efficiency that held sway, but considerations of the common good."[5]

In the historical back-and-forth of regulation and deregulation of the transportation sector, the middle of the twentieth century in West Germany appears as a high point of regulation and at the same time as a starting point for a long, steady deregulation, the pace of which accelerated in the 1980s. Within the national economy, transportation was seen as an exceptional sector; the goals of transportation policy were considerations of social and spatial policies. Precisely because the intentions were regulatory in nature, they could—within this perspective—be achieved only by a state that took vigorous action; a state that employed, to this end, the state-run railroad, local public transportation, and the state's postal service, the latter as a provider of regional bus service; that created a legal foundation for the special status of transportation; and, of course, planned and built roads.

At the same time, the transportation sector felt the tension from public, communal transportation enterprises like the state railroad and local streetcars and buses, on the one side, and private freight carriers and individually used automobiles, on the other. Transportation policy sought to meld this competition between monopoly and market into an orderly whole with a bundle of measures that provided charters, established regulations, and set rates. This field of tension was the basic pattern of transportation policy in the Federal Republic.

The elevated regulatory claim of transportation policy at the time corresponded with the relative absence of broad participation by the citizenry in the period under review. Moreover, transportation experts from academia and the bureaucracy took on a significant role in that they sought to set the direction of debates and were regularly consulted on specific questions pertaining to the technology and organization of transportation. To that end, the Federal Ministry of Transportation appointed two scientific advisory committees.

As one result of his study of the transportation policy of the Federal Republic, Klenke distinguished three phases. In the first legislative period from 1949 to 1953, the traditional transportation system, with the strong state guidance and oversight that I have described, was largely restored. The second phase is described as the "high point of the transportation crisis." This refers to excess capacities in freight hauling as a result of the growth of truck transportation, which, in combination with the first deficit for the federal railroad, turned transportation into a political issue. At the same time, the number of accidents in motorized individual transportation rose sharply, which was attributed in part to the poor condition of the transregional road network. In this "rail/road conflict," the federal government chose to pursue a containment of truck traffic, though it was not able to push this course through Parliament to the extent it wanted. According to Klenke, the beginning of a long and sustained motorization of individual transportation occurred in this phase. The year 1961 saw the beginning of a liberalization of the transportation markets and greater exertions devoted to road construction.[6]

In 1952, the nominal stock of passenger cars of the prewar period had been reached again, and throughout the 1950s, the rate of motorization—starting from a low basis—rose more than 20 percent a year. However, in the 1950s many Germans were still driving motorcycles instead of the relatively expensive cars; one important reason was reluctance of many consumers to make purchases in installments or on credit. The civilian Volkswagen that was finally built in the Lower Saxon company town of Wolfsburg was therefore all the more important; the ten millionth "Beetle" rolled off the assembly line in 1965. While under the tutelage of the British occupation authorities and especially after it was handed over to the governments of the state of Lower Saxony and the federal government in 1949, the Volkswagen plant and its products became the most visible signs of motorization: the promise of broad car ownership that the Nazi state failed to keep was fulfilled in the Federal Republic.[7]

Germany reached the state of mass motorization, usually defined by transportation economists as a statistical ratio of ten inhabitants per automobile, in 1961; in 1950, the ratio had been 97:1, and in 1955, 31:1. At the end of the period under review, 1970, the Federal Republic, after a period of making up ground rapidly, had a ratio of four inhabitants per car and was for the first time on a par with Great Britain and France. In comparison to the United States, West Germany reached the American motorization level of 1930 (five inhabitants sharing one car) by the late 1960s. The beginning of this decade was also a turning point as far as transportation services measured in kilometers per person was concerned, for the transport of persons was now achieved overwhelmingly by individual means of transportation rather than trains, buses, or trams. Toward the end of the 1950s, the stock of passenger cars in the Federal Republic surged, from 2.5 million vehicles in 1957 to 4.3 million in 1960. Wider circles of the working class also benefited from this trend. For the first time, automobiles became common consumer items.[8]

After the expansion of the federal autobahnen had long been on the back burner, the federal government provided significant funds for new road construction for the first time in 1958. A Road Building Financing Law was passed in 1960; by earmarking the fuel oil tax, it gave motor transportation a special status within the budget law. Through the tax revenue, the dynamic of motorization was translated directly into road building and was spurred on even more. As a result, the pace at which federally funded highways expanded grew considerably. At the end of the war there had been 2,100 kilometers of autobahnen in what became the Federal Republic; by 1966 the network had grown to 3,378, and, after ever greater expansion, reached 8,198 kilometers by 1985. Today, the unified Germany possesses more than 12,000 kilometers of autobahnen, a national number to be surpassed only by the U.S. interstate highway network of 68,500 kilometers (or 42,700 miles).

Opening ceremonies for autobahn sections were part of the political imagery of the Bonn Republic.[9] Meaningful broad, nationwide public opposition to autobahn construction did not appear until the early 1970s. Right up to the end of the period under discussion, the four-lane highways were largely unchallenged as transportation routes. In contrast to the practice under National Socialism, the *Bundeswehr* (West German army) was from the beginning systematically involved in the planning, though that had no bearing on the conflicts described here. New routes were consistently reviewed by the defense department in Bonn. Moreover, it requested several emergency landing strips for military airplanes on the autobahn, that is, short, dead straight sections of 1.5 to three kilometers in length. By 1968, six of these autobahn airport strips were completed, one was under construction, and fourteen were planned or investigated.[10] Incidentally, one unique development was the use of a five-kilometer-long, straight section of the autobahn near Landstuhl in Rhineland-Palatinate as a makeshift airstrip by the U.S. Army after 1951. The former autobahn subsequently became part of the Ramstein airbase and the freeway was redirected.[11] The autobahn had also played a role for the general occupation policy of the victorious World War II powers: after protracted negotiations, the autobahn section from Karlsruhe via Stuttgart to Ulm formed the boundary between the American and French zones of occupation in southwestern Germany.[12]

In the 1950s and especially the 1960s, the autobahn and above all automobiles became showcase emblems and instruments of the prospering postwar republic. Even if possession of a driver's license was for a long time still reserved mostly for men, driving or being driven in an automobile became the everyday means of transportation for work and vacation. New leisure activities such as autocamping now became for the first time possible on a broader scale and were widely used as the expression of individualized consumption in a new republic. However, the prerequisites for this kind of individualism were Fordist mass production and a growing industrialization. Nevertheless, ownership and operation of an automobile conveyed to many Germans a sense of independence.[13] Theodor Adorno was not alone in labeling the car a "medium and symbol of freedom."[14] The Cold War—or more precisely, the competition between the systems of the Federal Republic and East Germany—was always present in the background. As the *Deutsche Straßenliga*, a lobbying group for automobile interests primarily from the economic sector, expressed it with concise simplicity: "Motorization means more freedom for people. It is no surprise that the eastern world has poor roads and fewer automobiles." While such rhetoric was the most pronounced form of this competition, it was evident also in the field of landscape and technology.[15] It would help to explain why the autobahn has become synonymous with the absence of a speed limit. According to Klenke, it was chiefly an antitotalitarian feeling that equated speed limits with totalitarian control. In 1953, all speed limits were abolished in the Federal Republic, including those within built-up areas. Following protests from trauma surgeons, who were pointing to the growing number of accident victims, the legal maximum speed in built-up areas became 50 km/h in 1957. But it was only in 1972 that the Bundestag introduced a general speed limit of 100 km/h outside of built-up areas; generally, the autobahnen have remained exempted, even though the issue was often debated in the 1970s and 1980s.[16]

Building a federal highway system

After 1949, the autobahn's organizational statutes received a new footing. This change is crucial to understanding road building and landscape in the Federal Republic. As I have shown, in 1934 the German Reich, by establishing the central office of the Inspector-General for German Roads that was directly answerable to the Führer, had arrogated competencies in the area of road building that had previously belonged to the states. The planning, construction, and operation of transregional roads became tasks of the Reich. At the same time, roads were classified as Reich, state, or district roads. As a result, the greater part of the road network remained within the legal responsibility of the states. As part of the deliberations for the newly emerging Federal Republic after the war, the authors of the constitution decided to shift the competencies in road construction, which had been transferred to the Reich level under National Socialism, back to the states, at least in part. According to the Basic Law and the Federal Highway Law, classifying roads fell within the competency of the states; the federal government was left with overseeing federal highways. The Federal Highway Law defined them as public roads that form a connected network and serve an expansive transportation. In keeping with a uniform scheme, roads were classified into four levels, as federal superhighways, state highways (*Landstraßen*) of the first classification, highways of the second classification (also called district roads), and local roads.[17] Only the top layer of roads was under Bonn's control.

According to the constitutional setup, the job of the federal department of transportation was limited to rough planning and financing federal roads—and thus also the autobahnen while the states actually built and operated these superhighways, under federal oversight. The states naturally welcomed these added administrative functions, yet parts of the federal government and the road building industry criticized the setup, especially in the first years. Federal Minister of Transportation Hans-Christoph Seebohm (1903–1967) was largely alone among politicians in his desire for a powerful federal road office, for which he promised a "push toward a modern administration." Behind it stood the motivation to expand the administrative competencies of the federal government at the expense of the states, who, understandably enough, did not go along with this demand.[18] Seebohm served as minister of transportation in Bonn from 1949 to 1966, which made him one of the longest-serving secretaries of the Bonn republic. He preferred a strong interventionist, if not micromanaging, policy and exerted influence even on details of road construction, like the proper treatment of the median strip. Outside of transportation policy, Seebohm became known as a functionary of the Sudeten German expellees from Czechoslovakia through his notorious reactionary "Sunday speeches."[19]

Meanwhile, circles within the road construction industry criticized the way in which the states put projects out to bid, and the bureaucratic overlap with the competencies of the federal government. One article in a professional journal in 1959 criticized a cumbersome planning apparatus and mentioned the centralization of road construction "under Todt" as a positive counterexample.[20] The interest of these companies in predictable public contracts and their good memories of the abundant contracts during the Nationalist Socialist regime are obvious. The ideal was not federal democracy with a procedurally complex bureaucracy, but the rapid construction of projects determined by experts. In opposition to this position, federal bureaucrats denied that there was any great need for action. In a letter to the editor of the journal, the deputy head of the road building section in the Federal Ministry of Transportation requested that the public discussion of the topic not be pursued any further.[21] Not talking about centralization, especially by invoking the Nazi construction tycoon Todt, was preferable to talking about it.

Compared to the top-down planning approach of the Nazi autobahn, regional and local bodies and individual citizens had defined legal roles in the road-planning process of the new Federal Republic. Following the political decision on the need for a new road, its routing, and its construction costs, the planning determination process (*Planfeststellungsverfahren*) was the crucial part of the planning, since it resulted in the concrete road plan. In the plan preparation phase, the office that would bear the burden of building the road—in this case the respective state office at the behest of the Federal Ministry of Transportation—had to present a plan with all the relevant data, such as the routing and the number and scope of bridges. During the subsequent hearings, all involved agencies and affected citizens had an opportunity to present their suggestions and concerns. After the hearing process, the hearing agency drew up a statement on the basis of the presented plans and the complaints it had received. The relevant plan determination agency—in the case of the federal highways it was the chief State Road Construction Office—then signed off on the planning and thus brought it to a conclusion.[22]

With respect to the landscape design of the roads, this allocation of competency within the relationship between the federal government and the states reshuffled the status of landscape architects as well. The landscape architects of the erstwhile *Reichsautobahn* were knocking on the wrong door when they pushed for reemployment with the Federal Ministry of Transportation, as they did right after it had been set up. Simply on an administrative basis, the way in which road building was constituted in West Germany offered few points of contact to carry on the landscape integration on the federal level in the tradition of the *Reichsautobahnen*. After what they had experienced during the building of the autobahn up to 1945, the landscape architects had little interest in seeing a return of their uncertain status and of competencies that had to be continually renegotiated. Still, collaborating on the federal autobahn with their predetermined process seemed to them a potentially rewarding endeavor. However, their organized approaches to the Federal Ministry of Transportation were unsuccessful because of the distribution of competencies. Todt's central office with its concern for landscaping was extinct. Some road-building administrations of the states proceeded to employ landscape architects on a case-by-case basis. But that merely confirmed the fundamental and general absence of landscape architects on the federal level. When the impetuous and partly chaotic autobahn construction under National Socialism changed into the relative regularity and federally moderated resolution of conflicts under the Federal Republic, the group of landscape architects lacked, as they saw it, access to the top administrative echelons of road construction. Exemplary for this trend is how Alwin Seifert fared. Shortly after his denazification trial, the former Reich Landscape Advocate, nourished by his self-confidence and convinced that the administration of the autobahn would continue, demanded that he be restored to the top level of road building. In his denazification proceedings, Seifert was classified as "not incriminated" (*unbelastet*) in the fall of 1949 thanks to numerous exonerating letters from colleagues, and thus was eager to return to work.[23]

Even before the establishment of the Federal Republic, the Wiesbaden landscape architect Hirsch had tried to procure commissions for landscape advocates in the rebuilding of the roads, many of which had been destroyed by the Wehrmacht. In October 1948 he wrote to Seifert:

> Unfortunately my varied attempts to use the old landscape advocates again runs into the difficulty time and again that the "Old" is met with mistrust and the strongest misgivings. This is, of course, very sad, but I am convinced that one day people will return to it again, simply because the reason and experience of these people will win.[24]

That same fall, the landscape advocates met in Königswinter near Bonn in an effort to regain their former status. They wanted Seifert to head the group. In a letter to Hugo Koester, a former official in the agency of the Inspector-General who was now *Ministerialdirigent* in the Federal Ministry of Transportation, Seifert spoke about the alleged appreciation that the Allies had expressed for the way in which the autobahnen were integrated into the landscape. And if he had been in a position to "fully implement" his "from the outset completely correct intentions," and if he had not had to contend with the "active and passive resistance of the Reich Railroad people," the recognition from the victorious powers would have been even greater. "Our esteemed chief"—he was referring to Todt—had also listened far too long to false advisors. Seifert was thus reinterpreting the most recent past to his advantage by combining the mythos surrounding Todt since his plane crash in 1942 with a bow to the new political realities.[25] His remarks culminated in this demand:

> I would therefore like to ask you to prepare, as soon as possible, the reemployment of those landscape advocates who proved their worth ... I wish to reuse only some of the old landscape advocates, and would like those dropped who were forced upon us by the party. I myself would like to reserve only the restoration of the segment Munich-Salzburg. However, the landscape advocates who met last fall in Königswinter want me to assume some kind of leadership again. I guess I'll just become Federal Landscape Advocate![26]

It was Seifert's more-than-robust ego that allowed him to construct this seamless continuity from Reich Landscape Advocate to Federal Landscape Advocate with an undisguised craving for recognition. Evidently, he saw landscape design as a task above politics and beyond dictatorship and democracy. However, his rhetoric, and especially his ideas of a "kind of leadership" on his part, ran counter to the federal principles of the new republic. Added to this was the fact that Seifert, because of his exposed position under National Socialism, did not seem acceptable. Despite several letters to Federal Minister of Transportation Seebohm and to the Bavarian road-building administration, he remained largely excluded from work on the postwar autobahn.[27] And even though he regarded landscape integration as his "sole intellectual property," he was also not involved in the relevant institutional work. The Research Association for the Road System rebuilt its "landscape design" department under the leadership of Seifert's opponent Hans Lorenz; Wilhelm Hirsch and Ludwig Roemer worked in that department. Seifert noted as early as April 1950 that he did not believe that there was anything he could do for the autobahnen.[28] A few of Seifert's professional colleagues, however, participated in the rebuilding of the destroyed cities, as it was generally very easy for architects to establish a continuity between war and the postwar period.[29]

Seifert's collaboration thus remained sporadic. In 1952, Seifert was paid for participating in a trip on the autobahn from Bottrop to Wiesbaden as the basis for a study. Some voices within the Federal Ministry of Transportation criticized the neglect of autobahn planting. An internal statement explained that the inadequate care since the Second World War had continued in the first few years of the Federal Republic. Added to this was the fact that the glare shield plantings on the median strip were in many cases still inadequate. The purpose of Seifert's trip with two experts from the Ministry of Transportation was thus to gather some clues for guidelines for new plantings. To justify his participation it was noted that Seifert "enjoys a special reputation as landscape designer." His personal restitution failed in that he received no commissions from the Bonn administration for the new construction of autobahnen. Instead, the Federal Ministry of Transportation was more interested in formalizing the expertise gained under National Socialism and enshrining it in the form of guidelines. This can be seen as an act of recapturing the administrative sovereignty over the construction of the autobahn, and it went hand in hand with the call to place road building on a stronger scientific footing.[30]

Instead, Seifert's career in the Federal Republic focused on rivers, not roads: he became the leading landscape architect for the expansion of the Mosel River in the 1960s, designed landscaping plans for many industrial buildings and home gardens, and published an exculpatory autobiography, in which he played down his involvement in National Socialism.[31] He was one of the most highly regarded representatives within the conservative circles of conservation and landscape cultivation in the 1950s and 1960s and received high state honors. Seifert became honorary chairman of the *Bund Naturschutz* in Bavaria and was a signatory of the "Green Charter" of 1961, an appeal for an ecological rebuilding of Western Germany that was motivated by concerns of landscape cultivation.[32] With the help of a fantastic argumentation, by which he depicted himself as a victim of National Socialism, he secured a teaching position at the Technical University in Munich from 1953 to 1955. Seifert died in 1972, almost contemporaneously with the rise of environmental protection as a political topic and of the current environmental movement.

That the priorities had shifted when it came to the landscape design of the autobahnen is also confirmed by an exchange of letters pursued by the Working Circle of Landscape Advocates in 1952. This group was a loose union of like-minded professionals, in contrast to the professional representation of the League of German Garden Architects (*Bund Deutscher Gartenarchitekten*). That the name was modeled after Todt's "landscape advocates" is obvious; some of the members had already worked on the *Reichsautobahnen*.

Jointly with a regional group of the League of German Garden Architects, the Working Circle complained about the inadequate landscaping care of the autobahn section from Hamburg to Bremen. It charged that new plantings had been poorly planned and carried out; the plant material that had been used was paltry and there was no connection to the existing prewar planting. Criticism was leveled at the unprofessional pruning of shrubs in the median strip and of some pine trees along the side of the road, which made them look ugly. Some hawthorn bushes had not been pruned, as a result of which their overgrown condition made them appear unpleasant and unnatural. Two highway maintenance depots were given an evaluation of "disorderly." The landscape architects had observed that one recreation area situated at a lake was closed off with a chain-link fence, and the autobahn deserved better.[33]

On the whole, the critique shows just how strongly the landscape architects remained attached to the ideas of an autobahn that was spatially expansive and thoroughly staged. By pointing to the "originally intended and impressive picture of the spatial design of the autobahn," they were invoking bygone Nazi views of the construction of the *Reichsautobahn*. They explicitly noted that the earlier plantings had created an "organic and artistic unity between autobahn and landscape." That unity could be restored. An ideological argument was thus turned into one of personnel policy: the obviously deficient care, so went the criticism of the landscape architects, pointed to the urgent need for ongoing professional advice. Only an expert could protect the economic values and avoid the kind of misdirection that had happened so far. Concretely, the two groups demanded that their member Max Schwarz be "consulted on an ongoing basis."

The relevant civil servant in the Federal Ministry of Transportation conceded that there was "some justification" to the criticism of the professional garden architects, and noted "an excessively schematic treatment of the road with respect to design." The highway departments of the states of Hamburg and Lower Saxony were therefore asked to review the matter, even though it was clearly seen that the arguments by the two groups were driven by their own specific interests having to do with professional status and aimed, at their core, at winning reemployment for one of their members. The road-building department of Lower Saxony subsequently pursued the matter with little urgency; no reply can be found in the files. This incident confirms that the way the federal system allocated responsibilities for road building threw up obstacles for the cause of the landscape advocates, at least from their perspective. The loss of a single point of contact within the bureaucracy was an organizational shortcoming for the architects. To be sure, even during the building of the *Reichsautobahnen*, they had been dependent on the regional planning offices that were in charge on the ground. However, what set the federal system of road building apart from the organizational scheme of the Nazi state was that the Federal Ministry of Transportation no longer had the authority to issue directives in matters relating to landscape design, and that the authority concerning the employment of landscape architects was transferred to the state level.[34]

In this concrete case, the landscape architect Schwarz failed in his attempt to claim comprehensive competencies for the "landscape expert" on the autobahn. Although Schwarz did receive commissions after the intervention, he was merely charged with preparing planting plans. Schwarz complained about this in a letter to the Federal Ministry of Transportation in 1962, summarizing the competencies that should ideally belong to a landscape architect working on the autobahn. Interestingly enough, Schwarz, unlike Seifert, avoided a direct reference to the Nazi autobahnen by replacing the label "landscape advocate" with "landscape expert" (*Landschaftsfachmann*). Schwarz's goal was the construction of an expert independent of any particular era. "The work of the landscape expert should begin with alignment and excavation, and include the protection and care of the topsoil, the cultivation of the topsoil, the preparation of planting plans, and the supervision of the planting." Schwarz thus demanded the maximum palette of possible influences that landscape architects could exert on the process of planning and building the autobahn, a palette that had already been formulated in the 1930s and was not achieved back then, either. Closely connected with this was the request for commissions, which served personal interests.[35]

The response from Bonn was negative. The road-building administration of the *Landschaftsverband* Westphalia-Lippe, the road-building agency in charge, had dispensed with the use of freelance landscape architects; instead, it had established a "Section Landscape Building" (*Referat Landschaftsbau*) that was headed by a landscape architect with civil-servant status. This section directed landscape gardeners in their work on the newly constructed roads. The Federal Ministry of Transportation attested that this administrative practice had yielded "good experiences" and "remarkable success." The relevant administrator, in his personalized response to Schwarz, expressed his regret that, as a result of these firmly delineated competencies between agencies, there was no room for a landscape architect with a purely consultative function. "Things are simply different from what they once were, aren't they" was the justification, as telling as it was vague.[36]

In summary, we can note that the federal road-building administration stood in the way of a uniform responsibility for landscape architects. Only in 1976, after the end of the period under review here, did passage of the Federal Nature Conservation Law (*Bundesnaturschutzgesetz*) make landscape cultivation a compulsory part of road construction planning undertaken by the federal government.[37] Drawing on the centralized road building during the Nazi dictatorship, the landscape architects sought in vain to continue their work under the new political reality. Although the road-building department in the Ministry of Transportation in Bonn was largely staffed with former civil servants from the office of the Inspector-General, they had neither the authority nor the professional inclination to help the landscape architects achieve a position of systematic collaboration on the autobahn. At the level of the states, the landscape design of the roads during the period in question was evidently not given the high priority the landscape architects would have wished for.

A final verdict on how landscape planning on the autobahn was handled in the states must await regional studies. However, the sources I have examined permit the conclusion that a continuity of centrally regulated influence on road building in the Federal Republic—which is what the architects were after—was not attained. On the organizational level, the breakup and diffusion of authority over the building of the autobahn in the Federal Republic proved to be a complicating factor for the former landscape advocates. To be sure, the edifice of ideas about landscape integration that stemmed from the fast-paced and contradictory construction of the *Reichsautobahnen* was, as we shall see, formalized and bureaucratized within individual road-building administrations. However, the leeway of the federal states proved, especially in this regard, to be an obstacle to the uniform implementation of the criteria of landscape-bound construction. The building history of the autobahn during National Socialism already revealed that organizational and substantive criteria were interconnected when it came to the landscape design of these highways. That was even truer for the Federal Republic. While personal alliances and changing constellations of power under the Nazi dictatorship produced rhetorical successes and the occasional concrete result the landscape architects would have wished for, road construction after 1949, with its mixed organization on the federal and state levels and a more structured planning process, no longer offered the possibility of intervening by activating political connections to the top echelons of the administration. Their degree of organization was correspondingly weak, compared to what it had been under National Socialism, when their undefined status had driven, in response, a stronger internal group formation. That created even more pressure to invoke a "school of the *Reichsautobahn*" as a community of the initiated and as a historical entity that created a sense of identity.[38] The phenomenon of the landscape advocates who acted as a group in their work on the *Reichsautobahn* found no organizational continuation in the Federal Republic.

The postwar trust in numbers

In the history of the construction of the *Reichsautobahnen*, the quarrel over the generation of knowledge for the autobahnen had proved crucial in shaping the plans and the structure. While the landscape architects had—roughly speaking—presented an aesthetic approach to nature as the starting point and justificatory pattern for the technical parameters of road construction, the civil engineers tended to base their work on argumentation and calculations that could be academically verified. The given in these discourses was "the motorist," an amorphous figure based on inductive generalization. These different approaches came with different construction methods, which were also the product of conflicts. This can be seen most clearly in the quarrel between Todt and Seifert over straight and curvy routing. Both in the first phase of the construction of the *Reichsautobahnen*, in which the routing elements followed largely the ideas of the civil engineers to traverse space through long straightaways, and in the second phase, when the landscape architects with their demands for sinuous lines began to prevail, the top road construction agency of the Reich retained the power to define what was an appropriate, landscape-compatible route. In the Federal Republic, the weight shifted further in favor of the civil engineers. After the agency of the Inspector-General had attracted large parts of the personnel resources in road construction, many autobahn engineers ended up in the road-building department of the Federal Ministry of Transportation. Old alliances, an evolved institutional structure, and existing contacts played their part in making it possible for this department to preserve an "astounding capacity to assert itself internally" until the early 1970s among the departments of the ministry that were broken down by modes of transportation—rail, road, water, air. Before 1945, the function of the Reich Ministry of Transportation had been largely oversight over the railroad, a situation that changed fundamentally after 1949 with the existence of the road-building department. This was evident in the men who filled the supervisory positions. Both the head of the road building department from 1949 to 1959, Hermann Kunde (born 1903), and his deputy during those years and eventual successor from 1960 to 1963, Hugo Koester (born 1898), were representatives of the construction of the *Reichsautobahnen*. Kunde left the office in 1959 under a cloud of scandal; two years later he was sentenced to three years and eight months for bribery, tax evasion, and abuse of his office, and he died before he began serving his sentence.[39] Herbert Eymann (born 1905), who headed the road-building department from 1963 to 1970, and his successor, Wilhelm Heubling, had also gained professional experience on the *Reichsautobahnen*. Only a few top-level representatives from the Inspector-General's office had been too exposed to continue their official state employment. But there was private business: after being held captive by the Allies for two years, Todt's deputy, Eduard Schönleben, worked for the Afghan government and various German construction companies; Schönleben had been the author of a Todt encomium. Todt's former undersecretary and subsequent chief of Organization Todt headquarters, Xaver Dorsch, after the war established in Munich the consulting firm Dorsch-Consult, with worldwide operations.[40]

The road-building department of the Federal Ministry of Transportation, which can thus largely be seen as a West German successor organization to the office of the Inspector-General for the German Roads in terms of personnel and substance, was urged by Minister of Transportation Seebohm to "scientize" road building and refine the methods for road design and planning. At the center of the engineering discussion concerning road building in the 1950s stood the search for a scientifically justifiable way of giving form to highways that offered an opportunity to distance oneself ideologically from the construction of the *Reichsautobahnen*. In this process, mathematization of the alignment proved as much a method of calculation as a parameter for the discourse.

In what follows, the growing use of mathematical formulas for geometric forms in autobahn construction should be understood, not as the ineluctable result of an inner scientification of road building, but as the emergence of quantifying methods in one branch of science, a development that needs to be contextualized. Theodore Porter believes that the steady growth in the importance of quantification in science, technology, economics, and politics in the twentieth century raises larger questions about the generation of knowledge and the status of experts in a given society. In this kind of analysis, numbers, graphs, and formulas are seen as communicative strategies. With their help, social groups such as scientists and engineers can claim that the results of their research are universally valid, a claim that would be more difficult to sustain with other rhetorical methods of communication:

> Perhaps most crucially, reliance on numbers and quantitative manipulation minimizes the need for intimate knowledge and personal trust. Quantification is well suited for communication that goes beyond the boundaries of locality and community. A highly disciplined discourse helps to produce knowledge independent of the particular people who make it.

This establishes a close link between the organization of knowledge and the organization of science, though that link does not consist of a simple reaction on the part of scientists to the political circumstances. While Porter does not claim that quantification is nothing but a political solution to a political problem, he reckons that this "is surely one of the things that it is." The quantification of knowledge and a different way of generating knowledge must thus be examined as a social phenomenon. The questions that need to be asked are the following: Under what social and political conditions do scientists and engineers have recourse to quantifying methods in their work? What social goals do they pursue in the process? How does this change in the justifying argumentation modify the appearance of their scientific studies?[41]

It was Federal Transportation Minister Seebohm himself who combined criticism of the construction of the *Reichsautobahnen* with demands for more research. In a programmatic speech to the re-established Research Society for the Road System (*Forschungsgesellschaft für das Straßenwesen*) in 1950, he criticized the inadequate scientific foundation of decisions in the transportation section, and especially in the construction of the *Reichsautobahnen*. Seebohm, a mining engineer by training, challenged the primacy of engineers in making technical decisions. Instead, it was imperative that a scientific basis be established first. The minister of transportation reinforced this point further by pointing to the relative poverty in Germany immediately after the war and the high investment costs for transportation projects. For that reason it was necessary, especially in the transportation sector, to strengthen "the scientific work."

As an example for the lack of a scientific foundation, Seebohm mentioned the *Reichsautobahnen*. He argued "that especially certain experiences on the construction of these autobahnen should teach us how a good idea can sometimes be considerably compromised in its practical effect by hasty planning and implementation." The highest ranking transportation official in Germany reminded his listeners that transportation must be "servant and pillar of the economy" and should not take on a purpose of its own. For him, the network of the Nazi autobahn had been considerably short on functionality and rationality in terms of transportation policy. The interdependence of transportation route and mode of transportation had been neglected in this case: "In the past, one would have done much better to adjust the roads first of all to current transportation necessities and motorization, instead of reaching far into the future and leaving us with a road network that is encumbered with many mistakes."[42]

The cardinal problem in the eyes of the minister of transportation was the lack of an "organic" transportation policy, that is, the integration of roads into the existing transportation structures. Specifically he criticized the route of the autobahn from Kassel to Frankfurt, which ran past important economic centers and transportation hubs and therefore created long approaches for the users. Moreover, the excessive gradient of the roads was an impediment to trucks, which were in fact forced to seek alternate routes on highways rather than using the freeway. As we have seen, these gradients were the product of the efforts of Nazi road planners to stage the autobahnen, and they offered up the autobahn landscape for visual consumption. Alongside the achievements of road building one therefore also had to emphasize its mistakes, Seebohm told the assembled highway engineers. His criticism culminated in a personal attack, though he shied away from mentioning a name: "The man to whom we owe such much evil also made crucial mistakes here."[43]

In this reinterpretation of the Nazi propaganda, the autobahnen were thus retained as "Adolf Hitler's Roads," only now the dictator was held responsible for their functional deficiencies, which were described as the result of an irrational dictatorship. This perspective, in exculpatory fashion, blocked out the fact that the alignment of the roads was in fact the result of a process of negotiation between civil engineers, landscape advocates, and the political construction bureaucracy. However, the target audience of Seebohm's critique, highway engineers, was fully aware of the historical genesis of the truck-unfriendly gradients.

Incidentally, the civil engineers of the Research Society had already been criticized for the routing of the *Reichsautobahnen* at their first general meeting in 1947. The head of the central administration of roads in the American and British occupation zones lamented that under National Socialism, road research had borne traits of "research for its own sake." The lack of cooperation between research, science, and implementation had led to "pronounced misdirections." This philippic condemned the gradient of the autobahn Stuttgart-Ulm up to the plateau of the Swabian Jura as a bad example:

If the alignment of an autobahn segment—and it is not the only one in Germany—is laid out in such a way that the autobahn can hardly be traveled on by a commercial vehicle even under normal conditions, it is clear that a lot of thinking, but a lot of wrong thinking, has gone into this work. For us, a road is only usable if it is not run over the highest peaks of the mountains for the sake of some kind of nice vistas, but if it serves traffic, specifically, for the most part haulage traffic, which means, in turn, heavy haulage. All of you will have found it to be grotesque, and I find it grotesque every time I realize that, with the exception of few people who do not know the autobahn segment yet, nearly the entire traffic flows to Munich, not over the autobahn, but on Reich Road 10, namely on the old [incline called] Geislinger Steige, which was sensibly laid out—as much as one knew of such things under the conditions at the time.[44]

Minister of Transportation Seebohm continued this line of criticism and formulated a clear goal for the Research Society for the Road System: one should learn from past mistakes and not continue to go down the wrong path. The scarcity of funds demanded that one advocate an "organic structure." Seebohm's attention was directed especially at the development of new surface materials with lower maintenance costs and resistance to deicing salt, which would allow less money to be spent on upkeep and more on the construction of new roads.

For the future, the Federal Ministry was expecting the heightened research activity to produce a greater degree of efficiency and safety for the roads. These two functions were now seen as the highest goals of the autobahn; scientification, rationalization, and economizing formed the framework within which road planners and road builders wrote about the autobahnen and called for them on the public political stage. As early as 1950, Seebohm called for every effort to increase traffic safety. No country with a comparable level of motorization had accident figures as high as Germany's, he claimed. After two wars in half a century, "the health and labor power of our people" had priority. How popular such calls for safety were is shown by a breathless magazine article in 1960 entitled "The Autobahn Battlefield," which ended with this demand: "We don't want any luxury on Germany's supposedly famous roads. But we demand more safety! Safety through guardrails that prevent the flight of death across the median strip. Safety from well-built access and exit lanes. Safety through hedges on the median strips that eliminated the deadly dangerous glare from oncoming traffic."[45]

Glare protection on the autobahn even became the topic of a top-level cabinet session in 1959, with Chancellor Konrad Adenauer asking about the methods that would keep cars from crossing the median. In his response, Seebohm referred to tests with a lattice fence on concrete pilings in the median and to guardrails. Seebohm blamed the federal states, who, he claimed, were not installing enough guardrails in spite of available funds (see figure 7.1).[46] The mass deaths on the roads were a great social problem. In the early 1950s, the number of annual traffic fatalities stood at 8,000, by 1956 it had surged to 12,800. The numbers rose year after year and hit about 19,000 in 1972, which equaled more than 50 automotive deaths per day.[47]

Figure 7.1. More and more, drivers and citizens of the Federal Republic declared the primacy of aesthetics on the Nazi autobahn to be obsolete. Instead, many demanded safe roads as thousands of drivers were killed each year on the roads. Guardrails, which were installed on thousands of kilometers of autobahn after the war, were one of the answers to these requests. Planners increasingly paid attention to bad weather conditions such as fog and tried to provide roads that would offer a uniform driving experience throughout the seasons and in every part of West Germany.
Hans Lorenz, *Trassierung und Gestaltung von Straßen und Autobahnen* (Wiesbaden/Berlin: Bauverlag, 1971), 132.

To achieve the safety and scientific quality that was being called for, the minister of transportation recommended that the traffic engineers turn to statistical and comparative methods. Seebohm noted the differences between basic and applied research. While the former was shaped by the image of the discoverer-inventor and was pursued for its own sake, the latter was systematic and benefited from economic and organizational insights, in his eyes. That is why the minister of transportation explicitly accorded comparative methods scientific status, but only as long as the work was "neat and orderly." With his appeal to modernize the research work, Seebohm was aiming at greater systematization and plannability, qualities that were in turn closely linked to the repeatedly propagated goals of safety and economic efficiency. The idea was that the infusion of methodology would impose a systematic structure on road planning and its operation, and rationalize the work internally. The generation of knowledge was thus placed on a new, depersonalized basis.[48]

The design criteria for the roads in the landscape were subordinated to this new context of justification. At the second postwar meeting of the Research Society for the Road System, Seebohm mentioned the "proper landscape integration" of the roads as one of the worthwhile research topics. The point was to create works that not were merely technically first-rate, but also as "harmonious as possible, thereby giving to the entire landscape and also to the heart of people something that they could carry beyond the future." However, this demand is found only once in the speeches of the federal transportation minister at this meeting. It shows, on the one hand, that the call for harmonious technology was still sufficiently attractive even to Seebohm for him to at least mention it. On the other hand, the mere mention without context or further justification indicates that it no longer seemed to be a central theme. At least Seebohm did not go as far as some civil engineers, who, as we shall see, sought to throw off demands for landscape integration entirely as so much superfluous baggage after 1949. His demand for "proper" integration seems significant. It implies that there is also a wrong form of integration from which engineers must distance themselves. How and with what personnel this "proper" form could be achieved remained unresolved.[49]

This question appeared to have been already settled within the top administrative and scientific echelons of German road building. In 1954, Kunde, the head of the road building division within the Bonn Ministry of Transportation and chairman of the Research Society for the Road System, noted that in the face of the scale and speed of German traffic, it was no longer acceptable that the designs for highways and city roads were being worked on "from outdated perspectives or under the influence of regional (*landsmannschaftliche*) emotions." Because of the increased speed, so went the implication, regional considerations were becoming obsolete. Instead, uniformity promoted road safety: "Local deviations, no matter how interesting or even somewhat cheaper in price, disturb the uniform overall picture of the roads, unnecessarily impede the smooth flow of traffic, and reduce traffic safety." Under this approach, the goal of design was uniformity and linearity, not a dialogue between the road and the local conditions.[50]

And that was why the landscape design of roads also had to face up to new perspectives. After its "equally strong and fruitful development" during the construction of the *Reichsautobahnen*, landscape integration now required "once again more systematic cultivation and promotion." Moreover, the demands of landscape design had to accommodate themselves "in a reasonable way" to the demands of the constantly growing traffic. This vocabulary of reason and economic rationality implied that the landscape design of the *Reichsautobahnen* had sprung from unsystematic work. The systematization being called for aimed for scientization and uniformity under the overarching primacy of safety. In this context, standardization was seen as so important that even questions of cost had to take a backseat. The only thing left for "landscape" was a subordinate role; the focus now was on the uniform overall appearance of the roads.[51]

Within the parameters of this discourse that I have described, such as safety and uniformity, emphasis was also placed on the modernity of scientific road planning. The collective concept "modernity" made it possible to present parameters devised on the basis of repeatable methods as progressive and on the cutting edge; "regional (*landsmannschaftliche*) feelings," that is, approaches committed to regional criteria and based more on emotion than reasoned justification, could thus easily be dismissed as backward and premodern. At the same time, "modern" carried such power as a term that it required no further justification: "Let us not waste time on detailed justifications why modern routing had to come about, since it is self-evident to everyone of you that the fast motorcar needs a different road than the mail coach, and that today one can build different roads with excavators, tampers, and pavers than was once possible with shovels and wheelbarrows."[52]

New technological possibilities ("the fast motorcar") and means (excavators instead of the shovel) thus created what appeared to be an ineluctable constellation in which "modern" could function as a signal word for a scientifically underpinned complex of road design. In this context, engineers used technical determinism—the idea that technology and not humans was driving history—as a strong rhetorical argument. The goal in all of this was a "fast, safe, and economical" journey by car. It followed from this that the routing of the roads had to be adjusted to the demands of driving dynamics. Moreover, the layout of the road was understood as a psychological task, since cars were guided "by eye, brain, and hand." Instead of the aesthetics of the landscape, now it was the effect of the road on the motorist's psyche that was being negotiated. Introductory reflections on the relationship between man and machine were part of that process: because man was the older of the two, he "had not yet completely adjusted to the machine biologically."[53]

A vague psychology of the motorist thus took the place of the experience of landscape and the mobilization of geography that was an essential aspect of the *Reichsautobahnen*. To be sure, in the psychological justification one can still find echoes of past rhetoric—for example, when the "pleasure in driving through forests" is explained with reference to anthropological constants, according to which man had "lived for hundreds of thousands of years in open nature, and in our latitudes mostly in the forest." More significant in terms of results, however, was the mathematical demonstration that straight roads were more accident-prone than curvy ones, and the relief that this "long overdue" insight was now concrete. However, the justification was anecdotal and based on simplistic quantification: studies on the "curviness" of a highway section defined it as the ratio of the real length of a road and distance as the crow flies. Calculations yielded values of 1.0 to 1.2. Of five examined sections, all showed that "dozing accidents" (where the driver fell asleep) depended on curviness. This was supposedly true for passenger cars as well as for trucks, and for the latter "even with near-linear regularity."[54]

The Nuremberg civil engineer Lorenz—a former employee in the office of the Inspector-General, Seifert's antagonist before and after 1945, and a representative of the quantifying current—recommended generous curves in place of the "widely used broken lines of straightaways with short connecting arcs." As we have seen, the landscape advocates of the *Reichsautobahn* had already pursued that goal, but now civil engineers were endowing this demand with a different justifying logic. It was determined that in the curve, the transverse gradient possessed the correct dynamic position; moreover, zigzag lines were up to 4 percent longer and therefore more expensive than sinuous lines. Consistent with the framework of economic argumentation was also the assertion that good routing freed up transport capacities for "more profitable purposes." Summarizing, Lorenz described alignment as "the art of constant and steady change of direction in all three dimensions, determined by dynamic, psychological, and aesthetic considerations." Here, the layout of the roads was placed explicitly within an artistic context, even if the justification was given an economic thrust and the execution was mathematized. Moreover, the sequence of the criteria implied a ranking list. At the same time, it becomes clear that aesthetics was now a matter for engineers, and no longer only for landscape architects.[55]

Geometric patterns were recommended as the means for achieving a sinuous, fluid line. The steadiness aimed at by alignment was "in the final analysis a mathematical notion." Straightaways and circular arcs alone were not enough, one needed an additional routing element with a steadily increasing or decreasing curvature. "In most road-building countries," the clothoid, a "curve with a steadily increasing curvature," had come into use for these transition curves. The sought-after goal was a safe, cheaper, and aesthetically pleasing autobahn with "optical guidance" of the driver. This reflected the claim of road builders that they were using the constantly changing, lengthy curves to create a never-flagging attention on the part of the motorist.[56]

Especially after the slowdown in the construction of the *Reichsautobahn*, the clothoid was studied by academic engineers. Leopold Oerley, a professor in Vienna, had proposed it as early as 1937 as a design element "for reasons of driving dynamics." However, his proposal referred only to the curves of exit and entry ramps. Lorenz and his colleague Walter Schürba, evidently at Todt's suggestion, used this geometric form for the first time in a comprehensive way in autobahn planning when they drew up plans for the "transit autobahn" Breslau-Brno-Vienna through occupied Czechoslovakia. Accordingly, no landscape advocate was used for this section, because he was considered superfluous. At the end of 1940, Todt asked Schürba to prepare a plotting chart for transition curves based on the curvature law of the clothoid; it appeared in 1942, that is, after construction on the *Reichsautobahnen* had been suspended. Civil engineers could use this first clothoid chart to make their own, elaborate calculations of the curves easier.[57] In 1943, Lorenz described as the ideal the ability to calculate by means of geometric forms an aesthetic routing derived from artistic talents:

A supple and pleasant route that is drawn free hand (with the soft architect's pencil, so to speak), and which initially took no account of construction elements, can be mathematically modeled, calculated, and laid out without any greater problems, but with better success than before, when planners limited themselves unnecessarily to the rigid forms they could put together from straightaways and circular arcs.[58]

The hard mathematical formula of the engineer could thus replace the soft pencil of the (landscape) architect. Any "arc shape that is desired by the shape of the terrain but is not easy to grasp mathematically" could thus be modeled in order to do justice to the beauty of the line and to considerations of the psychology of the driver. Civil engineers, who by training and work were inclined to give credence to mathematical methods, were now also able to achieve a "supple and pleasing" line of transportation routes, without having to expand their canon of methodology by including the feeling for nature, which seemed unscientific. Aesthetically satisfying solutions could be generated by mathematical calculations. With this embrace of quantification, civil engineers secured additional legitimation and a position that the landscape advocates had still fought for before the war.

The formula of the clothoid embedded itself in additional attempts by builders of the *Reichsautobahnen* to grasp the spatial effect of the highways on the landscape with repeatable criteria. Planners suggested that a graphic representation take the form of a three-dimensional depiction, and in the hiatus of autobahn construction before 1958 (the result of financial constraints), artists, too, were commissioned to produce imaginary pictures of autobahnen yet to be built set within the landscape. This use of autobahn paintings must be distinguished from the propaganda function of autobahn painting that depicted and glorified construction sites and completed segments. These new artistic renderings were joined by gradient models, that is, wooden models visualizing the changing elevation.[59] But the formula of the clothoid offered the most visible expression and the greatest potential for establishing itself in "modern road construction." In 1953, the compilation of the formula charts was described as an aid for the "most fluid line imaginable today," which would thus become "supple, beautiful, and economical" (for an illustration of a clothoid see figure 7.2). Undersecretary Koester of the Federal Ministry of Transportation used the same arguments to praise the clothoid. A route that was "fluid, favorable to driving technique, and convincing in terms of driving psychology" guaranteed a good journey and saved "no small part of the construction costs," since it integrated itself functionally into the local terrain. That is why the clothoid was being used with ever greater frequency. He concluded in the form of an appeal: "The way for the application of the insights of the modern, fluid alignment has thus been prepared." It is revealing that in contrast to the justification of 1943, economic efficiency was now included in the chain of arguments. To that extent, the economization of the autobahn called for by Seebohm was showing its effect.[60]

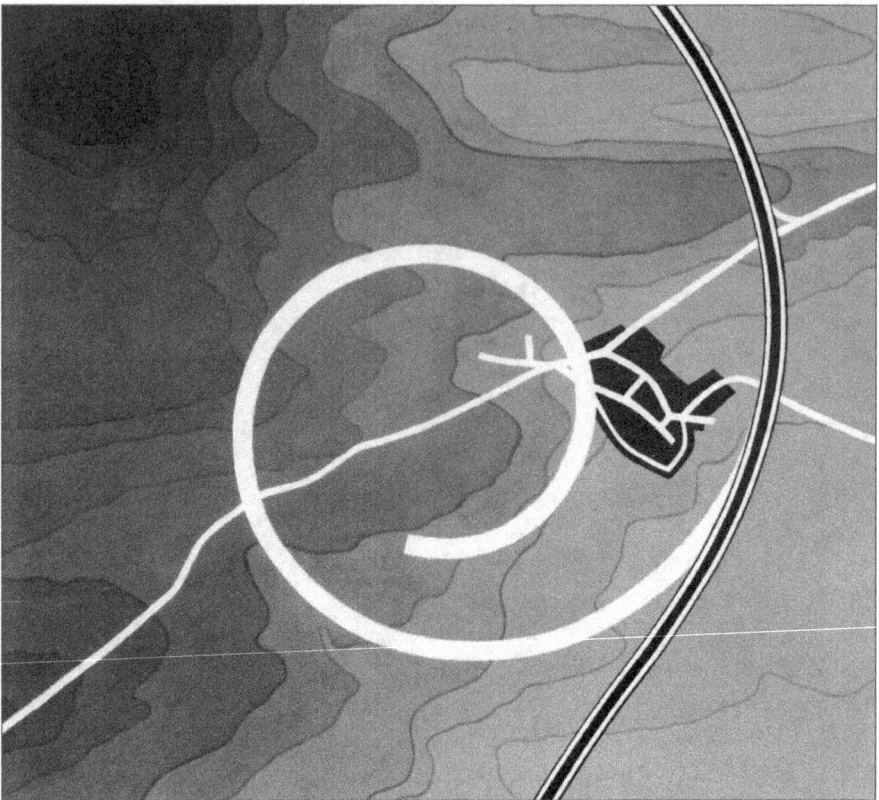

Figure 7.2. In the early years of the Federal Republic, autobahn designers tried to recouch the rhetoric and reasoning for the roads. Instead of serving a violent dictatorship, the roads were now portrayed as apolitical means of meeting traffic needs. Hand in hand with these efforts went the quest for more mathematically sound methods of road design, based on abstract mathematical formulae rather than intuitive experiences of the landscape. The geometric form of the clothoid was used extensively in postwar road design. This figure shows the cover illustration of a textbook on road design: The clothoid resembles a spiral curve from which the autobahn derives its form. The author had been active on the pre-1945 autobahn and was one of the leading proponents to destigmatize the roads after the war through mathematically grounded design methods.
Hans Lorenz, *Trassierung und Gestaltung von Straßen und Autobahnen* (Wiesbaden/Berlin: Bauverlag, 1971), illustration on cover.

At the beginning of the 1960s, the authors of a standard textbook were confident that the clothoid had carried the day. This change manifested itself most clearly in the altered justification of the clothoid as a third element for alignment alongside the straightaway and the circle. The need for the geometric form of the clothoid was now demonstrated mathematically. All other attempts to do so were described as inadequate, even if they produced the desired shape:

> They [previous justifications and proofs] are based in part on assumptions about the operation of the steering wheel, the sideways jolt, and the angle of the transverse

gradient, in part on studies about the driver's view of the road from an aesthetic and driver-psychological point of view, in part on lane analysis, comparisons of curves, and driving tests. Even though the known proofs in the end always lead to the clothoid, the practician often finds the assumptions to be too idealized, especially when it comes to proofs of driving dynamics.[61]

The textbook charts of 1961 dispensed completely with making inductive conjectures regarding driving dynamics the basis of its argumentation. This decision reflects a new quality of the ways in which knowledge was generated in road construction. Instead of basing decisions for or against certain technical parameters on patterns of driving behavior that were either assumed or arrived at with the beginnings of an empirical approach, or on presumed predilections of drivers with the corresponding accident frequency, road planning in the form of alignment became the task of finding and applying formulas, justified solely on mathematical grounds. Specifically, the standard work declared that the transition curve was being introduced "on the basis of a simple consideration." This deduction moved entirely within the realm of geometry. It was assumed that, so far, "almost exclusively" straightaways and circular arcs had been used for alignment. A straightaway has the curvature $1/R = 0$ (with R being the radius of the curvature, which is infinitely large in a straightaway); in the circle, the curvature is consistent at $1/R = C$. As a supplement to the routing elements of the straight and circle, "inadequate on their own," the mathematically next simplest curve with a constant change in curvature was introduced. Since the curvature was supposed to increase in linear fashion with the length (L) of the arc, this produced the formula $1/R = C \times L$. "The clothoid corresponds to this law of curvature."

This derivation of a formula makes clear how mathematization was used as a strategy and rhetoric of justification. The mathematical form was stripped of all nonmathematical conditions and preconditions in order to arrive at a geometric argument under ideal conditions. (This method is analogous to the assumption of "all else being equal" conditions in economics.) However, it proved impossible to do entirely without justifications that lay outside of the formula; that certain routing elements were "inadequate on their own" was styled into an unquestioned a priori fact.

A review of the first edition of the standard work on the clothoid emphasized the chance that the "new routing element" would do justice to the demands of modern traffic and help to shape the "face of the modern road." Pictures were used to compare the prewar autobahn with "unlovely pictorial effects" and the new, geometrically constructed autobahn. Modernity was, therefore, mathematically defined.[62]

Still, the case of the clothoid was not a linear and straightforward march to victory. To some extent, the mathematization of road construction and with it the appearance of the clothoid were contested also after 1949. The publications in the organ of the Research Society for the Road System reflect this clash within the community of civil engineers. In 1950, the complaint was heard within this community—evidently as a reaction to what was perceived as excessive mathematization—that the precision of the detailed implementations of the Guidelines for Country Highways (RAL) stood in no reasonable relationship to their practical importance. This remained a lone voice, however. Another highway engineer argued that considerations of driving technique and aesthetics could be satisfied only if the various routing elements were in tune with each other and in harmony with the environment. It was therefore necessary to determine "mathematically certain threshold values and proportion relationships." Yet another voice argued that the steering that occurred during driving corresponded exactly to the clothoid. Although this was a plausible assumption, it was supported only by personal, subjective experience.[63]

In 1952, the head of the road building department in the ministry of transportation listed, among the three most important research tasks, studies on "fluid spatial alignment and good optical layout." The studies mentioned above were so strongly in support of the clothoid that one article went so far as to ask: "Is the straightaway as a routing element condemned to extinction?" The beauty of the line achieved by the use of the clothoid largely continued to be accepted as an argument. However, the notion that the car was in a quieter position in the sloped curve was disputed. Since long straightaways seemed unmodern, the author recommended that attention be paid to good visibility: the radius of the chosen curves should be no less than ten kilometers in order to ensure good visibility for passing.[64]

The article triggered a debate in letters to the editor that was quite unusual for the professional journal *Straße und Autobahn*. One response from the Technical University in Braunschweig also placed the issue of passing front and center and described cases of smaller curve radii "where passing was entirely impossible." The author stood up for the straightaway as a routing element, arguing that it could not be rejected in every instance for reasons of aesthetics or driving psychology. It is evident that this kind of position could be assumed only out of a defensive posture. Viktor von Ranke, an engineer who favored three-dimensional depictions of the highways, responded to the rhetorical question about the extinction of the straightaway: "Well, it didn't die out. The empirical development of alignment is not that cruel." Instead, the straightaway certainly continued to have its place, for example, when crossing valleys or in feeder roads toward a city center. However, one had to be "careful and parsimonious" in the use of the straightaway since it came with an unstable driving characteristic. The author invoked modernity to justify embracing the clothoid, in the process labeling other views as premodern. "Modern research" on driving technique and driving psychology should not lead engineers to build racetracks, but should enable drivers to quietly and safely reach their goal. The most striking argument, however, was the reference to the decision-making power in the hands of the Federal Ministry of Transportation: a meeting at the ministry had revealed that there was a clear propensity toward a curvy line of the modern road. On his visit to Bonn he had heard few voices of doubt.[65]

This debate shows how the clothoid was increasingly accepted as a design element in the middle of the 1950s. It was far more than an encouraging admonition when it was authoritatively stated in 1958 that the clothoid was used "without exception." Kunde believed that the geometric evolution of the alignment had already come "to some kind of conclusion." He justified this assertion with the adaptation of this design formula in other countries, though he did not bother to mention them.[66]

This "evolution" became most obligatory in the Guidelines for Building Country Highways (*Richtlinien für die Anlage von Landstraßen*, RAL). These instructions were published by the semiofficial Research Society for the Road System and carried special weight in federal postwar Germany. After the war, the Society set up a working committee to oversee their revision. As early as 1947, it was described as the most urgent task to emphasize more clearly the "technical-economic interconnections." Now the search was on for methods of measurement in order to find a "balance after the previous period design based largely on feeling." The RAL should be expanded "toward the economic side" to make engineers pay more attention to the costs of their construction; they should become aware once again of how their decisions burdened or relieved the economy. At the same time, the author emphasized that the "design of the road as a work of art" should be pursued further to keep the cultural sense of responsibility of the road building engineers alive. However, the "emphatic impression of perfectly laid out roads, this rare harmony of human and natural creation," lost priority already in the version of 1947, in that such demands did not lead to practical suggestions, but were merely formulated as empty phrases that were not obligatory. By the 1950s, then, references to the cultural mission had disappeared completely from the discourse of the RAL.[67]

Following twelve years of preparatory work, a new version of the RAL was finally published in 1959. These guidelines were one of the most important foundations for the work of highway engineers. Because of the federal diffusion of competency in road building, the federal states were in charge of carrying out the actual work, which meant they also made the decision about the layout of the autobahnen and all other roads. These guidelines were issued by the Research Society for the Road System in its capacity as the professional association of highway engineers. As a result of the financial support from the Federal Ministry of Transportation for the work of the Research Society, and in the absence of the authority of the ministry in Bonn to issue directives, these guidelines became, if not obligatory, certainly strongly recommended. The introduction of the guidelines stated that the intent was to make insights available to the planners. The goal was the design of "good, safe, and productive roads." It was noted, however, that the civil engineers had sufficient leeway when laying out the route to do justice to the "variety of relationships between road, traffic, and landscape." The RAL thus represented the attempt to canonize the design knowledge in line with the given state of technology. At the same time, they expressed the desire for uniformity in road construction.[68]

The prescription hinted at by Kunde was clearly evident in the RAL, with the guidelines stating unambiguously that the transition curve should be designed in accordance with the mathematical law of the clothoid. Moreover, the slower pace of autobahn construction in the Federal Republic compared to the Third Reich also increased the likelihood that such authoritative pronouncements would in fact make their way into actual planning work.[69]

In the opinion of one observer, the substantial breakthrough of the clothoid as a design element in the layout of roads in the 1950s put an end "to nearly twenty years of passionate discussions about the correct and most advantageous form of the transition curve."[70] Mathematization offered civil engineers the possibility to satisfy the demands by the top echelons of politics and the bureaucracy for an economization and scientization of road building, and to present research on the autobahn in a modern, enlightened form. For all their differences, the rhetoric justifying this kind of planning was in agreement that emotional design was difficult to reconcile with the demands of the federal road bureaucracy for rationality and comprehensible results. In their rejection of emotional approaches to road building, the civil engineers as a group thus revealed a continuity to their behavior during the building of the *Reichsautobahnen*: the first steps toward making mathematization an issue had already appeared in the early 1940s.

However, it would be inaccurate to describe the clear upswing in mathematical criteria in road building as a linear development that was further accelerated by the political conditions of the Federal Republic. Rather, the road building engineers of the young Federal Republic pursued a remarkable policy of history by largely blocking out the clashes with the landscape advocates of the *Reichsautobahnen*, while at the same time continuing to appreciate their proposals, which they perceived as suggestions. This became evident not only in rhetorical bows to the landscape architects. As late as the mid-1950s, the Federal Ministry of Transportation promoted a posthumous publication by the Baden civil engineer and conservationist Hermann Schurhammer, whose reflections on road and landscape showed emotional formulations rather than mathematical formulas.[71] In his preface, Kunde described as a goal of road building "the beauty of form and the harmony in space." Schurhammer was hailed as a pioneer of this current. Kunde, however, avoided the technical term "landscape integration" and chose instead an awkward paraphrase that expressed the same idea.[72]

This preface with its reference to the idea of the integration of the *Reichsautobahnen* into the landscape and the superficial echoes of the *Heimatschutz* discourse of the 1930s only appeared to contradict the mathematization of road planning that was carried out in the everyday professional discussions of the 1950s. Rather, it becomes clear how the representatives of the ministry were slowly distancing themselves from the content and justificatory contexts of the prewar autobahn and their relationship to landscape. The twofold reference to "space (*Raum*)" as the foundation of design supplemented the concept of "landscape" which was much more highly charged intellectually and normatively. Kunde's subsequent explications on road building also show that the relationship between landscape and road was no longer one of the core concerns of road builders. The principles of design were "determined by purpose," a clear nod to instrumental rationality. In this regard, the functionality of the autobahn as a factor for accelerating automotive transportation prioritized its landscape effect.

Thus, the book forms a contradictory nexus between the 1930s and the 1950s. It was in a sense removed from both decades with their divergent approaches and sought to create a synthesis on the basis of older views, but such a synthesis could no longer be achieved in the 1950s. To that extent, the publication of this volume, as well as the financial support it received from the Federal Ministry of Transportation, was characteristic of a conflict-avoiding cultivation of tradition on the part of road building engineers, and, simultaneously, was untypical of the views of the authors who set the tone of the discourse in the 1950s. Added to this, on a personal level, is that the conservationist and road builder Schurhammer was probably the last actor examined here who combined in one person the full range of this contradiction. This publication can thus be seen as the last echo of the vanishing idea of a normatively charged landscape integration. The local nature of the understanding it propagated was increasingly overtaken by the anonymous, formulaic, repeatable, and abstract quantifying generation of knowledge.

The scientization of technology that becomes evident in this was no longer, as it had been in the late nineteenth century, an element of the struggle for the general social acceptance of engineers. Mathematization possessed a specific function within the context of the 1950s, when the professional silence about National Socialism covered up a social clash with the landscape architects over who would hold the status of experts for road construction. The goal was to use this quantifying methodology to push an erstwhile "powerful outsider" (Porter) into a position of reduced influence. This scientized form of knowledge had not only a heuristic, but also a social function.[73] The following section, introducing yet another level of analysis by looking at plantings, will look at the degree to which the relationship had to be renegotiated in the postwar years.

"An autobahn is not a hiking path": roadside plantings as safety devices

The change in meaning that came to the fore for landscape architects was already reflected in the terms that were used. The first postwar article about the relationship between road and landscape in the leading journal *Straße und Autobahn* in 1952 indicated, by its very title "Purposeful road greenery," a functionalization of language and content. The author of the article, a landscape architect, dispensed with a normative notion of landscape; indeed, he avoided the once widely used term entirely in the introduction and spoke instead of "biological-sociological formative powers of the local area." Although these powers were, along with the psychological behavior of motorists, juxtaposed to "static-physical-geometric quantities" as soft factors, the design claim encompassed a comprehensive combination of these factors "from a holistic formulation of the task." Within this functionally structured road planning, planting was assigned the role of a "purposive means of design and traffic guidance." Specifically, these were the purposes of securing the stability of the road's earthen body, directing traffic flow with a visual guideline, and enhancing traffic safety by providing a crash barrier.[74]

In view of this reinterpretation of road plantings, it already seemed necessary to emphasize that this purposive rationality did not contradict the demands of landscape care (*Landschaftspflege*). Clearly the easiest to integrate into the economized justification was the first purpose, that of securing the soil, which could be achieved economically and permanently through plantings. With respect to traffic flow, the author noted the heightened demands of fast-moving traffic, which required that road users be visually guided by perspective lines. This inductively justified demand was joined by the call for traffic safety, which could be achieved by plantings providing glare protection in the median and those protecting against snow and wind.

Within the context of the history of the construction of the autobahn, the article surprises with its unconditional subordination of planting to the newly defined functionalities of road building. Where landscape architects, in keeping with their professional title, had previously sought to defend inherent rights of landscape believed to be threatened, functional criteria for safe transportation now became the guideline for the planting of the roads. This change must be understood against the backdrop of the prescribed economization and scientization of road building, to which the author was trying to accommodate himself with a scientific-sounding jargon.

On a personal level, this article of 1952 can be seen as an attempt by the author, hitherto an outsider, to at least keep open the possibility of employment on the autobahn by using a different kind of language. By contrast, this pursuit of personal interests did not characterize the author of an article on "Safety plantings on the autobahn." Wilhelm Hirsch was still working as a "landscape advocate" in 1954 and had been commissioned with planting the median of the autobahn Frankfurt-Cologne and presented a preliminary result of his work.[75]

This planting work reflected the newly defined tasks of autobahn greenery and was the first larger planting on autobahnen in the Federal Republic. As early as November 1951, the Hesse Ministry of Economics submitted to the Federal Ministry of Transportation a cost estimate for plantings along the portion of the freeway in Hesse. In approving the request, the ministry in Bonn was insistent that the description "planting of the median" be changed in the future to "traffic safety planting and supplement to the general planting." Total costs for the planting were estimated at 300,000 DM. The pilot project served the purpose of standardizing the planting. To that end, Egon Barnard, head of the office for landscape cultivation with the *Landeshauptmann* in Münster, was invited, in his capacity as chairman of the Working Society of Landscape Architects, to a meeting at the Bonn department. The purpose of the meeting, which was chaired by Undersecretary Koester, was to find a uniform methodology when soliciting tenders and awarding contracts. To avoid failures in the selection of plants, the phytosociologist Reinhold Tüxen was asked to prepare an expert opinion on the vegetation of the area. Hirsch was eventually commissioned to carry out the planting. The special importance given to the planting between Cologne and Frankfurt is revealed by the directive from the ministry in Bonn to the road building agency of Lower Saxony to hold back with plantings until the results of the model test were known.[76]

The ministerial oversight articulated clear goals. The focus was not on local peculiarities, but on general principles that were broadly applicable. Achieving landscape effects through planting seemed outdated; instead, Hirsch designed "safety plantings." Especially glare protection, which landscape advocates had often opposed during construction of the *Reichsautobahnen*, was now central to the efforts of the autobahn bureaucracy to increase traffic safety. That was to be achieved by bushes, hedges, and trees planted in the median. In his article, Hirsch identified these stringently defined functions: first, plantings in the median were to cut down the glare from oncoming traffic at night; second, they should heighten the "clear alignment"; third, they should moderate gusts of wind. This catalogue moved planting into a utility thinking that included the subsequent economic efficiency of care and maintenance. Individual stands of trees made the cutting of grass with machines more difficult. This was given as the first reason for abandoning the "scattered, more garden-like arrangement" of the plants and embracing "larger, consistent area planting." Only then was it said that this form of planting represented the right scale vis-à-vis the large landscape area.[77]

The ideological elevation of the nativeness of the chosen plants under National Socialism, which was supposed to lead to a restoration of the German landscape, was turned into an economic factor: it was said that autochthonous greenery required less care and was more economical to maintain. For Hirsch, the amount of planting was also subordinated to the concerns of traffic safety. Plantings had to be sparse on inside curves so as not to obstruct visibility; outside curves, by contrast, allowed for tightly packed bush plantings, one reason being to prevent cars from being carried off the highways. In hilly terrain where visibility was reduced, plantings served to make the line of the roadways visible, "for otherwise the driver has the feeling that the road is leading nowhere." At dangerous points, the demands of clear visibility took priority. Along roads rich in panoramic vistas, however, the sightlines must not be blocked by dense plantings. Here looser plantings were appropriate, "which showed the driver the beauty of the landscape and thus eliminated the monotony of the line of the road." This last point was an echo of the aesthetic of the *Reichsautobahnen* and its goal of visual consumption, though in a milder form and adapted to the presumed needs of the motorist.[78]

At the same time, Hirsch was at pains to standardize autobahn planting. The exact distances between the individual plants and their rows, the mixture of plant communities, and the exact planting locations with their respective distances from the highway were precisely specified in order to make the actual work easier and to avoid "any arbitrariness." Moreover, the planting in rows promised a more rational approach. The landscape architect pointed out that it was problematic to plant autobahnen long after their construction phase was over. Because the layers of humus were by then strongly pervaded with roots, new plantings were slow to grow. This caused additional costs, and at the same time "years of plant development are lost, something that we cannot justify given the large volume of traffic today and its safety."[79] In addition, Hirsch criticized the fact that the practice of awarding contracts to the lowest bidder led the horticultural firms and nurseries to furnish plants of low quality, which would prove costly over the long run.

This article from the pen of a former collaborator on the Nazi autobahn reveals the changed status of the architects and the new functions that were ascribed to planting. At first glance, the commissions to Hirsch and Tüxen suggested a continuity to the *Reichsautobahn*; substantively, however, there was a discontinuity. Hirsch placed the entire complex of planting on a new foundation of definitions, without connecting to the thread of tradition of the planting of the *Reichsautobahnen*. The reference to the enjoyment of "beautiful landscape" does not contract this interpretation. Where the landscapes of the *Reichsautobahn* derived their justification from the adjective "German," this nationalized landscape could barely still be found in Hirsch in 1952; instead, it was merely an individual landscape consumption that was suggested. The stock of traditions of the Nazi autobahn proved incapable of continuation also when it came to the practical implementation of planting work. No firm consensus about the scope and supervision of the work had yet emerged between the road building bureaucracy, landscape architects, and companies doing the planting. Shoddy work raised the costs for the planting, which was already under pressure to justify its economic efficiency. At a joint meeting of the committees "Landscape Design" and "Road Planting" in 1953 on the topic "The road tree: seedling, planting, maintenance," participants lamented that the horticultural and technical knowledge about trees that once existed had been lost: "The trees that are delivered and used are (largely) unsuitably grown, without trunk-forming rank shoots, and on the roadside the trees are (again, for the most part) not treated correctly." Nurseries and road building administrations were therefore given pointers for a more effective planting work. However, it was clear to the participants "that the desired tradition cannot be pulled out of thin air." It would cost a good deal of effort, time, and money to get out of the current low point.[80]

All in all, planting as a component of landscape integration was on the defensive. The professional civil engineering journal *Brücke und Straße* (Bridge and Road) published violent polemics against tall-growing plantings, which culminated in the pronouncement: "An autobahn is not a hiking path."[81] The scope and nature of the plantings along the *Reichsautobahnen* were listed as a negative example for a Romantic attitude toward technology and the road. As a result, it was skepticism that predominated within the road-building bureaucracy of the Federal Ministry of Transportation. The planting project on the Frankfurt-Cologne route was seen explicitly as a test case that was intended to provide new insights for the strictly circumscribed purpose of glare effects.

The generation of knowledge about these plantings differed in its approach and claim from the structures of landscape integration in National Socialism. In keeping with Seebohm's directives, greater weight was now given to academic research and consistency in road planning. This can be demonstrated by the statements of landscape architects, their efforts to make a rhetorical connection, and the exceptional status of the planting project in the fifties. The designated main role in this desired process of scientization was played by the Research Society for the Road System. Although a working group "Landscape Design" had already existed there between 1935 and 1939 under Seifert's leadership, formalized guidelines mattered less than the crucial contacts and conflicts that took place—as we have seen—between the office of the Inspector-General and the landscape advocates themselves. In 1939, this working group was folded into the new working group "Planning, Road Design, and Traffic," and after the war it was not revived on the same level of the hierarchy. Instead, a working committee "Landscape Design" was set up under the leadership of the highway engineer Lorenz, and its first meeting took place in September 1950. At the same time, a working committee "Traffic Safety Plantings" headed by Hirsch was established within the same working group. Although the division into landscape design from an engineering perspective and landscape-architectural planting was abolished at the annual meetings, it did amount to a redefinition of the tasks of the landscape architects, whose area of work was now limited to plantings. The collaboration of road-building engineers and landscape advocates in laying out the route, which had still been considered the ideal case during the construction of the *Reichsautobahn*, thus gave way to the supremacy of the civil engineers also in the relevant committees of the Research Society.[82]

The tasks of the working committee "Landscape Design" included the publication of guidelines on planting. Preliminary work continued through the 1950s and 1960s; the regulations were published in 1960, 1964, and 1969. They represent the most extensive and the most thoroughly argued publications on the planting of the highways.[83] The 1960 guidelines had seven authors, five of whom hailed from the road-building administration. This group therefore had a clear preponderance of civil engineers and the bureaucracy over landscape architects, which indicates a shifting balance of power.[84]

The very first sentence of the introduction already placed road-building engineers in a dominant function: "A balanced, harmonious integration of the road into the landscape is one of the ways in which the road-building engineers can give the traveler on the road comfort and safety in equal measures." The supreme authority of the road builder was thus unopposed; moreover, the landscape integration of the road, reinforced by a pleonasm, was accorded a specific function. A well-designed road supposedly had a calming effect on the motoring person, promoted rest and relaxation, and thus promoted a smooth traffic flow. While meaning before 1945 had been derived from landscape, the functionalization of the road in the direction of an industrialized transport with high circulating speeds was now the main task. Nevertheless, given the massive impact of road building on the appearance of the landscape, the engineer's obligation to participate actively in the general landscape cultivation was mentioned. By means of appropriate plantings, engineers could help to put a stop to the "general desolation." Equally ambitious was the claim that in impoverished and disfigured landscapes, plantings could initiate a "better and richer redesign." The demands culminated in calls for creativity: "As part of the landscape, the road is given diversity, depth, and profile by its plantings. It is desirable that these plantings are carried out with imagination, a talent for design, and experience."[85]

The echoes of the engineer's artistic skill were even clearer in the comments on design, which explicitly called for an emotional approach when it came to planting (different from the layout of the route): "The integration of the earth shapes, the man-made structures, and the plantings into the landscape demands an *emotional understanding* of the *unique nature* and the *motifs* of this landscape." However, and this makes the change in the guidelines clear, the "character of the planned road" appeared on a par with this concern. This character was given by the width, the alignment, and the exigencies of traffic, and it had to be considered no less than the interests of the landscape. The guidelines demanded that these technical parameters should exert a determinative influence on the distances between plantings, the size of the groupings, and the growth forms of the plants. These basic reflections express the desire for a balance between the needs of landscape and road, a balance that had to be reflected in the plantings. As a result of the different backgrounds of the authors, the choice of these determinative factors already created a latent tension that could rise to the level of internal contradiction. This was reflected in the divergent approaches: on the one hand, "an emotional understanding of the unique nature," that is, an irreproducible feeling was to offer a basis for the plantings; on the other hand, their essential elements should be derived from numerically determined values such as the size and expected load of the road. This dilemma, however, was to be resolved not by the civil engineers by themselves, but by "experts designing with experience and a sure eye." Since the plantings were usually done by permanently employed qualified gardeners or self-employed landscape architects, it was they, and not the civil engineers, who had to bear the burden of these contradictory expectations.[86] The head of the working committee on landscape design, Lorenz, had drawn a similar distinction as early as 1952, and had spoken, for the relationship between road and landscape, of a technical (*handwerklich*) and an architectural (*baumeisterlich*) landscape design.[87] The former could be mastered by everyone, while the latter could be accomplished only by few. This distinction also applied to the planting, wrote Lorenz:

> Design as art cannot be learned by everyone. But in road planting there are many aspects that can be logically understood and carried out: planting against the runoff and sliding of embankments, plantings for the visual line, the arrangement of plantings with consideration for unencumbered visibility, the creation of a forest screen in front of torn forest edges, plantings as mechanical protection against cars plunging

over steep embankments, plantings that create a space-structuring connection to existing hedges, copses, and clumps of trees, and so on.

Lorenz was revealing his barely concealed disparagement of the publications of the landscape advocates of the *Reichsautobahn* by noting that when it came to architectural landscape design, "little that was coherent" had been written, and in its place he was introducing his own "manageable system." He was explicitly separating out the areas of landscape integration that were seen as artistic and allocated them to a separate group of experts, professionally organized landscape architects. What was left for the civil engineers were those areas that could be "logically grasped and carried out." These areas were thus closer to their conception of road building and could be so strongly rationalized with logical justifications and concrete directives that these areas were changed from something opaque into something useful.[88]

Within the guidelines for road planting, their tasks were narrowly defined and presented with rationally justifiable arguments. Specifically, four points were mentioned: technical tasks related to engineering and traffic, and tasks related to landscape and to biology. The technical engineering tasks of greenery included the stabilization of surfaces with grass or the prevention of embankment slides through the planting of suitable, supportive bushes and shrubs. Protection against snow and falling rocks was also in this category. Among technical traffic tasks, visual guidance was paramount, which was described as the attempt to structure the road space in depth to prevent accidents. In addition, plantings should create glare protection, and vehicles that veered off the road should be caught by bushes. Clear functional attributions to road greenery also came from the moderation of wind gusts and the reduction of "noise, visual, and olfactory nuisance" for parks, hospitals, and schools. By way of the functionalization of plantings, the effect of the road was expanded on the planning level to residents and not motorists, even if only in tentative and nonobligatory steps.[89] The list of landscape tasks was headed by the replanting of gravel pits and quarries where road-building materials had been excavated. In addition, it was stated very tersely that the road should be "integrated into the living structure of the surrounding landscape in a nature-appropriate way," though this challenge was not described in any greater detail. Moreover, plantings should serve to round out, reshape, and newly create landscape pictures. As for biological tasks, the publication mentioned shelter for pest-eating animals in the new plantings, their use as bee meadows, and a positive microclimatic effect. With respect to the plants themselves, the authors diluted the traditional dogma of nativeness. Although plant species meeting this requirement should be given preference, nonnative plants could be used if there was a "reasoned idea of the effect emanating from them," that is, if a landscape picture emerged that could be described as prevalent. Expert opinions from the perspective of phytosociology were recommended only in case the selection of species was not apparent from the landscape itself. An appendix described as a first suggestion introduced a plant chart that also called for nonnative species such as arborvitae ("only within built-up areas"), red maple, and chestnut ("for use only on the outskirts of the city").[90]

The chart also included the juniper (Juniper communis). At least on this point, the recommendations of the working committee ("use local breeds") diverged from the view of the Federal Ministry of Transportation that juniper be used only occasionally because of phytosociological concerns. The *Heimatschutz* and conservation committee of the Sauerland Mountain Club had asked the Federal Ministry of Transportation in 1952 to see to the reintroduction of the juniper, which many appreciated as a "moody shrub with a will of its own." The response, however, was restrained. The ministry pointed out that juniper could be planted only if it was in harmony with the phytosociological criteria that were seen as crucial to the planting and design in road building. More importantly, this matter was for the states to decide. In its explanation, the ministry put the phytosociology study in first place, while the authors of the guidelines recognized merely an auxiliary function of such scientific expertise. The phytosociological charting of new road segments that was initiated by the Nazis was not systematically continued on the federal level. Lorenz spoke disparagingly of plant sociologists as the "jurists among the biologists," whose insights were of little usefulness to construction practice.[91]

This brings us back to the guidelines for road plantings from 1960: in their concluding recommendations, the authors pushed for a stronger bureaucratization and standardization of planting. In the ideal case, this would be done with a planting plan with information about what plants were needed and where to get them. The respective road-building agency was supposed to entrust this to an employed or freelance landscape architect. The guidelines admonished the road-building engineer and the landscape architect to be in constant contact with each other. A hopeful tone also attached to the appeal that in purchasing land, one should, "if possible," acquire an area along the sides that corresponded to the width of the two-lane road. This last point referred to the economic efficiency of planting. It could not be uniformly regulated on the federal level, since the state agencies were largely autonomous in their decisions about landscape integration. That is why the guidelines remained nonobligatory for those making decisions at the state level. Their authors identified them explicitly as aids and suggestions for standard situations that occurred frequently. Therefore, the planting guidelines should not be confused with what were, by comparison, fixed parameters—such as the width of the road—in the guidelines for the building of highways and freeways.[92]

While the first part of the guidelines was devoted chiefly to the problems that arose during planning, the second part in 1964 summarized the prevailing views on how the road plantings should be carried out.[93] Concise descriptions were given especially of the treatment of topsoil and the preparation of compost heaps during the construction work. The discussions of grass and seed stock also sprang from efforts at systematization and standardization. Since most of the surface areas especially in autobahn construction were not planted with copses, grass was generally seeded to solidify the surface of the soil and prevent erosion.

What planners wanted were unfertilized, low-growth grass areas (*Magerrasen*), which would require the least possible maintenance and yet provide "a pleasant appearance throughout the year." In addition, shoulders and parking surfaces should be drivable, which required an especially resistant turf; embankments also required a thick turf and strong pervasion with roots to protect the soil against washout or wind erosion.[94]

The most controversial issue of lawns involved the seed mixture. The guidelines pointed out that it was impossible to indicate one single mixture for all of Germany, since the typical mix of different grasses was too different in each case due to types of soil, climate or slope condition. Even though the matter was seen as in need of local consultation, the appendix of the guidelines listed ten model seed mixtures differentiated according to the soil's humidity and acidity as a "rough outline" and a makeshift for those cases in which experts were not available. The guidelines explicitly advised against commercial embankment seed mixtures, since they were not controlled and were therefore unsuitable.[95]

However, this is exactly what appears to have taken place. To the chagrin of one landscape architect, it was left to the landscaper in charge to procure the grass seed, which meant that standard seed mixtures were used.[96] According to this author, as late as the early 1960s "thousands of centners" of cheap, unsuitable embankment mixtures were supplied and sown along the roads. Since the cheaper seed mixtures had to be applied in much greater volume and the resulting grass had to be cut up to three times a year, the costs were higher than with specific grass mixtures that were more expensive to procure. The landscape architect even demanded that the authorities prohibit these embankment mixtures. That did not happen, but the irate author was made coauthor of the guidelines for seedings.[97]

The landscape architects' desire to exert more influence on seeds remained largely unfulfilled, however. As late as 1974, a dissertation considered it to be well known that especially in seedings, not always the most suitable plant ensembles were chosen. This was a problem that was also significant in terms of sheer acreage. The construction of new autobahnen generated up to thirty-five square meters of area along the sides that needed to be newly covered in greenery for each meter of the route. On two-lane highways, the "road-accompanying acreage" was up to twenty square meters per meter of newly constructed roadway.[98]

Many times, it was charged, plantings were done that had great difficulty flourishing at their specific locations from the very outset. As far as the author could tell, the balance sheet after about a quarter of a century of road plantings in the postwar period was unambiguously negative, for only the first steps toward systematization were discernible. Valuable seed stock was frequently wasted. Incidentally, one ironic result of the grass seedings along the autobahnen was that the nature of the seed mixture barely influenced what kind of grassy areas would appear—at least over the long term. By the end of the 1960s along older segments, the stock of plants that had been planted during construction and the neighboring stock left untouched at the time had largely grown alike in their composition of species. Most species of grass had immigrated without any additional help from humans. There was only minor difference between the plant communities immediately along the autobahn and adjoining ones. Wind, water, and animals apparently had carried the plants that balanced out the original difference. However, observers did not conclude from this realization that research on seed composition should be given up, since its results were anyhow swallowed up. Rather, it was emphasized that these findings should not be generalized, and that especially the solidity of embankments called for specific plantings.[99]

In sum, one can note that the use and composition of grass mixtures for shoulders and medians of the autobahn lost out to the postwar demands for greater economic efficiency, systematization, and simplification. In the process, a gap became apparent between what was in many cases a clearly inadequate praxis of plantings and research that was lagging behind. While, apparently, the road-building administrations of the states largely left the seed mixtures up to the landscaping companies hired to do the work, it was only in the 1970s that economic demands came to guide the relevant research, which long clung to carefully designed, scientifically grounded plant communities. Only now did the realization prevail that the offerings of simple solutions had to appear more attractive within the newer context of their use. The agency of natural grass migrations, obvious to every gardener, had to be reckoned with scientifically. Not a botanist, Lorenz had stipulated as early as 1952: "Besides, every lawn remakes itself automatically over the years to the composition that is most suitable to its location. Unsuitable things die off, suitable seeds arrive on the wind and take root."[100]

Finally, the third part of the guidelines formalized the maintenance work on the road plantings. A chart captured the maintenance costs for both grassy areas and copses, with the latter being less costly in upkeep. Insecticides were recommended to protect against insect damage. Since plantings in the median were threatened by deicing salts, the most resistant kinds of woody plants should be selected.[101]

All in all, the three parts of the guidelines for road planting reflect the effort to systematize and rationalize road greenery. The justifications were placed increasingly within the context of roads where the emphasis was on safety, and whose accompanying greenery served as visual guiding lines and crash protection. Here and there one could still hear echoes of the emotional approach to nature, but such demands were externalized, as it were, and assigned to landscape architects. By finding an answer to the demands for safety in the form of road planting, road-building engineers were able to solidify their elevated status within traffic planning. These efforts to prevent accidents and accommodate the wishes of motorists were based more on suppositions than insights with even a modicum of empirical substantiation, as is revealed by the following passage on the building of rest areas: "Humans are more complicated than one might think. People don't just stop wherever a rest area has been situated. The desire to take a break builds up, and where fulfillment finally beckons, that is where people stop—even if it is not permitted at this particular location."[102]

Driving and resting behavior was clearly based on anthropological constants, which civil engineers—by virtue of their own driving experience and, more important still, their expertise on roads—were familiar with and made use of. Much the same was true of what was called the calming effect of a well-landscaped road.[103] Its effect on traffic safety was at best indirect, but the mere supposition was sufficient to justify plantings.

To what degree were these guidelines implemented? Even their authors appear to have been skeptical. Max Schwarz, a former landscape advocate of the *Reichsautobahnen* and collaborator on the second part of the guidelines, expressed profound doubt in a letter to the Federal Ministry of Transportation about his work in the committee on landscape design. He acknowledged that the committee members were trying hard. However, he sensed "no optimism" on the part of the civil engineers that the guidelines could be implemented in the future. The civil engineers were no longer open-minded about these questions. With a hidden reference to Todt, Schwarz mentioned the bygone training courses on these matters at universities, for professional engineers, and for maintenance workers. He concluded: "If it cannot be this way, there is no hope of accomplishing something, which is simply how it was intended from the beginning in road construction."[104]

Leaving aside Schwarz's tendency to idealize road building under National Socialism, his assessments indicate that the conception and scope of the landscape integration of the *Reichsautobahnen* did not establish a tradition that would have been apparent in the early 1960s, and that the efforts by some road-building engineers at catalogization and systematization were not aimed at reconstructing the pre-1945 expert knowledge, but sought to redefine it. The openly expressed frustrations indicate that within the context of competing ways of generating knowledge, landscape architects had little to contribute to the politically important academization, indeed, that they could be seen as its enemies. The head of the road-building department in the Federal Ministry of Transportation from 1970 to 1972, speaking about the relationship between engineers and architects, concluded that "this has created special problems, which in part have not been overcome to this day. In addition, some of the old opposition between engineers and landscape designers has erupted again, and in practice there was a struggle for what was common knowledge about landscape design that was shaped in the thirties. Much was too recent to have already become common property."[105] Although this assessment was too simplistic, it did describe the problems of meaning that the newly defined landscape design found itself subject to, especially in a federal system of autobahn construction. This situation also affected the status and job opportunities of landscape architects. They were becoming potentially superfluous with alignment work that was based on engineering standards, geometric formulas, and growing standardization. The layout of the line was becoming once again the domain of engineers, who subjected it to scientific criteria. Although landscape architects were employed on the functionalized autobahnen of the 1950s and 1960s on a case-by-case basis, their tasks were largely confined to utilitarian plantings in accordance with the guidelines I have looked at.[106] Compared to the situation that had prevailed under the *Reichsautobahn*, the radius of what the architects could do was thus clearly delineated and restricted. Unclear possibilities of negotiation and personal alliances were replaced with competencies that were circumscribed and limited from the outset, with a functional emphasis on safety and economic efficiency.

As we have seen, after 1945 leading engineers defined the emotional approach to nature by landscape advocates during the building of the *Reichsautobahnen* as pre- and unscientific. In this regard, quantification and mathematization were not only important methodological innovations for academically trained road builders, but a potent weapon to prevail against the competition from landscape architects in the production of knowledge. With the help of mathematization and formulas arrived at deductively, such as the clothoid, highway engineers succeeded in styling themselves as the dominant experts on the alignment of roads. In the process, scientization and the often-voiced demand for safety worked in the engineers' favor; they further reinforced this trend and appropriated it. By contrast, the landscape architects found themselves pushed on the defensive by the new discursive parameters of safety and rationality, a position that was hard to escape by reinterpreting trees and bushes as "safety plantings."

In the Federal Republic, mathematization also offered a chance to distance oneself from "Adolf Hitler's Roads," which carried a heavy ideological ballast. Without so much as addressing the prominence of the autobahnen in Nazi propaganda, by reducing their construction methodology to the supposedly pure rational core of mathematics, the leading engineers acquired a proven instrument to pursue a methodological discontinuity while preserving professional continuity. The landscape architects were left with the odium of a close involvement with the Nazi road project.[107]

Roadside greenery as a bone of public contention

So far, the main protagonists examined here have been experts. That is little surprise for the period of National Socialism, given the absence of a free public sphere. However, when it comes to the Federal Republic, one should ask how those who used these roads saw their relationship to the landscape. As we have seen, "the motorist" was a favorite rhetorical figure during turf battles within the circles of experts, and the preferences, desires, and experiences imputed to him were mostly deduced from personal perception. A few years after the establishment of the Federal Republic, however, the design of roads became a contentious issue that was increasingly fought over in public. The public nature of the conflict was evidently quite typical: according to Kurt Möser, transportation policy was one of the questions West Germans debated most vigorously. In fact, it has been said that citizen participation in and criticism of the state regulation of transportation was one of the most important areas of democratic controversy in the young republic.[108]

"The motorist" spoke up, and to the amazement of the road-building engineers, "he" was sometimes a woman. A point of critique was roadside trees, whose existence and numbers in the 1950s and 1960s became a subject of debates over safety and aesthetics. Many discussants, especially the automobile clubs, regarded the growing number of traffic fatalities as a result of the numerous trees lining the roads. And it is in fact true that many motorists died when their car hit a tree. Within the causal complex of road, car, and driver, the road and its very visible component, roadside trees, were often seen in those years as the most important reason behind traffic accidents. As a result, thousands of trees were cut down along roads and avenues in the 1960s and 1970s. In Bavaria alone, some 175,000 roadside trees were felled during the 1960s. In order to elucidate the debate and its results, I have analyzed 101 private letters to the Federal Ministry of Transportation, whose writers addressed roadside trees, landscape integration, glare or crash protection, or a combination of these issues. The letters either approved or disapproved of plantings on roads, and they date from the years 1953 to 1969.[109] As a whole, they offer unique insights into values regarding nature and technology.[110]

Very much in contrast to the orchestrated view of the autobahnen under National Socialism, they reveal the patterns of perception and demands on the part of broad segments of society. Still, the context matters: the writers were very much aware of who the recipients of their letters were. While sycophantic introductory phrases, such as the one wishing the Minister of Transportation a long life, were the exception and a bow to predemocratic supplications to those in power, all the writers were trying to influence processes that the experts of the ministerial bureaucracy were deciding professionally by virtue of their status.[111] The tone of the citizens' letters was accordingly varied. While a gesture of submission was rare, an aggressively demanding tone is found time and again. One writer asked the ministry: "Will you calmly watch as more people are smashed against the trees?," and he demanded the radical removal of all roadside trees.[112]

The number of letters sent each year increased dramatically over the course of time. Whereas only three inquiries were received in 1953, their number rose to twenty-two in a single year by 1969. Although the total distribution of voices pro and con was about equal, they were unevenly distributed chronologically. All in all, forty-three letter writers supported retaining or expanding the existing greenery along the roads; fifty-eight demanded the removal of trees and/or shrubs. While the number of supportive letters stayed within a narrow range of between 0 and 5 per year, the curve of letters opposed to roadside plantings shows a steep rise at the end of the 1960s. Twenty-eight of all negative letters are recorded in 1968 and 1969, almost half of this group. A first finding is thus that the number of tree opponents—to the extent that they manifested themselves in this source—rose sharply toward the end of the period under examination. This indicates a debate over roadside trees that grew increasingly intense, one in which opponents became more vocal while the number of supporters barely grew and thus fell behind in relative terms. An added factor was that the Social Democrat Georg Leber succeeded the conservative Seebohm as transportation secretary in 1966 and stayed in office until 1972, which led many letter writers to hope for a change in transportation policy and on the question of roadside trees, a change they sought to influence.[113]

While the geographic distribution of the letters' authors showed no particular trend, it is significant that eight of the letters were written by women. The debate over roadside greenery was thus to more than 90 percent a purely male debate, especially since the responsible officials in the Ministry of Transportation were exclusively men. It is striking that a majority of the female letter writers supported retaining trees and shrubs or adding more. The letter with the greatest degree of personal relevance is found among those sent by women. A thirty-three-year-old widow with three children who had lost her husband in a tree accident spoke accusingly about the existence of roadside trees. Writing a few days after her husband's death, she asked why there were still trees along the roads, since they were proving disastrous to huge numbers of motorists.[114]

On the part of the respondents, the combination of the two categories "woman" and "teacher" in one case provoked a predictable "male" reaction. The wish of a female teacher at a *Realschule* [secondary vocational school] to see more "fruit trees à la van Gogh" for drivers with a sense for natural beauty drew this grumbling aside comment from a clearly annoyed ministry official: "Typical 'female teacher'! One should wish to admire blooming fruit trees while *hiking* and not along *long-distance* roads!!" Thus the female author of this letter was denied the pleasurable trip she wanted.[115]

As far as occupational status was concerned, the single most important profession consisted of entrepreneurs, followed by physicians. Medical doctors as a group were overrepresented, compared to German society as a whole, and they laid claim to expert status by virtue of their profession. During the debate over safety and trees, they attempted successfully to establish themselves as experts for the relatively new field of trauma medicine, and thus exert influence on the design of roads and cars. According to a recent study, physicians in the Federal Republic dominated the discourse on traffic safety into the 1960s; systematic accident research did not begin until the end of the 1950s.[116]

Some letter writers boasted of their driving experience. One citizen from the city of Krumbach in Bavaria wrote that the campaign against traffic fatalities by minister of transportation Seebohm would be successful only if roadside trees were removed, underscoring his words with the comment, "This from a motorist who has already driven 300,000 kilometers."[117] This claim to long experience points to two circumstances: first, it indicates how strongly the debate over roadside trees was shaped by opinions from supposedly neutral authorities and experts. Second, it is clear that nonexperts also sought this status to lend weight to their arguments. The boundary between professionals and laypeople that the experts sought to draw was challenged by motorists who invoked their driving experience that supposedly gave them the authority to make especially important pronouncements.

Eight submissions were not just individual letters. Their authors sought to impress the authorities by collecting signatures, thus hoping to petition them more forcefully.[118] Only two of these collective efforts came from supporters of trees: in

1953, Peter Rieckmann from Stelle in the district of Harburg collected eleven signatures to protest the cutting of "large, beautiful" maple trees along Highway 4. A resolution by the hiking organization "Friends of Nature" ("Die Naturfreunde") in 1968 went beyond this purely local protest. This particular group, which was part of the workers' movement, urged that the existing stock of forest along the roads be secured and new forest be planted.[119] The resolution, adopted unanimously at the national congress, stated: "The national leadership [of the friends of nature] is directed to exert influence with the Federal Minister for Transportation, as well as with the relevant state ministries, to ensure that in all expansion and new construction on roads, the existing, in some cases valuable, stock of trees be spared wherever possible. Moreover, more attention should be paid once again to the planting of trees and shrubs along traffic routes, in the open landscape, traffic safety permitting. These efforts should be promoted through the preparation of landscape plans and through incorporation into the financing plans."

With this, the Friends of Nature were adopting the rhetoric of the conservation movement, which assumed a preservationist stance in the battle over roadside trees. This resolution, in particular, shows the transitional role of this association with respect to environmental policy: it sought to expand a topos like the pleasure in driving along tree-lined roads and the concern over these trees in the age of mass motorization to the driving workers, thereby implicitly regarding the former opposition by the unions to broad car ownership as a thing of the past.[120]

In contrast to these collective pro-tree sentiments, the opponents of roadside trees were able to tap into a much broader range of protest forms. The least degree of organization belonged to a meeting of thirty-two truck drivers in November 1967 in Hannover, who could not be given a response because their letter lacked a return address. These men who drove for a living criticized that trees in the median of the older autobahnen impeded the flow of traffic and made the roadway less easy to survey. Moreover, the leaves constituted a seasonal danger of skidding. As a replacement, the drivers suggested low grass, arguing that "the current tree plantings also disfigure the appearance of the landscape." By contrast, the newer autobahn sections, "without tree plantings and with a smooth cement bitumen coating and chalk lane markings ... [are] useful to long-haul traffic and safe!"[121]

These comments made it clear to the Ministry of Transportation that professional drivers applied different criteria to the roads than did some of the planners. They were less interested in vistas or transition curves than in an uneventful, unimpeded trip. This letter echoes a change in segments of the public discourse, one that regarded the road and its surroundings as a component of the built environment, a workplace, and not as a natural landscape.

With less numerical emphasis, four medical students from Erlangen argued in the fall of 1965 that the continuation of roadside trees was no longer justified in view of the danger of accidents. The Catholic Rural Youth Movement (*Katholische Landjugendbewegung*) in Meßkirch in Baden (incidentally the birth- and resting place of the philosopher Martin Heidegger) sounded an alarmist note in December of 1968 after one member of their group was killed when his car hit a tree. Twenty-four members and the local priest signed a resolution addressed to the Federal Ministry of Transportation. In it they asked: "Is it responsible that in our motorized age, whole series of 'barricades' exist along our transportation routes, whose existence many people have to pay for with their lives every year?"[122]

The growing importance of this issue is also reflected in the fact that local organizations of political parties began to take on roadside trees at the end of the 1960s. For example, the district association of the Junge Union, the youth organization of the conservative CSU, in Weilheim in Upper Bavaria called a protest meeting against roadside trees in March 1969, at which 674 signatures were collected for the removal of roadside greenery along "heavily trafficked and accident-prone roads" and were sent to the Federal Ministry of Transportation. All the attending speakers from road-building organizations, the ADAC (German Automobile Club), and the district were unanimous in calling for this removal. According to a press account, the county manager (*Landrat*) stated that "Preserving the landscape is probably the only thing we can still offer our citizens. ... But 'our landscape' is not along the roads. That is why the county has recognized the urgent call for help and has demanded roads without trees in the last few years." What the petitioners perceived as the dangerous effect of the roadside trees left no option but to cut them down. All one had to do was invoke the high number of traffic accidents to establish the relevant connection. Even the field of tension between safety and aesthetics in which trees were usually discussed was dissolved on that evening. The Weilheim county manager did concede that landscape protection was a binding political motivation. However, by removing the immediate environs of the roads from the landscape, he could present himself as an official who was committed to both landscape preservation and road safety. In his response, the responsible division head at the Federal Ministry of Transportation criticized the party organization for being too simplistic in its sweeping demands.[123]

Opposition to roadside trees extended across party lines. At the beginning of the social-liberal coalition in 1969, the local SPD organization from Türkenfeld-Moorenweis outside of Munich complained about "a kind of roadside tree ideology" along the federal highways. The road-building agencies were still clinging to "an antiquated tradition from the age of the stagecoach" by continuing to plant trees along roads. That is why no new trees should be planted, and existing ones should be cut down where they endangered the traffic. The Social Democrats gave examples from the county, but broadened their demand to include all of Germany. The Federal Ministry of Transportation declared in its response that this went too far. The party organization then made its demand more specific and called merely for the removal of all trees posing a potential accident hazard, especially along Federal Highway 2. Undersecretary Holger Börner, a Social Democrat and political appointee, responded to this with restrained agreement.[124]

The discussion over roadside trees that is found in the letters to the Federal Ministry of Transportation reflects the contradictory and vacillating public interest in roadside greenery. In the 1950s, the majority of letters were those calling for the planting of bushes and low trees along the roads for reasons of traffic safety and their aesthetic effect. But after the Federal Ministry of Transportation opted for guardrails in the median and the glare problem tended to be downplayed, tree advocates found themselves on the defensive. Their arguments were easy to brand as outdated and anti-modern, especially since their opponents were using the high accident figures in their own arguments. One thing that is striking is the increasingly sweeping and wholesale nature of the public controversy. Roadside trees became something to be passionately disliked or defended. The urgency was, of course, related to the exceedingly high death rates of automotive traffic in the postwar years, but it remains remarkable how deeply felt an altercation over landscape could be. The debate also cast the landscape integration of the roads, which had by now passed into the hands of the civil engineers, in a different light. Landscape integration could not be put under the heading of traffic safety, but was increasingly criticized by road users as a danger to traffic if it called for plantings and trees close to the road. In this context, motorists—in their capacity as citizens in a democratic republic—spoke out and began to challenge the expert status of engineers in the face of rising accident numbers.

In the final analysis, at the heart of the debate was the question of whether roadside trees were part of the landscape or part of the road. The cunning boundary work of the Bavarian local politician quoted above was, apparently, quite common. The German Council for Land Cultivation (*Deutscher Rat für Landespflege*, an alliance of landscape architects and some conservationists) took the position that roads, indeed, were a part of the landscape and should be treated as such. The Federal Ministry of Transportation disagreed. Minister of Transportation Seebohm maintained that roadside trees were part of the technological, constructed artifact of the road and were therefore subject to the functions allocated to the roads. After a meeting of the top leadership of the council, he put it in these words: "The median is part of the transportation structures and not of the landscape," whereas embankments *did* belong to the landscape. From Munich, Alwin Seifert commented mockingly: "A pleasant steppe trip, then, between guardrails painted white on all sides!" The median was not only rhetorically redefined, but also technologically rebuilt with thousands of kilometers of guardrails. Added to this was the fact that the massive use of melting salt during the winter beginning in the 1960s endangered the plantings. Instead of costly and labor-intensive mowing, some states were already experimenting with chemicals that retarded the growth of grass.[125] By 1970, West Germany's autobahn began to show a very different face to its users than thirty years earlier. The Fascist avenue to excitement had become a more quotidian transportation corridor.

Notes

1. The value of such epoch-spanning studies has been demonstrated for the history of technology by Kees Gispen, *Poems in Steel. National Socialism and the Politics of Inventing from Weimar to Bonn* (New York and Oxford, 2003). For an overview of science's and scientists' denazification, see Mitchell G. Ash, "Verordnete Umbrüche, konstruierte Kontinuitäten: Zur Entnazifizierung von Wissenschaftlern und Wissenschaften nach 1945," *Zeitschrift für Geschichtswissenschaft* 43 (1995), 903–923.
2. Volker Henschel, "Staat und Verkehr. Motive, Ziele und Mittel der Verkehrspolitik westlicher Industriestaaten seit 1880," in *Einflüsse der Motorisierung auf das Verkehrswesen*, ed. Hans Pohl (Stuttgart, 1988), 53–76; Ulrich van Suntum, *Verkehrspolitik* (Munich, 1986); Karl Oettle, *Verkehrspolitik* (Stuttgart, 1967); Trischler and Dienel, *Geschichte der Zukunft*, 22; Klenke, *Bundesdeutsche Verkehrspolitik*; Südbeck, *Motorisierung*. For a more detailed account see Zeller, *Straße, Bahn, Panorama*, 210–216.
3. Peter Czerwenka, "Verkehrsentwicklung im Zivilisationsprozeß," *Internationales Verkehrswesen* 44 (1992): 422–430; Klenke, *Bundesdeutsche Verkehrspolitik*, 124–133.
4. Winfried Süß, "'Wer aber denkt für das Ganze?' Aufstieg und Fall der ressortübergreifenden Planung im Bundeskanzleramt," in *Demokratisierung und gesellschaftlicher Aufbruch. Die sechziger Jahre als Wendezeit der Bundesrepublik*, ed. Matthias Frese, Julia Paulus, and Karl Teppe (Paderborn, 2003), 349–378; Matthias Frese and Julia Paulus, "Geschwindigkeiten und Faktoren des Wandels—die 1960er Jahre in der Bundesrepublik," ibid., 1–26.
5. Klenke, *Bundesdeutsche Verkehrspolitik*, 10; idem, *Freier Stau*.
6. Klenke, *Bundesdeutsche Verkehrspolitik*; idem, *Freier Stau*.
7. Kurt Möser, *Geschichte des Autos* (Frankfurt/New York, 2002), 193–194.
8. Schmucki, *Traum vom Verkehrsfluss*, 59–61; Klenke, *Freier Stau*, 51.
9. Klenke, *Freier Stau*, 50–59.
10. Hauptmann Kleinander, Federal Archives, Military Archive Freiburg, to the author, 4 January 2006.
11. Karl-Heinz Rothenberger, "Autobahnbau in der Pfalz nach dem Zweiten Weltkrieg," *Mitteilungen des Historischen Vereins der Pfalz* 100 (2002): 533–559, 537.
12. Tony Sharp, *The Wartime Alliance and the Zonal Division of Germany* (Oxford, 1975), 178.
13. Wolfgang Ruppert, "Das Auto: 'Herrschaft über Raum und Zeit,'" in *Fahrrad, Auto, Fernsehschrank. Zur Kulturgeschichte der Alltagsdinge*, ed. Wolfgang Ruppert (Frankfurt/Main, 1993), 119–161; idem, "Zur Konsumwelt der 60er Jahre," in *Dynamische Zeiten. Die 60er Jahre in den beiden deutschen Gesellschaften*, ed. Axel Schildt, Detlef Siegfried, and Karl Christian Lammers (Hamburg, 2000), 752–767; Arne Andersen, *Der Traum vom guten Leben. Alltags- und Konsumgeschichte vom Wirtschaftswunder bis heute* (Frankfurt and New York, 1997), 155–175.
14. Quoted after Möser, *Geschichte*, 196.
15. *Straße und Wirtschaft*, 21 (August 1958), quoted in Klenke, *Freier Stau*, 39. For a more detailed discussion of the East-West conflict in road construction see Doßmann, *Begrenzte Mobilität*.
16. Klenke, *Freier Stau*, 46–50.
17. The relevant articles of the Basic Law are Article 74, section 22, and Article 90, section 1. Jürgen Salzwedel, "Das Verkehrs- und Nachrichtenwesen. Straßen, Wasserstraßen und Luftverkehr," in *Deutsche Verwaltungsgeschichte*, ed. Kurt G.A. Jesserich, Hans Pohl, Georg-Christoph von Unruh, vol. 5, *Die Bundesrepublik Deutschland* (Stuttgart, 1987), 460–485, 467–468.
18. Salzwedel, "Verkehrs- und Nachrichtenwesen," 472; Hans-Christoph Seebohm, "Die Verwaltung der Bundesstraßen," *Straße und Autobahn* (hereafter cited as *SuA*) 4 (1953): 334–337; "Rede des Bundesministers für Verkehr Dr. Ing. Hans-Cristoph [sic] Seebohm auf der Mitgliederversammlung der Forschungsgesellschaft für das Straßenwesen e.V. am 7. September 1951 in München," *SuA* 2 (1951): 319–325, 324.

19. Klenke, *Freier Stau*. A look at how the construction of federal roads was handled in the states shows the full range of differences between the various bureaucracies. In Northrhine-Westphalia, the transportation section of the Ministry of Economics and Transportation was in charge of the road-building administrations in the *Landschaftsverbände* (country associations) of Rhineland and Westphalia-Lippe, below which were in turn Autobahn Offices, Offices for New Autobahn Construction, and others agencies to meet the state's needs. By contrast, the level below the ministry in Lower Saxony had only a single office. There, the section Road Construction within the State Administration Office stood under the professional oversight of the Ministry of Economics and Transportation, and under the administrative oversight of the Ministry of the Interior. In Bavaria, meanwhile, the Chief Construction Office within the State Ministry of the Interior was the point of contact for the Federal Ministry of Transportation. The road-building offices stood under the seven Bavarian district governments, while the two autobahn offices Munich and Nuremberg were on the same level within the hierarchy. A similar appreciation of intermediate authorities, in this case the *Regierungspräsidien*, is evident in Baden-Württemberg. Hesse and Rhineland-Palatinate set up such an intermediary authority with the Hesse State Office for Road Building and the Road Administration Rhineland-Palatinate. A state office of this kind was also established in Schleswig-Holstein in 1968. Dietrich Garlichs, *Grenzen staatlicher Infrastrukturpolitik. Bund/Länder-Kooperation in der Fernstraßenplanung* (Königstein/Taunus, 1980), 28–29; Salzwedel, "Verkehrs- und Nachrichtenwesen," 472–473. On Seebohm, see Pertti Ahonen, *After the Expulsion: West Germany and Eastern Europe, 1945–1990* (Oxford/New York, 2003), 62–63, 101, 159, 173.

20. Reinhold Klamm, "Grenzen des Föderalismus," *Der Straßenbau* 50 (1959): 436–438, 437.

21. Koester to the editors of *Der Straßenbau*, 20 December 1959, BAK B 108/20843.

22. Salzwedel, "Verkehrs- und Nachrichtenwesen," 472–475.

23. Initially, Seifert had been classified as a "Mitläufer" (nominal supporter), though in an appeal process he managed to clear himself completely. In rabulistic terms, Seifert claimed that he had become a victim of the Nazi state. "Urteil der Berufungskammer, 27. Oktober 1949," AGM VII 3702 Prof. Alwin Seifert.

24. Hirsch to Seifert, 10 October 1948, SN 130.

25. Since 1942, there has been a persistent rumor that Hitler had arranged Todt's plane crash, which served to enhance his posthumous appreciation far beyond 1945. Historians, however, have found neither a motive nor evidence for an assassination: Franz W. Seidler, "Der Flugzeugabsturz des Reichsministers Dr. Todt 1942. Attentat oder Unfall?" *Geschichte und Gegenwart* 4 (1985): 213–234; Norman Mörtzschky, "Wer profitierte vom plötzlichen Tod des Reichsministers für Bewaffnung und Munition, Dr. Fritz Todt?" *Historische Mitteilungen der Ranke-Gesellschaft* 11 (1998): 78–100.

26. Seifert to Koester, 27 November 1949, SN 226.

27. In 1958, the former *Reichsautobahn* propagandist Ostwald expressed his "personal satisfaction" that traffic safety now ranked higher than landscape design, and that "flower pot Alwin" Seifert was no longer involved in the autobahnen. Ostwald to Seiermann, 9 June 1958, BAK 108/18637.

28. Seifert to Rechenmacher, 19 July 1950; Seifert to Seebohm, 18 July 1950 and 18 July 1950. (These are two different letters with no response. It is not clear whether they were ever sent. Neither the original letter nor a response was found in the files of the department that was reponsible for landscape design in the Road Building Department of the Federal Ministry for Transportation.) Seifert to *Staatssekretär* Fischer, Regional Planning Office Munich, 18 July 1950; Seifert to Minister President Hans Ehard, 30 August 1950; Seifert to Spielmann, 6 April 1950, all SN 226; Seifert to Mrass, 9 April 1967, SN 200.

29. Werner Durth and Niels Gutschow, *Träume in Trümmern. Stadtplanung 1940–1950* (Munich, 1993); Jeffry M. Diefendorf, *In the Wake of War: The Reconstruction of German Cities after World War II* (Oxford, 1993). See chapter six, section "The landscape advocates seek power beyond the autobahn."

30. Note to file, signed Ilsemann, 23 August 1952, BAK B 108/18637. See Seifert to Ilsemann, 3 August 1952, ibid. (settlement of travel expenses). It would appear that Seifert enjoyed a better reputation in Switzerland as late as the 1960s: Walter Zschokke, "Von Schönheit wird nie gesprochen. Alwin Seifert: Vorreiter der landschaftlichen Einbindung von Straßenbauten," *Bauen+Wohnen* No. 1/2 (2000): 42–46, 46; Christian Pfister, "Landschaftsveränderung und Identitätsverlust. Akzentverschiebungen in der Modernisierungskritik von der Jahrhundertwende bis um 1970," *Traverse* 4, No. 2 (1997): 49–68, 58.
31. Sandra Chaney, "Water for Wine and Scenery, Coal and European Unity: Canalization of the Mosel River, 1950–1964," in *Water, Culture, and Politics in Germany and the American West*, ed. Susan C. Anderson and Bruce H. Tabb (New York, 2001), 227–252.
32. Kai F. Hünemörder, *Die Frühgeschichte der globalen Umweltkrise und die Formierung der deutschen Umweltpolitik (1950–1973)* (Stuttgart, 2004), 45–47. Seifert received the following awards in the Federal Republic: Großes Bundesverdienstkreuz (federal award, 1961), honorary chairman of the "Bund Naturschutz" in Bavaria (1964), honorary chairman of the League of Architects and Civil Engineers in Bavaria (Bund der Architekten und Bauingenieure in Bayern, 1966), Bavarian State Award (Bayerischer Verdienstorden, 1966).
33. "Arbeitskreis der Landschaftsanwälte e.V., Münster, und Bund Deutscher Gartenarchitekten, Landesgruppe Nordwest," to Federal Ministry of Transportation, Undersecretary Köster, 29 July 1952, BAK B 108/18637, 1–3. The following quotes are also from there.
34. Note, 24 September 1952, BAK B 108/18637; Federal Ministry of Transportation to Road Building Administrations Hamburg and Schleswig-Holstein, 26 September 1952, ibid.; Hansestadt Hamburg, Building Office, to Federal Ministry of Transportation, 4 December 1952, ibid.; Lower Saxony, Directorate of Road Building, to Federal Ministry of Transportation, 24 July 1953, ibid.
35. Schwarz to Ilsemann, Federal Ministry of Transportation (subsequently referred to as BMV or Bundesverkehrsministerium), 13 July 1962, BAK B 108/18638. Schwarz was 67 years old and died in 1963. Gröning and Wolschke-Bulmahn, *Grüne Biographien*, 357–358.
36. Ilsemann to Schwarz, 9 August 1962, BAK B 108/18638.
37. E.[rnst]-U.[lrich] Hiersche, "Umweltverträglichkeit beim Fernstraßenbau," *Straßenverkehr und Umwelt*, ed. Forschungsgesellschaft für Straßen- und Verkehrswesen (Cologne, 1980), 88–97.
38. In 1966 Seifert lamented that the "school of the *Reichsautobahn*" had not attracted the next generation. Seifert to BMV, 17 January 1966, BAK B 108/18639. He was told in response that landscape protection was "substantially taken into consideration" on federal and state roads, as the relevant guidelines showed. Eymann to Seifert, 22 January 1966, ibid.
39. Kunde (born 1903), obtained his doctorate in civil engineering from the Technical University of Berlin in 1933. Following a brief stint as university assistant and in private business, beginning in 1934 he worked as an expert (Dezernent) with the Regional Planning Office for the *Reichsautobahnen* in Munich. Thereafter he became a scientific aide and later the head of a division for the office of the Inspector-General. After the war, Kunde was director of the road-building division in the Central Administration for Transportation in Berlin for the Soviet occupation zone. After 1946 he functioned as a division head in the General Directorate for Road and Transportation in Bielefeld, for the English occupation zone. In 1947, he became head of the Road Building Department in the Main Administration for Roads in Bielefeld, and after 1949 in the Federal Ministry for Transportation. "Ministerialdirektor Dr.-Ing. Hermann Kunde 50 Jahre," *SuA* 4 (1953): 363. On the Kunde scandal see Doßmann, *Begrenzte Mobilität*, (Essen, 2003), 78, 243; Garlichs, *Grenzen*, 48. Koester was *Bezirksreferent* in the office of the Inspector-General and was appointed *Ministerialdirigent* in 1943. "Ministerialdirigent Hugo Koester-25 Jahre für den Straßenbau," *SuA* 4 (1953): 171–72; Böhm, *Straßenforschung*, 317–329.
40. Ludwig, *Technik*, 65; Doßmann, *Begrenzte Mobilität*, 71–79; Eduard Schönleben, *Fritz Todt. Der Mensch, der Ingenieur, der Nationalsozialist* (Oldenburg, 1943); "Ministerialdirektor a.

D. Dipl.-Ing. Eduard Schönleben 60 Jahre," *SuA* 9 (1958): 29. Erroneous on Eymann und Heubling: Zeller, *Straße, Bahn, Panorama*, 228.
41. Theodor M. Porter, *Trust in Numbers. The Pursuit of Objectivity in Science and Public Life* (Princeton, New Jersey, 1995), ix–x.
42. "Rede des Bundesverkehrsministers Dr. Ing. Seebohm auf der Mitgliederversammlung der Forschungsgesellschaft für das Straßenwesen in Hamburg am 22. Juni 1950," *SuA* 1 (1950), no. 7, 1–6, 32, 2–3.
43. Ibid., 4. On the rough planning of the north German autobahn segments as a "decentralized mesh net" see Rausch, "Einfluß des Geländes," 5. For an example of a postwar routing with the desired proximity to traffic sources see *Landesplanerisches Gutachten zur Linienführung der Autobahn Nordsüd in Niedersachsen* (Hannover, 1950), 4, 43.
44. "Ansprache des Leiters der Hauptverwaltung der Straßen des amerikanischen und britischen Besatzungsgebietes, Generaldirektor Dr. Schulz-Wittuhn," in *Straßenbauforschung. Vorträge gehalten auf der Mitgliederversammlung der Forschungsgesellschaft für das Straßenwesen am 21. Oktober 1947 in Bonn*, ed. E. Goerner (Berlin, Bielefeld, and Detmold, 1948), 7–10, 8.
45. "Rede des Bundesverkehrsministers," 6. "Schlachtfeld Autobahn," *Revue* 15 (August 1960), BAK B108/19035. On traffic accidents: F.A. Whitlock, *Death on the Road. A Study in Social Violence* (London, 1971); for a sociohistorical analysis see Sean O'Connell, *The Car and British Society. Class, Gender and Motoring 1896–1939* (Manchester and New York, 1998), 112–149; Kurt Möser, "Zwischen Systemopposition und Systemteilnahme: Sicherheit und Risiko im motorisierten Straßenverkehr 1890–1930," in Niemann and Hermann, *Geschichte*, 159–167.
46. "Blendschutz auf Autobahnen," Agenda item E, 81st. Cabinet session on 14 October 1959, http://www.bundesarchiv.de/kabinettsprotokolle, accessed 15 March 2005.
47. Klenke, *Freier Stau*, 46–50.
48. Hans-Christoph Seebohm, "Straßenplanung und Forschung. Vortrag vor der Straßenbautagung und Mitgliederversammlung der Forschungsgesellschaft für Straßenwesen am 24. Oktober 1952 in Düsseldorf," *SuA* 3 (1952): 361–380, 362.
49. "Rede des Bundesministers," 320.
50. Hermann Kunde, "Rationeller Straßenbau," *SuA* 5 (1954): 336–341, 338.
51. Kunde, "Rationeller Straßenbau," 338.
52. Hans Lorenz, "Moderne Trassierung," *SuA* 5 (1954): 370–373, 370. The following quotes also from there.
53. For some general reflections on such human-machine relationships see Barbara Schmucki, "Cyborgs unterwegs? Cyborgs und individuelle Mobilität seit dem 19. Jahrhundert," in *Technik und Gesellschaft* 10, ed. Gert Schmidt (Frankfurt and New York, 1999), 87–119. On technological determinism as a problem in the history of technology see Merritt Roe Smith and Leo Marx, eds., *Does Technology Drive History? The Dilemma of Technological Determinism* (Cambridge, Mass., 1994).
54. Lorenz, "Moderne Trassierung," 370–371.
55. Ibid., 371–72. On the notion of art see Ulrich Wengenroth, "Zur Differenz von Wissenschaft und Technik," in *Technikentwicklung und Industriearbeit*, ed. Daniel Bieber (Frankfurt and New York, 1997), 141–151.
56. Lorenz, "Moderne Trassierung," 372; Ludwig Altinger, "Optische Forderungen beim Straßenbau," *SuA* 5 (1954): 83–86. A clothoid is a level curve whose curvature radius is at every point inversely proportional to the length of its arc. A line made up of clothoid pieces resembles—grossly simplified—a slender s-curve. On the use of the clothoid in the U.S. see Louis Ward Kemp, "Aesthetes and Engineers: The Occupational Ideology of Highway Design," *Technology and Culture* 27 (1986): 759–797, 774–775. I thank Greg Baecher and Ali Haghani in the Department of Civil and Environmental Engineering, University of Maryland, for their terminological help.

57. Leopold Oerley, *Übergangsbogen bei Straßenkrümmungen* (Berlin, 1937); Walter Schürba, *Klothoiden-Abstecktafeln. Anleitung zu Entwurf, Berechnung und Absteckung* (Berlin, 1942); Hans Lorenz, "Sinn und Anwendung von Übergangsbögen," in *Trassierungsgrundlagen der Reichsautobahn*, ed. Hans Lorenz (Berlin, 1943), 43–55, 48; Hugo Kasper, Walter Schürba, and Hans Lorenz, *Die Klotoide als Trassierungselement* (Hannover, 1961), 5, 11.
58. Lorenz, "Sinn und Anwendung," 49; Walter Schürba, "Entwurf, Berechnung und Absteckung einer Klothoide als Straßenkrümmungsbogen mit Hilfe der Klothoiden-Abstecktafeln," in Lorenz, *Trassierungsgrundlagen*, 56–61, 56.
59. Viktor von Ranke, "Raumperspektive," in Lorenz, *Trassierungsgrundlagen*, 81–98; Emerich Schaffran, "Ein Maler erlebt die—erst im Plan vorhandene—Reichsautobahn," in ibid., 99–105; Hans Lorenz, "Gradientenmodelle," in ibid., 105–108; Windisch-Hojnacki, *Reichsautobahn*; Schütz and Gruber, *Mythos*, 112–115.
60. Kasper, Schürba, and Lorenz, *Klothoide*, 6; H. Koester, "Geleitwort," in ibid., 4.
61. Ibid., "Vorwort zur dritten Auflage," 7.
62. B., "Die Klotoide als Trassierungselement," *SuA* 5 (1954): 321; Hermann Kunde, "Ziele im Straßenbau," *SuA* 4 (1953): 338–342, here 339.
63. Rudolf Kraus, "Theorie und Praxis der Straßenkrümmung," *SuA* 1/3 (1950): 19–21; Johannes Schlums, "Räumliche Untersuchungen zur Bewertung von Straßenplanungen," *SuA* 1/4 (1950): 16–18; Gerhard Schramm, "Zu den Trassierungsgrundsätzen für Autobahnen," *SuA* 1/12 (1950): 21–23. For a more recent mathematical approach to the spatiality of transportation routes, see Hans Georg Schlichter, *Räumliche Linienführung von Verkehrswegen* (Karlsruhe, 1985).
64. Hermann Kunde, "Vordringlichste Forschungsaufgaben," *SuA* 3 (1952): 401–404. The other tasks he indicated were studies on the traction of roads and frost safety. Rolf Heering, "Ist die Gerade als Trassierungselement zum Aussterben verurteilt?," *SuA* 6 (1955): 42–44. On sight distances see also Kemp, *Aesthetes*.
65. Letter from Prof. Dr.-Ing. Albrecht, Technical University Braunschweig, *SuA* 6 (1955): 212–213, here 212; "Todesstoß der Geraden als Trassierungselement?," letter from V.J. Ch. v. Ranke, *SuA* 6 (1955): 213–214 (with anecdotal justification); "Am sichersten überholt man nicht in der Geraden," letter from Dipl-Ing. W. Blaschke, *SuA* 6 (1955): 214–215.
66. Hermann Kunde, "Neuzeitliche Straßenbautechnik in den westeuropäischen Ländern," *SuA* 9 (1958): 382–397, 384.
67. Heller, "Notwendigkeit und Ziel einer Neubearbeitung der Richtlinien für den Ausbau von Landstraßen (RAL)," in Goerner, *Straßenbauforschung*, 12–23, 23; Bruno Wehner, "Gedanken zur geplanten Neufassung der Richtlinien für die Anlage von Landstraßen (RAL)," *SuA* 9 (1958): 461–470; [no author given], *Bruno Wehner* (Bonn-Bad Godesberg, 1976).
68. "Entwurf der Richtlinien für die Anlage von Landstraßen," *SuA* 10 (1959): 467–475, 467.
69. Ibid., 472. A reference to curvy transition curves had been incorporated into the RAL as early as 1937. Wehner, "Gedanken," 465. However, as late as 1947 they were still described as a new method with which road builders still had to be acquainted. Heller, "Notwendigkeit und Ziel," 21.
70. Ernst-Ullrich Hiersche, "Straßenplanung und Straßenentwurf," in *Straßenforschung. 50 Jahre Forschungsgesellschaft für das Straßenwesen 1924–1974*, ed. Ehrtfried Böhm et al. (Bonn-Bad Godesberg, 1974), 235–252, 242.
71. It would appear that postmortem the term "Landschaftsanwalt" was permitted again: one obituary for landscape architect Hirsch ends with the words "German road building has lost one of its best landscape advocates." "Landschaftsarchitekt Wilhelm Hirsch†," *SuA* 9 (1958): 29; Hermann Schurhammer, *Straße und Landschaft. Ein Beitrag zur praktischen Landschaftspflege. Bearbeitet und mit Unterstützung des Bundesverkehrsministeriums herausgegeben von Diplomgärtner Hermann Schurhammer jr. Landschaftsarchitekt* (Bielefeld, 1955).
72. Hermann Kunde, "Geleitwort," in Schurhammer, *Straße und Landschaft*, 5. Following his university education at the Technical University in Karlsruhe, Schurhammer (1881–1952)

worked for the Water and Road Building Administration of Baden as a road-building engineer after 1906; from 1920 to 1937, he headed the road-building department of the town of Bonndorf in the Black Forest. At the same time he was active in conservation. "Oberregierungsbaurat Hermann Schurhammer†," *SuA* 4 (1953): 32.
73. Wengenroth, "Differenz"; Walter G. Vincenti, *What Engineers Know and How They Know It. Analytical Studies from Aeronautical History* (Baltimore and London, 1990). For an internalist view see Wolfgang Wirth, "Die Entwicklung der sicherheitsrelevanten Trassierungstechnik für moderne Kfz-Straßen," in *Geschichte der Straßenverkehrssicherheit im Wechselspiel zwischen Fahrzeug, Fahrbahn und Mensch*, ed. Harry Niemann and Armin Hermann (Bielefeld, 1999), 231–241.
74. Th. Spielmann, "Zweckgebundene Straßengrünflächen," *SuA* 3 (1952): 43–46, 43–44, 46.
75. Wilhelm Hirsch, "Sicherheitspflanzungen an den Autobahnen," *SuA* 5 (1954): 304–308, 304.
76. The Minister of Hesse for Labor, Agriculture, and the Economy to the Federal Ministry for Transportation, 7 November 1951, BAK B 108/18637; File note, 21 January 1952, ibid.; Note, 12 November 1951, ibid.; File note, 20 November 1951, ibid. (kilometer honorarium of 2 DM for Tüxen); Hirsch to BMV, Koester, 11 December 1953, ibid.; Koester to Hirsch, 30 January 1954, ibid.; Road Building Administration of Lower Saxony to BMV, 22 November 1952, ibid.; BMV to Road Building Administration of Lower Saxony, 16 December 1952, ibid.; Note, 22 April 1955, ibid.
77. Hirsch, "Sicherheitspflanzungen," 304; M. Leutzbach, "Blendschutz an Autobahnen," *SuA* 7 (1956): 318–320. The latter article provides a mathematical basis for glare protection.
78. Hirsch, "Sicherheitspflanzungen," 307–308.
79. Ibid., 306.
80. "Arbeitsausschuß Landschaftsgestaltung und Arbeitsausschuß Verkehrssicherheitspflanzungen," heading "Aus der Tätigkeit der Arbeitsgruppen der Forschungsgesellschaft für das Straßenwesen e.V.," *SuA* 4 (1953): 277–278. The complaint about the lost tradition in the area of road planting referred to the period "100 or 200 years ago."
81. Kurt Becker, "Straßenbautechnik und Straßenbaukunst," *Brücke und Straße* 3 (1951): 174. See "Der Autobahn-Mittelstreifen," ibid.: 116–118; G. Kübler, "Straßenbautechnik und Straßenbaukunst," ibid.: 118–119.
82. "Schaubild A6 Arbeitsgruppen 1924–1974," in Böhm, *Straßenforschung*, 335; "Arbeitsausschuß Landschaftsgestaltung," heading "Aus der Tätigkeit der Arbeitsgruppen der Forschungsgesellschaft für das Straßenwesen e.V.," *SuA* 1 (1950): 30; "Arbeitsausschuß Landschaftsgestaltung," heading "Aus der Tätigkeit," *SuA* 4 (1953), 277–278 ; "Arbeitsausschuß Landschaftsgestaltung," heading "Aus der Tätigkeit," *SuA* 9 (1958): 33 (Landscape Convention 1957 on the theme "Transitions, temporal and spatial"). A public appreciation of road-related landscape cultivation was promoted by the Federal Ministry of Agriculture, however. In 1961 it held a contest on the theme "Landscape cultivation on roads and footpaths," though it apparently was a one-time event without any lasting effects. Working Society for Garden and Landscape Culture (*Arbeitsgemeinschaft für Garten- und Landschaftskultur*), Kühn, to Koester, 28 November 1960, BAK B 108/18638; Pamphlet "Hilfe durch Grün," Competition 1961, ibid.; Working Society for Garden and Landscape Culture, minutes of the session of the federal prize jury on 30 November 1961, ibid.
83. Forschungsgesellschaft für das Straßenwesen e.V. Arbeitsausschuß Landschaftsgestaltung, *Richtlinien für Straßenbepflanzung (R Pf)*, part 1 (Cologne, 1960). According to a preliminary note on p. 2, the chief construction office in the Bavarian State Ministry of the Interior had helped to finance the work. Forschungsgesellschaft für das Straßenwesen e.V. Arbeitsausschuß Landschaftsgestaltung, *Richtlinien für Straßenbepflanzung (RPf 2)*, part 2: Ausführung von Straßenbepflanzungen (1964 edition, Cologne [reprint], 1967); Forschungsgesellschaft für das Straßenwesen e.V. Arbeitsausschuß Landschaftsgestaltung, *Richtlinien für Straßenbepflanzung (RPf 3)*, part 3: Pflege und Nacharbeiten an Straßenpflanzungen (Cologne, 1969).

84. Five authors came from the road-building administration: Lorenz, *Oberregierungsbaurat* Landgrebe (Chief Construction Office, Munich), *Landesbaurat* Barnard (Münster), *Oberregierungsbaurat* Heubling (Stuttgart), *Ministerialrat* Ilsemann (Federal Ministry of Transportation). *Regierungsforstrat* Pflug was described as an "expert for the biological measures in road construction, hydrological construction, land consolidation and so on in the Ministry for Agriculture, Viticulture, and Forests in Rhineland-Palatinate." Hans Lorenz and Wilhelm Heubling, ed., *Grünverbau im Straßenbau. Vorträge bei der Landschaftstagung der Forschungsgesellschaft für das Straßenwesen Koblenz 1961* (Bad Godesberg, 1962), 7. The freelance landscape architect Ludwig Roemer (Söcking near Starnberg) described himself as a student of Seifert's. In his application for the professorship in garden and landscape design at the Technical University in Munich in 1955 to succeed Seifert, he was ranked second among the applicants. Thomas Jakob, *Zur Geschichte der Landschaftsarchitektur an der TU München-Weihenstephan. Eine Dokumentation anläßlich des 40jährigen Jubiläums der Studienrichtung Landschaftsarchitektur 1996* (Freising-Weihenstephan, 1998), 10.
85. *Richtlinien für Straßenbepflanzung* (1960 edition), 5.
86. Ibid., 9. Emphases in original.
87. Hans Lorenz, "Straße und Landschaft," *Die Bauverwaltung* 1 (1952): 274–282. The author was challenging what he believed was a widespread notion that landscape design was a "mysterious science" which "liked to express itself in lovely words." Ibid., 274.
88. Ibid., 274–275, 276.
89. *Richtlinien für Straßenbepflanzung*, Part 1 (1960 edition), 36–37, 49. The most effective protection, however, was still to move the roads as far away as possible from such sites: ibid., 37.
90. Ibid., 37–38, 39, 63, Appendix: "Tabelle der Pflanzenarten in 5 Teilen."
91. "Sauerländischer Gebirgsverein, Heimat- und Naturschutzausschuß," Wilhelm Münker, to BMV, 15 February 1952, BAK B 108/18637; BMV to Münker, 10 March 1952, ibid. On the association, see Susanne Falk, "'Eine Notwendigkeit, uns innerlich umzustellen, liege nicht vor.' Kontinuität und Diskontinuität in der Auseinandersetzung des Sauerländischen Gebirgsvereins mit Heimat und Moderne 1918–1960," in *Politische Zäsuren und gesellschaftlicher Wandel im 20. Jahrhundert. Regionale und vergleichende Perspektiven*, ed. Matthias Frese and Michael Prinz (Paderborn, 1996), 401–417; Protocol about the founding meeting of the Working Community for Vegetation Cultivation (*Arbeitsgemeinschaft für Vegetationsbau*) on 8 May 1959 in Stolzenau on the Weser, B 108/18637; Note re: Working Meeting, 15 May 1959, ibid.; Lorenz to Ilsemann, 22 September 1959, ibid.
92. *Richtlinien für Straßenbepflanzung*, Part 1 (1960 edition), 64–65, 9.
93. *Richtlinien für Straßenbepflanzung*, Part 2 (1964 edition).
94. The planting of agriculturally useful grass meadows was not ruled out entirely, "provided they are accessible without endangering the traffic." Ibid., 11–12.
95. Ibid., 13.
96. Johannes Schad, "Einsaaten auf Straßenböschungen," in Lorenz and Heubling, *Grünverbau im Straßenbau*, 37–45, 37.
97. Ibid., 38, 45; *Richtlinien*, Part 2, 2. The guidelines also offered tips on the appropriate way to put a project out to bid. Relevant passages in the contract forms for the awarding of the work should ensure that the treatment of the topsoil and the grass seed was specified in detail and carried out according to the ideas of the landscape designer. Ibid., 38–39.
98. Ruprecht Rümler, "Zur Entwicklung von Rasenansaaten und ihrer Bedeutung für die ingenieurbiologische Sicherung von Straßenböschungen," Ph.D. dissertation, Rheinisch-Westfälische Technische Hochschule, Aachen, 1974, 2, 4.
99. Rümler, "Entwicklung von Rasenansaaten," 4–5. After computer-supported quantitative descriptions and studies of 293 individual areas in the Eifel and the Bergisches Land near Cologne, the author suggested a standard grass mixture composed of only five species of grass. This amounted to a substantial decrease in the number of species: during the construction of the *Reichsautobahnen*, von Kruedener had still proposed up to thirty-seven grass species for the grass mixtures for

ten different soil categories. The number of suggested species continued to decline especially during the 1960s. This was driven in part by the realization that the neighboring meadow areas spread their composition of grasses to the autobahn embankments. In addition, this also reflects the struggle for economic efficiency. Thus the author, when discussing highly expensive grass seeds, bluntly asked "whether their use is in fact worth it." Ibid., 134, 13, 16.

100. Hans Lorenz, "Straße und Landschaft," *Die Bauverwaltung* 1 (1952): 274–282, 274.
101. While the effort for grass surfaces—assuming one cut per year for a low-growth area—was put at 1.14 labor hours per square meter over a period of 40 years, maintenance costs for plantings of woody plants came to merely 0.28 labor hours per square meter over the same period. Because the same effort was continually necessary for grassy areas, their maintenance costs showed a linear growth in the period under examination, while the relative maintenance costs for woody plants increased only slightly. *Richtlinien für Straßenbepflanzung*, Part 3, 7, 23–24, 10.
102. Lorenz, "Straße und Landschaft," 277.
103. *Richtlinien für Straßenbepflanzung*, Part 1 (Cologne, 1960), 5.
104. Schwarz to Ilsemann, BMV, 22 November 1962, B 108/18638.
105. Wilhelm Heubling, "Straße und Umwelt," in Kühn, *Straßenforschung*, 253–264. See Hermann Landgrebe and Ludwig Roemer, "Landschaftliche Gestaltung moderner Schnellstraßen. Gutachten vom Oktober 1966 im Auftrage des Deutschen Rates für Landespflege," in *Landschaftpflege an Verkehrsstraßen. Empfehlungen, Untersuchungsergebnisse, Berichte und Stellungnahmen* (Bonn, 1968), 40–49.
106. This substitution also took place on a personal level, in that the construction official Lorenz formalized much of his knowledge and compiled it into a single-authored textbook: *Trassierung und Gestaltung von Straßen und Autobahnen* (Wiesbaden/Berlin, 1971). An unhappy Seifert noted that an honorary doctorate was being bestowed on Lorenz by "my own department." Seifert to Mrass, 9 April 1967, SN 200; Seifert, *Leben*, 85–86. For the request to grant Lorenz the honorary degree, see Technical University Munich, Department for Building Science, Dean, to Rector of the Technical University, 15 June 1959, HAUTUM Personnel file Hans Lorenz.
107. With a similar emphasis on continuity Doßmann, *Wie wir*, 239. Klenke, by contrast, interpreted the postwar automobile euphoria as a psychological coping with the war experience: "Die deutsche Katastrophe und das Auto. Zur 'Heils'geschichte eines nationalen Kultobjekts in den Jahren des Wiederaufstiegs," in *Moderne Zeiten. Technik und Zeitgeist im 19. und 20. Jahrhundert*, ed. Ilona Stölken-Fitschen and Michael Salewski (Stuttgart, 1994), 157–173.
108. Möser, *Geschichte*, 196. For Ulrich Herbert, the years after 1949 were marked by a rapid liberalization of German politics and society: Ulrich Herbert, ed., *Wandlungsprozesse in Westdeutschland: Belastung, Integration, Liberalisierung 1945–1980* (Göttingen, 2002).
109. Günter Bayerl, "Automobil und Umwelt in den 1950er und 1960er Jahren," in *Beiträge zur Geschichte der Binnenschiffahrt, des Luft- und Kraftfahrzeugverkehrs*, ed. Hans Jürgen Teuteberg (Cologne, 1994), 323–348; Alexander Gall: "'Gute Straßen bis ins kleinste Dorf!' Verkehrspolitik und Landesplanung 1945 bis 1976," *Bayern im Bund, vol. 1: Die Erschließung des Landes 1949 bis 1973*, ed. Thomas Schlemmer and Hans Woller (Munich, 2001), 119–204, 187. On gender aspects behind the wheel see Virginia Scharff, *Taking the Wheel: Women and the Coming of the Motor Age* (New York and Toronto, 1991); O'Connell, *Car*, 43–76. I evaluated the submissions collected in the files B 108/8982, 18637, 18638, 18639, 18640, and 18966. More recent letters were not accessible because files were still within the restrictive period. The examined letters were handed over to the expert whose sphere of work included landscape design. Along with direct letters to the BVM, the files also contain inquiries to the Office of the Chancellor, the Office of the President, or the *Petitionsausschuß* of the Bundestag that were passed on for review.
110. For reflections on letters, petitions, and public actions for social and environmental history, see Klaus Tenfelde and Helmuth Trischler, ed., *Bis vor die Stufen des Throns. Bittschriften und Beschwerden von Bergleuten im Zeitalter der Industrialisierung* (Munich, 1986), 9; Linse, *Bittschrift*.

111. Hans Ehras, Hartmannshof bei Hersbruck, to Seebohm, 23 October 1963, B 108/18638.
112. Hermann Deutsch, Bad Bertrich, to Seebohm, 24 May 1969, B 108/18640. This urgent tone points to another problem inherent in the letters. The senders were evidently in a state of agitation that was produced by a concern for the landscape or human lives. One must therefore be cautious about using an analysis of these letters to infer a widespread understanding of landscape. After all, it was precisely the upset and angry among the citizenry who expressed their unhappiness in these letters. Still, these remain valuable clues. These sources reveal when thresholds of tolerance had been crossed. Here it is important to mention that every analysis of newspapers and magazines would offer merely a certain sample. The sources I am dealing with here do not represent a sample, but represent the complete submissions to the Federal Ministry of Transportation. In this sense the genre of letters to a ministry are more insightful than an evaluation of letters to the editor in newspapers. It can be assumed that the surviving submissions are complete, especially since unanswered letters were also filed away.
113. For reasons of comparability, several letters from the same sender were evaluated as one letter. In no case did the renewed inquiries and responses generate a new perspective.
114. Ilse Zillig, Lampoding über Traunstein, to Seebohm, 24 October 1958, B 108/18637; Charlotte Plinke, Berlin, to Seebohm, 8 June 1959, B 108/18639; Nelly Heydorn, Hamburg-Wandsbek, to Seebohm, 7 August 1959, ibid.; Fr. v. Viebahn, St. Goar, to BMV, 10 March 1960, B 108/18638; Ilse Hedicke, Göttingen, to BMV, 15 May 1967, B 108/18639; Dr. med. Karin Pietschmann, Lemgo, to BMV, 18 January 1968, ibid.; Christine Weber, Westerburg, to Leber, 15 May 1968, B 108/18640; Widow Agnes Prumbau to Leber, 1 August 1969, B 108/18640. Viebahn protested against the planting of nut trees on the B 9 near Spay because of the danger from falling nuts; the trees were removed. (Ministry of Economics and Transportation Rhineland-Palatinate to BMV, 11 July 1960, B 108/18638.) The letter from this sender does not reveal whether she was generally opposed to trees along roadways. If this letter is included neither on the pro nor the contra side, we end up with a ratio of five pro to two contra voices among the female writers.
115. Handwritten notes in the margins of the letter by Ilse Hedicke, Göttingen, to BMV, 15 May 1967, B 108/18639. Emphasis original. Hedicke expressed her thanks on 17 June to the (more polite) response letter of 7 June 1967, saying it had "filled her with special satisfaction."
116. Forty-six of the 101 letter-writers could be identified in professional terms. In private letters, most senders indicated, if anything at all, a title or trained occupation, not an occupational designation. Twelve submissions came from entrepreneurs, four from general physicians, three from teachers, and the same number from journalists. Two certified economists are recorded, as are two foresters. The other occupations encompass a tax agent, a businessman (*Diplom-Kaufmann*), a dentist, a retired foreman, a graduate engineer (*Diplom-Ingenieur*), the owner of a farmstead, a farmer, an industrial sales apprentice, a truck farming company operator, a municipal senior clerk (*Gemeinde-Amtmann*), an authorized commercial representative (*Prokurist*), a student, a truck driver, and an insurance mathematician. All used their professional stationery, thus giving their letters a semiprivate character. "As a physician and driver (31 years without accident)," Dr. Carl Riedel called for a dense planting of the median strip; it had saved the life of one of his patients. Dr. Carl Riedel, Aachen, to Seebohm, 21 January 1958, B 108/18637. For physicians' involvement in traffic safety, see Heike Weishaupt, *Die Entwicklung der passiven Sicherheit im Automobilbau von den Anfängen bis 1980 unter besonderer Berücksichtigung der Daimler-Benz AG* (Bielefeld, 1999), 56, 66; Peter Voswinckel, *Arzt und Auto. Das Auto und seine Welt im Spiegel des Deutschen Ärzteblattes von 1907 bis 1975* (Münster, 1981); Heinrich Praxenthaler, "Die Geschichte der Verkehrssicherheit nach 1945," in Niemann and Hermann, *Geschichte der Straßenverkehrssicherheit*, 185–208; Klaus Kuhm, *Moderne und Asphalt: Die Automobilisierung als Prozess technologischer Innovation und sozialer Vernetzung* (Pfaffenweiler, 1997), 33–41.
117. Karl Bader, Krumbach/Schwaben, to BMV (handwritten postcard), 17 February 1968, B 108/18639.

118. For reflections on how environmental interests are organized, see Frank Uekötter, "Confronting the Pitfalls of Current Environmental History. An Argument for an Organisational Approach," *Environment and History* 4 (1998): 31–52.
119. Peter Rieckmann and Comrades to Seebohm, 25 November 1963, B 108/18637; Tourist Association "Die Naturfreunde" to Leber, 14 November 1968, B 108/18640.
120. On the reservedness of the unions in the 1950s see Axel Schildt, "Vom Wohlstandsbarometer zum Belastungsfaktor—Autovision und Autoängste in der westdeutschen Presse von den 50er bis zu den 70er Jahren," in Dienel and Trischler, *Geschichte,* 289–309. On the "Naturfreunde" see Williams, "The Chords"; Jochen Zimmer, ed., *"Mit uns zieht die neue Zeit." Die Naturfreunde: Zur Geschichte eines alternativen Verbandes in der Arbeiterkulturbewegung* (Cologne, 1984).
121. A group of thirty-two truck drivers to Seebohm, November 1967, B 108/18639. Since the senders threatened to get a Bundestag representative involved, the ministry took the precaution of preparing a response.
122. Volker Herold to Seebohm, 10 October 1965, B 108/18639; Katholische Landjugendbewegung Meßkirch to BMV, December 1968, B 108/18640.
123. Junge Union Bavaria, District Assocation Weilheim, to BMV, 6 June 1969, B 108/18640; "Langen Reden sollen Taten folgen," *Weilheimer Tagblatt,* 27 May 1969, ibid.; BMV to Junge Union Bavaria, District Assocation Weilheim, 2 July 1969, ibid. See also the petition from another Junge Union organization in Northern Bavaria with the same thrust: Junge Union, Regional Association Mittelfranken, Alfred Ragati, to BMV, 15 June 1967, B 108/18639; BMV to Junge Union, Regional Association Mittelfranken, Ragati, 11 July 1967, ibid.
124. SPD, local chapter Türkenfeld-Moorenweis to Federal Minister [of Health] Käthe Strobel, 5 April 1969, B 108/18640 (the letter was passed on for jurisdictional reasons); BMV to SPD, local chapter Türkenfeld-Moorenweis, 30 April 1969, ibid. BMV, Börner, to SPD, local chapter Türkenfeld-Moorenweis, 23 September 1969, ibid.
125. Marginal comment by Seebohm on a letter from the Deutscher Rat für Landespflege, Count Lennart Bernadotte, to Seebohm, 4 May 1964, 4, B 108/18639. Seifert, "Weg mit den Straßenbäumen!," letter to the editor, *Münchner Merkur,* 22 February 1964, 16, ibid.; BMV to Bundesanstalt für Straßenbau (Federal Office for Road Construction), 4 November 1963, BAK B 108/18638; Note re. keeping grass in the road area short through the use of chemical agents, 27 March 1963, ibid.; Seebohm to Mackenroth, 6 March 1961, BAK B 108/19035.

Chapter 8

Conclusion

The history of the autobahn and its landscapes is far more than an account of the development of a large-scale technological network. It mirrors Germany's changing political regimes and the varying ideological, professional, and cultural ideas driving them. Proposed unsuccessfully by a small pressure group under the Weimar Republic, autobahn ideas were embraced on a large scale by the National Socialist regime as the largest propaganda product of the Third Reich. While the civil engineers and landscape architects involved in the construction had enough in common ideologically to collaborate on the roads, they held different opinions on alignment and plantings. In what tended to be an anarchical atmosphere, these conflicts were postponed or only partially resolved under Todt's and Hitler's reign. Within the political system of the Federal Republic, the autobahnen were handed over to the joint responsibility of the federal government and the states. Thus, landscape design along the roads was largely a matter for the states. Some of the state road-building bureaucracies were quite willing to employ landscape architects. Their authority and leeway, however, were regulated and circumscribed from the outset. The regionally oriented landscape architects pushed in vain for centralization.

After 1949, the autobahn found itself under the politically driven commandment of rationalization and "scientization," by which was meant a mathematization of its design criteria. Federal Minister of Transportation Seebohm described the panoramic layout of the *Reichsautobahn* as counterproductive, pointing out that steep hills had made it often difficult, if not impossible, for trucks to use the freeways. The roadbuilding style of the autobahn thus suffered a remarkable downhill slide. The very same design features of the roads that once won them public praise now drew ridicule for the engineers. The autobahn of the Federal Republic would be placed under the desire for a rapid and safe form of transportation that was not primarily interested in vistas. Given

---

Notes for this section begin on page 246.

these changed parameters, civil engineers reinforced their desire to academicize the access to knowledge of road building and to determine the lay of the roads within the landscape with the help of quantifiable methods. The first geometric methodologies along these lines had been developed already in the 1930s. In postwar Germany, they offered a chance to attain a boost in status and to acquire the sheen of modernity by engaging in respectable scientific work.

The discomfort that civil engineers felt about their professional participation in "Adolf Hitler's Roads" is evident from three factors: their widespread silence about the meaning the National Socialist had imparted to the roads; occasional attempts at reinterpreting history along with the effort to posit a rational continuity (a professional policy about the past); and what were described as anti-Romantic attacks on the aesthetics of the road that was integrated into the landscape. Silence, in this respect, was more than denial; it was also a powerful strategy to strengthen a social position. Publications in the 1950s were at pains to stress that Hitler's autobahn had been based on the Hafraba plans, thus trying to disassociate them from the dictator. This allowed for the artificial separation of technology from its context. And the thrust against alleged Romanticism, which tied landscape concerns to the Nazi regime, could be used as the final blow. Within this constellation, the function of mathematization was as much scientific as it was political.[1] In this sense, the debate was part of a larger postwar controversy over the role of modern architecture, which Paul Betts has studied in the case of the Bauhaus. To the same degree that the Bauhaus was, according to Betts, interpreted in the Federal Republic as a modern German aesthetic that was not compromised by National Socialism, the mathematization of road building was called the end of a Romantic exceptionalism. This invocation of modernity was shaped by the competition between political and social systems in the Cold War.[2]

In the always-present rivalry with East Germany and its autobahnen, the mathematization of road building could be seen not only as a methodological advance, but also as a nonideological achievement. Hence, it should not come as a surprise that the clothoid was also used by East German autobahn planners. More obvious, of course, was the rapid growth of the West German autobahn network, while the autobahn in East Germany never achieved the dominant position within the transportation infrastructure that it had in the West.[3]

Moreover, this also meant that the power of definition and decision-making when it came to the building of the autobahnen and their layout in the landscape remained with the civil engineers, who no longer had to fear any systematic influence in this regard from the landscape architects. Their task was reduced to plantings, whereby the selection of plants was made difficult by the wish for standardization and uniformity. Like road planning itself, the greenery along the roads became a calculable factor in the hands of experts. This also made it possible to free the autobahnen from the prefix *Reich-*, to turn them into federal superhighways ("Bundesautobahnen" rather than "Reichsautobahnen") befitting a federal republic and thus to invoke instrumental rationality rather than the pet project of an unspeakable dictatorship. Unlike with the automobile, when it comes to roads in the period in question we generally do not find an explicit rhetoric of freedom with antitotalitarian overtones. Rather, the autobahn was reduced to the function of an efficient transportation machine, whose aesthetic, where it was in question, was largely the domain of insiders. Only when the issue of traffic safety crossed more and more attention thresholds did road building come under fire from public criticism. As the most visible and obvious element of the road structure, trees became the target of criticism especially at the end of the 1960s. Discussants from many parts of the political spectrum were able to reinterpret them as premodern relics in a society committed to modernity and to demand their large-scale removal. This became an increasingly popular demand, one that for the first time moved the discussion over road design among experts into a wider public arena, where it was newly negotiated.

In the process, the expert status of road-building engineers showed the first signs of cracks. The necessity of roads as such was hardly questioned during the period under examination, but their effects were, particularly when it came to safety. This means that one view that is found in the scholarly literature—that when it came to the construction of long-distance roads, it was more the image than the content of planning that was negotiated in the political arena up to the middle of the 1970s—is in need of correction.[4] During the 1960s, as well, roads were controversial among the public. It does seem accurate, however, that in the 1970s the criticism for the first time included road building projects as such, and not only their design. The problem of how to situate a road within the landscape, which was to be solved aesthetically, turned into the problem of finding a route that would cause the least ecological damage. The noise and exhaust pollution from the growing number of automobiles, the ecological fragmentation effects of roads, and damage to wildlife became dominant points of criticism. When critics of road building at the end of the 1970s pointed to the panoramic function of the *Reichsautobahn*, this was merely another argument for why roads were problematic (figure 8.1). In this process of change, planners, too, had to speak about the content of their planning and negotiate it with the public. Massive protests against individual segments shifted the parameters of planning. The effects of roads on the fauna were studied more systematically in the 1980s, after previously mostly the flora had been of interest. These conflicts have only begun to be studied historically.[5]

By this time, it was clear even to supporters that the panoramic autobahn of the 1930s was obsolete. With an untypical hint of self-criticism, the octogenarian Alwin Seifert warned in 1971: "The age of lovely views from the passing car is over. (The Irschenberg [on the Munich-Salzburg route] is a telling example for a planning that intended to be romantic but is wrong for our day and age.) The man behind the wheel must not take his eyes off the bumper of the car in front of him; looking the wrong way for a second can have dire consequences."[6]

Figure 8.1. The memory of Hitler's autobahn in the Federal Republic vacillated between subdued pride over the supposedly apolitical achievement and the realization that the extensive network had been a White Elephant, unthinkable without the dictatorship's massive support. In the 1970s, opposition to road building became one of the hallmarks of the post-war environmental movement. In this poster, critics of autobahn construction capitalized on the roads' Nazi past by referring to an alleged statement by Fritz Todt: "No landscape is too good for the Führer's autobahn!" Implicitly, they argued that in the Federal Republic, unlike during the dictatorship, some landscapes were worthy of protection from the roads.
Deutsches Historisches Museum, Berlin

Truth is, in the face of the high traffic density and high accident rate at the beginning of the 1970s, the role of the autobahn in landscape exploration became increasingly outdated. But this was in no way an inevitable result of the changes in the political parameters. Rather, in a complex process of negotiation, the modernity of the landscape-sensitive autobahn was replaced with a no less modern ideology of the efficient and safe circulation of people and goods. Social roles were at stake for the participants in this debate. For the roads, this meant a discursive shift out of a landscape that was partly defined in nonhuman terms and into a technologically shaped environment. This environment was shaped by the road itself and the driving experience that was linked with it, an experience that planners during the period in question understood increasingly as one of space, laying claim to its spatial design in its totality.[7]

*

In this study, I have examined the transportation system of the autobahnen in its connection to the physical and psychological construction of landscape. By placing landscape as a topic of historical study within the context of a methodological convergence of environmental history and the history of technology, technology and nature appear as a historical continuum, not as opposites. In this regard, the historical transformation of landscape represents the intersection of the seemingly opposing categories of technology and nature. This intersection very much becomes a zone of exchange. Precisely because landscape is normatively charged and the vehicle of multiple ideologies, it pays to wrestle with this difficult term and its historical constructions, reinterpretations, and contradictory uses. The relevant meaning of specific landscapes, like the transportation landscapes I have examined, changed and was subject to social transformation. Different societies and different groups within these societies accorded landscapes functions and meanings that were, in part, contradictory. Civil engineers, landscape architects, motorists, and propagandists could see the landscapes defined by roads as vehicles for a boost in social status, as a staging area for social conflicts, and as aesthetically pleasant or unpleasant, safe or unsafe, places of circulation. To that extent, landscape was not a refuge outside of society, but in its definition and design an eminently social phenomenon that was characterized by conflict and contradictory value ascriptions. In spite of all the efforts by various groups to attain the absolute power of interpretation, the meaning of these landscapes was never static, which makes them a rich topic for historians. More still: one finding of this study is that the history of environment and technology will be poorer if it continues to often disregard the study of a phenomenon as complex as landscape.

This study also analyzed the transportation landscapes that were the result of these conflicts as technological artifacts that need to be interpreted culturally. The roads in question were by no means neutral transportation corridors, but reflected cultural values and as such reverberated back upon the societies that produced them. In taking this approach, this study followed in the footsteps of similar analysis of technological structures. The parkways of the New York planner Robert Moses, which are widely discussed in science and technology studies and supposedly kept buses from using these roads, were certainly not as exclusionary as has been frequently assumed. Regular buses drive on these roads every day. Still, the question of for whom roads such as these parkways are built and who actually uses them, often against the intentions of the planners, remains one of the most exciting questions at the intersection of the history of technology and environmental history.[8] The ideological content of the autobahn shifted by 1970 from being a politically charged, mythically staged, and nature-appropriating construction project of a dictatorship, to being a supposedly apolitical space for the rapid, unimpeded circulation of goods and persons, presided over by academically trained experts.

The network of autobahnen appeared under National Socialist auspices in the 1930s and was most strongly expanded in postwar West Germany. Its change in meaning from an icon of dictatorship to the symbol of rapid automotive transportation also altered the justifying and accompanying discourse about the relationship between landscape and transportation. Landscape architects and civil engineers as the immediate expert groups each exerted different influence on the design and construction of the road network. Although the two groups examined the effect of the roads on the landscape along different pathways of knowledge, they kept their eyes on it, if with varying degrees of intensity.

The world of the autobahnen as originally imagined had its roots in the late 1920s. In the realm of passenger traffic, automobiles were no longer a curiosity to divert male elites, but they were also not yet an everyday means of transportation. The novelty factor of the car seemed to have worn off, and mass motorization à la the United States no longer appeared impossible. When sport motorists and urban elites proposed a network of separate transportation routes for the exclusive use of automobiles, they borrowed the name and concept from the chief transportation of the time, the railroad (*Eisenbahn*). These Auto-Bahnen remained exotic as long as they could be rejected as the pleasure sites of the happy few. As a project for legitimizing its rule, the Nazi dictatorship placed them within a context of work-procurement and mass motorization, creating in the process an economic failure and a tenacious propaganda project. The roads were far ahead of the need for them; as late as the 1950s, the Federal Republic possessed, in sheer mileage, more autobahn-quality roads than the United States. This country's engineers, who had regarded cost-benefit analysis since the 1920s increasingly as a precondition for the political implementation of large-scale projects, saw the German autobahnen as an example of false planning, an example of a policy of transportation infrastructure that anticipated need rather than responding to it.[9]

In Germany, even the minutiae of road design were subject to altercations. Although regulations about the arc length and length of the straightaways existed through the building period of the *Reichsautobahn*, the conflicts over the technical aspects reveal how minor a role these regulations played. They were handled in a very flexible manner; in the hectic construction climate, which was characterized by the contradictory demands of a timely opening of sections and the controlling zeal of the Reich Railroad's financial officials, the features of the propagandistically hyped landscape integration were negotiated in chaotic battles between various groups of experts. The differences between civil engineers and landscape architects, which were grounded in divergent visions of landscape and technology, were covered over by the authoritarian power of Todt's agency to make decisions. This agency sought to push through its own vision of a homogenized consumption of visually presented landscapes. To that extent, the findings of the present study call for emphatic corrections to the picture of landscape integration in the Third Reich that has been presented in the scholarly literature. The actors were by no means ideologically motivated conservationists, but landscape architects and engineers in search of professional status who occasionally found common ground in sporadic coalitions.

Contrary to the arguments of authors like Rollins, the autobahn project was also not an example of "environmental reform," but a peculiar mix of contradictory elements: the desire for accelerated transportation for a racially defined Germany, a symbolic boost for the Nazi dictatorship from modern technology, the desire for enhanced status on the part of the landscape architects and civil engineers, and a rhetorically attempted ecological restoration. The sources I have examined allow only one conclusion, namely that meaningful ecological restoration was not possible either ideologically or practically, given the few short years of prewar planning and the chaotic building conditions. The architects were trying to attain the ultimate authority of cultural interpretation by employing an increasingly radical ideology, whereby science and racism—as in the case of native plants—were obviously not mutually exclusive.

Compared to other large-scale scientific and technological projects of the Nazis, the landscape design of the Autobahn seems both more international and more insular. Unlike the short-lived "German Physics," which sought to replace quantum physics with a homegrown variation of the physical sciences, the landscape ideas revolving around the autobahn were strongly influenced by the discourse over the American parkways; in fact, the intellectual influence from that highly motorized country was a constant.

Todt's dislike of "landscape dreamers" and his emphatic preference for visual consumption, not ecological restoration, place the autobahn project within the context of a racially defined, emerging consumer society in the Third Reich, for which the automobile and its roads were both means and goals at the same time. To be sure, the popular enthusiasm for these highways and for automobilization was largely attributable to the regime's massive propaganda efforts; on the other hand, National Socialism exploited a latent enthusiasm for modern, fast transportation and its infrastructures, which was just as evident in the case of air travel. In this respect, "German Technology" in the form of the autobahn was more international than the insular "German Physics."[10]

The beginning ecological classification by phytosociologists amounted to a considerable boost for the institutionalization of this branch of science; this must be kept in mind, despite the bureaucratic muddle and the competition with engineering biology. In this regard, the landscapes of the autobahn were internationally notable and can be mentioned as examples for "normal science" under National Socialism.[11] For phytosociology in Hannover, which blossomed after the Second World War, the *Reichsautobahn* became an entry gate, as it were, into National Socialism, with its grounds for Nazi party congresses and camps that appeared to be in need of botanical experts.

At the same time, the nationalistic, at times racist, component of landscape design is impossible to overlook. The longing for a German landscape—more precisely, a modern German transportation landscape—remained the foundation underlying the demands of the landscape architects. To be sure, the call for the use of native plants grew louder only as it became increasingly clear that the landscape consultants were less relevant to the process. But the presumed, essentialist connection between man and land, and the notion that an improved land would bring forth a better people, already existed before 1933 and was further reinforced under National Socialism. In this regard, the landscapes of the autobahn were the result of a self-chosen insularity.

When it comes to the final result of the design of the autobahnen, we are left with the highly contradictory mix mentioned above. The question that Robert Proctor raised a few years ago, whether bad people can do good science, can be answered as follows in this case: in the final analysis, intermittent racists combined incompatible goals in the autobahn project, thereby producing an inconsistent technology that failed when measured against its own elevated claims of a harmonious integration into the landscape.[12] This is why the Nazis' green autobahn is a figment.

It was only in the Federal Republic that construction was standardized, a development to which the growing influence of the mathematization of the alignment contributed. This mathematization offered itself as a tried-and-true way for the engineers to solidify their expert status and to ensure their professional continuity through methodological discontinuity. The decreed "scientization" of the autobahnen consisted largely in the adaptation of quantifiable methods, which made central planning without local influences possible to an even greater degree and thus contributed to a twofold economization of the postwar autobahn. Internally, this economization was expressed in the desire for a safe and efficient management of the growing volume of traffic; externally, it meant the presentation of the road network as a plannable, economically justifiable, and profitable investment. Landscape was redefined into a space made up by the interplay of motorists, vehicle, and road. West German civil engineers, like their counterparts in the road-building bureaucracy in the United States, laid claim to and defended their hegemony through research, guidelines, and methodological innovations.[13]

On the German autobahnen, change toward what Klenke has called an "ecologization" began only toward the end of the 1970s. At that time there was a growing realization that the ecological damage of highways went beyond the visible loss of landscape. The most significant impacts are the barrier effects for ecological communities. Because of the insularization of their habitat, genetic changes have already occurred in some frog species in Germany. Even though one recent ecological publication maintains that by now more vertebrates are killed by cars than by hunting, ecologists evidently regard roadkill as an ecological problem only in local, exceptional cases. Numerous bridges and tunnels for wildlife are supposed to provide technological fixes for the problem.[14] It would appear that before 1960, neither civil engineers nor landscape architects were able to recognize these effects of autobahn construction, to a large degree because they were the result of the mass diffusion of automobiles and the unprecedented expansion of the road network. Still, it is not without irony that ecologists today refer to the side of the road as an "ecological frontier," while two generations of researchers ago, phytosociologists were using the road as a new area of work.

As we have seen, the landscape integration of the *Reichsautobahn* had no direct aftereffect in the Federal Republic, provoking instead methodological counterreactions on the part of civil engineers: methodological discontinuity was supposed to make it easier to maintain professional continuity. In any case, one finding of the present study is that another, profound change in perception had occurred already before road building became ecologized—a change in the way landscape was perceived, which Rosalind Williams has summarized this way: "A gash through the landscape once viewed as progress became viewed instead as desecration." The aesthetic appropriation of landscape by the motorist was increasingly rendered obsolete by the mass traffic of the 1960s, when rising accident rates raised questions about safety, not about the angles of panoramic vistas. As a look at private letters sent to the Ministry of Transportation on the topic of roadside trees has shown, it was easy to generate opposition to the "murderous trees." Already during the period of postwar reconstruction, the panoramic autobahn of the prewar period was rejected as unmodern and was made fit for long-distance heavy trucking. Beginning in the 1970s, the number of sections provided with noise barriers grew.[15]

The study of these landscapes has shown how their experience changed as a result of varying social demands and cultural interpretations. To put it in simplified form: the erstwhile promise of the autobahn, expressed in the metaphor of "opening up" ("Erschließung"), came to be overshadowed by the realization of loss—the loss of quiet areas outside of the realm of circulation. The emerging social protest against the building of new roads was based largely on the experience with autobahn construction in the 1960s and 1970s, which was seen increasingly as interference in ecologically sensitive cultural landscapes, not to mention as sources of pollution.[16]

In this respect, the difference in meaning I have examined should be seen as the gradual shrinking of the landscape to a humanly defined space. "The motorist," whose likes and dislikes experts had decided for decades, spoke up during the mass motorization of the 1960s, and most wanted a designed environment that was controlled and promised safety, rather than an eventful driving landscape. Fear, control, and safety, not experience, were the dominant motifs in this discourse, in which female drivers participated for the first time in larger numbers. The growing acceleration of industrial life that has been observed for the nineteenth century was therefore not the only form of perception in the twentieth century. Even if Germany is known as the country without a speed limit on the autobahnen, the search for safety was no less pronounced than the desire for a fast trip by car.[17]

In conclusion, I will place the examined landscapes within a larger historical context and ask about the relationship between landscape change and modernity. Only thirty years ago such a question would have been answered simply by dismissing critics of the massive changes that were understood as modernization as being antimodern agrarian romantics. Today, that is no longer possible. The disintegration of progress as an explanatory parameter not only in the history of technology, and the emphasis on local knowledge have made the critics of modernity appear at times as the better diagnosticians and overlooked voices of warning about the failure of progress. More recent works by James Scott and Dirk van Laak have criticized large-scale technological projects like those I have looked at as failed examples of an impatient perfectionism and of an authoritarian, state-guided modernity. It would be silly to deny the high costs of these projects to society and the landscape. Hitler's version of freeways is indeed the paragon of a white elephant. However, one should ask whether the "practical knowledge" that is invoked especially by Scott can be so clearly separated from the knowledge and claims of state planners. Based on the examples I have looked at, one could say, instead, that supporters and critics of the projects were part of the same system of a planning modernity. This kind of infrastructure at times absorbed some of the opposition, at least before 1970. In the case of the landscape architects, participation in state power seems to have been a significant professional impetus. More generally, one might ask whether the criticism of the landscape-altering effects of modernity was not already part of its repertoire by the 1930s. Critics and those they criticized could be seen, not as clashing opposites, but as part of a larger continuum. Analytically it is not very helpful to set up science and modernity, on one side, and landscape and local knowledge, on the other, as irreconcilable opposites. Rather, they operated within the same spectrum. Other studies might ask, for example, whether it was not the case that certain generations fought over ideas about a style of planning that could then be seen as unmodern by the next generation.[18]

Finally, this study appears to raise questions for future research. First, there is the comparative level. A comparison with other countries could show how the cultural production of landscape functioned in other national contexts and other mechanisms of creating meaning. Moreover, it should be noted that the turnaround from conservation to a more activist landscape design during the twentieth century has so far not been reflected in the historical literature. The historically important figure of the landscape architect has so far stood in the shadow of studies of conservationists and their motivation. Analogously, a look at roads is in many respects more promising in terms of environmental history than a look at nature preserves: in the 1980s, road corridors accounted for about 2 percent of the surface area of the Federal Republic, while nature preserves made up precisely half that, 0.99 percent. According to a more recent publication, between 15 and 20 percent of the area of the United States is affected by roads in ecological terms.

Finally, the present study raises questions about the relationship between aesthetically motivated ideas about nature and more technically oriented environmental protection. Historically, the two strands have often been at odds with each other, with public hygiene and health concerns on one end and bourgeois aesthetics on the other end of the spectrum. Scientific measurement was used in the former, while landscape was more difficult to quantify. Yet, one might ask whether these supposedly objective and subjective judgments were not in many cases the same fears and desires dressed in different garb.[19] In this regard it is to be hoped that the rediscovery of landscape and its historical shaping will remain a topic of historical scholarship. The historical look at landscape is worthwhile also in the age of disappearing daily panoramas.

That does not mean, however, that the culture-critical attitude toward the building of transportation routes is a thing of the past. With an eye toward other countries, one German observer has remarked:

> The routing of the roads in those countries is also very different from what it is here. In England and Holland, the roads are integrated into the landscape. Their line must conform to the topography, not vice versa. As a result they are curvier as well as narrower. In England, one drives between hedges that grow right up to the asphalt. It takes effort and time to constantly trim them back. In Holland, meadows are allowed to reach up to the road surface, highways are lined by trees and bushes, behind which there is usually also a wide bike path. In our country, the highways are built at an elevation, sometimes as high as railroad embankments. Depressions on both sides reinforce the sense that one is driving above the landscape, a truly imperial way of traversing the world. Trees and bushes have been banished from proximity to the roads. The roads are much wider, and it is not rare that far into the countryside they have three, sometimes four lanes. Curves are straightened, small elevations of the terrain are not crossed, but cut through or even leveled. The German highway seems like a mix between a runway and a racetrack, the English and Dutch counterpart is a country road covered in asphalt, an avenue approved for use by cars.[20]

What appears to be a demand for landscape integration from the middle of the twentieth century is in reality of much more recent date. This wish by the educated bourgeoisie for less traversing of the world and greater closeness to nature was penned in 1994. Apparently, cultured Germans still think of planting trees.

Notes

1 For a mostly internalist view see Hans Straub, *Die Geschichte der Bauingenieurkunst. Ein Überblick von der Antike bis in die Neuzeit*, ed. Peter Zimmermann, 4th ed. (Basel, Boston, 1992), 142–143. See also Reinhart Strecke, "Prediger, Mathematiker und Architekten. Die Anfänge der preußischen Bauverwaltung und die Verwissenschaftlichung des Bauwesens," in *Mathematisches Calcul und Sinn für Ästhetik. Die preußische Bauverwaltung 1770–1848* (Berlin, 2000), 25–36; Stefan Polónyi, "Der Einfluß des Wissenschaftsverständnisses auf das Konstruieren," in *Zur Geschichte des Konstruierens*, ed. Rainer Graefe (Stuttgart, 1989), 237–245; Herbert Ricken, *Der Bauingenieur. Geschichte eines Berufes* (Berlin, 1994). One example of such a constructed past is Kurt Kaftan, *Der Kampf um die Autobahnen: Geschichte und Entwicklung des Autobahngedankens in Deutschland, von 1907–1935, unter Berücksichtigung ähnlicher Pläne und Bestrebungen im übrigen Europa* (Berlin, 1955). Kaftan had been the public relations head for Hafraba and allegedly coined the term autobahn in 1926.

2 Paul Betts, "The Bauhaus as Cold-War Legend," *German Politics and Society* 14/2 (1996): 75–100. For analyses of coming to terms with the Nazi past, see Werner Bergmann, "Kommunikationslatenz und Vergangenheitsbewältigung," in *Vergangenheitsbewältigung am Ende des zwanzigsten Jahrhunderts*, ed. Helmut König, Michael Kohlstruck, and Andreas Wöll (Opladen/Wiesbaden, 1998), 393–408; Robert G. Moeller, "War Stories: The Search for a Usable Past in the Federal Republic of Germany," *American Historical Review* 101 (1996): 1008–1048; Norbert Frei, *Adenauer's Germany and the Nazi Past: The Politics of Amnesty and Integration*, transl. Joel Golb (New York, 2002).

3 Doßmann, *Begrenzte Mobilität*.

4 For this claim, see Heinrich Mäding, *Infrastrukturplanung im Verkehrs- und Bildungssektor. Eine vergleichende Untersuchung zum gesamtstaatlichen Planungsprozeß in der Bundesrepublik Deutschland* (Baden-Baden, 1978), 172.

5 Praxenthaler, *Geschichte*; Weishaupt, *Entwicklung*; Rainer Schmid, *Die Planung der Bundesautobahn von Stuttgart zum westlichen Bodensee* (Göttingen, 1972); Klenke, *Autobahnbau*; Peter Wuhrer, ed., *Land unter Beton* (Weingarten, 1985); Klaus Kamper, *Streitobjekt Autobahn: Bürger gegen DuBoDo* (Bochum, 1985); Peter M. Bode, ed., *Alptraum Auto: Eine hundertjährige Erfindung und ihre Folgen* (Munich, 1986); U. Fehlberg, "Ökologische Barrierewirkung von Straßen auf wildlebende Säugetiere—ein Tierschutzproblem," *Deutsche tierärztliche Wochenschrift* 101 (1994): 125–159. On the "freeway revolt" in the USA in the 1960s and 1970s see Mark H. Rose and Bruce E. Seely, "Getting the Interstate System Built: Road Engineers and the Implementation of Public Policy, 1955–1985," *Journal of Policy History* 2 (1990): 23–55; Tom Lewis, *Divided Highways: Building the Interstate Highways, Transforming American Life* (New York, 1997).

6 Alwin Seifert, "Vorplanung Autobahnring-Stadtnahe Südtrasse," here "Entwurf zur landschaftlichen Eingliederung," 3, 15 December 1971, SN 180. The eighty-one-year-old Seifert had prepared this study on the Autobahn ring around Munich for the engineering consultancy Dorsch-Consult (for Dorsch, see chapter five, section *Finding a niche for landscape architects*). On urban highways, see Barbara Schmucki, "Schneisen durch die Stadt—Sinnbild der 'modernen' Stadt. Stadtautobahnen und amerikanisches Vorbild in West- und Ostdeutschland, 1925–1975," *WerkstattGeschichte* 7/21 (1998): 43–63.

7 The American planners Donald Appleyard, Kevin Lynch, and John R. Myer, *The View from the Road* (Cambridge, Mass., 1964), 63, invoke this "new world of vision" and describe the parkways as obsolete (3).

8 Nye, *American Technological Sublime*; Robert A. Caro, *The Power Broker. Robert Moses and the Fall of New York* (New York, 1975), 318; Langdon A. Winner, "Do Artifacts Have Politics?," *Daedalus* 109 (1980): 121–136; Steve Woolgar and Geoff Cooper, "Do Artefacts Have Ambivalence? Moses's Bridges, Winner's Bridges, and other Urban Legends in S&TS," *Social Studies of Science* 29 (1999): 433–449; Bernward Joerges, "Do Politics Have Artefacts?," *Social Studies of Science* 29

(1999): 411–431; idem, "Brücken, Busse und andere Verkehrsteilnehmer—Zur Repräsentation undWirkung städtischer Artefakte," in *Technik und Gesellschaft 10*, ed. Gert Schmidt (Frankfurt and New York, 1999), 197–218; Matthew W. Roth, "Mulholland Highway and the Engineering Culture of Los Angeles in the 1920s," *Technology and Culture* 40 (1999): 545–575.

9   Bruce Seely, "Der amerikanische Blick auf die deutschen Autobahnen. Deutsche und amerikanische Autobahnbauer 1930–1965," *WerkstattGeschichte* vol. 7, no. 21 (1998): 11–28.

10 Alan D. Beyerchen, *Scientists under Hitler: Politics and the Physics Community in the Third Reich* (New Haven, 1977); Mark Walker, *German National Socialism and the Quest for Nuclear Power, 1939–1949* (Cambridge, 1989); Peter Fritzsche, *A Nation of Fliers: German Aviation and the Popular Imagination* (Cambridge, Mass., 1992); Guillaume de Syon, *Zeppelin! Germany and the Airship, 1900–1939* (Baltimore, 2002).

11 Margit Szöllösi-Janze, ed., *Science in the Third Reich* (Oxford and New York, 2001). Szöllösi-Janze uses the term in reference to Thomas Kuhn, the philosopher of science.

12 Robert N. Proctor, *The Nazi War on Cancer* (Princeton, 1999). For a study that emphasizes the strong importance that ideology had for a group of SS engineers see Michael Allen, *The Business of Genocide: The SS, Slave Labor, and the Concentration Camps* (Chapel Hill, 2002).

13 Bruce Seely, "The Scientific Mystique in Engineering: Highway Research in the Bureau of Public Roads, 1918–1940," *Technology and Culture* 25 (1984): 798–831.

14 Richard T.T. Formann and Lauren E. Alexander, "Roads and Their Major Ecological Effects," *Annual Review of Ecology and Systematics* 29 (1998): 207–231.

15 Klenke, "Autobahnbau und Naturschutz," 498; Rosalind Williams, quoted in Rose and Seely, "Getting the Interstate System," 53, note 45.

16 First approaches to the latter topic in Ueli Haefeli, "Luftreinhaltepolitik im Straßenverkehr in den USA, in Deutschland und in der Schweiz. Ein Vergleich zur Entwicklung nach 1945," *Traverse* vol. 6, no. 2 (1999): 171–191; Dietmar Klenke, "Das automobile Zeitalter—Die umwelthistorische Problematik im deutsch-amerikanischen Vergleich," in Bayerl, *Umweltgeschichte*, 267–281.

17 Joachim Radkau, "Auto-Lust: Zur Geschichte der Geschwindigkeit," in *Fortschritt vom Auto? Umwelt und Verkehr in den 90er Jahren*, ed. Tom Koenigs and Roland Schaeffer (Munich, 1991), 113–130.

18 For the older view, see Klaus Bergmann, *Agrarromantik und Großstadtfeindschaft* (Meisenheim am Glan, 1970); James C. Scott, *Seeing Like a State: How Certain Schemes to Improve the Human Condition Have Failed* (New Haven, Conn., 1998); Dirk van Laak, *Weiße Elefanten. Anspruch und Scheitern technischer Großprojekte im 20. Jahrhundert* (Stuttgart, 1999); Loren R. Graham, *What Have We Learned About Science and Technology from the Russian Experience?* (Stanford, Cal., 1998), 98–123; Williams, *Nature Out of Control*; Leo Marx, "Environmental Degradation and the Ambiguous Role of Science and Technology," in *Earth, Air, Fire, Water. Humanistic Studies of the Environment*, ed. Jill Ker Conway, Kenneth Keniston, and Leo Marx (Amherst, Mass., 1999), 320–338; Mark Roseman, ed., *Generations in Conflict. Youth Revolt and Generation Formation in Germany 1770–1968* (Cambridge, 1996).

19 Regina Rattay-Prade, *Die Vegetation auf Strassenbegleitstreifen in verschiedenen Naturräumen Südbadens-ihre Bewertung für den Naturschutz und ihre Bedeutung für ein Biotopverbundsystem* (Berlin, 1988), 3; Forman, *Roads*. For the United States: Brian Black, "Organic Planning: Ecology and Design in the Landscape of the Tennessee Valley Authority, 1933–45," in *Environmentalism in Landscape Architecture*, ed. Michel Conan (Washington, DC, 2000), 71–95; on Italy: Gabriele Zanetto, Francesco Vallerani, and Stefano Soriani, *Nature, Environment, Landscape: European Attitudes and Discourses in the Modern Period. The Italian Case, 1920–1970* (Padua, 1996). I am currently working on a comparison of parkways in the United States and Germany. On the separation of aesthetics and hygiene see Franz-Josef Brüggemeier, *Tschernobyl, 26. April 1986. Die ökologische Herausforderung* (Munich, 1998), 114.

20 Jürgen Manthey, "Glossa continua (XXIII)," *Merkur* 48 (1994), 743–746, 744.

Bibliography and Sources

Archival Sources

Bundesarchiv Koblenz (BAK)

Bestand Generalinspektor für das deutsche Straßenwesen R 65

Bestand Reichsstelle für Naturschutz B 245

Bestand Hauptarchiv der NSDAP-Fritz Todt NS 26

Bundesminister für Verkehr B 108

Note: Since using these files at the Bundesarchiv in Koblenz, R65 and NS26 have been moved to the new facility of the Bundesarchiv in Berlin-Lichterfelde.

Bundesarchiv, Abteilungen Potsdam (BAP)

Bestand Generalinspektor für das deutsche Straßenwesen 46.01

Bestand Generaldirektion der Reichsautobahnen 46.02

Note: Since using these files at the Bundesarchiv in Potsdam, they have been moved to the new facility of the Bundesarchiv in Berlin-Lichterfelde.

Berlin Document Center (BDC)

NSDAP-member file Alwin Seifert

Seifert-Nachlaß am Lehrstuhl für Landschaftsarchitektur und Entwerfen der Technischen Universität München-Weihenstephan (SN)

Alwin Seifert Papers, SN 1–521

Deutsches Museum, Munich, Archive (DM)
Alwin Seifert Papers, NL 133

Bayerisches Hauptstaatsarchiv Munich (BayHStA)
Personnel file Alwin Seifert MK 58957

Historisches Archiv der Technischen Universität München (HAUTUM)
Personnel file Hans Lorenz

Personnel file Alwin Seifert

Amtsgericht Munich, Registratur S (AGM)
Denazification Files Alwin Seifert

Institut für Zeitgeschichte, Munich, Archive (IfZ)
Prof. A. Seifert—R. Heß Korrespondenz 1934–1941 ED 32

Erinnerungen an Leben und Werk von Dr.-Ing. Fritz Todt von Dr.-Ing. E.h. Richard Auberlen Ms 392

Hafraba c.V., Satzung des Vereins und Eintrag ins Vereinsregister, 1926, Fa 84

Published Sources

Journals
Die Straße 1–10 (1934–1943)
Straße und Autobahn (SuA) 1–16 (1950–1965)

Primary sources
"An unsere Mitglieder!" *Bayerischer Heimatschutz* 29 (1933): 1.

Appleyard, Donald, Kevin Lynch, and John R. Myer. *The View from the Road*. Cambridge, Mass., 1964.

"Aus dem Jahresbericht des Bayerischen Landesvereins für Heimatschutz." *Bayerischer Heimatschutz* 30 (1934). 82–83.

Bonatz, Paul. *Leben und Bauen*. Stuttgart, 1950.

Braun-Blanquet, J.[osias]. "Die Pflanzensoziologie in Forschung und Lehre." *Der Biologe* 1 (1931/32): 175–180.

———. *Pflanzensoziologie. Grundzüge der Vegetationskunde*. Vienna, 1951.

Bundesminister für Verkehr Abteilung Straßenbau, ed. *Hafraba. Bundesautobahn Hansestädte-Frankfurt-Basel. Rückblick auf 30 Jahre Autobahnbau*. Wiesbaden and Berlin, 1962.

Deutsche Reichsbahn-Reichsbahn-Zentralamt. *Die Filme der Verkehrswissenschaften im Verleih der Reichsbahn-Filmstelle 1938 mit allgemeinem Überblick über den verkehrswissenschaftlichen Film des In- und Auslandes.* Berlin, no date.

Die Verkehrspolitik in der Bundesrepublik Deutschland 1949–1961. Ein Bericht des Bundesministers für Verkehr. Bad Godesberg, 1961.

Die Versteppung Deutschlands? (Kulturwasserbau und Heimatschutz). Sonderdruck mit Aufsätzen aus der Zeitschrift "Deutsche Technik." Leipzig, no date [1938].

Dittrich, Rudolf. *Autobahn-Fahrbahndecken 1934–1956. Grundlagen—Herstellung–Beanspruchung–Bewährung* (= Forschungsarbeiten aus dem Straßenwesen, new series 58). Bad Godesberg, 1964.

Fehlberg, U. "Ökologische Barrierewirkung von Straßen auf wildlebende Säugetiere–ein Tierschutzproblem." *Deutsche tierärztliche Wochenschrift* 101 (1994): 125–159.

Forschungsgesellschaft für das Straßenwesen e.V. Arbeitsausschuß Landschaftsgestaltung. *Richtlinien für Straßenbepflanzung (RPf)*, Part 1, 1960 edition. Cologne, 1960.

Forschungsgesellschaft für das Straßenwesen e.V. Arbeitsausschuß Landschaftsgestaltung. *Richtlinien für Straßenbepflanzung (RPf 2)*, Part 2, Ausführung von Straßenbepflanzungen. Cologne, 1964.

Forschungsgesellschaft für das Straßenwesen e.V. Arbeitsausschuß Landschaftsgestaltung. *Richtlinien für Straßenbepflanzung (RPf 3)*, Part 3. Pflege und Nacharbeiten an Straßenpflanzungen. Cologne, 1969.

Gesellschaft der Freunde des deutschen Heimatschutzes, ed., *Der deutsche Heimatschutz. Ein Rückblick und Ausblick.* Munich, 1930.

Goerner, E., ed. *Straßenbauforschung. Vorträge gehalten auf der Mitgliederversammlung der Forschungsgesellschaft für das Straßenwesen am 21. Oktober 1947 in Bonn* (= Forschungsarbeiten aus dem Straßenwesen. new series 1). Berlin, Bielefeld, and Detmold, 1948.

Gothein, Marie Luise. *Geschichte der Gartenkunst. Zweiter Band: Von der Renaissance in Frankreich bis zur Gegenwart.* Jena, 1914.

Hafen, Paul. *Das Schrifttum über die deutschen Autobahnen.* Bonn, 1956.

Hoffmann, Rudolf. "Neue verkehrs- und raumpolitische Entwicklungen." *Raumforschung und Raumordnung* no. 11 (1937): 455–462.

———. "Aktive Verkehrs- und Raumpolitik." *Raumforschung und Raumordnung* no. 4 (1937): 148–156.

Kasper, Hugo, Walter Schürba, and Hans Lorenz. *Die Klotoide als Trassierungslement.* Hannover, 1961.

Klamm, Reinhold. "Grenzen des Föderalismus." *Der Straßenbau* 50 (1959): 436–438.

Kruedener, Arthur Freiherr von. *Forstliche Standortanzeiger. Auslese zum Gebrauch im Walde.* 4th ed. Radebeul and Berlin, 1955.

———. *Ingenieurbiologie.* Munich and Basel, 1951.

Landesplanerisches Gutachten zur Linienführung der Autobahn Nordsüd in Niedersachsen (= Veröffentlichungen des Niedersächsischen Amts für Landesplanung und Statistik, Reihe G4). Hannover, 1950.

Landgrebe, Hermann, and Ludwig Roemer. "Landschaftliche Gestaltung moderner Schnellstraßen. Gutachten vom Oktober 1966 im Auftrage des Deutschen Rates für Landespflege." In *Landschaftpflege an Verkehrsstraßen. Empfehlungen, Untersuchungsergebnisse, Berichte und Stellungnahmen,* 40–49. Bonn, 1968.

Lange, Willy. *Gartengestaltung der Neuzeit.* 6th ed. Leipzig, 1928.

Leonhardt, Fritz. *Baumeister in einer bewegten Zeit.* Stuttgart, 1984.

Lindner, Werner. *Die Ingenieurbauten in ihrer guten Gestaltung.* Berlin, 1923.

———. *Bauten der Technik. Ihre Form und Wirkung. Werkanlagen.* Berlin, 1927.

———. and Conrad Matschoss, eds., *Technische Kulturdenkmale.* Munich, 1932.

Lorenz, Hans. "Straße und Landschaft." *Die Bauverwaltung* 1 (1952): 274–282.

———. *Trassierung und Gestaltung von Straßen und Autobahnen.* Wiesbaden/Berlin, 1971.

———. and Wilhelm Heubling. *Grünverbau im Straßenbau. Vorträge bei der Landschaftstagung der Forschungsgesellschaft für das Straßenwesen Koblenz 1961* (= Forschungsarbeiten aus dem Straßenwesen new series 51). Bad Godesberg, 1962.

Moore, J. J. "The Braun-Blanquet System. A Reassessment." *Journal of Ecology* 50 (1962). 761–769.

Müller-Hermann, Ernst. *Wettbewerb und Ordnung. Grundlage der Verkehrspolitik* (=Lebendige Wirtschaft 10B). Darmstadt, 1954.

Oerley, Leopold. *Übergangsbogen bei Straßenkrümmungen.* Berlin, 1937.

Person, Harlow Stafford. *Little Waters. A Study of Headwater Streams & Other Little Waters, Their Use and Relations to the Land.* Washington, D.C., 1936.

Rausch, Hans. "Über den Einfluß des Geländes auf die Netzbildung und Linienführung der Reichsautobahnen in Norddeutschland." Dissertation, Technical University Danzig, 1942.

Reichsministerium Speer, publ. *Das Erlebnis der Reichsautobahnen. Ein Bildwerk von Hermann Harz mit einer Einführung von Herybert Menzel.* Munich, no date [1943].

Reismann, Otto. *Deutschlands Autobahnen. Adolf Hitlers Straßen.* Bayreuth, 1937.

Riehl, Wilhelm Heinrich. "Das landschaftliche Auge," in idem, *Culturstudien aus drei Jahrhunderten,* 2nd ed. (Stuttgart, 1859), 57–79.

Roberts, Stephen D. *The House that Hitler Built.* New York, and London, 1938.

Rudorff, Ernst. "Über das Verhältniß [sic] des modernen Lebens zur Natur." *Natur und Landschaft* 65 (1990): 119–125.

Schaefer, Hans Ulrich. *Die Gesetze der Reichsautobahnen mit einschlägigen Vorschriften und Verweisungen* (= Stilles Rechtsbibliothek 161). Berlin, 1937.

Schönleben, Eduard. "Der Irschenberg." *Die Baukunst.* [supplement to] *Kunst im Deutschen Reich* (January 1942): 61.

Schönleben, Eduard. *Fritz Todt. Der Mensch. Der Ingenieur. Der Nationalsozialist.* Oldenburg, 1943.

Schultze-Naumburg, Paul. *Die Gestaltung der Landschaft durch den Menschen* (= Kulturarbeiten vols. 1–3). 3rd ed. Munich, 1928.

Schürba, Walter. *Klothoiden-Abstecktafeln. Anleitung zu Entwurf, Berechnung und Absteckung.* Berlin, 1942.

Schurhammer, Hermann (posthumous). *Straße und Landschaft. Ein Beitrag zur praktischen Landschaftspflege. Mit Unterstützung des Bundesverkehrsministeriums,* ed. by Diplomgärtner Hermann Schurhammer, Jr., landscape architect. Bielefeld, 1955.

Seifert, Alwin. *Die Heckenlandschaft.* Potsdam, 1944.

———. "Die Zukunft der ostdeutschen Landschaft." *Flüssiges Obst* 12 (1941): 108–110.

———. *Ein Leben für die Landschaft.* Düsseldorf and Cologne, 1962.

———. "Ewige Heimat der Deutschen." *Odal. Monatsschrift für Blut und Boden* 11 (1942): 113–116.

———. "Gedanken über bodenständige Gartenkunst." *Gartenkunst* 42 (1929): 118–123, 131–132, 175–178, 191–195.

———. *Im Zeitalter des Lebendigen. Natur-Heimat-Technik.* Planegg by Munich, 1942.

———. "Verkaufte Landschaft." *Blätter für Naturschutz,* ed. by the Bund Naturschutz in Bayern 29 (1949): 12–17.

Sloan Jr., Alfred P. *My Years with General Motors.* Garden City and New York, 1972 [orig. 1963].

Tansley, A.G. "The Use and Abuse of Vegetational Concepts and Terms." *Ecology* 16 (1935): 284–307.

Todt, Fritz. "Adolf Hitler and His Roads." In *Adolf Hitler: Pictures from the Life of the Führer 1931–1935.* New York and London, 1978, 88–95.

Tüxen, Reinhold. "Die Pflanzensoziologie in ihren Beziehungen zu den Nachbarwissenschaften." *Der Biologe* 1 (1931/32): 180–187.

Secondary sources

Adam, Thomas. "Parallele Wege. Geschichtsvereinigungen und Naturschutzbewegung in Deutschland." *Geschichte in Wissenschaft und Unterricht* 48 (1997): 413–428.

Adamek, Robert, and Fr. Saake. *Die Straßenkosten und ihre Finanzierung* (= Forschungsarbeiten aus dem Straßenwesen, new series 8). Bielefeld, 1962.

Adolf, Heinrich. "Technikdiskurs und Technikideologie im Nationalsozialismus." *Geschichte in Wissenschaft und Unterricht* 48 (1997): 429–444.

Ahonen, Pertti. *After the Expulsion: West Germany and Eastern Europe, 1945–1990.* Oxford/New York, 2003.

Allen, Michael. "The Puzzle of Nazi Modernism. Modern Technology and Ideological Consensus in an SS Factory at Auschwitz." *Technology and Culture* 37 (1996): 527–571.

———. *The Business of Genocide: The SS, Slave Labor, and the Concentration Camps.* Chapel Hill, 2002.

Andersen, Arne. "Heimatschutz. Die bürgerliche Naturschutzbewegung." In *Besiegte Natur. Geschichte der Umwelt im 19. und 20. Jahrhundert,* ed. Franz-Josef Brüggemeier and Thomas Rommelspacher, 143–157. Munich, 1989.

———. "Umweltgeschichte. Forschungsstand und Perspektiven." *Archiv für Sozialgeschichte* 33 (1993): 672–701.

———. *Der Traum vom guten Leben. Alltags- und Konsumgeschichte vom Wirtschaftswunder bis heute.* Frankfurt and New York, 1997.

Apel, Friedmar. *Deutscher Geist und deutsche Landschaft. Eine Topographie.* Munich, 1998.

Asendorf, Christoph. *Super Constellation-Flugzeug und Raumrevolution. Die Wirkung der Luftfahrt auf Kunst und Kultur der Moderne.* Vienna and New York, 1997.

Ash, Mitchell G. "Verordnete Umbrüche, konstruierte Kontinuitäten: Zur Entnazifizierung von Wissenschaftlern und Wissenschaften nach 1945," *Zeitschrift für Geschichtswissenschaft* 43 (1995), 903–923.

Autobahn-Bauamt Nuremberg, ed. *50 Jahre Autobahn in Nordbayern.* Nuremberg, 1984.

Baranowski, Shelley. *Strength Through Joy: Consumerism and Mass Tourism in the Third Reich.* Cambridge, 2004.

Barbour, Michael G. "Ecological Fragmentation in the Fifties." In *Uncommon Ground. Rethinking the Human Place in Nature*, ed. William Cronon, 233–255. New York, and London, 1996.

Barker, Theo, ed. *The Economic and Social Effects of the Spread of Motor Vehicles.* Basingstoke and London, 1987.

Bassin, Mark. "Imperialism and the Nation-State in Friedrich Ratzel's Political Geography." *Progress in Human Geography* 11 (1987): 473–495.

———. "Turner, Solov'ev, and the Frontier Hypothesis. The Nationalist Signification of Open Spaces." *Journal of Modern History* 65 (1993): 473–511.

Bätschmann, Oskar. *Entfernung der Natur. Landschaftsmalerei 1750–1920.* Cologne, 1989.

Bauer, Reinhard, and Ernst Piper. *München. Die Geschichte einer Stadt.* Munich and Zurich, 1993.

Bavaj, Riccardo. *Die Ambivalenz der Moderne im Nationalsozialismus. Eine Bilanz der Forschung.* Munich, 2003.

Bayerl, Günter. "Automobil und Umwelt in den 1950er und 1960er Jahren." In *Beiträge zur Geschichte der Binnenschiffahrt, des Luft- und Kraftfahrzeugverkehrs.* (= Schriftenreihe der Deutschen Verkehrswissenschaftlichen Gesellschaft B 169), ed. Hans Jürgen Teuteberg. Cologne, 1994, 323–348.

———. "Die Erfindung des Autofahrens. Technik als Repräsentation, Abenteuer und Sport." In *Sozialgeschichte der Technik. Ulrich Troitzsch zum 60. Geburtstag*, ed. Günter Bayerl and Wolfhard Weber (= Cottbuser Studien zur Geschichte von Technik, Arbeit und Umwelt 7), 317–329. Münster, 1998.

———. Norman Fuchsloch, and Torsten Meyer, ed. *Umweltgeschichte. Methoden, Themen, Potentiale. Tagung des Hamburger Arbeitskreises für Umweltgeschichte* (= Cottbuser Studien zur Geschichte von Technik, Arbeit und Umwelt 1). Münster, 1996.

Becker, Udo J. "Verkehrsökologie—was ist das?" *Internationales Verkehrswesen* 49 (1997): 440–446.

Begemann, Wolf, and Hugo Meinhard Schiechtl. *Ingenieurbiologie. Handbuch zum naturnahen Wasser- und Erdbau.* Wiesbaden and Berlin, 1986.

Belasco, Warren James. *Americans on the Road. From Autocamp to Motel, 1910–1945.* Baltimore and London, 1997 [orig. 1979].

Belhoste, Bruno. "Un modèle à l'épreuve. L'École polytechnique de 1794 au Second Empire." In Bruno Belhoste, Amy Dahan Dalmedico, and Antoine Picon, *La formation polytechnicienne 1794–1994*, 9–30. Paris, 1994.

Bending, Stephen. "The Improvement of Arthur Young. Agricultural Technology and the Production of Landscape in Eighteenth Century England." In *Technologies of Landscape. From Reaping to Recycling*, ed. David Nye, 241–253. Amherst, Mass., 1999.

Bensch, Margrit. *Die "Blut-und-Boden"-Ideologie. Ein dritter Weg der Moderne* (= Beiträge zur Kulturgeschichte der Natur 2). Berlin, 1995.

Bergmann, Werner. "Kommunikationslatenz und Vergangenheitsbewältigung." In *Vergangenheitsbewältigung am Ende des zwanzigsten Jahrhunderts* (= Leviathan Sonderheft 18), ed. Helmut König, Michael Kohlstruck, and Andreas Wöll, 393–408. Opladen and Wiesbaden, 1998.

Berman, Marshall. *All that is Solid Melts into Air. The Experience of Modernity.* New York, 1982.

Betts, Paul. "The Bauhaus as Cold-War Legend." *German Politics and Society* 14/3 (1996): 75–100.

———. "The New Fascination with Fascism: The Case of Nazi Modernism," *Journal of Contemporary History* 37 (2002): 541–558.

Beyerchen, Alan D. *Scientists under Hitler: Politics and the Physics Community in the Third Reich.* New Haven, 1977.

Biehl, Janet, and Peter Staudenmaier. *Ecofascism. Lessons from the German Experience.* Edinburgh and San Francisco, 1995.

Bijker, Wiebe E., Thomas Parke Hughes, and T.J. Pinch, eds., *The Social Construction of Technological Systems: New Directions in the Sociology and History of Technology.* Cambridge, Mass. 1987.

Birkefeld, Richard, and Martina Jung. *Die Stadt, der Lärm und das Licht. Die Veränderung des öffentlichen Raumes durch Motorisierung und Elektrifizierung.* Seelze, 1994.

Bitomsky, Hartmut. "Die Reichsautobahn." Television film. Westdeutscher Rundfunk, 1984.

Black, Brian. "Organic Planning. Ecology and Design in the Landscape of the Tennessee Valley Authority, 1933–45," in *Environmentalism in Landscape Architecture*, ed. Michel Conan, 71–95. Washington, DC, 2000.

———. *Petrolia. The Landscape of America's First Oil Boom.* Baltimore and London, 2000.

Bode, Peter M., ed. *Alptraum Auto. Eine hundertjährige Erfindung und ihre Folgen.* Munich, 1986.

Böhm, Ehrtfried et al. *Straßenforschung. 50 Jahre Forschungsgesellschaft für das Straßenwesen 1924–1974.* Bonn-Bad Godesberg, 1974.

Bollenbeck, Georg. *Tradition, Avantgarde, Reaktion. Deutsche Kontroversen um die kulturelle Moderne 1880–1945.* Frankfurt, 1999.

Bollmus, Reinhard. *Das Amt Rosenberg und seine Gegner. Zum Machtkampf im nationalsozialistischen Herschaftssystem.* Stuttgart 1970.

Borchardt, Rudolf. *Der Deutsche in der Landschaft.* Frankfurt, 1989 [orig. 1925].

Bork, Hans-Rudolf et al. *Landschaftsentwicklung in Mitteleuropa. Wirkungen des Menschen auf Landschaften.* Gotha and Stuttgart, 1998.

Borrmann, Norbert. *Paul Schultze-Naumburg 1869–1949. Maler—Publizist—Architekt.* Essen 1989.

Borscheid, Peter. "Lkw kontra Bahn. Die Modernisierung des Transports durch den Lastkraftwagen in Deutschland bis 1939." In *Die Entwicklung der Motorisierung im Deutschen Reich und den Nachfolgestaaten* (= Stuttgarter Tage zur Automobil- und Unternehmensgeschichte 2), ed. Harry Niemann and Armin Hermann, 23–38. Stuttgart, 1995.

Bortolotti, Lando. "Les prémieres propositions d'un système européen d'autoroutes, 1926–1937." In *European networks, 19th-20th Centuries. New Approaches to the Formation of a Transnational Transport and Communication System. Réseaux européens, XIXe-XXe siècles. Nouvelles approches sur la formation d'un système transnational de transports et de les communications. Proceedings of the Eleventh International Economic History Congress Milan, September 1994*, ed. Albert Carreras, Andrea Giuntini, and Michèle Merger, 47–59. Milan, 1994.

———. and Giuseppe De Luca. *Fascismo e autostrade. Un caso di sintesi. La Firenze-mare.* Milan, 1994.

Bramwell, Anna. *Blood and Soil. Richard Walther Darré and Hitler's Green Party.* Buckinghamshire 1985.

———. *Ecology in the 20th Century. A History.* London and New Haven, 1989.

Braudel, Fernand. *The Mediterranean and the Mediterranean World in the Age of Philip II.* 2 vols. Trans. Siân Reynolds. New York, 1972.

———. Georges Duby, and Maurice Aymard. *Die Welt des Mittelmeeres. Zur Geschichte und Geographie kultureller Lebensformen.* Frankfurt, 1987.

Brewer, John. "Was können wir aus der Geschichte der frühen Neuzeit für die moderne Konsumgeschichte lernen?" In *Europäische Konsumgeschichte. Zur Gesellschafts- und Kulturgeschichte des Konsums (18. bis 20. Jahrhundert)*, ed. Hannes Siegrist, Hartmut Kaelble, and Jürgen Kocka, 51–74. Frankfurt, and New York, 1997.

Brockhaus, Gudrun. *Schauder und Idylle. Faschismus als Erlebnisangebot.* Munich, 1997.

Brose, Eric Dorn. "Generic Fascism Revisited. Attitudes Toward Technology in Germany and Italy, 1919–1945." *German Studies Review* 10 (1987): 273–297.

Broszat, Martin. *The Hitler State.* Trans. John W. Hiden. London, 1981.

Brüggemeier, Franz-Josef. *Das unendliche Meer der Lüfte. Luftverschmutzung, Industrialisierung und Risikodebatten im 19. Jahrhundert.* Essen, 1996.

———. *Tschernobyl, 26. April 1986. Die ökologische Herausforderung.* Munich, 1998.

———. Mark Cioc, and Thomas Zeller, eds., *How Green Were the Nazis? Nature, Environment, and Nation in the Third Reich.* Athens, Ohio, 2005.

Buderath, Bernhard, and Henry Makowski. *Die Natur dem Menschen untertan. Ökologie im Spiegel der Landschaftsmalerei.* Munich, 1986.

Burckhardt, Martin. *Metamorphosen von Raum und Zeit. Eine Geschichte der Wahrnehmung.* Frankfurt, and New York, 1994.

Burrage, Michael. "Introduction. The Professions in Sociology and History." In *Professions in Theory and History. Rethinking the Study of the Professions*, ed. Michael Burrage and Rolf Torstendahl, 1–23. London, Newbury Park, and New Delhi, 1990.

Büschenfeld, Jürgen. *Flüsse und Kloaken. Umweltfragen im Zeitalter der Industrialisierung (1870–1918)*. Stuttgart, 1997.

Caro, Robert A. *The Power Broker: Robert Moses and the Fall of New York*. New York, 1975.

Chaney, Sandra Lynn. "Visions and Revisions of Nature. From the Protection of Nature to the Invention of the Environment in the Federal Republic of Germany, 1945–1975." Ph. D. Thesis, University of North Carolina at Chapel Hill, 1996.

———. "Water for Wine and Scenery, Coal and European Unity: Canalization of the Mosel River, 1950–1964," in *Water, Culture, and Politics in Germany and the American West*, ed. Susan C. Anderson and Bruce H. Tabb, 227–252. New York, 2001.

Cioc, Mark. *The Rhine: An Eco-Biography*. Seattle and London, 2002.

Cittadino, Eugene. *Nature as the Laboratory. Darwinian Plant Ecology in the German Empire, 1880–1900*. Cambridge, 1990.

Cohrs, Heinz Herbert. *Faszination Baumaschinen. Erdbewegung durch fünf Jahrhunderte*. Isernhagen, 1995.

Conford, Philip. *The Origins of the Organic Movement*. Edinburgh, 2001.

Cosgrove, Denis E. *Social Formation and Symbolic Landscape*. 2nd ed. Madison, Wisconsin, 1997.

———, "Landscape and *Landschaft*," *Bulletin of the German Historical Institute Washington D.C.*, No. 35 (Fall 2004): 57–71.

Crary, Jonathan. *Techniques of the Observer. On Vision and Modernity in the Nineteenth Century*. Cambridge, Mass., 1990.

Cronon, William. *Nature's Metropolis. Chicago and the Great West*. New York, and London, 1991.

———. ed. *Uncommon Ground. Rethinking the Human Place in Nature*. New York and London, 1996.

Daniels, Stephen. *Fields of Vision. Landscape Imagery and National Identity in England and the United States*. Princeton, 1993.

———. and Denis Cosgrove, eds. *The Iconography of Landscape*. Cambridge, 1989.

Davis, Timothy F. "Mount Vernon Memorial Highway. Changing Conceptions of an American Commemorative Landscape." In *Places of Commemoration. Search for Identity and Landscape Design*, ed. Joachim Wolschke-Bulmahn, 123–177. Washington, D.C., 2001.

Deléage, Jean-Paul. *Histoire de L'Ecologie. Une Science de L'Homme et de la Nature*. Paris, 1992.

Denecke, Dietrich, and Klaus Fehn, eds. *Geographie in der Geschichte* (= Erdkundliches Wissen 96). Stuttgart, 1989.

Diefendorf, Jeffrey M. *In the Wake of War: The Reconstruction of German Cities after World War II*. Oxford, 1993.

Dienel, Hans-Liudger, and Barbara Schmucki, eds. *Mobilität für alle. Geschichte des öffentlichen Personennahverkehrs in der Stadt zwischen technischem Fortschritt und sozialer Pflicht. Beiträge der Tagung "Öffentlicher Nahverkehr" in München, Dezember 1994* (= Vierteljahrschrift für Sozial- und Wirtschaftsgeschichte, Beiheft 129). Stuttgart, 1997.

Dimendberg, Edward. "The Will to Motorisation—Cinema and the Autobahn." In *Speed—Visions of an Accelerated Age*, ed. Jeremy Millar and Michiel Schwarz, 56–72. London, 1998.

DiNardo, R.L. *Mechanized Juggernaut or Military Anachronism? Horses and the German Army of World War II*. New York, 1991.

Ditt, Karl. "Nature Conservation in England and Germany, 1900–1970. Forerunners of Environmental Protection?" *Contemporary European History* 5 (1996): 1–28.

———. *Raum und Volkstum. Die Kulturpolitik des Provinzialverbandes Westfalen 1923–1945*. Münster, 1988.

———. "The Perception and Conservation of Nature in the Third Reich." *Planning Perspectives* 15 (2000): 161–187.

Dix, Andreas. *Industrialisierung und Wassernutzung. Eine historisch–geographische Umweltgeschichte der Tuchfabrik Ludwig Müller in Kuchenheim* (= Landschaftsverband Rheinland, Rheinisches Industriemuseum, Beiträge zur Industrie- und Sozialgeschichte 7). Cologne, 1997.

———. "Vorindustrielle Kulturlandschaften. Leitlinien ihrer historischen Entwicklung," in *Die Veränderung der Kulturlandschaft. Nutzungen-Sichtweisen-Planungen*, ed. Günter Bayerl and Torsten Meyer (Münster and New York, 2003), 11–31.

Doering-Manteuffel, Sabine. *Die Eifel. Geschichte einer Landschaft*. Frankfurt and New York, 1995.

Dominick, Raymond H. *The Environmental Movement in Germany. Prophets and Pioneers, 1871–1980*. Louisville, Kentucky, 1993.

Doßmann, Axel. "Auto-Suggestionen. Zur Autobahnplanung in der DDR bis 1961." *WerkstattGeschichte* vol. 7, no. 21 (1998): 65–85.

———. "Wie wir die Autobahnen lieben lernten. Strukturelle Leitbilder und Automobilismus in Deutschland bis in die sechziger Jahre." *Sozialwissenschaftliche Informationen* 25 (1996): 235–242.

———. *Begrenzte Mobilität. Eine Kulturgeschichte der Autobahnen in der DDR*. Essen, 2003.

Dupuy, Gabriel, and Vaclav Stransky. "Cities and Highway Networks in Europe." *Journal of Transport Geography* 4 (1996): 107–121.

Durth, Werner. *Deutsche Architekten. Biographische Verflechtungen 1900–1970*. Braunschweig and Wiesbaden, 1986.

———. "Die getarnte Moderne. Planung und Technik im Dritten Reich." In *"Die Axt hat geblüht." Europäische Konflikte der 30er Jahre in Erinnerung an die frühe Avantgarde*, ed. Jürgen Harten, Hans-Werner Schmidt, and Marie Luise Syring, 358–367. Düsseldorf, 1987.

———. and Niels Gutschow. *Träume in Trümmern. Planungen zum Wiederaufbau zerstörter Städte im Westen Deutschlands 1940–1950*, 2 vols. Braunschweig and Wiesbaden, 1988.

Edelmann, Heidrun. *Vom Luxusgut zum Gebrauchsgegenstand. Die Geschichte der Verbreitung von Personenkraftwagen in Deutschland*. Frankfurt/Main, 1989.

Eidenbenz, Mathias. *"Blut und Boden." Zu Funktion und Genese der Metaphern des Agrarismus und Biologismus in der nationalsozialistischen Bauernpropaganda R. W. Darrés*. Bern, 1993.

Eisel, Ulrich, and Stefanie Schultz, eds. *Geschichte und Struktur der Landschaftsplanung.* Berlin, 1991.

Eisenberg, Christiane. *"English Sports" und deutsche Bürger. Eine Gesellschaftsgeschichte.* Paderborn 1999.

Emmerich, Wolfgang, and Carl Wege, eds. *Der Technikdiskurs in der Hitler-Stalin-Ära.* Stuttgart, 1995.

Evernden, Neil. *The Social Creation of Nature.* Baltimore and London, 1992.

Fachbereich Stadt- und Landschaftsplanung der Gesamthochschule Kassel, ed. *Leberecht Migge 1881–1935. Gartenkultur des 20. Jahrhunderts.* Kassel, 1981.

Falk, Susanne. "'Eine Notwendigkeit, uns innerlich umzustellen, liege nicht vor.' Kontinuität und Diskontinuität in der Auseinandersetzung des Sauerländischen Gebirgsvereins mit Heimat und Moderne 1918–1960." In *Politische Zäsuren und gesellschaftlicher Wandel im 20. Jahrhundert. Regionale und vergleichende Perspektiven,* ed. Matthias Frese and Michael Prinz, 401–417. Paderborn, 1996.

Febvre, Lucien. *Der Rhein und seine Geschichte.* Frankfurt, 1994.

——. *A Geographical Introduction to History.* Westport, Conn., 1974 (orig. 1925).

Fehn, Klaus. "Persistente Kulturlandschaftselemente. Wichtige Quellen für Historische Geographie und Geschichtswissenschaft." In *Menschen, Dinge und Umwelt in der Geschichte. Neue Fragen der Geschichtswissenschaft an die Vergangenheit,* ed. Ulf Dirlmeier and Gerhard Fouquet, 1–26. St. Katharinen 1989.

——. "Rückblick auf die "nationalsozialistische Kulturlandschaft" unter besonderer Berücksichtigung des völkisch-rassistischen Mißbrauchs von Kulturlandschaftspflege." *Informationen zur Raumentwicklung* 5/6 (1999): 279–290.

Fiege, Mark. *Irrigated Eden. The Making of an Agricultural Landscape in the American West.* Seattle and London, 1999.

Fischer, Helmut. *Deutscher Heimatbund. 90 Jahre für Umwelt und Naturschutz. Geschichte eines Programms.* Bonn, 1994.

Fischer, Norbert. "Der neue Blick auf die Landschaft." *Archiv für Sozialgeschichte* 36 (1996): 434–442.

Flik, Rainer. "Ford-Legende und Wirklichkeit. Die Motorisierung des Straßenverkehrs in Europa und Übersee im Vergleich, bis 1939." *Traverse* vol. 6, no. 2 (1999): 125–142.

Frank, Hartmut. "Bridges: Paul Bonatz's Search for a Contemporary Monumental Style." In *The Nazification of Art. Art, Design, Music, Architecture and Film in the Third Reich,* ed. Brandon Taylor and Wilfried van der Will, 144–157. Winchester, 1990.

Frei, Norbert. *Der Führerstaat. Nationalsozialistische Herrschaft 1933 bis 1945.* Munich, 1987.

——. *Adenaner's Germany and the Nazi Past: The Politics of Amnesty and Integration,* transl. Joel Golb. New York, 2002.

——. "Wie modern war der Nationalsozialismus?" *Geschichte und Gesellschaft* 19 (1993): 367–387.

Frese, Matthias, Julia Paulus, and Karl Teppe, eds. *Demokratisierung und gesellschaftlicher Aufbruch. Die sechziger Jahre als Wendezeit der Bundesrepublik.* Paderborn, 2003.

Fritzsche, Peter. *A Nation of Fliers. German Aviation and the Popular Imagination.* Cambridge, Mass., 1992.

———. "Nazi Modern." *Modernism/modernity* 3 (1996): 1–21.

Gall, Alexander. "'Gute Straßen bis ins kleinste Dorf!' Verkehrspolitik und Landesplanung 1945 bis 1976." In *Bayern im Bund, vol. 1: Die Erschließung des Landes 1949 bis 1973,* ed. Thomas Schlemmer and Hans Woller, 119–204. Munich, 2001.

Gall, Lothar, and Manfred Pohl, eds. *Die Eisenbahn in Deutschland. Von den Anfängen bis zur Gegenwart.* Munich, 1999.

Garlichs, Dietrich. *Grenzen staatlicher Infrastrukturpolitik. Bund/Länder-Kooperation in der Fernstraßenplanung* (= Politikverflechtung IV, Schriften des Wissenschaftszentrums Berlin, Internationales Institut für Management und Verwaltung 11). Königstein/Taunus, 1980.

Geden, Oliver. *Rechte Ökologie. Umweltschutz zwischen Emanzipation und Faschismus.* Berlin, 1995.

Gillespie, Angus Kress, and Michael Aaron Rockland. *Looking for America on the New Jersey Turnpike.* New Brunswick, New Jersey, 1992.

Gispen, Kees. "National Socialism and the Technological Culture of the Weimar Republic." *Central European History* 25 (1992): 387–406.

———. *New Profession, Old Order: Engineers and German Society, 1815–1914.* Cambridge and New York, 1989.

———. *Poems in Steel. National Socialism and the Politics of Inventing from Weimar to Bonn.* New York and Oxford, 2003.

Gläser, Hermann H. *Via Strata. Roman der Straße. Die durchaus persönlich gesehene Geschichte des Straßenbaus von den Anfängen bis zur Autobahn.* Wiesbaden and Berlin, 1987.

Gottwaldt, Alfred. *Julius Dorpmüller, die Reichsbahn und die Autobahn. Verkehrspolitik und das Leben des Verkehrsministers bis 1945.* Berlin, 1995.

Graham, Loren R. *What Have We Learned About Science and Technology from the Russian Experience?* Stanford, Cal., 1998.

Groh, Ruth, and Dieter Groh. "Natur als Maßstab—eine Kopfgeburt." In Landeshauptstadt Stuttgart, Kulturamt, ed., *Zum Naturbegriff der Gegenwart,* vol. 2, 15–37. Stuttgart-Bad Cannstatt, 1994.

———. *Weltbild und Naturaneignung. Zur Kulturgeschichte der Natur.* Frankfurt/Main, 1991.

Gröning, Gert, and Ulfert Herlyn, eds. *Landschaftswahrnehmung und Landschaftserfahrung. Texte zur Konstitution und Rezeption von Natur als Landschaft.* Munich, 1990.

Gröning, Gert, and Joachim Wolschke. "Naturschutz und Ökologie im Nationalsozialismus." *Die alte Stadt* 10 (1983): 1–17.

Gröning, Gert, and Joachim Wolschke-Bulmahn. *1887–1987. DGGL: Deutsche Gesellschaft für Gartenkunst und Landschaftspflege e.V. Ein Rückblick auf 100 Jahre DGGL.* Berlin, 1987.

———. *Die Liebe zur Landschaft. Teil I. Natur in Bewegung. Zur Bedeutung natur- und freiraumorientierter Bewegungen der ersten Hälfte des 20. Jahrhunderts für die Entwicklung der Freiraumplanung.* Munich, 1986.

———. *Die Liebe zur Landschaft. Teil III. Der Drang nach Osten. Zur Entwicklung der Landespflege im Nationalsozialismus und während des Zweiten Weltkrieges in den "eingegliederten Ostgebieten."* Munich, 1987.

———. *Grüne Biographien. Biographisches Handbuch zur Landschaftsarchitektur des 20. Jahrhunderts in Deutschland.* Berlin, 1997.

———. "Some Notes on the Mania for Native Plants in Germany." *Landscape Journal* 11 (1992): 116–126.

Großheim, Michael. *Ökologie oder Technokratie? Der Konservatismus in der Moderne.* Berlin, 1995.

Gruner, Wolf. "Juden bauen die 'Straßen des Führers'. Zwangsarbeit und Zwangsarbeiterlager für nichtdeutsche Juden im Altreich 1940 bis 1943/44." *Zeitschrift für Geschichtswissenschaft* 44 (1996): 789–808.

Gugerli, David, ed. *Vermessene Landschaften. Kulturgeschichte und technische Praxis im 19. und 20. Jahrhundert.* Zurich, 1999.

Guse, John Charles. "The Spirit of the Plassenburg." Ph. D. Thesis, University of Nebraska at Lincoln, 1981.

Haber, Wolfgang. "Naturschutz und Landschaftspflege—Ursprünge, Gegenwartsprobleme und Zukunftsperspektiven aus naturwissenschaftlicher Sicht." In *Naturschutz- und Landschaftspflegerecht im Wandel, 8. Trierer Kolloquium zum Umwelt- und Technikrecht vom 23. bis 25. September 1992,* ed. Jörg Berkemann et al., 5–27. Heidelberg, 1993.

Haefeli, Ueli. "Luftreinhaltepolitik im Straßenverkehr in den USA, in Deutschland und in der Schweiz. Ein Vergleich zur Entwicklung nach 1945." *Traverse* vol. 6, no. 2 (1999): 171–191.

Hard, Gerhard. *Die "Landschaft" der Sprache und die "Landschaft" der Geographen. Semantische und forschungslogische Studien zu einigen zentralen Denkfiguren in der deutschen geographischen Literatur* (= Colloquium Geographicum 11). Bonn, 1970.

Hård, Mikael. "German Regulation. The Integration of Modern Technology into National Culture." In *The Intellectual Appropriation of Technology. Discourses on Modernity, 1900–1939,* ed. Andrew Jamison and Mikael Hård, 33–67. Cambridge, Mass., 1998.

Harrington, Anne. *Reenchanted Science. Holism in German Culture from Wilhelm II to Hitler.* Princeton, 1996.

Harris, Neil. *Building Lives. Constructing Rites and Passages.* New Haven, Conn., and London, 1999.

Hartmannsgruber, Friedrich. "'...ungeachtet der noch ungeklärten Finanzierung': Finanzplanung und Kapitalbeschaffung für den Bau der Reichsautobahnen 1933–1945." *Historische Zeitschrift* 278 (2004): 625–681.

Hascher, Michael, and Stefan Zeilinger. "Verkehrsgeschichte Deutschlands im 19. und 20. Jahrhundert. Verkehr auf Straßen, Schienen und Binnenwasserstraßen. Ein Literaturüberblick über die jüngsten Forschungen." *Jahrbuch für Wirtschaftsgeschichte* (2001): 165–183.

Haubner, Barbara. *Nervenkitzel und Freizeitvergnügen. Automobilismus in Deutschland 1886–1914.* Göttingen, 1998.

Heckmann-Strohkark, Ingrid. "Der Traum von einer europäischen Gemeinschaft. Die Internationalen Autobahnkongresse 1931 und 1932." In *Die Schweizer Autobahn,* ed. Martin Heller and Andreas Volk, 32–45. Zurich, 1999.

Heinrich-Hampf, Vroni. "Über Gartenidylle und Gartenarchitektur im Dritten Reich." In *Faschistische Architekturen. Planen und Bauen in Europa 1930 bis 1945*, ed. Hartmut Frank, 271–281. Hamburg, 1985.

Heller, Martin and Volk, Andreas, eds. *Die Schweizer Autobahn*. Zurich, 1999.

Henderson, George. "'Landscape is Dead, Long Live Landscape.' A Handbook for Sceptics." *Journal of Historical Geography* 24 (1998): 94–100.

Henning, Hansjoachim. "Kraftfahrzeugindustrie und Autobahnbau in der Wirtschaftspolitik des Nationalsozialismus 1933–1936." *Vierteljahrschrift für Sozial- und Wirtschaftsgeschichte* 65 (1978): 217–242.

Henschel, Volker. "Staat und Verkehr. Motive, Ziele und Mittel der Verkehrspolitik westlicher Industriestaaten seit 1880." In *Einflüsse der Motorisierung auf das Verkehrswesen*, ed. Hans Pohl, 53–76. Stuttgart, 1988.

Herbert, Ulrich, ed. *Wandlungsprozesse in Westdeutschland: Belastung, Integration, Liberalisierung 1945–1980*. Göttingen, 2002.

Herbst, Ludolf. *Das nationalsozialistische Deutschland*. Frankfurt/Main, 1996.

Herf, Jeffrey. *Reactionary Modernism. Technology, Culture, and Politics in Weimar and the Third Reich*. Cambridge, 1984.

———. "Der nationalsozialistische Technikdiskurs. Die deutschen Eigenheiten des reaktionären Modernismus." In Emmerich and Wege, *Technikdiskurs*, 72–93. Stuttgart, 1995.

Hermand, Jost. *Grüne Utopien in Deutschland. Zur Geschichte des ökologischen Bewußtseins*. Frankfurt/Main, 1991.

Hermann Mattern 1902–1971. Gärten, Gartenlandschaften, Häuser. Ausstellung der Akademie der Künste und der Technischen Universität. Berlin vom 17. Oktober bis 17. November 1982. Berlin, 1982.

Herzberg, Marcel. *Raumordnung im nationalsozialistischen Deutschland* (= Dortmunder Materialien zur Raumplanung 25). Dortmund, 1997.

Heskett, John. "Design in Inter-War Germany." In *Designing Modernity. The Arts of Reform and Persuasion 1885–1945. Selections from the Wolfsonian*, ed. Wendy Kaplan, 257–285. New York, 1995.

Heuser, Marie-Luise. "Was grün begann endete blutigrot. Von der Naturromantik zu den Reagrarisierungs- und Entvölkerungsplänen der SA und SS." In *Industrialismus und Ökoromantik. Geschichte und Perspektiven der Ökologisierung*, ed. Dieter Hassenpflug, 43–64. Wiesbaden, 1991.

Hitzer, Hans. *Die Straße. Vom Trampelpfad zur Autobahn*. Munich, 1971.

Hochman, Elaine S. *Architects of Fortune. Mies van der Rohe and the Third Reich*. New York, 1989.

Höfig, Carolyn. "Engineered Like No Other. German Society and the Automobile." In *Breakdown, Breakup, Breakthrough. Germany's Difficult Passage to Modernity*, ed. Carl F. Lankowski, 155–174. New York, 1999.

Hölz, Christoph. "Verkehrsbauten." In *Bauen im Nationalsozialismus. Bayern 1933–1945. Ausstellung des Architekturmuseums der Technischen Universität München und des Münchner Stadtmuseums*, ed. Winfried Nerdinger, 54–97. Munich, 1993.

Hoskins, W.G. *The Making of the English Landscape. With an Introduction and Commentary by Christopher Taylor*. London, 1988.

Hottenträger, Grit. "New Flowers—New Gardens. Residential Gardens Designed by Karl Foerster, Hermann Mattern and Herta Hammerbacher (1928–c. 1943)." *Journal of Garden History* 12 (1992): 207–227.

Howard, Peter. "Painter's Preferred Places." *Journal of Historical Geography* 11 (1985): 138–154.

Hughes, Thomas P. "Ideologie für Ingenieure." *Technikgeschichte* 48 (1981): 308–323.

Hünemörder, Kai F. *Die Frühgeschichte der globalen Umweltkrise und die Formierung der deutschen Umweltpolitik (1950–1973).* Stuttgart, 2004.

Hunt, John Dixon. "Arrêts de hasard sur l'autoroute." In *Autoroute et Paysages,* ed. Christian Leyrit and Bernard Lassus, 85–99. Paris, 1994.

Hunter, James M. *Perspectives on Ratzel's Political Geography.* Lanham etc., 1983.

Irwin, William. *The New Niagara. Tourism, Technology, and the Landscape of Niagara Falls, 1776–1917.* University Park, PA, 1996.

Jackson, John Brinckerhoff. *A Sense of Place, A Sense of Time.* New Haven and London, 1994.

——. *Discovering the Vernacular Landscape.* New Haven and London, 1984.

Jakle, John. "Landscapes Redesigned for the Automobile." In *The Making of the American Landscape,* ed. Michael Conzen, 293–310. Boston 1990.

Jakob, Thomas. *Zur Geschichte der Landschaftsarchitektur an der TU München-Weihenstephan. Eine Dokumentation anläßlich des 40jährigen Jubiläums der Studienrichtung Landschaftsarchitektur 1996* (= Schriftenreihe des Lehrstuhls für Landschaftsarchitektur und Entwerfen der TU München-Weihenstephan, ed. C. Valentien, 3). Freising-Weihenstephan, 1998.

Jarausch, Konrad H. *The Unfree Professions. German Lawyers, Teachers and Engineers, 1900–1950.* New York, and Oxford, 1990.

——. and Hannes Siegerist, eds. *Amerikanisierung und Sowjetisierung in Deutschland 1945–1970.* Frankfurt, am Main and New York, 1997.

Jay, Martin. "Vision in Context. Reflections and Refractions." In *Vision in Context. Historical and Contemporary Perspectives on Sight,* ed. Teresa Brennan and Jay Martin. New York and London, 1996.

Jefferies, Matthew. "Heimatschutz. Environmental Activism in Wilhelmine Germany." In *Green Thought in German Culture. Historical and Contemporary Perspectives,* ed. Colin Riordan, 43–54. Cardiff, 1997.

Joerges, Bernward. "Brücken, Busse und andere Verkehrsteilnehmer—Zur Repräsentation und Wirkung städtischer Artefakte." In *Technik und Gesellschaft* 10, ed. Gert Schmidt, 197–218. Frankfurt, and New York, 1999.

——. "Do Politics Have Artefacts?" *Social Studies of Science* 29 (1999): 411–431.

Jones, Caroline A. and Peter Galison, with Amy Slaton, eds. *Picturing Science, Producing Art.* New York, 1998.

Josephson, Paul, and Thomas Zeller. "The Transformation of Nature under Hitler and Stalin." In *Science and Ideology. A Comparative History,* ed. Mark Walker, 124–155. London and New York, 2003.

Kaftan, Kurt. *Der Kampf um die Autobahnen. Geschichte und Entwicklung des Autobahngedankens in Deutschland von 1907–1935 unter Berücksichtigung ähnlicher Pläne und Bestrebungen im übrigen Europa.* Berlin, 1955.

Kamper, Klaus. *Streitobjekt Autobahn. Bürger gegen DuBoDo.* Bochum, 1985.

Kaufmann, Stefan, ed. *Ordnungen der Landschaft. Natur und Raum technisch und symbolisch entwerfen* (= Identitäten und Alteritäten 12), Würzburg, 2002.

Keitz, Christine. *Reisen als Leitbild. Die Entstehung des modernen Massentourismus in Deutschland.* Munich, 1997.

Kemp, Louis Ward. "Aesthetes and Engineers. The Occupational Ideology of Highway Design." *Technology and Culture* 27 (1986): 759–797.

Kerbs, Diethart and Jürgen Reulecke. *Handbuch der deutschen Reformbewegungen 1880–1933.* Wuppertal, 1998.

Kershaw, Ian. *The "Hitler Myth:" Image and Reality in the Third Reich.* Oxford, 1987.

———. *The Nazi Dictatorship: Problems and Perspectives of Interpretation.* 4th ed. London, 2000.

———. *Hitler, 1889–1936. Hubris.* Oxford, 1998.

Kittler, Friedrich. "Auto Bahnen." In Emmerich and Wege, *Technikdiskurs*, 114–122.

Klemperer, Victor. *I Shall Bear Witness. The Diaries of Victor Klemperer.* Abridged and translated by Martin Chalmers. London, 1998.

Klenke, Dietmar. *"Freier Stau für freie Bürger." Die Geschichte der bundesdeutschen Verkehrspolitik.* Darmstadt, 1995.

———. "Autobahnbau und Naturschutz in Deutschland. Eine Liaison von Nationalpolitik, Landschaftspflege und Motorisierungsvision bis zur ökologischen Wende der siebziger Jahre." In *Politische Zäsuren und gesellschaftlicher Wandel im 20. Jahrhundert. Regionale und vergleichende Perspektiven*, ed. Matthias Frese and Michael Prinz, 465–498. Paderborn, 1996.

———. *Bundesdeutsche Verkehrspolitik und Motorisierung. Konfliktträchtige Weichenstellungen in den Jahren des Wiederaufstiegs* (=Zeitschrift für Unternehmensgeschichte, Beiheft 79). Stuttgart, 1993.

———. "Die deutsche Katastrophe und das Auto. Zur 'Heils'geschichte eines nationalen Kultobjekts in den Jahren des Wiederaufstiegs." In *Moderne Zeiten. Technik und Zeitgeist im 19. und 20. Jahrhundert*, ed. Ilona Stölken-Fitschen and Michael Salewski, 157–173. Stuttgart, 1994.

Klepsch, Thomas. *Nationalsozialistische Ideologie. Eine Beschreibung ihrer Struktur vor 1933.* Münster, 1990.

Kloepfer, Michael. *Zur Geschichte des deutschen Umweltrechts* (= Schriften zum Umweltrecht 50). Berlin, 1994.

Klueting, Edeltraud, ed. *Antimodernismus und Reform. Zur Geschichte der deutschen Heimatbewegung.* Darmstadt, 1991.

Knaut, Andreas. "Ernst Rudorff und die Anfänge der deutschen Heimatbewegung." In Klueting, *Antimodernismus und Reform*, 20–49.

———. *Zurück zur Natur! Die Wurzeln der Ökologiebewegung.* Greven, 1993.

König, Wolfgang. *Bahnen und Berge. Verkehrstechnik, Tourismus und Naturschutz in den Schweizer Alpen 1870–1939.* Frankfurt, and New York, 2000.

Konold, Werner ed., *Naturlandschaft-Kulturlandschaft. Die Veränderung der Landschaften nach der Nutzbarmachung durch den Menschen.* Landsberg, 1996.

Kopper, Christopher. "Modernität oder Scheinmodernität nationalsozialistischer Herrschaft. Das Beispiel der Verkehrspolitik." In *Von der Aufgabe der Freiheit. Politische Verantwortung und bürgerliche Gesellschaft im 19. und 20. Jahrhundert. Festschrift für Hans Mommsen,* ed. Christian Jansen, Lutz Niethammer, and Bernd Weisbrod, 399–411. Berlin, 1995.

———. *Handel und Verkehr im 20. Jahrhundert.* Munich, 2002.

Körner, Stefan. *Der Aufbruch der modernen Umweltplanung in der nationalsozialistischen Landespflege* (= Beiträge zur Kulturgeschichte der Natur 1). Berlin, 1995.

Kornrumpf, Martin. *HAFRABA e.V. Deutsche Autobahn-Planung 1926–1934.* Bonn, 1990.

Kos, Wolfgang, ed. *Die Eroberung der Landschaft. Semmering, Rax, Schneeberg. Katalog zur Niederösterreichischen Landesausstellung Schloss Gloggnitz 1992.* Vienna, 1992.

———. *Über den Semmering. Kulturgeschichte einer künstlichen Landschaft.* Vienna, 1984.

Koshar, Rudy. *German Travel Cultures.* Oxford/New York, 2000.

———. *Germany's Transient Paths. Preservation and National Memory in the Twentieth Century.* Chapel Hill and London, 1998.

Kuhm, Klaus. *Moderne und Asphalt. Die Automobilisierung als Prozess technologischer Innovation und sozialer Vernetzung* (= Stadt, Raum und Gesellschaft 9). Pfaffenweiler, 1997.

Kühn, Herbert, ed. *Strassenforschung. 50 Jahre Forschungsgesellschaft für das Straßenwesen 1924–1974.* Bonn-Bad Godesberg, 1974.

Kühne, Thomas. "Massenmotorisierung und Verkehrspolitik im 20. Jahrhundert. Technikgeschichte als politische Sozial- und Kulturgeschichte." *Neue Politische Literatur* 41 (1996): 196–229.

Küppers, Günter, Peter Lundgreen, and Peter Weingart. *Umweltforschung—die gesteuerte Wissenschaft? Eine empirische Studie zum Verhältnis von Wissenschaftsentwicklung und Wissenschaftspolitik.* Frankfurt/Main, 1978.

Küster, Hansjörg. *Geschichte der Landschaft in Mitteleuropa. Von der Eiszeit bis zur Gegenwart.* Munich, 1995.

Laak, Dirk van. *Weiße Elefanten. Anspruch und Scheitern technischer Großprojekte im 20. Jahrhundert.* Stuttgart, 1999.

Lane, Barbara Miller. *Architecture and Politics in Germany, 1918–1945.* Cambridge, Mass., 1985.

Lärmer, Karl. *Autobahnbau in Deutschland. Zu den Hintergründen.* East Berlin, 1975.

Lash, Scott, and John Urry. *Economies of Signs and Space.* London, 1994.

Latour, Bruno. *Aramis or the Love of Technology.* Cambridge, Mass., 1996.

Lay, Maxwell G. *Geschichte der Straße. Vom Trampelpfad zur Autobahn.* Frankfurt/Main 1994.

Lekan, Thomas M. "Regionalism and the Politics of Landscape Preservation in the Third Reich." *Environmental History* 4 (1999): 384–404.

——. *Imagining the Nation in Nature: Landscape Preservation and German Identity, 1885–1945.* Cambridge, Mass., 2004.

——. and Thomas Zeller (eds.), *Germany's Nature: Cultural Landscapes and Environmental History.* New Brunswick, New Jersey, 2005.

Lenk, Hans. "Der Macher der Natur? Über operativistische Fehldeutungen von Naturbegriffen der Neuzeit." In *Natur als Gegenwelt. Beiträge zur Kulturgeschichte der Natur,* ed. Götz Großklaus and Ernst Oldemeyer, 59–86. Karlsruhe, 1983.

Lenz, Gerhard. *Verlusterfahrung Landschaft. Über die Herstellung von Raum und Umwelt im mitteldeutschen Industriegebiet seit der Mitte des neunzehnten Jahrhunderts.* Frankfurt and New York, 1999.

Leonhard, Martin. *Umweltverbände. Zur Organisation von Umweltschutzinteressen in der Bundesrepublik Deutschland.* Opladen, 1986.

Lewis, Tom. *Divided Highways. Building the Interstate Highways, Transforming American Life.* New York, 1997.

Linse, Ulrich. *Ökopax und Anarchie. Eine Geschichte der ökologischen Bewegungen in Deutschland.* Munich, 1986.

——. et al. *Von der Bittschrift zur Platzbesetzung. Konflikte um technische Großprojekte. Laufen, Walchensee, Wyhl, Wackersdorf.* Berlin and Bonn, 1988.

Lippert, Frank. *Lastkraftwagenverkehr und Rationalisierung in der Weimarer Republik. Technische und ökonomische Aspekte fertigungsstruktureller und logistischer Wandlungen in den 1920er Jahren.* Frankfurt/Main, 1995.

Livingstone, David. *The Geographical Tradition.* Oxford, 1992.

Lorenz, Armin. "Straße und Umwelt im Wandel." In *150 Jahre Oberste Baubehörde im Bayerischen Staatsministerium des Innern,* 63–68. Munich, 1980.

Louter, David. "Glaciers and Gasoline. The Making of a Windshield Wilderness, 1900–1915." In *Seeing and Being Seen. Tourism in the American West,* ed. David Wrobel, 240–270. Lawrence, Kan., 2001.

Ludwig, Karl-Heinz. "Politische Lösungen für technische Innovationen 1933–1945. Eine antitechnische Mobilisierung, Ausformung und Instrumentalisierung der Technik." *Technikgeschichte* 62 (1995): 333–344.

——. ed. *Technik, Ingenieure und Gesellschaft. Geschichte des Vereins der Deutschen Ingenieure.* Düsseldorf, 1981.

——. *Technik und Ingenieure im Dritten Reich.* Düsseldorf, 1979 [orig. 1974].

Maase, Kaspar. *Grenzenloses Vergnügen. Der Aufstieg der Massenkultur 1850–1970.* Frankfurt/Main, 1997.

Mäding, Heinrich. *Infrastrukturplanung im Verkehrs- und Bildungssektor. Eine vergleichende Untersuchung zum gesamtstaatlichen Planungsprozeß in der Bundesrepublik Deutschland.* Baden-Baden, 1978.

Maier, Helmut. "Kippenlandschaft, 'Wasserkrafttaumel' und Kahlschlag. Anspruch und Wirklichkeit nationalsozialistischer Naturschutz- und Energiepolitik." In *Umweltgeschichte,* ed. Bayerl, Fuchsloch, Meyer, 247–266.

——. "Nationalsozialistische Technikideologie und die Politisierung des 'Technikerstandes.' Fritz Todt und die Zeitschrift 'Deutsche Technik.'" In *Technische Intelligenz und "Kulturfaktor Technik". Kulturvorstellungen von Technikern und Ingenieuren zwischen Kaiser-*

reich und früher Bundesrepublik Deutschland, ed. Burkhard Dietz, Michael Fessner, and Helmut Maier, 253–268. Münster, 1996.

———. "'Unter Wasser und unter die Erde'. Die süddeutschen und alpinen Wasserkraftprojekte des Rheinisch-Westfälischen Elektrizitätswerks (RWE) und der Natur- und Landschaftsschutz während des 'Dritten Reiches.'" In *Die Veränderung der Kulturlandschaft. Nutzungen-Sichtweisen-Planungen,* ed. Günter Bayerl and Torsten Meyer, 139–175. Münster and New York, 2003.

———. "'Weiße Kohle' versus Schwarze Kohle. Naturschutz und Ressourcenschonung als Deckmantel nationalsozialistischer Energiepolitik." *WerkstattGeschichte* 3 (1992): 33–38.

Margedant, Udo. "Entwicklung des Umweltbewußtseins in der Bundesrepublik Deutschland." *Aus Politik und Zeitgeschichte* B 29 (1987): 15–28.

Markowitz, Irene. "Ausblicke in die Landschaft." In *"Landschaft" und Landschaften im 18. Jahrhundert. Tagung der Deutschen Gesellschaft für die Erforschung des 18. Jahrhunderts, Herzog-August-Bibliothek Wolfenbüttel 20. bis 23. November 1991,* ed. Heike Wunderlich, 121–155. Heidelberg, 1995.

Marx, Leo. "Environmental Degradation and the Ambiguous Role of Science and Technology." In *Earth, Air, Fire, Water. Humanistic Studies of the Environment,* ed. Jill Ker Conway, Kenneth Keniston, and Leo Marx, 320–338. Amherst, Mass., 1999.

———. "The American Ideology of Space." In *Denatured Visions. Landscape and Culture in the Twentieth Century,* ed. Stuart Wrede and William Howard Adams, 62–78. New York, 1991.

———. *The Machine in the Garden. Technology and the Pastoral Ideal in America.* New York, 1964.

Matless, David. *Landscape and Englishness.* London, 1998.

Mauch, Christof, and Thomas Zeller (eds.), *The World Beyond the Windshield: Driving and the Experience of Landscape in 20th Century Europe and America.* Athens, Ohio, 2007.

McNeill, John R. *The Mountains of the Mediterranean World.* New York, 1992.

———. *Something New Under the Sun. An Environmental History of the Twentieth-Century World* (New York/London, 2000).

McShane, Clay. *Down the Asphalt Path. The Automobile and the American City.* New York, 1994.

Mehrtens, Herbert. "Kollaborationsverhältnisse. Natur- und Technikwissenschaften im NS-Staat und ihre Historie." In *Medizin, Naturwissenschaft, Technik und Nationalsozialismus. Kontinuitäten und Diskontinuitäten,* ed. Christoph Meinel and Peter Voswinckel, 13–32. Stuttgart, 1994.

Merki, Christoph Maria. "Die verschlungenen Wege der modernen Verkehrsgeschichte." *Schweizerische Zeitschrift für Geschichte* 45 (1995): 444–457.

———. "Unterwegs in unwegsamem Gelände. Historische Straßenverkehrsforschung in der Schweiz." *Traverse* 6/2 (1999): 37–54.

Mielke, Hans-Jürgen. *Die Autobahn Berlin-Helmstedt. Über 160 km Langeweile?* Berlin, 1984.

Mierzejewski, Alfred C. *The Most Valuable Asset of the Reich. A History of the German Railway Company.* Vol. 1: 1920–1932. Chapel Hill and London, 1999.

———. *The Most Valuable Asset of the Reich. A History of the German Railway Company.* Vol. 2: 1933–1945. Chapel Hill and London, 2000.

Mitchell, Don. *Cultural Geography. A Critical Introduction.* Oxford and Malden, Mass., 2000.

Mitchell, Sandra D. "The Superorganism Metaphor. Then and Now." In *Biology as Society. Society as Biology. Metaphors,* ed. Sabine Maasen, Everett Mendelsohn, and Peter Weingart, 231–247. Dordrecht, 1995.

Mitchell, W.J.T. *Landscape and Power.* Chicago, 1994.

Mock, Wolfgang. *Technische Intelligenz im Exil. Vertreibung und Emigration deutschsprachiger Ingenieure nach Großbritannien 1933 bis 1945.* Düsseldorf, 1986.

Moeller, Robert G. "War Stories. The Search for a Usable Past in the Federal Republic of Germany." *American Historical Review* 101 (1996): 1008–1048.

Mom, Gijs. "Das 'Scheitern' des frühen Elektromobils (1895–1925). Versuch einer Neubewertung." *Technikgeschichte* 64 (1997): 269–285.

Mommsen, Hans, and Manfred Grieger. *Das Volkswagenwerk und seine Arbeiter im Dritten Reich.* Düsseldorf, 1996.

Mörtzschky, Norman. "Wer profitierte vom plötzlichen Tod des Reichsministers für Bewaffnung und Munition, Dr. Fritz Todt?" *Historische Mitteilungen der Ranke-Gesellschaft* 11 (1998): 78–100.

Möser, Kurt. "World War I and the Creation of Desire for Automobiles in Germany." In *Getting and Spending. European and American Consumer Societies in the Twentieth Century,* ed. Susan Strasser, Charles McGovern, and Matthias Judt, 195–222. Cambridge, 1998.

———. *Geschichte des Autos.* Frankfurt and New York, 2002.

Mosse, George L. "War and the Appropriation of Nature." In *Germany in the Age of Total War. Essays in Honour of Francis Carsten,* ed. Volker Berghahn and Martin Kitchen, 102–122. London and Towota, NJ, 1981.

Mrass, Walter. *Die Organisation des staatlichen Naturschutzes und der Landschaftspflege im Deutschen Reich und in der Bundesrepublik Deutschland seit 1935, gemessen an den Aufgabenstellungen einer modernen Industriegesellschaft.* Stuttgart, 1970.

Mücke, Hubert. *Historische Geographie als lebensweltliche Umweltanalyse. Studium zum Grenzbereich zwischen Geographie und Geschichtswissenschaft.* Frankfurt/Main, 1988.

Muir, Richard. *Approaches to Landscape.* Lanham, 1999.

Müller, Gerhard H. *Friedrich Ratzel (1844–1904). Naturwissenschaftler, Geograph, Gelehrter. Neue Studien zu Leben und Werk und sein Konzept der "Allgemeinen Biogeographie."* Stuttgart, 1996.

Müller, Gunter. "Zur Geschichte des Wortes Landschaft." In *"Landschaft" als interdisziplinäres Forschungsproblem. Vorträge und Diskussionen des Kolloquiums am 7./8. November 1975 in Münster* (= Veröffentlichungen des Provinzialinstituts für westfälische Landes- und Volksforschung des Landschaftsverbandes Westfalen-Lippe Reihe 1, Heft 21), ed. Alfred Hartlieb von Wallthor and Heinz Quirin, 4–12. Münster, 1977.

Müller, Uwe. *Infrastrukturpolitik in der Industrialisierung. Der Chauseebau in der preußischen Provinz Sachsen und dem Herzogtum Braunschweig vom Ende des 18. Jahrhunderts bis in die siebziger Jahre des 19. Jahrhunderts* (= Schriften zur Wirtschafts- und Sozialgeschichte 57). Berlin, 2000.

Museum für Verkehr und Technik, ed. *Ich diente nur der Technik. Sieben Karrieren zwischen 1940 und 1950.* Berlin, 1995.

Nerdinger, Winfried, ed. *Architekturschule München 1868–1993. 125 Jahre TU München.* Munich, 1993.

Niemann, Harry, and Armin Hermann, eds. *100 Jahre Lkw. Geschichte und Zukunft des Nutzfahrzeugs* (= Stuttgarter Tage zur Automobil- und Unternehmensgeschichte. Eine Veranstaltung des Daimler-Benz Archivs, Stuttgart, 3). Stuttgart, 1997.

——. *Die Entwicklung der Motorisierung im Deutschen Reich und den Nachfolgestaaten* (= Stuttgarter Tage zur Automobil- und Unternehmensgeschichte 2). Stuttgart, 1995.

——. *Geschichte der Straßenverkehrssicherheit im Wechselspiel zwischen Fahrzeug, Fahrbahn und Mensch* (= Stuttgarter Tage zur Automobil- und Unternehmensgeschichte 4). Bielefeld, 1999.

Nietfeld, Annette. *Reichsautobahn und Landschaftspflege. Landschaftspflege im Nationalsozialismus am Beispiel der Reichsautobahnen* (= Werkstattberichte des Instituts für Landschaftsökonomie 13). Berlin, 1985.

Nipperdey, Thomas. *Deutsche Geschichte 1866–1918.* Vol. 1: Arbeitswelt und Bürgergeist. Munich, 1990.

Nolan, Mary. *Visions of Modernity. American Business and the Modernization of Germany.* New York, 1994.

Noseda, Irma. "Die Eroberung der Schweizer Talböden." *Werk, Bauen+Wohnen* 1/2 (2000): 34–41.

Novak, Barbara. *Nature and Culture. American Landscape and Painting 1825–1875.* New York and Oxford, 1995.

Nye, David. *American Technological Sublime.* Cambridge, Mass., and London, 1994.

——. ed. *Technologies of Landscape. From Reaping to Recycling.* Amherst, Mass., 1999.

O'Connell, Sean. *The Car and British Society. Class, Gender and Motoring 1896–1939.* Manchester and New York, 1998.

Olwig, Kenneth R. "Recovering the Substantive Nature of Landscape." *Annals of the Association of American Geographers* 86 (1996): 630–653.

——. *Landscape, Nature, and the Body Politic: From Britain's Renaissance to America's New World* (Madison, 2002).

Osterhammel, Jürgen. "Die Wiederkehr des Raumes. Geopolitik, Geohistoire und historische Geographie." *Neue Politische Literatur* 43 (1998): 374–397.

Ott, Konrad et al. "Über die Anfänge des Naturschutzgedankens in Deutschland und den USA im 19. Jahrhundert." In *Naturnutzung und Naturschutz in der europäischen Rechts- und Verwaltungsgeschichte* (= Jahrbuch für europäische Verwaltungsgeschichte 11), ed. Erk Volkmar Heyen, 1–56. Baden-Baden, 1999.

Otto, Christian F. "Modern Environment and Historical Continuity. The Heimatschutz Discourse in Germany." *Art Journal* 43 (1983): 148–157.

Overy, Richard J. "Cars, Roads, and Economic Recovery in Germany, 1932–1938." In Richard J. Overy, *War and Economy in the Third Reich,* 68–89. Oxford, 1994.

——. "Heralds of Modernity. Cars and Planes from Invention to Necessity." In *Fin de Siècle and its Legacy,* ed. Mikuláš Teich and Roy Porter, 54–79. Cambridge, 1990.

Patton, Phil. *Open Road. A Celebration of the American Highway.* New York, 1986.

Peters, Tom F. *Building the Nineteenth Century.* Cambridge, Mass., 1996.

Peukert, Detlev J.K. *The Weimar Republic: The Crisis of Classical Modernity.* Trans. Richard Deveson. New York, 1989.

Pfister, Christian. "Landschaftsveränderung und Identitätsverlust. Akzentverschiebungen in der Modernisierungskritik von der Jahrhundertwende bis um 1970." *Traverse* 4/2 (1997): 49–68.

Picon, Antoine. *L'Invention de l'ingénieur moderne. L'École des ponts et chaussées 1747–1851.* Paris, 1992.

Piepmeier, Rainer. "Das Ende der ästhetischen Kategorie 'Landschaft'. Zu einem Aspekt neuzeitlichen Naturverhältnisses." *Westfälische Forschungen* 30 (1980): 8–46.

——. "Landschaft." In *Historisches Wörterbuch der Philosophie*, vol. 5, ed. Joachim Ritter and Karlfried Gründer, cols. 11–28. Basel and Stuttgart, 1980.

Pierre, Francis. *Faszination Baumaschinen. Straßenbau-Geschichte.* Isernhagen, 1998.

Pohl, Manfred. *Die Strabag 1923 bis 1998.* Munich and Zurich, 1998.

——. *Philipp Holzmann. Geschichte eines Bauunternehmens 1849–1999.* Munich, 1999.

Polónyi, Stefan. "Der Einfluß des Wissenschaftsverständnisses auf das Konstruieren." In *Zur Geschichte des Konstruierens*, ed. Rainer Graefe, 237–245. Stuttgart 1989.

Porter, Theodore M. *Trust in Numbers. The Pursuit of Objectivity in Science and Public Life.* Princeton/NJ, 1995.

Potthast, Thomas. *Die Evolution und der Naturschutz. Zum Verhältnis von Evolutionsbiologie, Ökologie und Naturethik.* Frankfurt and New York, 1999.

Prinz, Michael. "Die soziale Funktion moderner Elemente in der Gesellschaftspolitik des Nationalsozialismus. In *Nationalsozialismus und Modernisierung*, ed. Michael Prinz and Rainer Zitelmann, 297–327. Darmstadt, 1991.

Proctor, Robert N. *The Nazi War on Cancer.* Princeton, 1999.

Puschner, Uwe, Walter Schmitz, and Justus H. Ulbricht, eds. *Handbuch zur "Völkischen Bewegung" 1871–1918.* Munich, 1999.

Rabinbach, Anson. "The Aesthetics of Production in the Third Reich," *Journal of Contemporary History* 11 (1976): 43–74.

——. "Nationalsozialismus und Moderne. Zur Technik-Interpretation im Dritten Reich." In Emmerich and Wege, *Technikdiskurs*, 94–113.

Radde, Bruce. *The Merritt Parkway.* New Haven, Conn., 1993.

Radkau, Joachim. *Natur und Macht. Eine Weltgeschichte der Umwelt.* Munich, 2000.

——. *Technik in Deutschland. Vom 18. Jahrhundert bis zur Gegenwart.* Frankfurt/Main, 1989.

——. "Technik- und Umweltgeschichte." *Geschichte in Wissenschaft und Unterricht* 48 (1997): 479–497, 50 (1999): 250–258, 356–384.

——. "Unausdiskutiertes in der Umweltgeschichte." In *Was ist Gesellschaftsgeschichte? Positionen, Themen, Analysen*, ed. Manfred Hettling et al., 45–53. Munich, 1991.

———. "Was ist Umweltgeschichte?" In *Umweltgeschichte. Umweltverträgliches Wirtschaften in historischer Perspektive* (= Geschichte und Gesellschaft Sonderheft 15), ed. Werner Abelshauser, 11–28. Göttingen, 1994.

Rasp, Hans-Peter. *Eine Stadt für tausend Jahre. München—Bauten und Projekte für die Hauptstadt der Bewegung.* Munich, 1981.

Reichel, Peter. *Der schöne Schein des Dritten Reiches. Faszination und Gewalt des Faschismus.* Munich and Vienna, 1991.

Reininghaus, Wilfried and Karl Teppe, eds. *Verkehr und Region im 19. und 20. Jahrhundert. Westfälische Beispiele* (= Westfälisches Institut für Regionalgeschichte, Landschaftsverband Westfalen-Lippe Münster, Forschungen zur Regionalgeschichte 29). Paderborn, 1999.

Renneberg, Monika and Mark Walker (eds.), *Science, Technology, and National Socialism.* Cambridge, 1994.

Ricken, Herbert. *Der Bauingenieur. Geschichte eines Berufes.* Berlin, 1994.

Riechers, Burkhardt. "Naturschutz im Nationalsozialismus. Versuch einer Skizzierung." *Grüner Weg 31a. Zeitschrift des Studienarchivs Arbeiterkultur und Ökologie, Baunatal* 8 (1994): 11–16.

Rigele, Georg. *Die Großglockner-Hochalpenstraße. Zur Geschichte eines österreichischen Monuments.* Vienna, 1998.

———. *Die Wiener Höhenstrasse. Autos, Landschaft und Politik in den dreißiger Jahren.* Vienna, 1993.

Ritter, Joachim. "Landschaft. Zur Funktion des Ästhetischen in der modernen Gesellschaft." In Joachim Ritter, *Subjektivität.* Frankfurt/Main, 1974, reprint 1989.

Rohde, Heidi. *Transportmodernisierung contra Verkehrsbewirtschaftung. Zur staatlichen Verkehrspolitik gegenüber dem Lkw in den 30er Jahren.* Frankfurt/Main, 1999.

Rohkrämer, Thomas. "Antimodernism, Reactionary Modernism and National Socialism. Technocratic Tendencies in Germany, 1890–1945," *Contemporary European History* 8 (1999): 29–50.

———. *Eine andere Moderne? Zivilisationskritik, Natur und Technik in Deutschland 1880–1933.* Paderborn, 1999.

Rollins, William H. *A Greener Vision of Home. Cultural Politics and Environmental Reform in the German Heimatschutz Movement, 1904–1918.* Ann Arbor, 1997.

———. "Whose Landscape? Technology, Fascism, and Environmentalism on the National Socialist Autobahn." *Annals of the Association of American Geographers* 85 (1995): 494–520.

Rose, Mark H. *Interstate. Express Highway Politics, 1939–1989.* Knoxville/TN, 1990.

———. and Bruce E. Seely. "Getting the Interstate System Built. Road Engineers and the Implementation of Public Policy, 1955–1985." *Journal of Policy History* 2 (1990): 23–55.

Roseman, Mark, ed. *Generations in Conflict. Youth Revolt and Generation Formation in Germany 1770–1968.* Cambridge, 1996.

Rosenstock-Huessy, Eugen. *Out of Revolution. Autobiography of Western Man.* Providence, RI, and Oxford, 1993 (orig. 1938).

Rössler, Mechtild. "'Area Research' and 'Spatial Planning' from the Weimar Republic to the German Federal Republic." In *Science, Technology and National Socialism*, ed. Monika Renneberg and Mark Walker, 126–138. Cambridge, 1994.

——. *Wissenschaft und Lebensraum. Geographische Ostforschung im Nationalsozialismus.* Berlin and Hamburg, 1990.

—— and Sabine Schleiermacher. *Der Generalplan Ost. Aspekte der nationalsozialistischen Planungs- und Vernichtungspolitik.* Berlin, 1993.

Roth, Matthew W. "Mulholland Highway and the Engineering Culture of Los Angeles in the 1920s." *Technology and Culture* 40 (1999): 545–575.

Roth, Roland, and Dieter Rucht, eds. *Neue soziale Bewegungen in der Bundsrepublik Deutschland.* Frankfurt and New York, 1987.

Rothenberger, Karl-Heinz."Autobahnbau in der Pfalz nach dem Zweiten Weltkrieg." *Mitteilungen des Historischen Vereins der Pfalz* 100 (2002): 533–559.

Rubner, Heinrich. *Deutsche Forstgeschichte 1933–1945. Forstwirtschaft, Jagd und Umwelt im NS-Staat.* 2nd ed. St. Katharinen, 1997.

Rümler, Ruprecht. "Zur Entwicklung von Rasenansaaten und ihrer Bedeutung für die ingenieurbiologische Sicherung von Straßenböschungen." Ph.D. dissertation Rheinisch-Westfälische Technische Hochschule Aachen, 1974.

Runge, Karsten. *Die Entwicklung der Landschaftsplanung in ihrer Konstitutionsphase 1935–1973* (= Landschaftsentwicklung und Umweltforschung. Schriftenreihe des Fachbereichs Landschaftsentwicklung der TU Berlin, 73). Berlin, 1990.

Ruppert, Wolfgang. "Das Auto: 'Herrschaft über Raum und Zeit'." In *Fahrrad, Auto, Fernsehschrank. Zur Kulturgeschichte der Alltagsdinge*, ed. Wolfgang Ruppert, 119–161. Frankfurt/Main, 1993.

Sachs, Wolfgang. *Die Liebe zum Automobil. Ein Rückblick in die Geschichte unserer Wünsche.* Reinbek, 1984.

Saldern, Adelheid von. "Cultural Conflicts, Popular Mass Culture and the Question of Nazi Success. The Eilenriede Motorcycle Races, 1924–1939." *German Studies Review* 15 (1992): 317–338.

Salzwedel, Jürgen. "Das Verkehrs- und Nachrichtenwesen. Straßen, Wasserstraßen und Luftverkehr." In *Deutsche Verwaltungsgeschichte, vol. 5, Die Bundesrepublik Deutschland*, ed. Kurt G.A. Jeserich, Hans Pohl, and Georg-Christoph von Unruh, 460–485. Stuttgart, 1987.

Sandgruber, Roman. *Strom der Zeit. Das Jahrhundert der Elektrizität.* Linz, 1992.

Sauer, Walter. "Der Mythos des Naturerlebnisses in der Jugendbewegung." In *Typisch deutsch. Die Jugendbewegung. Beiträge zu einer Phänomengeschichte*, ed. Joachim Knoll and Julius H. Schoeps, 55–70. Opladen, 1988.

Schäfer, Hans-Dietrich. *Das gespaltene Bewußtsein. Über deutsche Kultur und Lebenswirklichkeit 1933–1945.* Munich, 1981.

Schama, Simon. *Landscape and Memory.* New York, 1995.

Scharff, Virginia. *Taking the Wheel. Women and the Coming of the Motor Age.* New York and Toronto, 1991.

Schefold, Klaus, and Alois Neher, eds. *50 Jahre Autobahnen in Baden-Württemberg. Eine Dokumentation im Auftrage des Autobahnamtes Baden-Württemberg.* Stuttgart [1986].

Schiegerl, Gertrud, and Armin Stiegler. "Die Gärten Alwin Seiferts." Diploma thesis, Lehrstuhl für Landschaftsarchitektur und Entwerfen, Technical University Munich-Weihenstephan, 1985.

Schildt, Axel, Detlef Siegfried, and Karl Christian Lammers, eds. *Dynamische Zeiten. Die 60er Jahre in den beiden deutschen Gesellschaften.* Hamburg, 2000.

Schipperges, Heinrich. "Natur." In *Geschichtliche Grundbegriffe. Lexikon zur politisch-sozialen Sprache in Deutschland,* ed. Reinhart Koselleck, Otto Brunner, and Werner Conze, vol. 4, 215–244. Stuttgart, 1978.

Schivelbusch, Wolfgang. *Railway Journey: The Industrialization of Time and Space in the 19th Century.* Berkeley, Calif., 1986.

Schmädicke, Jürgen. "Bessere Straßen braucht das Land. Der deutsche Straßenbau zwischen den Weltkriegen unter den Anforderungen des Lastkraftwagenverkehrs." In Niemann and Hermann, *100 Jahre Lkw,* 356–368.

Schmid, Rainer. *Die Planung der Bundesautobahn von Stuttgart zum westlichen Bodensee.* Göttingen 1972.

Schmidt, Alexander. *Reisen in die Moderne. Der Amerika-Diskurs des deutschen Bürgertums vor dem Ersten Weltkrieg im europäischen Vergleich.* Berlin, 1997.

Schmithüsen, Josef. *Was ist eine Landschaft?* (= Erdkundliches Wissen, Schriftenfolge für Forschung und Praxis 9). Wiesbaden, 1964.

Schmucki, Barbara. "'Verkehrsnot in unseren Städten!' Leitbilder in der Verkehrsplanung Ost- und Westdeutschlands (1945–1990)." *Technikgeschichte* 63 (1996): 321–342.

———. "Automobilisierung. Neuere Forschungen zur Motorisierung." *Archiv für Sozialgeschichte* 35 (1995): 582–597.

———. "Cyborgs unterwegs? Cyborgs und individuelle Mobilität seit dem 19. Jahrhundert." In *Technik und Gesellschaft* 10, ed. Gert Schmidt, 87–119. Frankfurt and New York, 1999.

———. *Der Traum vom Verkehrsfluß. Städtische Verkehrsplanung seit 1945 im deutsch deutschen Vergleich.* Frankfurt and New York, 2001.

———. "Schneisen durch die Stadt—Sinnbild der 'modernen' Stadt. Stadtautobahnen und amerikanisches Vorbild in West- und Ostdeutschland, 1925–1975." *WerkstattGeschichte* 7/21 (1998): 43–63.

Schoenbaum, David. *Hitler's Social Revolution: Class and Status in Nazi Germany 1933–1939.* New York, 1967.

Schultz, Hans-Dietrich. *Die deutschsprachige Geographie von 1800 bis 1970. Ein Beitrag zur Geschichte ihrer Methodologie.* Berlin, 1980.

———. "Land-Volk-Staat. Der geographische Anteil an der 'Erfindung' der Nation." *Geschichte in Wissenschaft und Unterricht* 51 (2000): 4–16.

Schulz, Jürgen. "Raumwissenschaft und Raumplanung als Rahmen der Entwicklung der Profession und der Hochschuldisziplin der Landschaftsplanung." In *Geschichte und Struktur der Landschaftsplanung,* ed. Ulrich Eisel, Stefanie Schultz, 192–246. Berlin, 1991.

Schütz, Erhard. "'… eine glückliche Zeitlosigkeit.' Zeitreise zu den 'Straßen des Führers.'" In *Reisekaltur in Deutschland. Von der Weimarer Republik zum "Dritten Reich,"* ed. Peter J. Brenner, 73–99. Tübingen, 1997.

———. "'… verankert fest im Kern des Bluts.' Die Reichsautobahn—mediale Visionen einer organischen Moderne im 'Dritten Reich.'" In *Faszination des Organischen. Konjunkturen einer Kategorie der Moderne*, ed. Hartmut Eggert, Erhard Schütz, and Peter Sprengel, 231–266. Munich, 1995.

———. "'Jene blaßgrauen Bänder.' Die Reichsautobahn in Literatur und anderen Medien des 'Dritten Reiches.'" *Internationales Archiv für Sozialgeschichte der deutschen Literatur* 18/2 (1993): 76–120.

———. and Eckhard Gruber. *Mythos Reichsautobahn. Bau und Inszenierung der "Straßen des Führers" 1933–1941*. Berlin, 1996.

Schwarz, Angela. "Der Hitler-Mythos aus zeitgenössischer Sicht. Stephen Roberts. 'The Home that Hitler Built.'" *Archiv für Kulturgeschichte* 73 (1991): 469–481.

———. *Die Reise ins Dritte Reich. Britische Augenzeugen im nationalsozialistischen Deutschland (1933–39)* (= Veröffentlichungen des Deutschen Historischen Instituts London, 31). Göttingen and Zurich, 1993.

Schwarze, Thomas. "Landschaft und Regionalbewußtsein—Zur Entstehung und Fortdauer einer territorialbezogenen Reminiszenz." *Berichte zur deutschen Landeskunde* 70 (1996): 413–433.

Scott, James C. *Seeing Like a State. How Certain Schemes to Improve the Human Condition Have Failed*. New Haven, Conn. 1998.

Seely, Bruce. "Der amerikanische Blick auf die deutschen Autobahnen. Deutsche und amerikanische Autobahnbauer 1930–1965." *WerkstattGeschichte* 7/21 (1998): 11–28.

———. "The Scientific Mystique in Engineering: Highway Research in the Bureau of Public Roads, 1918-1940." *Technology and Culture* 25 (1984): 798-831.

———. *Building the American Highway System. Engineers as Policymakers*. Philadelphia, 1987.

Seidler, Franz W. "Der Flugzeugabsturz des Reichsministers Dr. Todt 1942. Attentat oder Unfall?" *Geschichte und Gegenwart* 4 (1985): 213–234.

———. *Die Organisation Todt. Bauen für Staat und Wehrmacht 1938–1945*. Koblenz, 1987.

———. *Fritz Todt. Baumeister des Dritten Reiches*. Berlin, 1986.

Seifert, Manfred. *Kulturarbeit im Reichsarbeitsdienst. Theorie und Praxis nationalsozialistischer Kulturpflege im Kontext historisch-politischer, organisatorischer und ideologischer Einflüsse* (= Internationale Hochschulschriften 196). Münster and New York, 1996.

Semlinger, Franz. *Die Autobahn von Hienberg bis Nürnberg. Bau und Bedeutung 1934 bis heute*. Neunkirchen am Sand, 1998.

Shand, James D. "The Reichsautobahn. Symbol for the Third Reich." *Journal of Contemporary History* 19 (1984): 189–200.

Sieferle, Rolf Peter. "Einleitung. Naturerfahrung und Naturkonstruktion." In *Natur-Bilder. Wahrnehmungen von Natur und Umwelt in der Geschichte*, ed. Rolf Peter Sieferle and Helga Breuninger, 9–18. Frankfurt and New York, 1999.

———. "Entstehung und Zerstörung der Landschaft." In *Landschaft*, ed. Manfred Smuda, 238–265. Frankfurt/Main, 1986.

———. *Fortschrittsfeinde? Opposition gegen Technik und Industrie von der Romantik bis zur Gegenwart*. Munich, 1984.

———. "Heimatschutz und das Ende der romantischen Utopie." *Arch+ 81* (1985): 38–42.

——. *Rückblick auf die Natur. Eine Geschichte des Menschen und seiner Umwelt.* Munich, 1997.

Silverman, Dan P. *Hitler's Economy. Nazi Work Creation Programs, 1933–1936.* Cambridge, Mass., London, 1998.

Smuda, Manfred, ed. *Landschaft.* Frankfurt/Main, 1986.

Snow, William Brewster, ed. *The Highway and the Landscape.* New Brunswick, N.J., 1959.

Söderqvist, Thomas. *The Ecologists. From Merry Naturalists to Saviours of the Nation. A Sociologically Informed Narrative Survey of the Ecologization of Sweden 1895–1975.* Stockholm, 1986.

Soulé, Michael E., and Gary Lease. *Reinventing Nature? Responses to Postmodern Deconstruction.* Washington, DC, and Covelo, CA, 1995.

Speck, Artur. *Via Vita. Lebensgeschichte eines Straßenbauers im Zeitalter des Kraftwagens.* Bad Godesberg, no date.

Speich, Daniel. "Wissenschaftlicher und touristischer Blick. Zur Geschichte der 'Aussicht' im 19. Jahrhundert." *Traverse* 3 (1999): 83–99.

Speitkamp, Winfried. "Denkmalpflege und Heimatschutz in Deutschland zwischen Kulturkritik und Nationalsozialismus." *Archiv für Kulturgeschichte* 70 (1988): 149–193.

Spoerer, Mark. "Die Automobilindustrie im Dritten Reich. Wachstum um jeden Preis?" In *Unternehmen im Nationalsozialismus*, ed. Lothar Gall and Manfred Pohl, 61–72. Munich, 1998.

Steinbacher, Sybille. *"Musterstadt" Auschwitz. Germanisierungspolitik und Judenmord in Oberschlesien.* Munich, 2000.

Steingräber, Erich. *Zweitausend Jahre europäische Landschaftsmalerei.* Munich, 1985.

Sternberger, Dolf. *Panorama oder Ansichten vom 19. Jahrhundert.* Frankfurt/Main, 1974.

Stier, Bernhard. "Auf der Wasserstraße in die Moderne. Der Bau des Neckarkanals im Spannungsfeld von Technik, Ästhetik und Politik 1920–1935." *Zeitschrift für Geschichte des Oberrheins* 143 (1995): 287–351.

Stilgoe, John R. *Metropolitan Corridor. Railroads and the American Scene.* New Haven and London, 1983.

Stine, Jeffrey K., and Joel A. Tarr. "At the Intersection of Histories. Technology and the Environment." *Technology and Culture* 39 (1998): 601–640.

——. and Joel A. Tarr. "Technology and the Environment. The Historian's Challenge." *Environmental History Review* 18 (1994): 1–7.

Stockmann, Dieter. *Strecke 46. Die Reichsautobahn zwischen Spessart und Rhön.* Veitshöchheim, 1999.

Stolz, Michael. "Am Beginn des modernen Straßenbaus—Sächsische Straßenbaupolitik und Straßenbautechnik zur Zeit der Weimarer Republik." *Bautechnik* 75 (1998): 391–402.

Stommer, Rainer, ed. *Reichsautobahn. Pyramiden des Dritten Reiches. Analysen zur Ästhetik eines unbewältigten Mythos.* Marburg, 1982.

Straub, Hans. *Die Geschichte der Bauingenieurkunst. Ein Überblick von der Antike bis in die Neuzeit*, ed. Peter Zimmermann. 4th ed. Basel, Boston, Berlin, 1992.

Strecke, Reinhart. "Prediger, Mathematiker und Architekten. Die Anfänge der preußischen Bauverwaltung und die Verwissenschaftlichung des Bauwesens." In *Mathematisches Calcul und Sinn für Ästhetik. Die preußische Bauverwaltung 1770–1848. Ausstellung des Geheimen Staatsarchivs Preußischer Kulturbesitz in Zusammenarbeit mit der Kunstbibliothek der Staatlichen Museen zu Berlin*, 25–36. Berlin, 2000.

Südbeck, Thomas. *Motorisierung, Verkehrsentwicklung und Verkehrspolitik in der Bundesrepublik Deutschland der 1950er Jahre. Umrisse der allgemeinen Entwicklung und zwei Beispiele. Hamburg und das Emsland* (=Vierteljahrschrift für Sozial- und Wirtschaftsgeschichte, Beiheft 113). Stuttgart, 1994.

Suntum, Ulrich van. *Verkehrspolitik*. Munich, 1986.

Syon, Guillaume de. *Zeppelin! Germany and the Airship, 1900–1939*. Baltimore, 2002.

Szöllösi-Janze, Margit, ed. *Science in the Third Reich*. Oxford and New York, 2001.

Teuteberg, Hans-Jürgen. "Entwicklung, Methoden und Aufgaben der Verkehrsgeschichte." *Jahrbuch für Wirtschaftsgeschichte* (1994): 173–194.

Thompson, George F., ed. *Landscape in America*. Austin, Tex., 1995.

Tobey, Ronald C. *Saving the Prairies. The Life Cycle of the Founding School of American Plant Ecology, 1895–1955*. Berkeley, 1981.

Trepl, Ludwig. *Geschichte der Ökologie. Vom 17. Jahrhundert bis zur Gegenwart*. Frankfurt/Main, 1987.

——. "Ökologie als konservative Naturwissenschaft. Von der schönen Landschaft zum funktionierenden Ökosystem." In *Geographisches Denken*, ed. Ulrich Eisel and Hans-Dietrich Schultz, 467–492 (= Urbs et Regio. Kasseler Schriften zur Geographie und Planung, Sonderband 65/1997). Kassel, 1997.

——. "Was ist Landschaft?" *Der Bürger im Staat* 44 (1994): 2–6.

Trischler, Helmuth, and Hans-Liudger Dienel, eds. *Geschichte der Zukunft des Verkehrs. Verkehrskonzepte von der Frühen Neuzeit bis zum 21. Jahrhundert*. Frankfurt/Main, 1997.

Troitzsch, Ulrich. "Die technikgeschichtliche Entwicklung der Verkehrsmittel und ihr Einfluß auf die Gestaltung der Kulturlandschaft." *Siedlungsforschung. Archäologie-Geschichte-Geographie* 4 (1986): 127–143.

Troll, Carl. "Die geographische Landschaft und ihre Erforschung." *Studium Generale* 3 (1950): 163–181.

Trommer, Gerhard. *Natur im Kopf. Die Geschichte ökologisch bedeutsamer Naturvorstellungen in deutschen Bildungskonzepten*. 2nd ed. Weinheim, 1993.

Trommler, Frank. "Amerikas Rolle im Technikverständnis der Diktaturen." In Emmerich and Wege, *Technikdiskurs*, 159–174.

——. "The Avant-Garde and Technology. Toward Technological Fundamentalism in Turn-of-the-Century Europe." *Science in Context* 8 (1995): 397–416.

Uekötter, Frank. "Confronting the Pitfalls of Current Environmental History. An Argument for an Organisational Approach." *Environment and History* 4 (1998): 31–52.

Urban, Josef. "Die geplante Reichsautobahnbrücke über das Kleinziegenfelder Tal. Zur Geschichte des Natur- und Landschaftsschutzes im Landkreis Lichtenfels." *Vom Main zum Jura* 3 (1986): 59–87.

Urry, John. *Consuming Places*. London, 1995.

Vahrenkamp, Richard. "Der Autobahnbau 1933 bis 1939 und das hessische Autobahnnetz." *Zeitschrift des Vereins für hessische Geschichte und Landeskunde* 109 (2004): 225–266.

Vierhaus, Hans-Peter. *Umweltbewußtsein von oben. Zum Verfassungsgebot demokratischer Willensbildung* (= Schriften zum Umweltrecht 48). Berlin, 1994.

Vierle, Claudia. *Camillo Schneider. Dendrologe und Gartenbauschriftsteller. Eine Studie zu seinem Leben und Werk* (= Materialien zur Geschichte der Gartenkunst 4). Berlin, 1998.

Vincenti, Walter G. *What Engineers Know and How They Know It. Analytical Studies from Aeronautical History.* Baltimore and London, 1990.

Voglmaier, Edelgard. *Hans Grässel: Architekt und städtischer Baubeamter in München 1860–1939.* Munich, 1994.

Vogt, Gunter. *Entstehung und Entwicklung des ökologischen Landbaus im deutschsprachigen Raum.* Bad Dürkheim, 2000.

Voswinckel, Peter. *Arzt und Auto. Das Auto und seine Welt im Spiegel des Deutschen Ärzteblattes von 1907 bis 1975.* Münster, 1981.

Wagner, Arfst. "Anthroposophen und Nationalsozialismus. Probleme der Vergangenheit und Gegenwart." *Flensburger Hefte* 32 (Spring 1991): 16–78.

Walker, Mark. *German National Socialism and the Quest for Nuclear Power, 1939–1949.* Cambridge, 1989.

———, ed., *Science and Ideology. A Comparative History.* London and New York, 2003.

Wamberg, Jacob. "Abandoning Paradise. The Western Pictorial Paradigm Shift around 1420." In Nye, *Technologies of Landscape*, 69–86.

Warnke, Martin. *Politische Landschaft.* Munich, 1992.

Wasser, Bruno. *Himmlers Raumplanung im Osten. Der Generalplan Ost in Polen 1940–1944.* Basel, Berlin, and Boston, 1993.

Weishaupt, Heike. *Die Entwicklung der passiven Sicherheit im Automobilbau von den Anfängen bis 1980 unter besonderer Berücksichtigung der Daimler-Benz AG* (= Wissenschaftliche Schriftenreihe des DaimlerChrysler Konzernarchivs 2). Bielefeld, 1999.

Wengenroth, Ulrich. "Zur Differenz von Wissenschaft und Technik." In *Techcnikentwicklung und Industriearbeit*, ed. Daniel Bieber, 141–151. Frankfurt and New York, 1997.

Werner, Uwe. *Anthroposophen in der Zeit des Nationalsozialismus (1933–1945).* Munich, 1999.

Wessolleck, Winfried. *Die Ökologiebewegung.* Cologne, 1985.

Wettengel, Michael. "Staat und Naturschutz 1906–1945. Zur Geschichte der Staatlichen Stelle für Naturdenkmalpflege in Preußen und der Reichsstelle für Naturschutz." *Historische Zeitschrift* 257 (1993): 355–399.

Wey, Klaus-Georg. *Umweltpolitik in Deutschland. Kurze Geschichte des Umweltschutzes in Deutschland seit 1900.* Opladen, 1982.

Wienecke, Carl. *Entwicklungsgeschichtliche Betrachtung des deutschen Straßenwesens in den Jahren 1871–1945.* Bielefeld, 1956.

White, Richard. "'Are You an Environmentalist or Do You Work for a Living?' Work and Nature." In Cronon, *Uncommon Ground*, 171–185.

———. *The Organic Machine. The Remaking of the Columbia River.* New York, 1995.

Whitlock, F.A. *Death on the Road. A Study in Social Violence.* London, 1971.

Willeke, Stefan. *Die Technokratiebewegung in Nordamerika und in Deutschland zwischen den Weltkriegen. Eine vergleichende Analyse.* Frankfurt/Main, 1995.

Williams, John Alexander. "'The Chords of the German Soul are Tuned to Nature.' The Movement to Preserve the Natural *Heimat* from the Kaiserreich to the Third Reich." *Central European History* 29 (1996): 339–384.

Williams, Rosalind. "Nature Out of Control. Cultural Origins and Environmental Implications of Large Technical Systems." In *Cultures of Control*, ed. Miriam R. Levin, 41–68. Amsterdam, 2000.

Wilson, Alexander. *The Culture of Nature. North American Landscape from Disney to Exxon Valdez.* Cambridge and Oxford, 1992.

Windisch-Hojnacki, Claudia. "Die Reichsautobahn. Konzeption und Bau der RAB, ihre ästhetischen Aspekte sowie ihre Illustration in Malerei, Literatur, Fotografie und Plastik." PhD Dissertation, University of Bonn, 1989.

Winiwarter, Verena. "Alpenblumengrüße." In *Katalog zur Ausstellung "Wo i leb ... Kulturlandschaften in Österreich,"* 87–94. Linz, 1997.

———. *Was ist Umweltgeschichte?* (= Soziale Ökologie 54). Vienna, 1998.

Winner, Langdon A. "Do Artifacts Have Politics?" *Daedalus* 109 (1980): 121–136.

Winter, James. *Secure from Rash Assault. Sustaining the Victorian Environment.* Berkeley, 1999.

Wirth, Wolfgang. "Die Entwicklung der sicherheitsrelevanten Trassierungstechnik für moderne Kfz-Straßen." In *Geschichte der Straßenverkehrssicherheit im Wechselspiel zwischen Fahrzeug, Fahrbahn und Mensch*, ed. Harry Niemann and Armin Hermann, 231–241. Bielefeld, 1999.

Wohl, Robert. *A Passion for Wings. Aviation and the Western Imagination, 1908–1918.* New Haven and London, 1994.

Wolf, Winfried. *Eisenbahn und Autowahn. Personen- und Gütertransport auf Schiene und Straße. Geschichte, Bilanz, Perspektiven.* Hamburg and Zurich, 1992.

Wolschke-Bulmahn, Joachim. *Auf der Suche nach Arkadien. Zu Landschaftsidealen und Formen der Naturaneignung in der Jugendbewegung und ihrer Bedeutung für die Landespflege.* Munich, 1989.

———. "Biodynamischer Gartenbau, Landschaftsarchitektur und Nationalsozialismus." *Das Gartenamt* 42 (1993): 590–595, 638–642.

———. "Political Landscapes and Technology. Nazi Germany and the Landscape Design of the *Reichsautobahnen* (Reich Motor Highways)." *Council of Educators in Landscape Architecture (CELA) Annual Conference Papers* VII (1995): 157–170.

———. *1913–1988. 75 Jahre Bund Deutscher Landschafts-Architekten BDLA, Teil 1. Zur Entwicklung der Interessenverbände der Gartenarchitekten in der Weimarer Republik und im Nationalsozialismus.* Bonn, 1988.

———. "The Ideology of the Nature Garden. Nationalistic Trends in Garden Design in Germany during the Early Twentieth Century." *Journal of Garden History* 12 (1992): 73–80.

———. and Gert Gröning. "Regionalistische Freiraumgestaltung als Ausdruck autoritären Gesellschaftsverständnisses? Ein historischer Versuch." *Kritische Berichte* 1/12 (1984): 5–47.

Woolgar, Steve, and Geoff Cooper. "Do Artefacts Have Ambivalence? Moses's Bridges, Winner's Bridges, and other Urban Legends in S&TS." *Social Studies of Science* 29 (1999): 433–449.

Worster, Donald. *Dust Bowl. The Southern Plains in the 1930s.* Oxford and New York, 1979.

———. *Nature's Economy. A History of Ecological Ideas.* Cambridge, 1985.

Wuhrer, Peter, ed. *Land unter Beton.* Weingarten, 1985.

Yago, Glenn. "Ursprünge der deutschen Autolobby. Zur Motorisierungspolitik im Dritten Reich." *Blätter für deutsche und internationale Politik* 25 (1980): 717–727.

Zanetto, Gabriele, Francesco Vallerani, and Stefano Soriani. *Nature, Environment, Landscape. European Attitudes and Discourses in the Modern Period. The Italian Case, 1920–1970* (= Quaderni del Dipartimento di Geografia 18). Padua, 1996.

Zatsch, Angela. *Staatsmacht und Motorisierung am Morgen des Automobilzeitalters.* Konstanz, 1993.

Zeller, Thomas. "Consuming Landscapes. The View from the Road in Germany and the United States, 1910–1995." *Bulletin of the German Historical Institute Washington, DC,* 32 (Spring 2003): 117–126.

———. "'Ganz Deutschland sein Garten.' Alwin Seifert und die Landschaft des Nationalsozialismus." In *Naturschutz und Nationalsozialismus,* ed. Joachim Radkau and Frank Uekötter, 273–302. Frankfurt and New York, 2003.

———. "'Ich habe die Juden möglichst gemieden.' Ein aufschlußreiches Briefwechsel zwischen Heinrich Wiepking und Alwin Seifert." *Garten + Landschaft. Zeitschrift für Landschaftsarchitektur* no. 8 (1995): 4–5.

———. "Landschaft als Gefühl und Autobahn als Formel. Der Autobahnbau in der frühen Bundesrepublik als Abgrenzungsversuch gegen die 'Straßen Adolf Hitlers.'" *WerkstattGeschichte* 7/21 (1998): 29–41.

———. "Landschaften des Verkehrs. Autobahnen im Nationalsozialismus und Hochgeschwindigkeitsstrecken für die Bahn in der Bundesrepublik." *Technikgeschichte* 64 (1997): 323–340.

———. "Molding the Landscape of Nazi Environmentalism. Alwin Seifert (1890–1972) and the Third Reich." In *How Green Were the Nazis? Nature, Environment and Nation in the Third Reich,* ed. Franz-Josef Brüggemeier, Mark Cioc, and Thomas Zeller. Athens, Ohio, 2005, 147–170.

———. *Straße, Bahn, Panorama. Verkehrswege und Landschaftsveränderung in Deutschland 1930 bis 1990.* Frankfurt/New York, 2002.

———. "'The Landscape's Crown.' Landscape, Perceptions, and Modernizing Effects of the German Autobahn System, 1934 to 1941." In Nye, *Technologies of Landscape,* 218–238.

———. "Weichenstellung. Verkehr als Ordnung und Ausdruck von Freiheit." *Sozialwissenschaftliche Informationen* 25 (1996): 243–249.

Ziegler, Volker. "Il progetto autostradale tedesco fra città e territorio, 1925–1955." *Storia urbana* 26, 3 (2002): 85–120.

Zimmer, Jochen, ed. *"Mit uns zieht die neue Zeit." Die Naturfreunde. Zur Geschichte eines alternativen Verbandes in der Arbeiterkulturbewegung.* Cologne, 1984.

Zorn, Wolfgang. "Idee und Erscheinungsformen des Landschaftsschutzes aus sozial- und wirtschaftshistorischer Sicht." In *Kulturlandschaft in Gefahr,* ed. Peter Cornelius Mayer-Tasch, 23–35. Munich, 1976.

Zschokke, Walter. *Die Strasse in der vergessenen Landschaft. Der Sustenpass.* Zurich, 1997.

——. "Technische Bauten und der gelungene Versuch ihrer Aussöhnung mit der Landschaft." In *Moderne Architektur in Deutschland 1900 bis 1950. Reform und Tradition,* ed. Vittorio Magnago Lampugagni and Romana Schneider, 221–243. Stuttgart, 1992.

——. "Von Schönheit wird nie gesprochen. Alwin Seifert. Vorreiter der landschaftlichen Einbindung von Straßenbauten." *Bauen+Wohnen* 1/2 (2000): 42–46.

INDEX

A

accidents, *see* safety issues
ADAC (German Automobile Club), 222
Adenauer, Konrad, 48, 196
Adorno, Theodor, 185
AEG (Allgemeine Elektrizitäts-Gesellschaft/
   General Electric), 24-5
agriculture, 23, 35, 70, 82-3, 112
Agricultural University (Landwirtschaftliche
   Hochschule), Berlin, 40
alignment, *see* road planning considerations
Allinger, Gustav, 88, 89, 94-6
Alps, 6, 138-42, 167
anthroposophy, 35, 39, 87-8
   Anthroposophical Society, 87
anti-Americanism, 67-9, 166
   see also United States
anti-Semitism, 38, 39, 61, 67-70, 166
   of Henry Ford, 52
anti-totalitarianism, 185, 237
Association of German Engineers (*Verein
   Deutscher Ingenieure*, VDI), 28-9, 66, 79
Association of German Garden Architects
   (*Verband Deutscher Gartenarchitekten*),
   87, 92
Association of German Garden Designers
   (*Verband Deutscher Gartengestalter*), 88
Association of German Landscape
   Architects (*Bund Deutscher Landschafts-
   Architekten*), 40
Association for the Preparation of Reich
   Planning and Regional Planning
   (*Gesellschaft zur Vorbereitung der
   Reichsplanung und Raumordnung*), 56
Association for the Preparation of the
   Reichsautobahn, see Gezuvor
Association Reichsautobahnen, 35-7, 55-9,
   61-2, 98-104
   see also German Reich Railroad
Augsburg, 133
Auschwitz, 154

Austria, 16, 58, 59, 138-42, 156, 159, 188,
   237
autobahn segments:
   Bamburg-Lanzendorf, 112
   Berlin-Magdeburg, 135, 150
   Berlin-Stettin, 135
   Bremen-Lübeck-Hamburg-Frankfurt-
      Basel, 48
   Breslau-Brno-Vienna, 59, 200
   Breslau-Liegnitz, 135
   Cologne-Bonn, 69
   Frankfurt-Cologne, 208-11
   Frankfurt-Darmstadt-Heidelberg, 48,
      57, 59, 130, 135, 141, 149
   Frankfurt/Oder-Posen, 61, 135
   Hamburg-Bremen, 60, 135, 190
   Hamburg-Lübeck, 111, 113
   Kassel-Frankfurt, 195
   Kassel-Siegen-Cologne, 94
   Königsberg-Elbing, 88
   Lanzendorf-Bayreuth-Nuremberg, 150
   Lauterbach-Odelzhausen, 133
   Munich-Austria, 58, 64, 138-42,
      156, 159, 188, 237
   Munich-Garmisch, 153
   Munich-Holzkirchen, 83-4, 86, 98
   Munich-Mangfall Bridge, 135, 139
   Posen-Lodz-Warsaw-Minsk, 114
   Salzburg-Vienna, 59, 141-42
   Stuttgart-Heilbronn, 111
   Stuttgart-Munich, 141
   Ulm-Augsburg, 104
   Ulm-Stuttgart, 148, 185, 195-96
automobile production, 51, 52, 183, 185
autostrada (Italy), 48

B

Baden, 24, 25, 221
Bamberg, 112
Barnard, Egon, 208
barrages, 24-6

Basel, 47-8
Bauch, Werner, 87, 89-90, 157, 165
Bauhaus, 26, 27, 29, 90
Bavaria, 24, 35, 59, 60, 112, 219, 220
Bayerlein, Fritz, 65 fig. 4.1
Bayreuth, 112, 150
Belgium, 136
Bensheim, 48
Bergisches Land, 151
Berlin, 24, 50, 135, 150
Betts, Paul, 236
biodynamic agriculture, 35, 87-8, 97, *see also* anthroposophy
bioengineering (Ingenieurbiologie), 152-56, 170
biology, 145
Black Forest, 13
"blood and soil" (*Blut und Boden*), 70, 171
Bonatz, Paul, 25-6, 30
Bonn, 48, 69
Börner, Holger, 222
"Bornum Circle," 90-1
botany, 34, 37
Bramwell, Anna, 3
Braun-Blanquet, Josias, 145-46, 153, 154
Bremen, 48, 60, 135, 190
Breslau (Wroclaw), 59, 200
bridges, 26, 59, 61, 111, 112-14, 139-40, 162-63, 243
    Inn Bridge, 139
    Lahn Bridge – Hesse, 59
    Mangfall Bridge – Upper Bavaria, 59, 139
Broszat, Martin, 57
Brücke und Straße (Bridge and Road), 210
Brüning, Heinrich, 49
Brünn (Brno), 59
Bundestag, 185
Bundeswehr, 184
Bund Heimatschutz, 28, 29, 33, 35, 111
Bund Naturschutz, 83, 189

C

Central Europe, 14, 165
centralization under the National Socialist regime, 55, 85, 185, 192
Chiemsee Lake, 139, 140, 156
civil engineers, 6, 28, 29
    and the clothoid, 200-07, 216-18
    design and construction of the autobahn, 57, 66-8, 108-09, 114
    in the Federal Republic, 5, 192-7, 200-07, 211-13, 216-18, 236-37,
    and landscape advocates, 99-100, 102-05, 107, 108-09, 116, 129, 137, 143, 153-55, 169, 206, 214
Clements, Frederick, 145

clothoid, 200-07, 236
Cold War, 185
Cologne, 48, 69
communism/Communist Party, 91-2
Comte, Auguste, 145
conservation and conservationists, 6, 22, 70, 97, 109-17, 164-67, 171, 189, 221, 244-45
    see also Heimat and the *Heimatschutz* movement, nature preserves/ nature protection
Conwetz, Hugo, 24
Cosgrove, Denis, 15, 16
cost of construction, *see* economic issues
curvilinear roads, *see* road planning considerations
Czechoslovakia, 59, 186, 200

D

dams, 23, 28
Danzig, 24
Darmstadt, 48
Darré, Richard Walther, 167
Darwin, Charles, 36
Denmark
    motorization rate, 52
Depression, *see* Great Depression
Deutscher Heimatbund, 165-66
Deutsche Straßenliga, 185
Deutsche Technik, *see* German Technology
Deutsche Technik (journal), 66
Deutscher Werkbund, 28, 86
Deutsches Museum, 29
Die Gartenschönheit, 88
Die Ingenieurbauten in ihrer guten Gestaltung (Well- Designed Civil Engineering Works), 28
Die Straße, 60, 63, 133, 134
Dorpmüller, Julius, 51, 56, 59, 101, 103
Dorsch, Xaver, 95, 193
Dresden, 23
Dresdner Bank, 24-5
drivers licenses, 129, 185
Duisburg, 113

E

Eastern Europe, 114
    see also specific countries
ecoforestry, 115
ecology, 82-3, 111-12, 142-46, 170-72, 243-44
economic issues in constructing the autobahnen:
    compensation of landscape advocates, 98-102
    construction costs, 53, 61-2, 163, 201, 205

planting costs, 83, 150-51, 160, 162-63, 208-10
employment and autobahn construction, 1, 50, 59-62, 64
    see also labor issues in building the autobahnen
engineers, see civil engineers
England, see Great Britain
environmental history, 2-3, 6-7, 15, 22-31, 115, 170-71, 244-45
    and relation to history of technology, 15-17, 239-45
Erlangen, 221
Erxleben, Guido, 88, 89, 106, 113
Europe, 2
    European integration, 49
    traffic issues, 47
    see also specific countries
Experience of the Reichsautobahnen, The, 161

F

Feder, Gottfried, 53-5, 66
Federal Ministry of Transportation, 134, 182, 183, 186-92, 193, 196, 204-07, 208, 214, 217, 219-23, 243
    see also Seebohm, Hans-Christoph
Federal Nature Conservation Law (1976), 191
Federal Republic of Germany:
    environmental consciousness, 221, 232
    federalism, 185-87, 190-92
    governance, 185-87
    transportation policy, 185-87, 218-23, 235-36
finances, see economic issues
Fischer, Theodor, 33
Foerster, Karl, 90
forced labor, 60
Ford, Henry, 52
Ford Motor Company, 52
Forstenried Park (Munich), 153-4
Four Year Plan, 54, 69, 163
France, 55, 66, 83
    motorization rate, 52, 184
Franconian Switzerland, 112, 113
Frankfurt, 47-9, 57, 59, 61, 113, 135, 141, 149
freight traffic, 51, 56, 141, 170, 183, 195-96, 199-200, 221, 235
Friedrich, Caspar David, 15
Friends of Nature (*Die Naturfreunde*), 221
Fritzsche, Peter, 171
Fuchs, Carl Johannes, 24
Fürst Pückler Society, 79

G

gardens and garden architecture, 27, 34-5, 39-40, 144, 147, 171
General Motors, 48
Gerlach, Hans, 89, 94, 99
German Automobile Club (*Automobilclub von Deutschland*, AvD), 49
German Council for Land Cultivation (*Deutscher Rat für Landespflege*), 223
German history, 2, 3, 62-3, 67, 85
German Labor Front, 52, 60, 85, 91-2
German National People's Party (*Deutschnationale Volkspartei*), 38
German Physics (*Deutsche Physik*), 241
German Reich Railroad (*Deutsche Reichsbahn*), 49, 51, 52, 55-7, 61, 98-102, 08, 130-31, 162, 168, 188
    Association Reichsautobahnen, 35-7, 55-59, 61-2, 98-104
German Road Building Association (*Deutscher Straßenbauverband*) 48
German Society for Horticulture, 95
German Technology (*Deutsche Technik*), 65-71, 85, 97, 103, 116, 167, 241
German Trade Association, 47
Gestapo, 60
Gezuvor (*Gesellschaft zur Vorbereitung der Reichsautobahn*), 55-6, 114
Giesler, Hermann, 39
glare shields, see safety issues
Goethe, Johann Wolfgang von, 27, 152
Göring, Hermann, 54, 112, 113, 115
Göritz, Hermann, 96
Gräbner, Rudolf Wilhelm, 88
gradient, see road planning considerations
Grässel, Hans, 35
Great Britain, 5, 15, 66, 67, 128, 245
    motorization rate, 52, 184
Great Depression, 35, 49, 50
"Green Charter" of 1961, 189
Gröning, Gert, 4, 171
Großheim, Michael, 67
Gruber, Eckhardt, 4
Guidelines for Building Country Highways (RAL), 204, 205-7

H

Haeckel, Ernst, 36
Hafraba Association, 47-51, 53, 55, 57, 63, 91, 110, 113, 129-30, 134, 169, 226
Hamburg, 47-8, 60, 111, 113, 135, 190
Hammerbacher, Herta, 90
Hannover, 152, 165
Hausendorff, Erhard, 115
Haverbeck, Werner, 81, 84
hedgerows, 82-3, 111-12
Heicke, Carl, 110

Heidelberg, 25-6, 48
   Heidelberg Castle, 26
   Heidelberg University, 26
Heimat and the *Heimatschutz* movement, 21-31, 35-6, 64-5, 70, 79, 81-5, 97, 109, 146, 159, 206, 214
Herf, Jeffrey, 67
Hermand, Jost, 3
Heß, Ilse, 38
Heß, Rudolf, 38, 39, 59, 81, 82
Hesse, 59, 141, 208
Heubling, Wilhelm, 193
hiking, 32-3
   see also Wandervogel movement
Hildebrand, Bruno, 89, 107
Hirsch, Wilhelm, 87, 107-08, 130, 165, 166, 188, 189, 208-11
Hitler, Adolf, 51-3, 55, 56-9, 61, 63, 101, 128, 139, 195
Hoemann, Reinhold, 88, 89, 94, 96, 108, 150-51
Hof, Willy, 47, 51-2, 110
Hofoldinger Forest, 83-4, 139
Hogarth, William, 27
Hoher Meißner mountain, 33
holism, 36, 132, 208; *see also* ecology
Holland, 245
Holzkirchen, 152
Hönig, Eugen, 81
Hoskins, William George, 127
Hübotter, Wilhelm, 88, 106, 152
hydroelectric power, 142, 167
   Laufenburg plant, 24-5, 26, 70

I

industrialization, 24-6, 39
Inn Bridge, 139
Inspector General of the German Roads, 51, 54-9, 80, 86-8, 92-3, 98 , 112-14, 115-17, 129-31, 137, 149-51, 155, 161, 168-69, 185, 1 93
   see also, Todt, Fritz
Irschenberg Mountain, 138-42, 237
Isar River, 32
Italy, 2
   autostrada, 48
   motorization rate, 52

J

Jews:
   as autobahn labor, 61
   engineers, 67
   see also anti-semitism
journalists, 13
Jünger, Ernst, 67
Junge Union, 223

K

Kampenwand mountain, 139
Kampfbund Deutscher Architekten und Ingenieure, 66
Karlsruhe, 25
Kassel, 33, 141, 195
   Kassel conference of 1933, 79, 81-2
Kayser, Hans, 88
Kempff, Wilhelm, 90
Kerrl, Hanns, 114
Kershaw, Ian, 56
Kleinziegenfeld Valley, 112
Klemperer, Victor, 169
Klenke, Dietmar, 182-3, 243
Koester, Hugo, 188, 193, 201, 208
Kollwitz, Käthe, 90
Königsberg, 86, 88
König, Wolfgang, 16
Kopper, Christopher, 51
Koshar, Rudy, 140
Kraft durch Freude, 60
Kraftwerk, 1
Kragh, Gert, 165
Kruedener, Arthur von, 152-3
Kühn, Erich, 165-6
Kulmbach, 112
Kulturarbeiten (Schultze-Naumburg), 26-8, 30
Kultursteppe, 82, 143, 148, 155
Kunde, Hermann, 193, 198, 205-07
Kurz, Otto, 104-05
Küster, Hansjörg, 14

L

Laak, Dirk van, 244
labor issues in building the autobahnen, 60, 61, 163
labor unions, 52
Lammers, Hans Heinrich, 57
Landsberg, 63
landscape (as concept)
   definitions, 5-6, 13-17, 80, 128, 167-68, 242-43
landscape and technology, 14, 16-17, 28, 69-71
landscape and the traveler, 37, 128, 169-70
   see also motorist; visual consumption
landscape advocates in the Third Reich, 22
   compensation, 98-10, 163, 168-69
   relationship with civil engineers: 99-100, 102-05, 107, 108-09, 116, 129, 137, 143, 153-55, 169, 206, 214,
   responsibilities and ideology: 55, 86-7, 98, 102-06, 110, 111-15, 157-61, 164-69,
   and road planning, 129, 131-34, 137, 161-62

selection of, 85-98
landscape architecture, 34-7, 39-41
    in the Federal Republic, 187-92, 207-18
landscape integration, 30-1, 103, 136, 145, 155, 162-64, 169, 188, 198, 211-18, 223, 241, 243
landscape painters/paintings, 13, 15, 16, 25, 64
Landschaft, 13-14, 15
Landstuhl, 184
Lange, Max, 90
Lange, Willy, 146
Langerhans, Oswald, 88
Lanzendorf, 112
large scale technological projects, 16, 24-6, 33, 40-1, 49, 62-5, 69, 241, 244
Laufenburg
    hydroelectric power plant, 24-5, 25, 70
League of German Garden Architects (*Bund Deutscher Gartenarchitekten*), 189-90
Leber, Georg, 219
Léger, Ferdinand, 15
Leibig, Josef, 165, 166
Lindner, Werner, 28-30, 35, 39, 81, 83-4
Lorenz, Hans, 95-6, 150, 189, 197 fig. 7.1, 200-03, 212-16
Lower Saxony, 52, 190, 209
Lübeck, 47-8
Ludwig, Karl-Heinz, 4
Lüneburg Heath, 14

M

Mangfall bridge, 59, 139
Mannheim, 48
mathematics and road planning, 193-207, 218, 236, 242
Mattern, Hermann, 86, 90-5, 168
media, 63-4
    see also propaganda
Mehrtens, Herbert, 106
Menzel, Adolph von, 15
Meyer-Jungclaussen, Hinrich, 88, 103
Mies van der Rohe, Ludwig, 50, 169
Migge, Leberecht, 90, 97
military purpose of the autobahn, 1, 53, 54, 56, 136, 184
military vehicles, 52
Ministry of Transportation, *see* Federal Ministry of Transportation
modernism, 1, 15, 26, 29, 167, 171, 199, 244
    anti-modernism, 23-4
    "reactionary modernism," 67-8
Monet, Claude, 15
Mosel river, 189
Möser, Kurt, 218

Moses, Robert, 240
Mosse, George, 32-3
motorists and motoring adventure, 6, 137, 159, 182, 192, 199, 218, 243-44
    see also visual consumption
motorization rates, 8
    in Germany, 48, 52, 59, 128, 182-84, 196
    comparative countries, 49-50, 52, 184
Müller, Max, 88
Munich, 29, 37-8, 53, 58, 63, 64, 83-4, 86, 98, 133, 138, 153
Münster, 208
Mussolini, Benito, 48

N

National Socialism, 30-1, 36, 155
    administrative structures, 39, 51, 57, 85, 98, 115
    and autobahn propaganda, 1-2, 21, 28, 53, 56, 59, 62-5, 70, 148, 162, 241
    building projects, 41
    Deutsche Technik, 66-71
    and environmental history, 3-5, 115-17, 171-72
    transportation policy, 51-3, 59
    see also NSDAP
National Socialist League of German Technology (*Nationalsozialitscher Bund Deutscher Technik*, NSBDT), 66
native flora and nativeness (*bodenständig*), 34-5, 50, 83, 90, 96, 98, 110, 113, 115, 143-55, 170, 209, 213-14, 242
nature preserves/nature protection, 3, 4, 14, 23-4, 39, 115-17, 245
    see also conservation; *Heimat* and the *Heimatschutz* movement
Naturschutz, 109
Naumann, Friedrich, 25
Nazi regime, *see* Hitler, Adolf; National Socialism
Neckar River
    barrages, 24-6, 70
Netherlands, 15
New York Times, 169
Neutra, Richard, 90
New Jersey Turnpike, 132
Nietfeld, Annette, 4
Nipperdey, Thomas, 23
North Rhine-Westphalia, 14
NSDAP, 53-5, 66, 89-97
    and landscape advocates, 87, 89-98, 108, 168
    Main Office for Technology, 54, 66, 93-4
    Office for the Cultivation of Art, 95

Nur-Autostraßen, 47
Nuremberg, 63, 112, 154
Nye, David, 14

O

Oerley, Leopold, 200
Olympic Games of 1936, 92, 153
    Olympic Stadium, 92
"On the Relationship of Modern Life to Nature"(Rudorff), 22-3
Orff, Carl, 38
Organization Todt, 54, 92, 106, 107-08, 193
Otzen, Robert, 47, 49
Overy, Richard, 59

P

Palestine, 67
Panama Canal, 32
parkways (U.S.), 141, 169, 170, 240, 241
Peukert, Detlev, 67
phytosociology (*Pflanzensoziologie*), 37, 145-46, 151-56, 170, 213-14, 242
plantings on the autobahn, 50, 83, 96, 98, 110, 113, 142-44, 149-56, 170, 207-18
    roadside trees, 218-23
    see also native flora and nativeness
Plassenburg Castle, 66, 112, 136
Poelzig, Hans, 90
Poland, 61
    attack on in 1939 and the effect that had on autobahn construction, 59, 107, 114, 135
pollution, 8, 237
polycracy, 85, 98
Porsche, Ferdinand, 52
Porter, Theodore, 194, 207
Posener, Julius, 27
Prien, 156
Prinz, Michael, 3, 171
prisoners of war as a labor source, 61
Proctor, Robert, 242
propaganda and the autobahn, 1-2, 21, 52, 53, 56, 57, 59, 62-5, 70, 148, 162, 168-70, 241
    movies produced, 63:
        "*Auf Deutschlands neuen Autostraßen*" (On Germany's New Highways)
        "*Bahn Frei*" (Open Road)
        "*Schnelle Straßen*" (Fast Roads)
        "*Straßen der Zukunft*" (Roads of the Future)
        "*Straßen machen Freude*" (Roads are Fun)
Provincial Office for Natural Monument Preservation, 152
Prussian Ministry of Culture, 24
Prussian Rhine province, 48, 113, 165

public activism, 24-25, 218-23, 243-44
Puricelli, Piero, 48

R

race tracks, 50
racism, 21-2, 30-1, 36-9, 68, 171
    see also anti-Semitism
Radkau, Joachim, 7
railroads, 15, 16, 56, 127-28
railway construction, 34, 37, 55, 127-28
    as a model and negative model for the autobahn, 55, 127-28, 134-35, 169, 240
railway travel and the landscape experience, 15-16
Ramstein airbase, 184
Ranke, Viktor von, 204
Rathenau, Walter, 25
Raumforschung und Raumordnung (Spatial Research and Regional Planning), 114
regional planning generally and regional planning offices (*Oberste Bauleitungen*), 32, 84-5, 86, 129-30, 150, 157, 168
Regional Planning Office Altona near Hamburg, 87, 104, 111
Regional Planning Office Berlin, 88, 91, 97, 135
Regional Planning Office Breslau, 88
Regional Planning Office Cologne, 88, 89
Regional Planning Office Dresden, 87, 89-90, 157, 165
Regional Planning Office Essen, 88
Regional Planning Office Frankfurt/Main, 87, 88
Regional Planning Office Halle, 88, 101, 103
Regional Planning Office Hannover, 87, 88, 95, 102-04
Regional Planning Office Kassel, 91, 93-4, 99
Regional Planning Office Königsberg, 89, 99
Regional Planning Office Munich, 104, 105, 140
Regional Planning Office Nuremberg, 87, 88
Regional Planning Office Stettin, 88, 94-6
Regional Planning Office Stuttgart, 87
Reich Association of the Automobile Industry (*Reichsverband der Automobilindustrie*), 49
Reich Association of German Horticulture (*Reichsverband des Deutschen Gartenbaus*), 88
Reich Audit Office, 99
Reich Chancellery, 57, 167
Reich Economics Ministry, 54
Reich Food Estate (*Reichsnährstand*), 97, 112
Reich Forestry Office, 166
Reich Labor Ministry, 61
Reich Labor Service, 60, 117

Reich Nature Protection Law of 1935, 115-17, 164
Reich Office for Area Planning, 114
Reich Office for Conservation, 81, 113
Reich Office for Job Planning and Unemployment Insurance, 60, 61
Reich Office for Nature Protection, 109, 112, 166, 167
Reich Railroad, *see* German Reich Railroad
Reich Security Main Office (RSHA), 39, 61
Reich Transportation Ministry, 51
Reichsbund Volkstum und Heimat, 81, 84
Reichstag, 49
Reichswehr, 56
Research Association for the Road System, 106, 112, 188-89, 194-98, 203, 205, 211
Research Office for Bioengineering, 152
Rhine river, 16, 24-5
Rhineland, 113
Rhineland-Palatinate, 184
Rieckmann, Peter, 221
Riehl, Wilhelm Heinrich, 13, 14
road planning considerations:
    alignment (sinuous vs. straight), 27, 122, 127, 170, 192-93, 199-206, 240-41
    construction, 53-4
    gradient, 135, 141, 170, 195
    railway models, 127-28, 131
    routing, 111-15, 127-28, 161-62, 187, 192-93, 198, 235-39
Roemer, Ludwig, 166, 189
Rohkrämer, Thomas, 67
Röhnick, Wilhelm, 89
Rollins, William, 4, 171, 241
Romanticism and anti-romanticism, 6, 15, 81, 107, 210
Rosenheim, 59
Rosenstock-Huessy, Eugen, 1, 9
Rudolphi, Karl, 99, 102-3
Rudorff, Ernst, 22-4, 29, 79, 109, 111
    "On the Relationship of Modern Life to Nature," 22-3
Ruhr region, 25, 113
Russia, *see* Soviet Union
Rust, Bernhard, 115

S

safety issues, 128-29, 132-33, 141-42, 170, 196-97, 199, 216, 219-23, 237-39, 244
    accidents, 135, 183, 185, 196, 213, 239
    glare shields, 149, 189, 196, 209, 213
    speed limits, 1, 185, 244
Salzkammergut, 141-42
Salzburg, 59, 138, 141-42, 237
Sauerland Mountain Club, 214

Schama, Simon, 4, 16, 171
Scharoun, Hans, 90, 92
Schimmelpfennig, Alexander, 50, 91, 94
Schimper, Andreas Franz Wilhelm, 145
Schivelbusch, Wolfgang, 16, 127-8
Schlageter, Leo, 89
Schleswig-Holstein, 111-12
Schneider, Camillo, 87, 95, 96, 102, 104, 150
Schnizlein, Ludwig, 88
Schoenichen, Walther, 109-10, 112, 116
Schönleben, Eduard, 95, 100, 133, 134, 135, 138, 193
Schulte-Frohlinde, Julius, 92
Schultze-Naumburg, Paul, 23, 29-30, 34, 35, 39, 66, 70, 83, 127
    Kulturarbeiten, 26-8, 30
Schürba, Walter, 200
Schurhammer, Hermann, 165, 206-07
Schütz, Erhard, 4, 171
Schütze, Kurt, 88
Schwarz, Max K., 87, 104, 105, 106, 111-12, 165, 166, 190-91, 217
Schwenkel, Hans, 111, 116, 166
science and road planning, 193-207
    anti-science, 23
    and mathematics, 193-207, 242
    and nature, 23, 144-47
    and rationalism, 36-7
    see also, anthroposophy; phytosociology
Scott, James, 244
Seebohm, Hans-Christoph, 186, 193-98, 201, 211, 219, 223, 235
Seehamer Lake, 139
Seidler, Franz, 98, 171
Seifert, Alwin, 4, 21, 64, 70, 127, 223
    biography and career, 31-9, 156-60, 187-89
    compensation of landscape advocates, 98-102
    in the Federal Republic, 182-89
    and *Heimatschutz*, 27-8, 35-7, 81-5
    and nativeness/native flora, 34-7, 142-55
    and Fritz Todt, 39, 82-5, 132, 156-60, 149-54, 156-62, 169, 188
    road planning and routing, 69, 131-35, 140, 192, 237
    role of landscape advocates, 157-62, 166-67
    selection of landscape advocates, 86-98
Siebengebirge mountain range, 113
Siegloch, Carl, 87, 95, 103, 111
Siemens Bauunion, 60
social protest, *see* public activism
Society of the Friends of the German *Heimatschutz*, 79
Sombart, Werner, 25, 49

Soviet Union, 69
  motorization rate, 52
SPD, 222
speed limits, 1, 185, 244
  see also safety issues
Speer, Albert, 54, 91-2
Spengler, Oswald, 67, 145
SS, 61, 92, 166
Stanford University, 26
Starnberg, Lake, 53
Staße und Autobahn, 204, 207
state control of roads:
  Federal Republic, 185-87, 190-92, 205
  Nazi era, 55, 108
  Weimar era, 48
Steiner, Rudolf, 35
Steppefication (*Versteppung*), 82, 167
Sternberg Castle meeting of 1941, 165-66
Stifter, Adalbert, 140
Stommer, Rainer, 4
Streicher, Julius, 63
Stück, Fritz, 91, 93-4, 99
Stuttgart, 25, 111, 141, 148, 185, 195-96
Swabian Jura, 111, 141, 195-96
Switzerland, 16
  motorization rate, 52

T

Technical University, Berlin, 90
Technical University, Braunschweig, 204
Technical University, Hannover, 47
Technical University, Munich, 33, 34, 35, 37, 146, 189
technology, 15
  Deutsche Technik, 66-71
  and environmental history, 15-17, 39-45
  history of, 2, 6-7, 67, 80, 239-42
  integration with nature and the landscape, 16-17, 28-30, 69-71, 152-56
Thule Society, 38
Todt, Fritz, 31, 37, 51, 186, 238
  administration of the Inspector General's office, 57-9, 61, 63, 64, 66-7, 115-17
  biography and career, 53-5, 85
  Bown memorandum, 53-4
  and *Heimatschutz*, 79
  ideology, 53, 129-32, 241
  and landscape advocates, 79, 92, 93-4, 96-8, 101, 102, 106, 108-09, 149-56, 162, 169, 170, 171
  road planning, 38-42, 113, 128-29, 131-36, 160-62, 192, 200
  and Alwin Seifert, 39, 82-7, 89, 101, 102, 132, 156-60, 188

  and the Western Wall, 54, 60
  see also Inspector General for the German Roads
toll roads, 47, 48, 49, 50, 56, 162
Traub, Gottfried, 33
Trepl, Ludwig, 13, 144
transportation policy:
  Federal Republic, 181-87, 193-200, 205-07, 218-23, 235-36
  National Socialist, 51-53, 59
  Weimar Republic, 47-50, 53
trucks/trucking, see freight traffic
Tucholsky, Kurt, 32
Türkenfeld-Moorenweis, 222
Turner, Joseph Mallord William, 15
Tüxen, Reinhold, 145, 152-5, 170, 209-10

U

Ulm, 104, 148, 185, 195-96
Ungewitter, Rudolf, 88, 106
United States, 3, 5, 6-7, 67, 242, 245
  anti-Americanism, 67-9, 166
  highways, 132, 184
  motorization rates, 48, 49, 52, 184, 240
  parkways, 141, 169, 170, 240, 241
  as a reference point, 2, 24, 48, 49, 169, 170, 184, 240, 241
University of Tübingen, 24
Unterhaching, 58
Urry, John, 80

V

vegetation science, see phytosociology
Vienna, 59, 141-42
visual consumption, 138-42, 161, 169-72, 195
Volkswagen, 52, 183

W

Wagner, Martin, 90
Wagner, Richard, 38
Wandervogel movement, 31-3, 90, 93
Warming, Eugenius, 145
Warnke, Martin, 15-16, 25
Weber, Christian, 154
Weber, Max, 25
Wehrmacht, 56, 59, 107-08, 139, 188
Weilheim, 35, 67, 222
Weimar Republic
transportation policy, 47-50, 53
Weinheim, 48
Weltanschauung, 69, 132, 144
Wessel, Horst, 89
Western Wall, 54, 59, 60, 69
West Prussian Provincial Museum, 24

Wetekamp, Wilhelm, 24
Widar Circle, 38
Wiepking-Jürgensmann, Heinrich, 38, 40, 92, 97, 166
Wiesbaden, 49
Williams, Rosalind, 243
Wolfsburg, 52, 183
Wolschke-Bulmahn, Joachim, 4, 171
Working Asscoiation for Nature and Landscape Protection Frankfurt and Environs, 110
Working Circle of Landscape Advocates, 106-07, 189-91
World War I, 33-4
World War II, 59, 61, 107-08, 135, 165, 166
Württemberg, 24, 25, 111

Y

Yellowstone National Park, 24
Youth Movement, 31-2, 97

Z

Zitelmann, Rainer, 3

www.ingramcontent.com/pod-product-compliance
Lightning Source LLC
Chambersburg PA
CBHW071334080526
44587CB00017B/2834